Refining Child Pornography Law

The legal definition of child pornography is, at best, unclear. In part because of this ambiguity and in part because of the nature of the crime itself, the prosecution and sentencing of perpetrators, the protection of and restitution for victims, and the means for preventing repeat offenses are deeply controversial. In an effort to clarify the questions and begin to formulate answers, in this volume, experts in law and the social sciences examine child pornography law and its consequences. Focusing on the roles of language and crime definition, the contributors present a range of views about the increasingly visible role child pornography plays in the national conversation on child safety, as well as the wisdom of the punishment of those who produce, distribute, and possess materials that may be considered child pornography.

Carissa Byrne Hessick is Professor of Law at the University of North Carolina School of Law.

Law, Meaning, and Violence

The scope of Law, Meaning, and Violence is defined by the wide-ranging scholarly debates signaled by each of the words in the title. Those debates have taken place among and between lawyers, anthropologists, political theorists, sociologists, and historians, as well as literary and cultural critics. This series is intended to recognize the importance of such ongoing conversations about law, meaning, and violence as well as to encourage and further them.

Series Editors: Martha Minow, Harvard Law School
Austin Sarat, Amherst College

RECENT TITLES IN THE SERIES

Refining Child Pornography Law: Crime, Language, and Social Consequences, edited by Carissa Byrne Hessick

The First Global Prosecutor: Promise and Constraints, edited by Martha Minow, C. Cora True-Frost, and Alex Whiting

Hybrid Justice: The Extraordinary Chambers in the Courts of Cambodia, by John D. Ciorciari and Anne Heindel

The Justice of Mercy, by Linda Ross Meyer

Dying Inside: The HIV/AIDS Ward at Limestone Prison, by Benjamin Fleury-Steiner with Carla Crowder

Sacred Violence: Torture, Terror, and Sovereignty, by Paul W. Kahn

Punishment and Political Order, by Keally McBride

Lives of Lawyers Revisited: Transformation and Resilience in the Organizations of Practice, by Michael J. Kelly

Among the Lowest of the Dead: The Culture of Capital Punishment, by David Von Drehle

Punishing Schools: Fear and Citizenship in American Public Education, by William Lyons and Julie Drew

Suing the Gun Industry: A Battle at the Crossroads of Gun Control and Mass Torts, edited by Timothy D. Lytton

Transformative Justice: Israeli Identity on Trial, by Leora Bilsky

Jurors' Stories of Death: How America's Death Penalty Invests in Inequality, by Benjamin Fleury-Steiner

The Jurisprudence of Emergency: Colonialism and the Rule of Law, by Nasser Hussain

Communities and Law: Politics and Cultures of Legal Identities, by Gad Barzilai

From Noose to Needle: Capital Punishment and the Late Liberal State, by Timothy V. Kaufman-Osborn

The Limits to Union: Same-Sex Marriage and the Politics of Civil Rights, by Jonathan Goldberg-Hiller

Pain, Death, and the Law, edited by Austin Sarat

Bad Boys: Public Schools in the Making of Black Masculinity, by Ann Arnett Ferguson

Whispered Consolations: Law and Narrative in African American Life, by Jon-Christian Suggs

Refining Child Pornography Law

Crime, Language, and Social Consequences

Edited by Carissa Byrne Hessick

UNIVERSITY OF MICHIGAN PRESS

Ann Arbor

Published in the United States of America by the
University of Michigan Press
Manufactured in the United States of America
♾ Printed on acid-free paper

2019 2018 2017 2016 4 3 2 1

A CIP catalog record for this book is available from the British Library.

Library of Congress Cataloging-in-Publication Data

Names: Hessick, Carissa Byrne, editor.
Title: Refining child pornography law : crime, language, and social consequences / Edited by Carissa Byrne Hessick.
Description: Ann Arbor : University of Michigan Press, 2016. | Series: Law, meaning, and violence | Includes bibliographical references and index.
Identifiers: LCCN 2015039989| ISBN 9780472119769 (hardback) | ISBN 9780472121663 (ebook)
Subjects: LCSH: Child pornography—United States. | Child abuse—Law and legislation—United States.
Classification: LCC KF9323 .R44 2016 | DDC 345.73/0274—dc23
LC record available at http://lccn.loc.gov/2015039989

Acknowledgments

This book would not have been possible without the help and encouragement of many people. First, many thanks to Melody Herr, who first suggested that I explore the idea of a book on child pornography law, and whose tireless help and vision shaped the book as it appears today. Second, many thanks to Judy Stinson—an amazing associate dean and an even better friend—who encouraged me to pursue this project and who gave me the flexibility while I was on the faculty of the Sandra Day O'Connor College of Law to do so. Third, I am indebted to the University Research Committee at the University of Utah for awarding a research grant that allowed me to complete this book.

I would also like to thank the many people whose research assistance helped me to complete this book: Beth DiFelice, Lee Warthen, Kristin Martinez, Amy Coughenour, Jennison Cox, and K. Clint Metheney.

Finally, my deepest thanks and appreciation go to Andy Hessick. He read a number of draft proposals and chapters, which helped make this book much better. What is more, his unflagging personal support and his constant willingness to do more than his fair share of child care and housework gave me the time and the motivation needed to complete this professional project (and many others).

Contents

Introduction

Carissa Byrne Hessick

> *The desire to have collections of a large number of photographs of children seems to be a common, although not universal, characteristic of many pedophiles. Some of this exchange of photographs takes place in person, a great deal takes place through the mails, and recently a significant amount of the exchange has taken place by the use of computer networks through which users of child pornography let each other know about materials they desire or have available.*
>
> —Attorney General's Commission on Pornography (1986)

When Attorney General Edwin Meese published his report on pornography more than twenty-five years ago, he could not have known how much computers and the Internet were going to affect child pornography. Technological advances have led to a proliferation of child pornography images. Technology has also wrought significant changes in the detection and prosecution of child pornography crimes. Simply put, the past twenty years have seen a child pornography revolution.

In the decades since child pornography first came to the attention of the American criminal justice system, it has been the subject of many state and federal laws and a number of high-profile Supreme Court cases. Child pornography is presently the focus of countless media stories, increasingly severe punishment, and some of the biggest modern sentencing controversies.

Despite this sustained attention, the law surrounding child pornography is far from settled. Serious questions remain about what types of images qualify as "child pornography." The modern trend of increasingly harsh criminal sentences for those who possess child pornography has met with significant resistance from some judges. And whether there is a link between those who view child pornography and sex crimes against children has become a hotly contested issue in the criminal justice community. In other words, as a matter of language, as a matter of criminal sanctions, and as a matter of social policy, child pornography requires further study and reflection.

Refining Child Pornography Law: Crime, Language, and Social Consequences adds nuance and depth to the public discussion surrounding child pornography. This volume brings together experts in law and related disciplines who study child pornography law and the consequences of that law. Focusing on language and crime definition in the child pornography debate, this volume includes chapters representing a number of different views about the increasingly visible role child pornography plays in the national conversation on child safety, as well as the wisdom of the current legal penalties that are imposed on those who produce, distribute, and possess child pornography.

Underscoring the importance of language in the child pornography debate is the controversy surrounding the term "child pornography." A growing number of academics and activists contend that the term ought not be used to refer to sexually explicit images of minors. They argue that the term "child pornography" fails to capture the horrible nature of the harm suffered by the children who are depicted. As Professor Mary Leary notes in her chapter, *The Language of Child Sexual Abuse and Exploitation*, the term "child pornography" "likely conjures up images of younger looking adults striking provocative poses, as opposed to the reality of an increasingly violent collections of photographs and video depicting younger and younger children being violently victimized."

In using the term "child pornography" both in the title of the book and in this introduction, I do not mean to ignore the arguments that Professor Leary and others have made about the importance of language nor the possibility that a term that includes the word "pornography" may lead some to misapprehend the nature of the images. Rather, I use the term because it continues to be most widely recognized term used to refer to these images.

Before previewing the contents of the book, this introduction will provide a brief overview of the development of American child pornography law. The overview is intended to give readers only a passing familiarity with legal developments in this area. More complete and nuanced discussions of the major Supreme Court cases in this area and other legal developments are provided in the individual chapters.

Child pornography laws are of a relatively recent vintage.[1] The first American jurisdiction to prohibit child pornography was California. In 1961 it passed a law prohibiting individuals from using a minor to "prepare[], publish[], print[], exhibit[], distribute[], or offer[] to distribute, . . . any obscene matter." Any individual who engaged in that prohibited behavior was guilty of a misdemeanor and could be fined up to two thousand dollars and imprisoned for up to one year.[2] North Dakota passed legislation in 1975 that made the production of child pornography a Class C felony.[3] Tennessee enacted a similar prohibition that same year.[4] A number of other states and the federal government enacted anti-child-pornography laws in 1977 and 1978.[5]

This spate of child pornography legislation appears to have been prompted by media reports.[6] For example, in 1977, the *Chicago Tribune* ran a series of articles on "child predators." The series ran on the front page for four consecutive days, and it included an article devoted to child pornography.[7] That same year, one member of Congress noted:

> A year ago who had ever heard of child pornography or even imagined that children were being abused in this manner? . . . All of a sudden there it was. In newspapers, in Time magazine, on television, and, inevitably, on the House floor. The revelations were shocking and disgusting. Children, ages 3 to 16, being used, sold, traded, photographed for sexual purposes.[8]

While media reports of exploited children captivated the public and lawmakers, these initial child pornography statutes resembled laws criminalizing obscenity. That is to say, most of the laws prohibiting child pornography criminalized the production and distribution of child pornography images that were obscene.[9] Because obscenity was already widely prohibited in American jurisdictions,[10] the new child pornography laws provided little in the way of added protection for children. The states presumably wrote their laws in this fashion because they wanted to avoid First Amendment problems. Images are ordinarily protected by the free speech guarantees of the First Amendment, and legislatures may criminalize sexualized images of children only when those images are not entitled to constitutional protection. Obscenity is a well-established exception to the First Amendment, and so in limiting their laws against child pornography to images that were obscene, the states were able to avoid any constitutional questions.

One notable exception to this trend was New York, which adopted a statute criminalizing the production and distribution of child pornography and a separate statute criminalizing the distribution of obscene material.[11] The United States Supreme Court upheld the New York law in *New York v. Ferber*.[12] In that opinion, the Supreme Court announced that child pornography was entitled to no First Amendment protection and that states could criminalize its production and distribution even if the images were not obscene. After *Ferber* was decided in 1982, state and federal laws criminalizing the creation, distribution, and possession of child pornography proliferated.

In addition to omitting the obscenity requirement, some jurisdictions expanded their child pornography laws by prohibiting the possession of images.[13] For example, Ohio amended its child pornography laws in 1988 to include private possession.[14] Because the Supreme Court had previously stated that the private possession of obscene materials was protected by the First Amendment,[15] some believed that laws such as Ohio's were unlikely to survive constitutional challenge.[16] But the Supreme Court upheld Ohio's law in *Osborne v. Ohio*.[17] The Supreme Court explained that although the private possession of other obscene materials was constitutionally protected, child pornography was different because the process of creating child pornography harmed the child.

As American states and Congress expanded the scope of their child pornography laws, and as enforcement agencies began to target distributors and collectors of child pornography, the number of child pornography images in circulation dropped. The successful identification and prosecution of child pornography offenders led many to conclude that the commercial circulation of child pornography images had essentially ceased by the early 1990s.[18] But "[j]ust when suppression of the child pornography trade seemed within sight, . . . the Internet arrived on the scene."[19]

The rise of the Internet, as well as the rapid development of several other technologies, allowed for fast, widespread, and anonymous distribution of child pornography. Before the advent of the Internet, distributing child pornography was a time-intensive and expensive undertaking. A distributor would have to physically copy an image,[20] expend effort to identify interested recipients (such as taking out advertisements in pornographic magazines or otherwise actively attempting to meet others interested in acquiring child pornography), and physically mail or otherwise transfer a package to the intended recipient. Because images would significantly deteriorate in quality after a few copies, distribution was extremely limited.

Contrast that situation with distribution in the Internet era: Any individual who possesses pornographic images on his or her computer and who visits a file-sharing site will "distribute" those images to countless individuals,[21] even with no affirmative action on his or her part. There is no cost associated with duplicating a digital image, and the quality of an image does not noticeably deteriorate, even if it is many copies removed from the original image. To obtain images, individuals can search and download from websites anonymously. In short, technology facilitates the widespread distribution of child pornography.

As the Internet led to increasing availability of child pornography, legislators sharply increased the sentences imposed on child pornography offenders. For example, in 1990, federal law punished the possession of child pornography by up to ten years in prison.[22] In 1996, the maximum penalty was increased to fifteen years,[23] and it was raised again in 2003 to twenty years.[24] Many states also dramatically increased their penalties.[25]

While judges generally, and the Supreme Court in particular, were at first supportive of legislative efforts to combat child pornography, they have become more skeptical in recent years. For example, in a 2002 decision, *Ashcroft v. Free Speech Coalition*,[26] the U.S. Supreme Court struck down a federal statute that prohibited virtual child pornography—that is, pornographic images created wholly by technological means. More recently, a number of federal judges have refused to impose the severe sentences required by the federal sentencing guidelines for child pornography offenders.[27] These refusals have not only prompted a number of media stories[28] but also have led the United States Sentencing Commission to suggest that Congress limit sentencing discretion of federal judges.[29]

The most recent child pornography issue to reach the U.S. Supreme Court involved victim restitution. A federal statute requires courts to order defendants convicted of certain crimes, including child pornography offenses, to pay the victim "the full amount of the victim's losses."[30] Doyle Randall Paroline pled guilty to possessing a number of child pornography images, including two images of a young girl who sought restitution under the pseudonym "Amy." Amy was sexually abused by her uncle when she was eight and nine years old, and photographs the uncle took during that abuse have been widely distributed on the Internet. Amy has suffered significant emotional harm from that distribution, which has required ongoing psychological treatment. When she became an adult, Amy sought more than $3 million in restitution from Paroline to compensate her for the costs of her ongoing treatment and lost wages.

The issue before the Supreme Court in *Paroline v. United States*[31] was the amount of restitution to require from Paroline. The restitution question was difficult because the losses Amy suffered were caused not only by Paroline, but also by the many other individuals who distributed and possessed those images. The Court held that restitution under the federal statute is appropriate only to the extent the defendant's offense proximately caused a victim's losses. But proximate cause is a slippery concept. To say that someone's conduct proximately caused a result is to say not only that the conduct actually caused the result, but also that the conduct had a "sufficient connection to the result."[32]

Causation is especially tricky in child pornography possession cases. In an ordinary case, causation does not exist if the loss would not have occurred but for the defendant's actions. But in cases of child pornography possession it is difficult to establish that the victim would have suffered harm if one particular defendant had not possessed the relevant images. For example, thousands of individuals have possessed the images of Amy that were created by her uncle; she would presumably have lost the same amount of income and required the same amount of treatment if one fewer person possessed the images of her. To establish that Paroline played any role in causing Amy's losses, the Court relied on a common law rule that allows for a finding of causation where the losses would have occurred even if the defendant had not engaged in the particular conduct. The rule recognizes a defendant as an actual cause of harm when the cumulative effects of multiple actors' conduct results in the harm. This aggregation concept allowed the Court to find that Paroline caused Amy's losses even though she would have suffered those same losses if Paroline had not possessed the images.

But while the Supreme Court concluded that Paroline was a cause of Amy's losses, it did not give much guidance about how much of her losses could be attributed to Paroline under the concept of proximate causation. That is to say, while the Court resolved whether Paroline could be held responsible for some amount of Amy's losses, it did not clarify how much. The Court said that judges should order restitution in child pornography cases "in an amount that comports with the defendant's relative role in the causal process that underlies the victim's general losses."[33] In making that assessment, the Supreme Court suggested that lower courts look to a number of factors, including:

> the number of past criminal defendants found to have contributed to the victim's general losses; reasonable predictions of the number of future offenders likely to be caught and convicted for crimes contributing to the victim's general losses; any available and reasonably reliable estimate of the broader number of offenders involved (most of whom will, of course, never be caught or convicted); whether the

> defendant reproduced or distributed images of the victim; whether the defendant had any connection to the initial production of the images; how many images of the victim the defendant possessed; and other facts relevant to the defendant's relative causal role.

It also cautioned lower courts against making "trivial restitution orders."[34]

The Supreme Court's analysis in *Paroline* leaves a number of questions unanswered. Most importantly, it fails to provide much guidance to lower courts about how to calculate restitution awards—a point made forcefully by Chief Justice Roberts in his dissent. Although the Supreme Court's directions to lower courts are vague, they clearly instruct those courts to engage in a comprehensive analysis of the various sources of harm to child pornography victims. As a result, we should expect to see restitution cases that attempt to assess the relative wrongdoing of child pornography defendants, cases that could enhance the current conversations surrounding child pornography crimes.

At present, however, the discussions surrounding child pornography are underdeveloped. Although child pornography law is a matter of sustained public interest, a number of important issues have remain underexplored. For example, there are serious disputes about the relationship between child pornography offenders and child sex abuse. While the national discourse on child pornography often seems to assume that those who possess child pornography also pose a physical threat to children, research in this area has failed to definitely support that assumption.

It is against this backdrop that the chapters of this book explore the language, criminal sanctions, and public policy surrounding child pornography crimes. All the important issues surrounding child pornography cannot be explored in a single volume. This book does not, for example, attempt to settle the ongoing controversy about whether child pornography offenders also have sexually abused children. Instead, the book focuses on two distinct but related goals. First the book highlights the importance of language and legal definitions in child pornography law, which, as the first part of the book illustrates, are extremely important for both constitutional and policy reasons. Second, the book provides a primer on some of the most visible, ongoing controversies in the application of child pornography law. While the chapters address a number of different topics and include a number of different methodological approaches, each chapter demonstrates that the crimes associated with child pornography are contested and contestable.

The book begins by exploring the definitional issues associated with child pornography crimes. In particular, the first two chapters address constitutional issues associated with child pornography. In chapter 1, *The Context and the Content of* New York v. Ferber, James Weinstein situates the Supreme Court's child pornography cases within the broader framework of the Supreme Court's First Amendment jurisprudence. As Professor Weinstein notes, at the time the Supreme Court decided *New York v. Ferber*, its free speech cases were overwhelmingly predisposed against exempting entire categories of speech from constitutional protection; instead the Court had developed a new framework, in which it asked whether the relevant law was a restriction on the content of speech and, if it was, whether that restriction satisfied strict scrutiny based on the harm that the speech could cause. In deciding the *Ferber* case, the Court refrained from affirming the New York child pornography prohibition based on the harm that such speech could cause. Instead, the Court elected to uphold the law based on the harm that was done to children during the production of those images. This harm, according to the Court, was sufficient to create a categorical exception to the First Amendment. While the New York law likely qualified as a content restriction, Professor Weinstein stresses the significance of the Court's decision not to analyze the child pornography law under this framework. That is to say, the Court did not characterize the New York law as a content restriction and then conclude that the state's interest in protecting children satisfied strict scrutiny. Professor Weinstein suggests that the Court did not take this approach because it might have undermined the Court's new methodology if it were to uphold a law as satisfying strict scrutiny. The chapter goes on to describe how, in subsequent child pornography decisions, the Court has resisted attempts to broaden the categorical free speech exception it created in *Ferber*. In sum, by evaluating *Ferber* in the broader context of the Supreme Court's twentieth-century free speech cases, Professor Weinstein concludes that *Ferber* is in many ways a remarkably speech-*protective* decision.

Chapter 2, *Setting Definitional Limits for the Child Pornography Exception*, proposes a specific limitation on the definition of child pornography—namely, that the child pornography exception to the First Amendment include only those images created through the sexual abuse or exploitation of a child. In proposing this limited definition for child pornography, the chapter notes that much of the analysis in the Supreme Court's child pornography cases focuses on the harms that children suffer in the production of child pornography images. Although the Court also expresses concern over the reputational and privacy harms that child pornography victims suffer when the images are later distributed, the chapter concludes that those harms, standing alone, should not be sufficient to transform an image into child pornography. Changing the definitional limits for the child pornography exception to the First Amendment would prevent prosecutors from pursuing charges in several categories of cases, including so-called "teen sexting" cases, which have garnered significant media attention in recent years. The proposed definitional change would also affect morphed and surreptitiously created images, which are often not created through either child sex abuse or exploitation.

After examining broad constitutional issues associated with the definition of child pornography crimes, the book then presents two chapters that examine various consequences of the current legal definition. In chapter 3, *The "Dost Test" in Child Pornography Law: "Trial by Rorschach Test,"* Amy Adler evaluates the prevailing legal test for assessing when an image that depicts a "lascivious exhibition of the genitals" qualifies as child pornography. According to Professor Adler, the *Dost* test poses not only constitutional problems, but also cultural ones. In particular, she argues that *Dost* is vague and arguably overbroad and that the cases decided under *Dost* seem inconsistent with Supreme Court cases in this area. In addition to these constitutional concerns, Professor Adler argues that to the extent *Dost* has been interpreted to incorporate the pedophile's perspective in evaluating images, the test invites us to view nonsexual pictures of children through the gaze of the pedophile, transforming these images into child pornography. As Professor Adler notes, one harm done by child pornography is that it changes the way we perceive children; ironically, when *Dost* requires us to take on a "perception of children as sexual objects," then child pornography *law* changes the way we perceive children.

Despite her criticisms of the *Dost* test, Professor Adler seems to conclude that some similar test may be necessary because the Supreme Court has made clear that nudity is *not* the dividing line between protected speech and child pornography, and because a number of federal courts have concluded that a picture can be criminalized as "lascivious" even if it contains *no* nudity. What is more, Professor Adler concedes that the unpredictability and malleability of *Dost* may be a positive feature of the test; a more limited test would mean that some child abusers would go free and that some abusive, harmful images would be permitted to circulate. In short, her chapter identifies a number of shortcomings with the test and leaves the reader to decide whether the costs of *Dost* outweigh its benefits.

In chapter 4, *The Language of Child Sexual Abuse and Exploitation*, Mary Leary contends that many of the common terms used to describe child pornography and other forms of child exploitation ought to be revised. She notes that precision and content in language are, as a general matter, exceedingly important. In the context of child sex abuse and child exploitation, she argues that the conduct and the social reaction are complicated and thus the language used to discuss these issues must be precise. For example, Professor Leary notes ambiguity surrounding the term "child." Different American jurisdictions use the words "child" or "minor" to refer to individuals of varying ages. In the context of child abuse and exploitation, she proposes that the term "child" should be universally understood to refer to all individuals under the age of eighteen. While she does not dispute that individuals do (and should) accrue certain legal rights before that age, Professor Leary concludes that just as the criminal justice system treats all criminal offenders under the age of eighteen differently than adults, so too should our understanding of victims as children be anchored at the age of eighteen.

In addition to noting certain ambiguous terms, Professor Leary also argues that a number of common terms do not sufficiently reflect the true nature of victimization. In particular, she criticizes the terms "child pornography," "child prostitution," and "sexting." Applying the principle of fair labeling, which originated in discussions over how to revise the British criminal code, Professor Leary explains in detail why the term "sexually abusive images of children" should be used in place of the term "child pornography," as well as why the term "child sex trafficking" should be used in place of "child prostitution." Professor Leary's discussion of the term "sexting" is especially noteworthy, as she identifies the extremely wide range of images to which the media has applied this label, and she notes that the conditions under which an image was created vary wildly: some were taken with the permission of the subject, some were not; some depict consensual sex acts, some depict sexual assaults. Noting that these differences are exceedingly important, Professor Leary suggests a few different labels for these images, including "child-produced sexually abusive images."

The definitional chapters are followed by a number of chapters that assess the wisdom of current child pornography law and that offer suggestions for improvement. The first three of these chapters tackle the specific challenges posed by the current legal treatment of those defendants who possess child pornography images. Chapter 5, *Questioning the Modern Criminal Justice Focus on Child Pornography Possession*, criticizes the modern trend of increasing the criminal justice resources spent to detect, prosecute, and punish those who possess child pornography. It argues that possessing child pornography is one of the least serious crimes involving the sexual abuse of children; for example, those who possess child pornography pose less of a threat and cause less harm than those who create or distribute child pornography, and they are obviously less dangerous and less culpable than those who sexually assault children. Drawing an analogy to the war on drugs, the chapter explains why focusing criminal justice resources on possession cases not only seems less fair, but also does not seem calculated to sensibly reduce the availability of child pornography. After criticizing the arguments that are often given in support of enforcement techniques that focus on child pornography possessors, the chapter concludes that resources are better spent detecting, prosecuting, and punishing crimes that are more directly tied to sexual abuse and exploitation.

In chapter 6, *The Dignitary Harm of Child Pornography—From Producers to Possessors*, Audrey Rogers challenges the traditional categories that have been used to distinguish among child pornography defendants. American criminal justice systems regularly treat child pornography defendants differently depending on whether they have produced, distributed, or merely possessed child pornography images. As Professor Rogers notes, modern technology has blurred these categories to such an extent that it has become difficult to defend different punishment for child pornography defendants based on these distinctions. In particular, she argues that child pornography possessors—the category of child pornography defendants whose criminal punishments are most often criticized as too severe—are no longer easily distinguished from those who receive or distribute child pornography. Professor Rogers' chapter also documents the extensive dignitary harm that child pornography possessors cause to their child victims. In so doing, she specifically challenges the claim, which is advanced in previous chapters of the volume, that morphed and surreptitiously created images ought not be treated the same as other child pornography images.

In chapter 7, *Not Just "Kiddie Porn": The Significant Harms from Child Pornography Possession*, Paul Cassell, James Marsh, and Jeremy Christiansen directly dispute the idea that possessing child pornography is not a serious crime—that while those who create (or perhaps distribute) child pornography inflict severe harms on their child victims, those who merely possess images are not significantly blameworthy. Focusing in particular on the argument as it has arisen in the context of restitution for child pornography victims, the authors explain why each individual who collects and views child pornography causes significant losses for which victims should receive significant compensation. The endless collecting and viewing of a victim's child sex images subjects victims to continuous invasions of privacy, producing lasting psychological injury and significant economic losses.

The chapter explains in detail why the prevailing view in child pornography restitution cases—namely, that the proper way to assess the harm caused by a child pornography defendant is to calculate how many defendants have viewed the image, and then to estimate what proportion of the victim's losses are attributable to each defendant—is deeply flawed. As the authors note, trying to apportion financial losses among tens of thousands of criminals invariably neglects the significant psychological harm each crime causes. What is more, this analysis suggests that the larger the number of criminals who view a victim's images, the less responsible any particular criminal is for the harm caused to the victim. Rather than attempting to quantify the economic harm that is attributable to each defendant, the authors argue that each individual defendant should be held jointly and severally liable for all the harms child pornography possession causes, an argument that they trace to basic principles of tort law, which identify all who contribute to a single harm as being responsible for paying compensation for the entire harm.

The final three chapters address the challenges facing those who write child pornography laws, those who investigate and prosecute child pornography crimes, and those who sentence child pornography defendants. The first of these chapters, *Challenges in Investigations and Prosecutions of Child Pornography Crimes*, uses data from the National Juvenile Online Victimization Study—the most comprehensive study available on Internet-related sex crimes against minors—to explore the growth and complexity of child pornography crimes. In particular, the chapter identifies and explores the challenges faced by law enforcement investigators and prosecutors of child pornography crimes. As the chapter authors note, while law enforcement and prosecutors identify a number of challenges they face in detecting and prosecuting child pornography offenders, enforcement of child pornography laws has been quite successful. Law enforcement is increasingly engaged in proactive investigations of child pornography crimes; prosecutors pursue charges in a large number of cases, they obtain a high percentage of guilty pleas to child pornography charges, and the study identified no cases that ended in acquittal after trial.

Notably, a number of challenges government officials identified were related to definitional issues surrounding child pornography. Because prosecutors must prove that images fit within particular statutory definitions of child pornography, the content of those definitions may pose particular problems, such as whether the child depicted is young enough or whether a particular image is graphic or explicit enough to fit the prevailing definition of child pornography. One particular definitional challenge that prosecutors face is the burden of showing that an image depicts a real child. (This burden is the result of the Supreme Court's *Ashcroft v. Free Speech Coalition* decision, which limited the constitutional category of child pornography to exclude virtual or computer-generated images.) The chapter notes that prosecutors use multiple methods to meet their various definitional burdens under child pornography statutes. The chapter concludes with data on a child pornography definition issue that is still in flux: teen sexting. Sexting often falls within states' legal definitions of child pornography, and many jurisdictions have struggled with how to treat those cases. The chapter reports data from prosecutors who have worked on sexting cases, noting that prosecutors often present minors with a wide range of alternative outcomes rather than automatically charging those juveniles under the state's child pornography laws.

The final two chapters focus on the highly visible and hotly contested sentencing scheme for federal child pornography offenders. A number of federal judges have begun to object to the federal sentencing regime, refusing to impose the lengthy sentences, and drawing media attention in the process. In chapter 9, *A Critical Evaluation of the Federal Sentencing Guidelines for Child Pornography Offenses*, Troy Stabenow walks readers through the decisions that a federal judge must make when sentencing a typical federal child pornography offender. As Mr. Stabenow's hypothetical sentencing exercise illustrates, the various circumstances that the federal sentencing guidelines use to increase punishment for child pornography defendants apply in nearly every case. What is more, some of the factual findings that will significantly affect a judge's sentencing decision seem, upon reflection, irrelevant—such as whether a defendant viewed child pornography on his computer or on his television. The criticisms this chapter raise lie at the heart of the current controversy over federal sentencing for child pornography offenders. And by framing his chapter as a hypothetical sentencing decision, Mr. Stabenow effectively conveys the frustration that many judges feel when they are required to base their sentencing decisions on seemingly arbitrary distinctions between defendants.

In chapter 10, *Political and Empirical Controversies Threaten the Federal Child Pornography Guidelines*, Melissa Hamilton frames the federal sentencing controversy as a power struggle between three powerful institutions: Congress, the federal courts, and the U.S. Sentencing Commission. She notes that the Supreme Court's 2005 opinion in *United States v. Booker*, which transformed the federal sentencing guidelines from presumptive rules into advisory guidelines, has placed the Sentencing Commission at the center of a tug of war between Congress and federal judges over federal sentencing policy for child pornography offenders. She focuses in particular on the legal question of whether federal sentences should be based on empirical study—a question that has featured prominently in judicial opinions about child pornography sentences and that has resulted in a significant divergence of judicial opinion. Dr. Hamilton's chapter details these political and empirical controversies, identifies the differences in ideologies and legal analysis that fuel these controversies, and provides a wealth of information about recent child pornography cases and sentences.

The law and the public discussion surrounding child pornography are ever-changing. At the time of writing, the United States Sentencing Commission has asked Congress to revise federal child pornography laws, and federal courts are just beginning to grapple with the Supreme Court's opinion in *Paroline v. United States*, which directs judges to award restitution in child pornography cases by assessing which harms suffered by a child pornography victim are attributable to individual possessors of child pornography. Another high-profile child pornography case could trigger additional legislation at any time.

By bringing together experts in different fields and with different viewpoints, this volume aims to influence the legal and policy discussions surrounding child pornography. In particular, it seeks to identify the important role that the definition of child pornography plays in those discussions, to highlight the uncertainty that has been created by imprecision in the language describing and defining child pornography, and to illustrate how language and definition are important components in improving the law surrounding child pornography. By refining the scope of child pornography language and debates, we hope to ensure that child pornography laws become more effective at protecting children.

NOTES

1. *See* NATIONAL RESOURCE CENTER FOR CHILD ADVOCACY AND PROTECTION, CHILD SEXUAL EXPLOITATION: BACKGROUND & LEGAL ANALYSIS 111 (1984).
2. 1961 Cal. Stat., c. 2147 § 5, p. 4428–29.
3. 1975 N.D. Stat., c. 119, p. 429–31 ("It shall be a class C felony to permit a minor

to participate in a performance which is harmful to minors"). Notably, the definition of material that is harmful to minors mirrored the statutory definition of obscene material. *Id.*

4. Tenn. Code Ann. § 39-3013 (1975).

5. *See* Jennifer M. Payton, Note, *Child Pornography Legislation*, 17 J. FAM. L. 505, 520 (1978–79) (noting the "wave of child pornography legislation that swept the statehouses *circa* 1977 and 1978"); *see also* T. Christopher Donnelly, *Protection of Children from Use in Pornography: Towards Constitutional and Enforceable Legislation*, 12 U. MICH. J.L. REFORM 295, 305–306 n.64–67 (1979) (collecting statutes).

6. *See* IAN O'DONNELL & CLAIRE MILNER, CHILD PORNOGRAPHY: CRIME, COMPUTER AND SOCIETY 17 (2007). One author traces public awareness of child pornography in the United States to the cleanup operation launched in New York City in 1979 prior to the Democratic National Convention. TIM TATE, CHILD PORNOGRAPHY: AN INVESTIGATION 63 (1990).

7. Richard S. Pope, *Child Pornography: A New Role for the Obscenity Doctrine*, 1978 U. ILL. L.F. 711, 713–14 n.10; *see also* Donnelly, *supra* note 5, at 295 n.1 (collecting media sources).

8. 123 CONG. REC. H10068 (daily ed. Sept. 26, 1977) (remarks of Rep. Quie).

9. *See* Pope, *supra* note 7, at 712 ("Ten of the thirteen jurisdictions that had enacted child pornography legislation by early 1978 either based their statutes on the obscenity exception to first amendment protection, or did not punish speech, and thus did not need an obscenity requirement."); *see also* NATIONAL RESOURCE CENTER, *supra* note 1, at 112–13 (noting different approaches to obscenity issue in the states); Payton, *supra* note 5, at 521–31 (same).

10. *See generally* FREDERICK F. SCHAUER, THE LAW OF OBSCENITY 8–29 (1976)

11. New York v. Ferber, 458 U.S. 747, 749–52 (1982) (distinguishing between N.Y. Penal Law, § 263.10 and § 263.15 (McKinney 1980)).

12. *Id.*

13. *See* Josephine R. Potuto, Stanley + Ferber = *The Constitutional Crime of At-Home Child Pornography Possession*, 76 KY. L.J. 15, 18 n.18 (1978) (collecting statutes criminalizing the possession of child pornography); *see also* Susan G. Caughlan, Note, *Private Possession of Child Pornography: The Tensions Between* Stanley v. Georgia *and* New York v. Ferber, 29 WM. & MARY L. REV. 187, 201 (1987) (similar). Earlier assessments of child pornography laws were analyzed, *inter alia*, according to whether they prohibited production, distribution, or both; possession was not mentioned. *See* NATIONAL RESOURCE CENTER, *supra* note 1, at 111, 133–41; Donnelly, *supra* note 5, at 305–306.

14. 1988 H 51, eff. 3-17-89, *codified at* Ohio Rev. Code Ann. § 2907.323.

15. Stanley v. Georgia, 394 U.S. 557 (1969).

16. *E.g.*, Caughlan, *supra* note 13. *But see* Potuto, *supra* note 13.

17. 495 U.S. 103 (1990).

18. *E.g.* O'DONNELL & MILNER, *supra* note 6, at 20; TATE, *supra* note 6, at 17.

19. O'DONNELL & MILNER, *supra* note 6, at 28.

20. This action would have required a significant effort in the days before easy access to technology such as digital scanners and CD burners.

21. *See, e.g.*, United States v. Dyer, 589 F.3d 520 (1st Cir. 2009).

22. *See* 18 U.S.C. § 2252(b) (1990).

23. *See* Child Pornography Prevention Act of 1996, Pub. L. No. 104-208, § 121(5),

110 Stat. 3009–26, 3009–30, *invalidated by* Ashcroft v. Free Speech Coal., 535 U.S. 234 (2002).

24. *See* PROTECT Act, Pub. L. No. 108–21, § 103(a)(1)(B)(i), 117 Stat. 650, 652 (2003) (codified as amended at 18 U.S.C. § 2252(b)(1)). The maximum penalty was increased from fifteen to twenty years for "receiving" child pornography. The legislation also increased the maximum penalty for possession from five to ten years. PROTECT Act § 103(a)(1)(C)(i). Because receipt is a necessary component for possession, it is the twenty-year maximum penalty that represents the true exposure for offenders who possess child pornography.

25. *See, e.g.*, Carissa Byrne Hessick, *Disentangling Child Pornography from Child Sex Abuse*, 88 WASH. U. L. REV. 853, 857–60 (2011).

26. 535 U.S. 234 (2002).

27. *See, e.g.*, United States v. Cruikshank, 667 F. Supp. 2d 697 (S.D. W. Va. 2009); United States v. Beiermann, 599 F. Supp. 2d 1087 (N.D. Iowa 2009); United States v. Grober, 595 F. Supp. 2d 382 (D.N.J. 2008); United States v. Johnson, 588 F. Supp. 2d 997 (S.D. Iowa 2008); United States v. Hanson, 561 F. Supp. 2d 1004 (E.D. Wis. 2008); United States v. Grinbergs, No. 8:05CR232, 2008 WL 4191145 (D. Neb. Sept. 8, 2008); United States v. Ontiveros, No. 07-CR-333, 2008 WL 2937539 (E.D. Wis. July 24, 2008).

28. *E.g.*, Amir Efrati, *Judges Trim Jail Time for Child Porn*, WALL ST. J., Jan. 19, 2010, at A2; Lynne Marek, *Sentences for Possession of Child Porn May Be Too High, Judges Say*, NAT'L L.J., Sept. 10, 2009, http://www.law.com/jsp/nlj/PubArticleNLJ.jsp?id=1202433693658.

29. *See* U.S. SENTENCING COMMISSION, REPORT ON THE CONTINUING IMPACT OF *United States v. Booker* ON FEDERAL SENTENCING Part A at 6, 47–49, 60, 67–68, 87, 106 Part C-10, C-11 (2012) (identifying child pornography and fraud as offenses where the federal sentencing guidelines have lost influence and suggesting that Congress adopt proposals that would decrease the independence of federal judges).

30. 18 U.S.C. § 2259(a).

31. 134 S. Ct. 1710 (2014).

32. *Id.* at 1719.

33. *Id.* at 1727.

34. *Id.* at 1728.

Part I (A) | Defining Child Pornography Crimes

Constitutional Issues

1 | The Context and Content of *New York v. Ferber*

James Weinstein

In *New York v. Ferber*, the United States Supreme Court held that child pornography—visual depictions of actual children engaged in explicit sexual conduct—was categorically devoid of First Amendment protection.[1] Most of this chapter will be devoted to a detailed discussion of *Ferber* and its progeny, including *Ferber*'s revival of a discredited free speech methodology and its reliance on a rationale that avoided consideration of the effects of child pornography on the viewer. But before focusing directly on *Ferber*, it will be useful to locate this decision in the vast expanse of the Court's free speech jurisprudence. So contextualized, *Ferber* can be more accurately evaluated both for its specific holding and for its implications for free speech generally. In particular, consideration of the larger doctrinal background will suggest, surprisingly, that *Ferber* is in many ways a remarkably speech-*protective* decision.

Doctrinal Context

By 1982, the year *Ferber* was decided, American free speech doctrine provided extraordinarily strong protection to speech that vehemently challenged the status quo. For instance, the Court had a decade earlier upheld the right of an antiwar protestor to wear a jacket in public bearing the message "Fuck the Draft."[2] But the right of dissent in the United States was not always so secure. Just seven years after the First Amendment was ratified, Congress passed the Sedition Act of 1798, which made it a crime to publish any "false, scandalous, and malicious writing" with the intent to "defame" the government or bring it "into contempt or disrepute" or to excite against the government "the hatred of people of the United States." Several prominent newspaper publishers critical of the Adams administration were prosecuted and convicted under this law. Although the Supreme Court never had an occasion to rule on the constitutionality of the Sedition Act, lower court judges, including Supreme Court justices sitting as trial court judges, unanimously upheld its constitutionality.[3]

It was not until 1919 that the Supreme Court, in *Schenck v. United States*, issued its first significant free speech decision.[4] From the perspective of protecting dissent in a democratic society, this debut was nothing short of disastrous. In this decision, which announced the famous "clear and present danger" test, and in other cases decided shortly thereafter, the Court unanimously upheld convictions under the Espionage Act of 1917 of protestors for vehemently condemning American involvement in World War I as motivated by capitalist interest.[5] One of these decisions upheld the conviction of Eugene Debs, the leader of the Socialist Party and presidential candidate, sentenced to twenty years' imprisonment for praising fellow socialists convicted of obstructing the draft. In the absence of any meaningful restriction on the prosecution of anti-war speech, the government prosecuted more than two thousand people under the Espionage Act and obtained more than a thousand convictions.[6] As a prominent free speech commentator would later aptly observe, the Court's performance in World War I Espionage Act cases was "simply wretched."[7]

During the next several decades the Court issued some significant speech-protective decisions.[8] Still, as late as the 1950s it had not yet formulated a doctrine adequate to protect dissent that must be allowed in a free and democratic society. For instance, in a now much-reviled 1951 decision, the Court upheld the conviction of the leaders of the American Communist Party for conspiring to advocate the overthrow of the United States government by teaching material such as THE COMMUNIST MANIFESTO.[9] It would take nearly two more decades for the Court to transform the "clear and present danger" test into a truly speech-protective standard. In *Brandenburg v. Ohio*, a 1969 decision that has become a cornerstone of American free speech doctrine and which, as we shall see, sets sharp limits on the government's ability to prohibit child pornography, the Court reversed the conviction of a Ku Klux Klan leader convicted under a state law that forbade "advocat[ing] crime, sabotage, violence, or unlawful methods of terrorism as a means of accomplishing industrial or political reform."[10] In doing so, the Court explained that the First Amendment prevents the government from prohibiting "advocacy of the use of force or of law violation except where such advocacy is directed to inciting or producing imminent law violation and is likely to incite or produce such action."[11] This test provides extraordinarily strong protection for political advocacy: it grants absolute immunity to advocacy of law violation short of incitement to such conduct, and it immunizes incitement unless the government can show that it was likely to lead to imminent lawless conduct.

The importance of *Brandenburg* in finally providing adequate protection to speech denouncing particular laws, such as those governing conscription or, more generally, to expression vehemently agitating against the entire legal system, including the American form of government, cannot be overestimated. But a grossly underprotective "clear and present danger" test that *Brandenburg* remedied was not the only substantial defect in the Court's First Amendment jurisprudence. In addition, the methodology utilized by the Court in a seminal 1942 decision created several gaping holes in the web of free speech protection. In *Chaplinsky v. New Hampshire*, the Court upheld a disorderly conduct conviction of a Jehovah's Witness for using so-called "fighting words"—face-to-face insults—in a confrontation with a law enforcement official.[12] In the course of this holding, the Court observed:

> There are certain well-defined and narrowly limited classes of speech, the prevention and punishment of which have never been thought to raise any Constitutional problem. *These include the lewd and obscene, the profane, the libelous, and the insulting or 'fighting' words* . . . . It has been well observed that such utterances are no essential part of any exposition of ideas, and are of such slight social value as a step to truth that any benefit that may be derived from them is clearly outweighed by the social interest in order and morality.[13]

Unlike speech advocating law violation, which even under the pre-*Brandenburg* reformulation of the "clear and present danger" test was at least theoretically protected unless the government could demonstrate the necessary imminent danger, the Court here identified certain types of speech as categorically devoid of First Amendment protection. This means that with respect to lewd, obscene, profane, libelous, or personally insulting speech, the government need not show that the particular instance of the speech at issue caused harm; rather, all the government need do to punish this speech consistent with the First Amendment was to show that it came within the parameters of one of these forlorn categories of expression. As an abstract matter, such a free speech methodology seems sound, for by definition any speech it suppresses has de minimis First Amendment value and is at the same time manifestly and immediately harmful. But as Justice Holmes aptly observed, "The life of the law has not been logic: it has been experience,"[14] and experience proved that *Chaplinsky*'s categorical approach impaired valuable expression.

The categorical exclusion of libel vividly demonstrates Holmes's aphorism. In 1960, an Alabama jury had awarded a police commissioner $500,000 in damages against the *New York Times* and several civil rights activists, finding libelous an advertisement carried by the paper complaining about police treatment of protestors involved in civil rights demonstrations led by Dr. Martin Luther King, Jr. The finding was based on several inaccurate statements in the advertisement, such as that Dr. King had been arrested seven times by the Montgomery police for his protest activities, when in fact he had been arrested only four times. Because *Chaplinsky* had cast libelous statements beyond the ambit of the First Amendment and because these statements were technically libelous at common law, there were no First Amendment constraints on the power of the Alabama courts to render an onerous judgment against the defendants in this case, including imposing strict liability on the newspaper. In *New York Times v. Sullivan*, the Court reversed this judgment, famously observing that "debate on public issues should be uninhibited, robust and wide-open and . . . may well include vehement, caustic, and sometimes unpleasantly sharp attacks on government and public officials."[15] In order to give free expression adequate "breathing space," that Court held that public officials cannot recover for defamatory statements about their official duty unless they can show by clear and convincing evidence that the statements were made with "actual malice"—that is, with knowledge that the statements were false or with reckless disregard for the truth.[16]

More generally, the Court in *Sullivan* and subsequent cases recognized the danger that the exclusion of entire categories of speech can pose to free expression.[17] As a result, the Court did away altogether with some of the exceptions to First Amendment coverage that *Chaplinsky* had recognized and greatly narrowed the rest. An example of the Court's extinguishing an exception in its entirety is the case mentioned above, in which the Court extended First Amendment coverage to profanity in upholding the right of an antiwar protester to use the word "fuck" in public to condemn the draft. An example of the narrowing approach is that today only libel of private individuals devoid of public concern remains beyond First Amendment coverage.[18] Another example, and one that is of particular relevance to the government's ability to suppress child pornography, was a series of decisions attempting to define and for the most part narrowing the category of obscenity, culminating in the 1973 in opinion *Miller v. California*, which confined the category of obscenity to "hard core" pornography.[19] Prior to these decisions, government had routinely banned as obscene books and films of notable artistic and literary value due to their frank discussion or portrayal of sex.[20] Similarly, despite *Chaplinsky*'s suggestion of a broader reach, the Court has limited the category of "fighting words" to the use of words directed to an individual or a small group of individuals in a face-to-face confrontation.[21] So it was remarkable that the Court in *Ferber* bucked this trend by adopting the *Chaplinsky* methodology in holding child pornography categorically beyond the protections of the First Amendment.

New York Times v. Sullivan and *Brandenburg v. Ohio* were plainly conscious reactions to the failure of doctrine to provide adequate protection to dissent during the first half of the twentieth century and before. In particular, both decisions represent strategic "overprotection" of speech to counteract the tendency of prosecutors, juries, and even courts, including on occasion even the Supreme Court itself, to overestimate the danger of speech that vehemently attacks society's sacred cows, particularly in times of social unrest. But while these two cases provide strong protection to government criticism and political protest in two important doctrinal areas—defamation of public officials and advocacy of law violation—neither establishes a general rule for measuring the validity of speech restrictions. The genesis of such an overarching rule is to be found in *Chicago Police Department v. Mosley*,[22] a 1971 case in which the Court articulated what was to become the leitmotif of contemporary free speech doctrine: the rule against content discrimination.

At issue in *Mosley* was an ordinance that banned all picketing or demonstrations within 150 feet of schools while in session but exempted "peaceful picketing of any school involved in a labor dispute." Mosley, who had for months prior to the enactment of the ordinance quietly picketed outside a Chicago high school carrying a sign accusing the school of practicing racial discrimination, challenged the ban as violating both the First Amendment and the Equal Protection Clause of the Fourteenth Amendment. In invalidating the ordinance, Justice Thurgood Marshall's opinion for the Court observed:

> Above all else, the First Amendment means that government has no power to restrict expression because of its message, its ideas, its subject matter, or its content. To permit the continued building of our politics and culture, and to assure self-fulfillment for each indi-

vidual, our people are guaranteed the right to express any thought, free from government censorship. The essence of this forbidden censorship is content control. Any restriction on expressive activity because of its content would completely undercut the 'profound national commitment to the principle that debate on public issues should be uninhibited, robust, and wide-open.'[23]

During the next decade the Court frequently cited *Mosley's* condemnation of content regulation,[24] and by the time *Ferber* was decided in 1982, the foundation had been laid for the central rule of contemporary free speech jurisprudence: content-based speech restrictions are invalid unless the government can demonstrate that the restriction in question is "justified by a compelling government interest and is narrowly drawn to serve that interest."[25] Such "strict scrutiny" imposes "a very exacting and rarely satisfied standard" on the government defending a content-based speech regulation.[26] In sharp contrast, content-neutral regulation of expression—such as ordinances regulating the time, place, or manner of speech without regard to its message—are readily upheld.[27]

The Child Pornography Problem

Having learned a hard lesson from its inadequate protection of free speech during the first half of the twentieth century, the Supreme Court by the early 1980s had firmly in place a free speech jurisprudence calculated to protect the right of Americans to vehemently challenge the status quo through offensive, inflammatory, and even dangerous expression. At about this same time, however, perhaps in part because of the existence of this highly protective free speech jurisprudence, an industry devoted to the production and distribution of child pornography was flourishing. The legislative response was massive, with the federal government and forty-seven states passing laws addressing the problem.[28] These laws took three basic forms: (1) twelve states prohibited only the production of child pornography; (2) fifteen states and the federal government prohibited the distribution of material depicting children engaged in sexual conduct but only if the material also met the *Miller* standard for obscenity; and (3) twenty states, including New York, prohibited distribution of child pornography even if it was not legally obscene.[29]

Despite being part of a production that is photographed or filmed, the promotion of sexual activity by children was not considered "speech" for purposes of the First Amendment, but rather "conduct" constituting serious child abuse.[30] Banning the use of children in the production of pornography therefore did not present any substantial free speech problem. Similarly, since obscenity is expression beyond the scope of the First Amendment, the banning of a particularly harmful type of obscenity also did not raise a difficult free speech question. It was only laws that banned the *distribution* of *non-obscene* child pornography that presented a serious First Amendment question. Indeed, it appeared as if the extremely protective free speech doctrine developed by the Court over the previous several decades might well have made laws prohibiting the distribution of child pornography unconstitutional. This was the holding of the only two federal court decisions to address the issue prior to *Ferber*.[31] It was also the view of the New York Court of Appeals (the highest court in New York state judicial system) in rendering the decision below in the *Ferber* case itself.[32]

Enacted in 1977, the New York child pornography law made it a felony to distribute any motion picture or photograph of a child less than sixteen years of age engaged in sexual conduct.[33] Paul Ferber, the proprietor of a Manhattan bookstore specializing in sexually oriented material, was convicted under this law for selling two films "devoted almost exclusively to depicting young boys masturbating."[34] The New York Court of Appeals found the New York law unconstitutional because it prohibited photographic images that were not legally obscene.[35] In addition, duly reflecting the antipathy to content-based speech restrictions expressed in recent Supreme Court opinions, the court condemned the law for "discriminat[ing] against films and other visual portrayals of nonobscene adolescent sex solely on the basis of their content."[36] Demonstrating the tension between bans on child pornography and the highly speech-protective doctrine it had developed in previous decades, the United States Supreme Court, though reversing the Court of Appeals decision, acknowledged that the lower court's position was "not unreasonable in light of our decisions."[37]

The *Ferber* Decision

Justice Byron White began his opinion for the Court by observing that in recent years, "the exploitive use of children in the production of pornography has become a serious national problem."[38] The challenge for the Court was how to permit government sufficient leeway to address this problem without undermining the strong protection of free speech the

Court had painstakingly constructed during the prior three decades. A key component of this bulwark against government suppression of dissent, was, as we have seen, the Court's intense hostility to content regulation of speech, an attitude that would within a few years be reified into a rule forming the cornerstone of contemporary free speech jurisprudence. Moreover, motion pictures and photographs had long been considered expression protected under the First Amendment.[39] And, as the Court of Appeals noted, New York's law manifestly discriminated on the basis of the content of the photograph or film, targeting material that depicted children engaged in sexual conduct. "Serious national problem" that use of children in the production of pornography may have been, it would have been a large step backwards to the weak speech protection of the first part of the century for the Court simply to have invoked this harm as justifying an exception to its injunction that "[a]bove all else, the First Amendment means that government has no power to restrict expression because of its message, its ideas, its subject matter, or its content."

A crucial though not often enough articulated lesson from the Court's "wretched" performance in applying the "clear and present danger" test to antiwar protests during World War I and to speech of Communist Party members during the McCarthy era is the counterintuitive precept that even serious harm is not sufficient reason to suppress speech connected to democratic self-governance.[40] As Learned Hand, one of the few judges willing to protect speech vehemently denouncing America's involvement in World War I, astutely observed, antiwar speech has the capacity to cause grave harm. "Virulent attacks" upon America's involvement in the war, he explained, "enervate public feeling at home . . . and encourage the success of the enemies of the United States abroad." Moreover, joining such criticism of the war with condemnation of conscription "tends to promote a mutinous and insubordinate temper among the troops." Nonetheless, Hand, in sharp contrast to almost all of his contemporary jurists, including the entire Supreme Court, held that such speech should be allowed in a free and democratic society despite the harm it caused.[41] Similarly, the expression of virulent racist ideas can cause grievous harm both through the psychic injury it can inflict on minorities defamed by such speech and through persuading others to discriminate against members of these groups. Yet at the time *Ferber* was before the Court, there were strong indications that, like virulent antiwar speech, hate speech too was protected by the First Amendment despite the harm it can cause.[42] The Court would later confirm this view of hate speech.[43]

Fortunately for both the protection of children and for free speech, the

Court in *Ferber* declined either to mechanically find that the rule against content discrimination rendered the New York law unconstitutional or to hold that the serious harm associated with child pornography was sufficient to justify an exception to this fundamental precept of free speech jurisprudence. Rather, the Court commendably paid careful attention both to the free speech values that would likely be impaired by the suppression of child pornography and to *the mechanism* of the harm this expression caused.[44]

The Court emphasized that the free speech value of photographic reproduction of children engaged in "lewd sexual conduct" is "exceedingly modest, if not *de minimis*."[45] In the Court's view it was unlikely that "visual depictions of children performing sexual acts or lewdly exhibiting their genitals" would often constitute "an important and necessary part" of an artistic performance or a scientific or educational work. The Court added that if such depictions were thought necessary to the value of these works, a person over the age limit but who looked younger could be employed or, alternatively, that prohibited acts forming the basis of the depiction could be simulated. Finally, the Court was confident that there was no "question here of censoring a particular literary theme or portrayal of sexual activity."[46] Accordingly, the Court concluded that the only First Amendment interest impaired by the law was the ability to render the portrayal of sexual activity engaged in by children "somewhat more 'realistic'" by photographing children actually engaged in the sexual activity prohibited by the law.[47]

Having thus assessed the free speech interests impaired by bans on child pornography, the Court then turned to the harm caused in the production of this material, citing studies that showed, unsurprisingly, that the use of children as subjects of pornographic films and photographs "is harmful to the physiological, emotional, and mental health of the child." It then observed that "safeguarding the physical and psychological well-being" of children is a "compelling" state interest, and in particular, that "prevention of sexual exploitation and abuse of children constitutes a government objective of surpassing importance."[48] It remained, however, to explain why a ban on *the distribution* of child pornography was required to prevent the harm caused by the use of children *in the production* of such material. The Court gave two reasons.

First, the Court noted that because these materials are a "permanent record" of the child's participation in the activity, their distribution exacerbates the harm to the child caused by the events recorded in the materials. Second, and more significantly, the Court concluded that the "distribution network must be closed if the production of material which requires the sexual exploitation of children is to be effectively controlled." The Court relied on the legislature's conclusion that it would be "difficult, if not impossible" to put an end to the sexual exploitation of children by prosecuting only those involved in the production of the movies and photographs. It noted that although the production of child pornography was a "low-profile, clandestine industry," it required a "visible apparatus" to market its wares. Accordingly, it agreed with the conclusion of Congress and thirty-five states that the "most expeditious if not the only practical method" of preventing children from being sexually abused in the production of these films was "to dry up the market" for this material by imposing severe criminal penalties on those who distribute it.[49]

The Court then rejected the argument that New York could accomplish this goal by punishing only those who distribute child pornography that is legally obscene under the *Miller* standard. It explained that the criteria for legal obscenity do not reflect the state interest in protecting children from the harms arising from their use in the production of pornography. Thus, the Court pointed out, *Miller's* first two requirements, that the work "appeal to the prurient interest of the average person" and be "patently offensive," have no bearing on whether a child has been physically or psychologically harmed in the production of the work. Similarly irrelevant, the Court explained, is the *Miller* test's inquiry whether the work, "taken as a whole, contains serious literary, artistic, political, or scientific value." Judged in its entirety, a work could possess such value yet still embody "the hardest core of child pornography," the production of which was extremely harmful to a child.[50]

Having documented both the minimal First Amendment interests impaired by the prohibition on the distribution of child pornography and the reasons for forbidding such distribution, the Court declared child pornography to be "a category outside the protection of the First Amendment." Such categorical exclusion, the Court explained, is appropriate where, as in the case of child pornography, "it may be appropriately generalized that within the confines of the given classification, the evil to be restricted so overwhelmingly outweighs the expressive interests, if any, at stake that no process of case-by-case adjudication is required."[51] Accordingly, in a prosecution for the distribution of child pornography, the government does not have to show that a government interest in suppression of the material in that particular case outweighs the First Amendment interests of the defendant in its distribution. Relatedly, defendants are not able to invoke the First Amendment even if they can show that no significant physiological or psychological harm befell children in the production of the particular material they were charged with distributing, or that in this instance suppressing the material will not substantially serve the goal of preventing harm in the production. Rather, so far as First Amendment constraints are concerned, the government need show only that the material falls within the category of expression that it declared beyond the purview of the First Amendment.

However, in excluding child pornography from the scope of the First Amendment, the Court cautioned that "there are, of course, limits on the category of child pornography . . . unprotected by the First Amendment." It noted that the prohibited material must be "adequately defined by the applicable state law" and similarly that "the category of 'sexual conduct'" depicted in the proscribed material must be "suitably limited and described" in the law. But most importantly, the Court held that in light of the "nature of the harm to be combated," the category of child pornography beyond the ambit of the First Amendment must be limited to works that "*visually* depict sexual conduct by children below a specified age."[52] Though emphasizing that the "test for child pornography is separate from the obscenity standard enunciated in *Miller*," the Court compared the two tests "for the purposes of clarity." It explained that unlike obscenity under the *Miller* test, child pornography need not appeal to "the prurient interest of the average person" nor portray sexual conduct in a "patently offensive manner." And in accordance with its previous discussion of why banning only obscene material depicting children was not sufficient to combat the harms of child pornography, the Court held that in contrast to the requirement for a finding of obscenity, the material at issue in a child pornography prosecution "need not be considered as a whole."[53] As a result, the fact that an hour-long film contains only a single fifteen-second scene depicting children engaged in sexual activity will not save the work from being deemed child pornography beyond the scope of the First Amendment.

Finally, the Court rejected the argument that the New York law was unconstitutionally overbroad because it banned material with "serious literary, scientific or educational value." As part of its overall goal of strengthening protection of free speech, the Court had developed what had become known as the "overbreadth doctrine," which permits someone whose own speech might have been constitutionally proscribed by a more narrowly drawn prohibition to ask a court to invalidate the law in its entirety on the grounds that it sweeps up a substantial amount of protected speech.[54] The purpose of this doctrine is to prevent a law from chilling the exercise of First Amendment rights of those not before the court. Invoking this doctrine, the New York Court of Appeals found the law under which Ferber was charged to be fatally overbroad because it prohibited showing and distributing medical or educational materials depicting children engaged in sexual activity. The Supreme Court disagreed. It noted, first, that it was uncertain how often, if ever, children needed to be used to produce pictorial representation in medical or educational material. It then added that in any event it was highly doubtful that these arguably impermissible applications of the statute amounted to more than "a tiny fraction of the material within the statute's reach." The Court accordingly found that the statute was not "substantially overbroad."[55]

Justice Sandra Day O'Connor joined the opinion of the Court but wrote separately to emphasize that the majority opinion did not hold that the category of material it identified as beyond the scope of the First Amendment contains an exemption for material with "serious literary, scientific or educational value." To the contrary, in her view the majority opinion's focus on the harm to children in the production of child pornography suggests that literary, scientific, or educational value is insufficient to vest such material with First Amendment protection. Justice O'Connor explained, however, that certain visual depictions of children engaged in sexual activity, such as those that might appear in medical textbooks or "pictures of children engaged in rites widely approved in their cultures, such as those that might appear in issues of National Geographic," might not threaten the harms identified by the Court and thus might be protected by the First Amendment.[56]

Justice William Brennan, joined by Justice Marshall, filed an opinion concurring in the judgment noting that he agreed with "much of what is said in the Court's opinion." Justice Brennan, however, took the opposite tack than had Justice O'Connor, explaining that prohibition of depictions of children engaging in sexual activity that have "serious literary, artistic, scientific, or medical value" would violate the First Amendment. Emphasizing the Court's reasoning that child pornography is properly excluded from the scope of the First Amendment because such material has "exceedingly 'slight social value,'" he observed that the free speech value of depictions of children engaged in sexual activity that "are in themselves serious contributions to art, literature, or science, is by definition, simply not '*de minimis*.'"[57]

The majority opinion in *Ferber* is remarkable in two related respects: its categorical exclusion of child pornography from First Amendment coverage and the type of harm on which the Court relied in holding that this material may constitutionally be suppressed. A mainstay of the Court's free speech jurisprudence in the 1940s and 1950s, the categorical exclusion methodology had fallen into disuse, arguably even disrepute, by the time *Ferber* reached the Court. Not only had the Court failed to identify any categories of unprotected speech beyond the ones it had specified in *Chaplinsky*, the 1941 decision that had originated the categorical exclusion methodology, but by the time *Ferber* was decided, the Court had reversed course and extended First Amendment coverage to several categories of speech identified in *Chaplinsky* as unprotected. And subsequent to *Ferber*'s categorical exclusion of child pornography, the Court has not recognized any other category of speech as beyond the First Amendment's purview. To the contrary, it has adamantly rebuffed pleas, including by the United States, to recognize other categories of unprotected speech.[58] The *Ferber* Court's selective revival of the categorical exclusion approach thus cries out for explanation.

One obvious reason for *Ferber*'s use of this approach is that child pornography easily fits *Chaplinsky*'s criteria of unquestionably harmful expression whose prohibition would, at most, only minimally impair free speech values.[59] But while this may constitute a necessary condition for invocation of the categorical exclusion approach, the Court's persistent refusal to exclude other categories of speech sharing these criteria shows that it is not sufficient to exclude speech from First Amendment coverage.[60] Interestingly, by the time the *Ferber* case reached the Court, the *Chaplinsky* categorical exclusion approach had become so antiquated that New York quite understandably did not even suggest that the Court add child pornography to by then greatly diminished list of speech categorically beyond the purview of the First Amendment. Rather, the state argued that the ban on child pornography survived "strict scrutiny," the test for content-based restrictions on speech, which required the government to demonstrate that the prohibition "furthers a compelling state interest and is the least restrictive alternative to achieve that interest."[61]

The Court readily acknowledged that protecting children against sexual abuse was a compelling state interest. So why then didn't it simply agree with New York's argument that the ban on child pornography survived "strict scrutiny" rather than revive a seemingly defunct and plainly problematic free speech methodology? One possibility is that even though the test for content-based speech regulations is not an absolute bar against such provisions but permits such restrictions if they are the least restrictive means to serving a compelling state interest, the Court wanted this test to function as a nearly *per se* rule against content discrimination. Especially because this crucial feature of modern free speech jurisprudence was still in a relatively early stage of development, the Court may have feared that upholding any content-based provision was likely to dilute the exacting version of strict scrutiny it intended this test to impose.[62] So although use of the categorical exclusion approach presented its own risks to the Court's overarching concern with building a speech-protective First Amendment jurisprudence, the Court may well have thought it preferable to revive this methodology for this one occasion than to risk undermining a newly laid cornerstone of its free speech jurisprudence.[63]

This underlying premise of this hypothesis—that the Court intended the test applicable to content-based restrictions of speech to be a virtually *per se* rule against such provisions—is consistent with language in *Chicago Police Department v. Mosley*, the progenitor of the rule against content discrimination, which condemns such provisions in unqualified terms, and more significantly by the fact that today there is only one Supreme Court majority opinion that is still good law in which a content-based restriction survived strict scrutiny.[64] But whether or not the Court consciously made such a calculus, its use of the categorical exclusion methodology rather than holding that the ban on child pornography met the "strict scrutiny" standard for content-based restrictions on speech was on the whole a speech-protective move.

Another speech-protective feature of the Court's methodology in *Ferber* is the type of harm on which the Court relied—and, more importantly, on which it did *not* rely—in concluding that the First Amendment did not extend to child pornography. In regulating the content of speech, the harm that government seeks to avoid almost always flows from the *communicative impact* of the speech, typically the concern that the speech at issue will lead the audience to engage in some detrimental conduct, ranging from draft resistance to violence against women to some disfavored economic activity.[65] In its brief to the Court in *Ferber*, the state invoked just this type of harm, citing studies "suggesting a link between the sale of these materials and the commission of sex crimes against children."[66] Significantly, however, in discussing the harm of child pornography that justified excluding such expression from First Amendment coverage, the Court eschewed reliance on this communicative-related harm.[67] Rather, in what has come to be known as the "harm-in-the-production" rationale, the Court focused exclusively on another type of harm, also documented by the state:[68] the physiological and psychological harm arising from "the use of children as subjects in pornographic materials."[69]

By declining the state's invitation to rely on harm caused by the audience's reaction to child pornography and focusing instead on harm unrelated to the communicative effect of this material, the Court rendered its decision speech-protective in two important respects. First, banning the distribution of child pornography on the grounds that it may lead viewers to commit sex crimes disrespects the individual autonomy of the viewers and thus would have implicated a norm that many believe lies at the heart of the First Amendment.[70] In addition, a rationale turning on the power of speech to influence its audience is applicable to a wide variety of expression and is thus difficult to cabin. So if the Court had accepted the state's rationale for prohibiting child pornography, it would have created precedent for the suppression of other types of material that studies showed might contribute to the audience's engaging in harmful or even illegal behavior, such as pornography that arguably contributes to men's aggressive behavior toward women or racist propaganda that that might well lead to discrimination against minorities.[71] In contrast, the harm-in-the-production rationale is easily confined, for by definition it applies only to a limited class of harms resulting from film or photographic production.[72]

I do not want to overstate *Ferber*'s speech-protectiveness, for there are features of the decision that look in the opposite direction. The primary weakness of the categorical exclusion approach is that categories of speech that seem in the abstract to encompass only expression of little or no First Amendment value in actual operation turn out to include speech that has considerable First Amendment value. A related problem is that if the category is not defined with adequate precision it can sweep up expression that is not in fact harmful. With regard to this latter problem, several commentators have persuasively demonstrated how child pornography laws have been applied to material that does not present the harm that justified excluding child pornography from the First Amendment's ambit in the first place.[73] Since other contributions to this volume discuss this problem in detail,[74] I will focus instead on another speech-restrictive consequence permitted, if not required, by *Ferber* and one that, moreover, arguably trenches on a fundamental free speech interest.

Osborne v. Ohio and Possession of Child Pornography

In 1969, the Court held in *Stanley v. Georgia*[75] that even though obscene material was categorically beyond the scope of the First Amendment, it was nonetheless unconstitutional for government to criminalize its mere possession. "If the First Amendment means anything," the Court declared in an opinion by Justice Marshall, "it means that a State has no business telling a man, sitting alone in his own house, what books he may read or what films he may watch. . . . Our whole constitutional heritage rebels at the thought of giving government the power to control men's minds."[76] So when Clyde Osborne was arrested and charged under Ohio law for the possession of child pornography in his home, his lawyers might have been reasonably confident that although *Ferber* had several years earlier declared child pornography categorically unprotected by the First Amendment, Osborne nonetheless had a right to possess this material in the privacy of his home.[77] Any such confidence, however, was misplaced.

As he had in *Ferber*, Justice White wrote for the Court in *Osborne v. Ohio*.[78] Unlike the unanimous result in *Ferber*, however, three justices dissented in an opinion by Justice Brennan. White began the majority opinion by reciting *Ferber*'s assessment that the value of child pornography was "exceedingly modest, if not de minimis." This observation was beside the point in two separate respects. First, in making this assessment, the Court in *Ferber* was focusing on the minimal detriment that the inability to use children engaged in sexual acts would have on "a literary performance or scientific or educational use," not the affront to individual autonomy and privacy interests with which *Stanley* was concerned. In addition, like child pornography, obscenity is beyond the scope of the First Amendment precisely because of its exceedingly limited First Amendment value. But as the Court in *Stanley* made clear, the right to receive information and ideas does not depend on "their social worth." So it was quite disingenuous for Justice White to question whether under *Stanley* Osborne had any "First Amendment interest in viewing and possessing child pornography" and then merely to assume only "for the sake of argument" that he did.[79]

The Court found firmer ground for distinguishing *Stanley* in observing that "the interests underlying child pornography prohibitions far exceed the interests justifying the Georgia law at issue in *Stanley*." The Court accurately recounts that in *Stanley*, Georgia sought to prohibit the private possession of obscenity because it was concerned that viewing the material would "poison the minds of its viewers." In contrast, the Court emphasized, Ohio did not rely "on a paternalistic interest in regulating Osborne's mind" but rather has enacted the ban on possession of child pornography to "protect the victims of child pornography; it hopes to destroy a market for the exploitative use of children." And it was "surely reasonable," the Court continued, "for the State to conclude that it will decrease the production of child pornography if it penalizes those who possess and view the product." Finally, the Court credited Ohio's argument that since *Ferber* was decided, "much of the child pornography market has been driven underground; as a result, it is now difficult, if not impossible, to solve the child pornography problem by only attacking production and distribution."[80]

The Court acknowledged that in *Stanley*, Georgia had argued that its prohibition of the private possession of obscenity was "a necessary incident to its proscription on obscenity distribution." Georgia's argument, however, the Court insisted, must be viewed in light of the "weak interests asserted by the State in that case"[81] and contrasted it with the interest in "'safeguarding the physical and psychological well-being of a minor'" furthered by Ohio's ban on possession of child pornography, an interest which the Court in *Ferber* declared to be "compelling."[82] In addition, the Court noted two "other interests" supporting Ohio's ban on possession. First, as the Court had noted in *Ferber*, materials produced by child pornographers "permanently record the victim's abuse" and can continue to haunt the victim years after the film is made. The ban on possession encourages the possessor of these materials to destroy them, thus reducing the harm to the victim. Second, "because evidence suggests that pedophiles use child pornography to seduce other children into sexual activity," a law promoting the destruction of this material also serves the interest in protecting children.[83]

In dissent, Justice Brennan, joined by Justices Marshall and John Paul Stevens, objected that Ohio had already enacted "a panoply of laws prohibiting the creation, sale, and distribution of child pornography" but had not demonstrated why these laws were "inadequate and why the State must forbid mere possession [of child pornography] as well."[84] He characterized as "speculat[ive]" the Court's assumption that, in light of these other provisions, outlawing private possession of child pornography will decrease the production of child pornography. He added that even if he were to accept the Court's "empirical assumptions," he would nevertheless find its approach foreclosed by *Stanley*. Brennan noted that in response to Georgia's argument in that case that a ban on possession of obscenity was a "necessary incident" to its ban on distribution because of the difficulty of proving intent to distribute or in adducing evidence of distribution, the Court stated:

> We are not convinced that such difficulties exist, but even if they did we do not think that they would justify infringement of the individual's right to read or observe what he pleases. Because that right is so fundamental to our scheme of individual liberty, its restriction may not be justified by the need to ease the administration of otherwise valid criminal laws.[85]

One can fairly fault the dissent with not coming to grips with the majority's argument that in light of the far weightier interests government has in combating the harm associated child pornography than with obscenity, *Stanley*'s injunction against prohibiting possession "to ease the administration" of related laws should not be controlling. More pertinently, the dissent fails to explain why the far greater state interests involved in combating the harm in the production of child pornography does not entitle the state to correspondingly greater leeway to prohibit possession to combat this upstream harm. Still, the dissent does persuasively demonstrate that the First Amendment interest "to read or observe what [one] pleases" in the privacy of one's home is an interest that, far from being "exceedingly modest, if not de minimis," is one that had previously been recognized as a *fundamental* liberty. So *Osborne*'s holding that this liberty interest may be infringed based on a showing considerably shy of conclusive evidence that Ohio's ban on possession of child pornography was strictly necessary to combat the harm in production suggests that this interest is not nearly as weighty as *Stanley* declared it to be. And to the extent that *Ferber* and it methodology contributed to the diminution of the status of the liberty interest recognized in *Stanley*, *Ferber* is in this respect a speech-restrictive decision.

The Limits of the Child Pornography Exception

There are two related yet conceptually distinct types of limits to the child pornography exception: definitional and justificatory. Definitional limits are those imposed by the Court's linguistic formulation of the type of material constituting child pornography categorically excluded from First Amendment protection. Justificatory limits, which undergird and accordingly should control the definitional limits, are those imposed by the rationales for the exclusion. In *Ferber* and its progeny the Court provides little in the way of explicit definitional limits on the category of unprotected speech. The most significant definitional limit the Court has provided, and one it expressly tied to the primary justificatory limit on the child pornography exception, is *Ferber*'s statement that "the nature of the harm to be combated requires" the category of child pornography be limited to works that "*visually* depict sexual conduct by children."[86] As has often been remarked upon, the Court declined to give any explicit definition of the "sexual conduct" the visual depiction of which is beyond the scope of the First Amendment.[87] It did, however, implicitly provide a definition of at least the core of this conduct by approving New York's definition. It signaled that further definition of this conduct, including its outer boundaries, should be fleshed out by legislatures in the first instance and then by reviewing courts, both paying careful attention, as the Court itself did in limiting the child pornography to visual depictions, to the harm-in-the-production rationale.[88] These laws and decisions and the tests they have produced are described in detail in other contributions to this volume.[89] So I will focus here on the guidance, limited and inferential though it may be, that the Court has provided about the meaning of "sexual conduct" the visual depiction of which may be prohibited under the child pornography exception to the First Amendment.

Definitional Limits

In addition to limiting the category of child pornography unprotected by the First Amendment to visual depictions of sexual conduct, the Court in *Ferber* announced that any prohibited material of this nature must be "adequately defined by the applicable state law" and, further, that the "the category of 'sexual conduct'" depicted in the proscribed material be "suitably limited and described." The New York law upheld in *Ferber* defined "sexual conduct" as "actual or simulated sexual intercourse, deviant sexual intercourse, sexual bestiality, masturbation, sado-masochistic abuse, or lewd exhibition of the genitals."[90] The Court readily held that this provision defined the forbidden visual depictions of sexual acts with "sufficient precision" and "sufficiently describes a category of material the production and distribution of which is not entitled to First Amendment protection." So even though *Ferber* did not offer explicit guidelines or criteria for determining whether visual depictions qualify as "sexual conduct" devoid of First Amendment protection, the decision does make clear, for instance, that pictures showing children engaged in actual sexual intercourse, masturbating, or lewdly exhibiting their genitals plainly qualify. *Ferber* thus helpfully identifies the core of the category of expression that it held to be without First Amendment protection.[91] In contrast, *Ferber* reveals little about the outer boundaries of the exception. For example, "though mere nudity is undoubtedly insufficient"[92] to constitute "sexual conduct" the depiction of which is unprotected by the First Amendment, what additional elements or circumstance render visual depictions of nude children beyond the ambit of the First Amendment? This was a question raised but not resolved in *Massachusetts v. Oakes*.[93]

Douglas Oakes was convicted under a Massachusetts child pornography law for taking topless photographs of his physically mature fourteen-year-old stepdaughter, who at the time was attending modeling school. The photographs depicted the girl "sitting, lying, and reclining on top of a bar, clad only in a red and white striped bikini panty and a red scarf [which did] not cover [her] breasts."[94] The Massachusetts law prohibited adults from posing minors "in a state of nudity" in photographs or motion pictures and defined nudity to include the uncovered "post-pubertal" female breast.[95] The Massachusetts Supreme Judicial Court invalidated the law as unconstitutionally overbroad. The five justices of the United States Supreme Court who reached the overbreadth issue divided sharply as to whether the law was substantially overbroad.[96] Justice Brennan, in an opinion joined by Justices Marshall and Stevens, objected that by its terms the law imposed severe criminal penalties on parents who photographed their naked infants or toddlers in the bath or romping on the beach. In addition, Brennan faulted the law for criminalizing "nonexploitative" topless photographs or films of adolescent girls, for instance, at the pool or on a beach where such nudity is permitted, as well as for banning professional nude modeling by teenagers not involving sexually explicit conduct. In light of such extensive application to protected speech, Brennan found the law to be unconstitutionally overbroad.[97]

Justice Antonin Scalia, in an opinion joined by Justice Harry Blackmun, took issue with Brennan's conclusion that the law was substantially overbroad. Unlike Brennan, he expressed doubt as to whether nonpornographic, artistic photographs or films of nude children, including those depicting topless adolescent minors, constituted expression protected by the First Amendment. Rather, since he suspected that most adults would not want to be nude models "whatever the intention of the photographer or artist, and however unerotic the pose" and because there "is no cause to think children are less sensitive," it was not unreasonable in his view for the state to deem the use of even consenting minors as nude models "a form of child exploitation." Indeed, Scalia was not even certain that family photographs of nude infants or toddlers in the bath or on the beach was protected expression, though he was willing to assume for the sake of argument that prohibiting such photographs was unconstitutional "as opposed to merely foolish." Still, given the extent of child pornography in general "and of pornographic magazines that use young female models" in particular, the legitimate scope of the law in his view "vastly exceed[ed]" any unconstitutional application and therefore was not substantially overbroad.[98]

The disagreement in *Oakes* about when depictions of child nudity also constitute child pornography unprotected by the First Amendment is no doubt merely a specific manifestation of what were and still are significantly different views among the justices about the proper boundaries of the child pornography exception. Indeed, *Ferber*'s remarkable failure to provide any explicit definition of child pornography or even guidelines for determining what materials fall within this category may well mask such disagreement. And just as differences about the definitional limits of child pornography came to the fore in *Oakes*, disagreement about justificatory limits of arose when the Court considered a federal ban on "virtual" child pornography.

Justificatory Limits: Harm in the Production, "Virtual" Child Pornography, and Ashcroft v. Free Speech Coalition

An attractive feature of the Court's decision in *Ferber* is that it firmly tethered its upholding the ban on child pornography to the prevention of a palpable and indisputably serious injury: harm to children in the production of pornography, a rationale that eschews any reliance on audience reaction to the proscribed expression. This harm-in the-production rationale has in the decades since *Ferber* was decided withstood powerful expansionary pressures that would have greatly distended a less narrowly confined and firmly anchored principle. Arguably, the Court extended this rationale to its limits in *Osborne* when it upheld a ban on possession in the absence of rigorous proof that the ban would significantly reduce harm in the production.[99] But when Congress pushed that rationale well beyond its breaking point by outlawing computer-generated images of children engaged in sexual activity and even the use of adult actors who looked like children, the Court pushed back.

As originally enacted and in several subsequent amendments, the federal ban on child pornography applied only to visual depictions using actual children.[100] In 1996, however, Congress passed the Child Pornography Prevention Act ("the CPPA"), which contained as its key provision a prohibition on the distribution or possession of "any visual depiction" that "is, or appears to be, of a minor engaging in sexually explicit conduct."[101] By virtue of the "or appears to be" specification, the law applied not just to depictions of actual children but also to "virtual" child pornography, including computer-generated images of children engaged in sexual activities, as well as to depictions of adult actors who look like children.[102] In *Ashcroft v. Free Speech Coalition*,[103] in an opinion by Justice Anthony Kennedy joined by four other justices, the Court invalidated this provision as substantially overbroad.[104] At the beginning of its opinion, the Court emphasized that by "prohibiting child pornography that does not depict an actual child," the law "goes beyond" *Ferber*, which had upheld the suppression of child pornography because of "the State's interest in protecting the children exploited by the production process." The Court observed that by its literal terms, the statute embraced "a Renaissance painting depicting a scene from classical mythology" depicting what "appears to be a minor engaging in sexually explicit conduct," as well as "Hollywood movies, filmed without any child actors," if an actor "'appears to be' a minor engaging" in such conduct. The Court again stressed that these images "do not involve, let alone harm, any children in the production process."[105]

The Court then considered the severity of the penalties imposed by the CPPA, noting that a first offender may be imprisoned for fifteen years and that a repeat offender faces a minimum of five years and a maximum of thirty years in prison. "With these severe penalties in force," the Court concluded, "few legitimate movie producers or book publishers . . . would risk distributing images in or near the uncertain reach of this law." Having noted this potential of the CPPA to prohibit or chill a massive amount of speech, the Court then turned to the government's various justifications for prohibiting any visual depiction that "appears to be" a minor engaging in sexually explicit conduct. The government offered two arguments tied to the harm-in-the-production rationale that the Court adopted in *Ferber* and two additional rationales more generally related to preventing sexual abuse of children, all of which the Court rejected.[106]

With respect to harm in the production, the government argued first that eliminating the market for pornography using real children required prohibition of virtual images because virtual images are indistinguishable from real ones, are part of the same market, and are often exchanged. For this reason, the government insisted, virtual images promote trafficking in works in whose production actual children were harmed. The Court found the premise of this argument "somewhat implausible." If virtual images were in fact indistinguishable from pornography using real children, the latter images, the Court reasoned, would be driven from the market by virtual child pornography because pornographers would not risk prosecution by abusing real children if computerized images would suffice. In addition, the Court noted that creation of the speech involved in *Ferber* was "itself the crime of child abuse" and that the prohibition of that expression deterred the crime by "removing the profit motive." In contrast, with respect to the creation of virtual child pornography prohibited by the CPPA, the Court pointed out that "there is no underlying crime at all" to deter.[107]

In an additional attempt to tie the ban on virtual pornography to harm in the production, the government argued that the existence of virtual child pornography makes it difficult to prosecute producers of pornography involving real children because experts may have difficulty determining whether the material in question was made using actual children or computer-generated images. Accordingly, the government argued that it was necessary to prohibit both kinds of images. The Court firmly rejected this argument, retorting that government "may not suppress lawful speech as the means to suppress unlawful speech. Protected speech does not become unprotected merely because it resembles the latter." Indeed, the Court explained, such an approach "turns the First Amendment upside down" and is precisely what the overbreadth doctrine prohibits.[108]

Perhaps realizing that the Court would likely reject as too tenuous any asserted connection between virtual child pornography and harm to actual children in the production of pornography, the government advanced two additional arguments in support of the "appears to be a child" provision. First, it claimed that the ban on virtual pornography was necessary to prevent pedophiles from using this material to seduce children. This rationale had a long and checkered history in child pornography litigation: it was advanced by the state though ignored by the Court in *Ferber* but then relied on by the Court in *Osborne* as one of two "other" interests besides deterring harm in the production that supported a ban on possession of child pornography involving actual children.[109] In *Free Speech Coalition*, however, the Court again switched course and found the interest in preventing pedophiles from using child pornography to seduce children to be an insufficient reason to ban virtual child pornography. In rejecting this rationale, the Court relied on the well-established principle that "speech within the rights of adults to hear may not be silenced completely in an attempt to shield children from it."[110]

The government also sought to justify the prohibition against virtual child pornography by claiming that it "whets the appetite" of pedophiles, thereby leading them to sexually abuse children. The Court also firmly rejected this rationale, explaining that "the mere tendency of speech to encourage unlawful acts is not a sufficient reason for banning it" and that the government "cannot constitutionally premise legislation on the desirability of controlling a person's private thoughts." More specifically, the Court found that the rationale offered by the government was inconsistent with a cornerstone of its modern free speech jurisprudence, the test it carefully crafted in *Brandenburg v. Ohio* for determining when speech constitutes incitement. That decision, the Court explained, allows government to "suppress speech for advocating the use of force or a violation of law only if 'such advocacy is directed to inciting or producing imminent lawless action and is likely to incite or produce such action.'" The Court found that the government here had shown only "a remote connection between speech that might encourage thoughts or impulses and any resulting child abuse." In the absence of a "significantly stronger, more direct connection," the Court concluded, "the Government may not prohibit speech on the ground that it may encourage pedophiles to engage in illegal conduct." Accordingly, because this and all the reasons proffered by the government for prohibiting the large category of expressive activity constituting virtual child pornography had "no justification in [the Court's] precedents or in the law of the First Amendment," the Court held this key provision of the CPPA be overbroad and unconstitutional.[111]

Justice Clarence Thomas filed an opinion concurring in the Court's judgment. In his view the government's strongest argument was that those who possess and disseminate sexually graphic images of actual children might raise reasonable doubt as to their guilt by claiming that the images are computer generated. But because the government was unable to point to a single case in which a defendant had been acquitted based on such a defense, he concluded "this speculative interest" was insufficient to support the broad scope of the CPPA. He added, though, that if technology evolves to such a state where prosecutions of actual child pornography are thwarted by such defenses, the government should not be foreclosed from enacting an appropriately narrow ban on computer-generated child pornography.[112]

Justice O'Connor filed an opinion concurring in the Court's judgment that the "appears to be . . . of a minor" provision was unconstitutionally overbroad to the extent that the prohibition covered sexually graphic images of adults who look like children.[113] Joined in this part of her opinion by Chief Justice William Rehnquist and Justice Scalia, however, O'Connor dissented from the Court's judgment to the extent that it held that the provision was overbroad as applied to completely computer-generated images of children engaged in sexually explicit conduct. In her view, the ban on computer-generated material survived the strict scrutiny applicable to content-based restrictions. She found that the ban on computer-generated images of children engaging in explicit sexual conduct promote the nation's compelling interest in protecting children because these images "whet the appetite" of child molesters who may use them to seduce young children. An even more serious concern, in her view, is that those engaged in the production, distribution, or possession of pornography produced with actual children "may evade liability by claiming that the images attributed to them are in fact computer-generated."

O'Connor acknowledged that the language "appears to be . . . of a minor" seemed not to be "narrowly tailored" to serve these compelling interests in that it would, for instance, "capture even cartoon-sketches or statues of children that were sexually suggestive," images not likely be used to seduce children. She therefore interpreted "appears to be . . . of" to mean "virtually indistinguishable from." In light of this narrowing construction, O'Connor found that the ban on computer-generated child pornography passed strict scrutiny and was not substantially overbroad.[114]

Chief Justice Rehnquist filed a dissenting opinion,[115] which Justice Scalia joined.[116] In his view, the term "sexually explicit conduct" as used in CPPA should be narrowly construed to apply only to "hard core" child pornography. Under that interpretation, the law would ban only "visual depictions of youthful looking adult actors engaged in *actual* sexual activity; mere *suggestions* of sexual activity, such as youthful looking adult actors squirming under a blanket" would not be prohibited. So construed, the CPPA would not reach any material not previously banned by federal law other than computer-generated images virtually indistinguishable from child pornography using real children.[117]

Justificatory Limits: The Uncertain Status of the "Harm-in-the-Circulation" Rationale

The harm-in-the-production rationale may be the primary justification invoked by Court for the exclusion of child pornography from First Amendment coverage, but it is not the only justification. In addition, it will be recalled, *Ferber* noted that "the materials produced are a permanent record of the children's participation [in the making of the materials] and the harm to the child is exacerbated by their circulation."[118] And in *Osborne*, the Court invoked this harm-in-the-circulation rationale as a reason for upholding the constitutionality of a ban on the possession of child pornography. The Court, however, "has not made clear whether the harm of circulation, standing alone, is sufficient to justify the [First Amendment] exception for child pornography."[119] The Court's statement in *Ferber* that the harm in the production is "exacerbated" by the circulation of the material suggests that this rationale depends entirely on the harm in the production, as does the Court's observation in the immediately prior sentence that distribution of the material "is intrinsically related to the sexual abuse of children" inherent in the making of child pornography.[120] However, the Court's quotation of an authority describing the recording of the event to be "an even greater threat to the child victim" than sexual abuse[121] suggests that the interest in preventing the circulation of images of a child engaged in sexual activity is an independent rationale for banning the distribution and possession of child pornography.

As Carissa Hessick explains in an insightful recent article[122] and in this volume,[123] whether the harm-in-the-circulation rationale is independent from or derivative of the harm-in-the-production justification has important consequences for the limits of the child pornography exception. For instance, if is it purely derivative, then it would not support categorizing as child pornography a "morphed" computer images that "pastes" the face of an actual child on the body of an adult involved in sexual conduct.[124] Similarly, the typical case of "sexting" could not be prosecuted as child pornography devoid of First Amendment protection.[125] In contrast, if the harm-in-the-circulation rationale is an independent justification for the categorical exclusion of child pornography from First Amendment protection, then this material is logically eligible for inclusion as child pornography. This same definitional issue would also arise with regard to photographs surreptitiously taken of young children engaged in sex play with no instigation from an adult. Indeed, the question of whether material is properly classified as child pornography is presented by any visual depiction of actual children engaged in sexual conduct that did not involve child abuse. Since distribution of sexually explicit visual depictions of children would often be prohibited by laws other than by bans on child pornography, such as by obscenity and invasion of privacy laws, the major practical significance of whether such material can be classified as child pornography is whether mere possession of such material can be constitutionally prohibited. Another practical consequence is the availability of draconian penalties commonly imposed by child pornography laws[126] but typically not by other laws applicable to distribution of sexually explicit visual depiction of children.

Because the Court in *Ferber* declined to provide a definition of child pornography, lower courts and the Court itself in subsequent cases have had to rely on the justifications for the child pornography exception in order to determine whether material banned by various child pornography laws comes within the constitutional definition of child pornography. In *Ashcroft v. Free Speech Coalition*, the Court helpfully confirmed that the harm-in-the-production rationale was the primary justification for the categorical exclusion of child pornography for First Amendment protection, held that the interest in preventing pedophiles from using sexually explicit images of children to seduce minors was not itself a sufficient rationale for banning such material, and firmly rejected the argument that material that "whets the appetite" of child molesters is grounds for banning these images. However, the Court has yet to squarely decide whether its reference in *Ferber* to the harm resulting from the existence of a permanent record of the child participating in sexual conduct is a justification independent of the harm-in-the-production rationale or merely an aspect of it. The uncertain status of this harm-in-the-circulation rationale in turn creates uncertainty as to the definition and the limits of the child pornography exception.

Conclusion

From its dismal failure to protect speech in the first part of the twentieth century the Court learned the critical importance of formulating precise, cabinable rationales for upholding restrictions on expression. This is particularly true of restrictions targeting speech in media essential to the formation of public opinion or for artistic expression such as books, magazines, newspapers, or film. From suppression of antiwar speech, to banning of literary masterpieces, to libel awards against newspapers for speech critical of official conduct, experience had shown the dire consequences of failing to articulate narrow and confineable rationales for upholding content-based speech restrictions. The harm-in-the-production rationale invoked by the Court as the primary and arguably the only sufficient justification for suppression of child pornography has, as we have seen, remained closely confined despite attempts by Congress and state legislatures to expand the scope of the material prohibited by child pornography laws. There have, it is true, been problematic applications of child pornography laws upheld by the lower courts. Significantly, however, these cases usually involve justifications other than the harm-in-the-production rationale, such as harm in the circulation.[127]

The harm-in-the-production rationale has, moreover, not only has proved confineable in its application to sexually oriented material depicting children, but it also has resisted appropriation as a rationale for categorical exclusion of other types of speech from First Amendment protection. In 1999, Congress enacted a law prohibiting the commercial creation, sale, or possession of visual or auditory depictions of animal cruelty.[128] In defending this law, the government urged the Court to find such depictions categorically devoid of First Amendment protection, and in support of this position invoked among other arguments *Ferber*'s harm-in-the-production rationale.[129] In invalidating this law as unconstitutionally overbroad, the Court firmly rejected the contention that this expression was categorically devoid of First Amendment protection.[130]

Upholding a content-based restriction aimed at crucial media for political or artistic expression such as photographs and film is fraught with danger not just from the restriction at hand but from the precedent the decision sets for the suppression of a wider variety of speech. Cognizant of this danger, the Court in *Ferber* and in subsequent child pornography decisions has for the most part done a commendable job of upholding suppression of photographs and film whose production involves "a most serious crime and an act repugnant to the moral instincts of a decent people,"[131] while at the same time maintaining First Amendment doctrine staunchly protective of expression essential to a free and democratic society.

NOTES

1. 458 U.S. 747 (1982).
2. Cohen v. California, 403 U.S. 15 (1971).
3. See Geoffrey R. Stone, *The Story of the Sedition Act of 1798: "The Reign of Witches,"* in FIRST AMENDMENT STORIES 35 (R. Garnett & A. Koppelman eds. 2012).
4. 249 U.S. 47 (1919).
5. *Id.* at 52–53. See also Frohwerk v. United States, 249 U.S. 204 (1919); Debs v. United States, 249 U.S. 211 (1919).
6. Geoffrey R. Stone, *The Origins of the "Bad Tendency" Test: Free Speech in Wartime*, 2002 SUP. CT. REV. 411, 414, n.11.
7. HARRY KALVEN, JR., A WORTHY TRADITION: FREEDOM OF SPEECH IN AMERICA 147 (1988).
8. *E.g.*, Fiske v. Kansas, 274 U.S. 380 (1927); Stromberg v. California, 283 U.S. 359 (1931); Near v. Minnesota, 283 U.S. 697 (1931); De Jonge v. Oregon, 299 U.S. 353 (1937); Cantwell v. Connecticut, 310 U.S. 296 (1940); Thornhill v. Alabama, 310 U.S. 88 (1940); Winters v. New York, 333 U.S. 507 (1948).
9. Dennis v. United States, 341 U.S. 494 (1951).
10. 395 U.S. 444 (1969).
11. *Id.* at 447.
12. 315 U.S. 568, 573–74 (1942).
13. *Id.* at 571–72.
14. OLIVER WENDELL HOLMES, THE COMMON LAW 1 (1881).
15. 376 U.S. 254, 270 (1964).
16. *Id.* at 279–80.
17. *See id.* at 269 (explaining that "libel can claim no talismanic immunity from constitutional limitations").
18. *See* Phila. Newspapers Inc, v. Hepps, 475 U.S. 767, 775 (1986); Dun & Bradstreet, Inc. v. Greenmoss Builders, Inc., 472 U.S. 749 (1985).

19. 413 U.S. 15, 27–28 (1973).

20. *See* HOWL ON TRIAL: THE BATTLE FOR FREE EXPRESSION 8–12 (B. Morgan and N. Peters eds. 2006).

21. *See* Terminiello v. Chicago, 337 U.S. 1 (1949); Street v. New York, 394 U.S. 576, 592 (1969).

22. 408 U.S. 92 (1972).

23. *Id.* at 95–96.

24. *E.g.*, Erznoznik v. Jacksonville, 422 U.S. 205, 209, 215 (1975); Hudgens v. N.L.R.B., 424 U.S. 507, 520 (1976); Young v. Am. Mini Theatres, Inc., 427 U.S. 50, 64–65 (1976); City of Madison, Joint Sch. Dist. No. 8 v. Wis. Emp't Relations Comm'n, 429 U.S. 167, 175–76 (1976); First Nat'l Bank of Boston v. Bellotti, 435 U.S. 765, 784–85 (1978); Carey v. Brown, 447 U.S. 455, 461–62 (1980); Consol. Edison Co. of N.Y., Inc. v. Pub. Serv. Comm'n of N.Y., 447 U.S. 530, 537–38 (1980).

25. Brown v. Entm't Merchs. Ass'n, 131 S. Ct. 2729, 2738 (2011); see also R.A.V. v. St. Paul, 505 U.S. 377, 395 (1992); Simon & Schuster, Inc. v. Members of N.Y. State Crime Victims Bd., 502 U.S. 105, 115 (1991); Boos v. Barry, 485 U.S. 312 (1988); Carey v. Brown, 447 U.S. 455, 461 (1980). As an exception to the rule against content discrimination, the Court has recognized that the First Amendment permits "restrictions upon the content of speech in a few limited areas," such as obscenity, incitement, and fighting words, *Brown*, 131 S. Ct. at 2733. In my view, the "exceptions" are far more extensive than the Court acknowledges, with the rule against content discrimination operating primarily in the realm of public discourse. *See* James Weinstein, *Participatory Democracy as the Central Value of American Free Speech Doctrine*, 97 VA. L. REV. 491, 493–97 (2011).

26. Hill v. Colorado, 530 U.S. 703, 735 (2000) (Souter, J., concurring); see also, e.g., Turner Broad. Sys., Inc. v. FCC, 512 U.S. 622, 624 (1994) ("Our precedents thus apply the most exacting scrutiny to regulations that suppress, disadvantage, or impose differential burdens upon speech because of its content.") (citations omitted). Indeed, *Holder v. Humanitarian Law Project*, 561 U.S. 1 (2010), is the only Supreme Court majority opinion that is still good law that has upheld a content-based speech restriction under strict scrutiny.

27. *E.g.*, Ward v. Rock Against Racism, 491 U.S. 781 (1989); *see also* James Weinstein, *How Theory Matters: A Commentary on Robert Selder's "The 'Law of the First Amendment' Revisited"*, 58 WAYNE L. REV. 1105, 1116–17 (2013).

28. *Ferber*, 458 U.S. at 749.

29. *See id.* at 749–50; *see also* Frederick Schauer, *Codifying the First Amendment*: New York v. Ferber, 1983 SUP. CT. REV. 285, 288–89.

30. *See* Griffin v. State, 396 So. 2d 152, 156 (Fla. 1981); Payne v. Commonwealth, 623 S.W.2d 867, 872 (Ky. 1981).

31. Graham v. Hill, 444 F. Supp. 584 (W.D. Tex. 1978); St. Martin's Press, Inc. v. Carey, 440 F. Supp. 1196 (S.D.N.Y. 1977), *rev'd on other grounds*, 605 F. 2d 41 (2d Cir. 1979) (finding that plaintiff had failed to show any real threat of prosecution).

32. People v. Ferber, 52 N.Y.2d 674 (1981).

33. N.Y. Penal Law, Art. 263. The law more broadly prohibited "the use" of a child less than sixteen years of age in "a sexual performance." § 263.05. "Sexual performance" was defined as "any performance . . . which includes sexual conduct by a child less than sixteen years of age" (§ 263.00(1)). "Sexual conduct," in turn, was defined as "actual or

simulated sexual intercourse, deviate sexual intercourse, sexual bestiality, masturbation, sado-masochistic abuse, or lewd exhibition of the genitals." § 263.00(3). Finally, "performance" was defined as "any play, motion picture, photograph or dance" or "any other visual representation exhibited before an audience." § 263.00(4).

34. *Ferber*, 458 U.S. at 752. Ferber was also indicted under another section of the law that prohibited obscene material, but he was acquitted of this charge.

35. *Id.* at 678. The Court noted that the sweep of the law would prohibit material such as medical and educational material depicting children engaged in sexual activity. *Id.*

36. *Id.* at 681 (citing *Erznoznik*, 422 U.S. at 215). The dissenting justices argued that because the law was "not concerned with the effect of this sexually exploitive material upon the community" but rather "seeks to inhibit the maintenance of a market" which leads to the sexual abuse of children, the law was not content based. *Id.* at 682–83 (Jasen, J., dissenting). Though not claiming that the law was content neutral, the United States Supreme Court adopted without attribution the dissent's argument about inhibiting the market for child pornography as a means of combating the harm to children caused in the production of the material. *Ferber*, 458 U.S. at 760.

37. *Id.* at 753.

38. *Id.* at 749. Justice White's opinion was joined in full by Chief Justice Warren Burger and Justices Lewis Powell, William Rehnquist, and Sandra Day O'Connor. Justice O'Connor also filed a concurring opinion. Justice William Brennan, joined by Justice Thurgood Marshall, filed an opinion concurring in the judgment. Justice John Paul Stevens also wrote an opinion concurring in the judgment. Justice Harry Blackmun concurred in the result without an opinion.

39. *See* Joseph Burstyn, Inc. v. Wilson, 343 U.S. 495 (1952), *overruling* Mutual Film Corp. v Industrial Comm'n, 236 U.S. 230 (1915) (film exhibition not protected by the First Amendment).

40. *See* James Weinstein and Ivan Hare, *General Introduction: Free Speech, Democracy, and the Suppression of Extreme Speech Past and Present*, in EXTREME SPEECH AND DEMOCRACY 6 (I. Hare & J. Weinstein eds., 2009).

41. *See* Masses Publishing Co. v. Patten, 244 F. 535 (S.D.N.Y.), *rev'd*, 246 F. 24 (1917); see also James Weinstein, *Extreme Speech, Public Order, and Democracy: Lessons from the Masses*, in EXTREME SPEECH AND DEMOCRACY 41–42, *supra* note 40.

42. *See* Nationalist Socialist Party v. Skokie, 432 U.S. 43 (1977).

43. *See* R.A.V. v. City of St. Paul, 505 U.S. 377 (1992).

44. *Ferber*, 458 U.S. at 771–72.

45. *Id.* at 762.

46. *Id.* at 763. Even by the Court's own account, however, the New York law was partially motivated by a desire to censor a particularly offensive portrayal of sexual material. Thus the Court notes that in addition to protecting children from the harm of exploitation from sexual performances, "the legislature found [that] 'the sales of these movies, magazines and photographs depicting the sexual conduct of children to be so abhorrent to the fabric of our society that it urge[d] law enforcement officers to aggressively seek out and prosecute . . . the peddlers of this filth.'" *Id.* at 757 n.8

47. *Id.* at 763.

48. *Id.* at 756–57.

49. *Id.* at 759–60. The Court also noted that the advertising and selling of child pornography was not entitled to First Amendment protection because these activities "pro-

vide an economic motive for the production of such materials" and are thus an integral part" of an illegal activity. *Id.* at 762 (*citing* Giboney v. Empire Storage & Ice Co., 336 U.S. 490 (1949)). The "integral part of an illegal activity" rationale for stripping speech of constitutional protection has, however, been aptly criticized as "indeterminate, dangerous, and inconsistent with more recent cases." Eugene Volokh, *Speech as Conduct: Generally Applicable Laws, Illegal Courses of Conduct, "Situation-Altering Utterances," and the Uncharted Zones*, 90 CORNELL L. REV. 1277, 1285 (2005). Accord, Schauer, *supra* note 29 at 300 (suggesting that the Court's giving this justification "little more than en passant mention . . . is best explained by the logical flaws" of the rationale.)

50. *Ferber*, 458 U.S. at 761.

51. *Id.* at 763–64.

52. *Id.* at 764.

53. *Id.* at 764–65. In contrast, the Court stated that under the obscenity laws "criminal responsibility may not be imposed without some element of scienter" and noted that the New York law "expressly includes a scienter requirement." Subsequently and more specifically, the Court explained in *United States v. X-Citment Video, Inc.*, 513 U.S. 64, 78 (1994), that a "statute completely bereft of a scienter requirement as to the age of the performers would raise serious constitutional doubts." Consequently, the Court read into the federal ban on the distribution of child pornography a requirement that the defendant know that material contained sexually explicit images of minors.

54. *See, e.g.*, Gooding v. Wilson, 405 U.S. 518 (1972).

55. *Ferber*, 458 U.S. at 773–74.

56. *Id.* at 774–75 (O'Connor, J., concurring).

57. *Id.* at 775–77 (Brennan, J., concurring).

58. *See* Brown v. Entm't Merch. Ass'n, 131 S. Ct. 2729 (2011) (rejecting the claim that violent videogames directed to children are categorically without First Amendment protection); United States v. Stevens, 559 U.S. 460 (2010) (rejecting the claim that visual depictions of animal cruelty are categorically without First Amendment protection).

59. Also, as discussed above, under the categorical exclusion approach it is not open to a defendant to argue that no harm befell children in the production of the particular material as it might be under a strict scrutiny analysis. In this way, categorical exclusion of child pornography makes prosecution of child pornography cases somewhat easier than under a strict scrutiny standard.

60. *See* supra note 58 and accompanying text.

61. *See* Brief and Appendices for Petitioner at 30, New York v. Ferber, 458 U.S. 747 (1982) (No. 81–55).

62. Additionally, although protecting children from sexual abuse is plainly a compelling state interest, the Court may have had some doubt that prohibiting distribution of the material was the "least restrictive alternative" available to the state to prevent this harm.

63. This hypothesis is similar to Frederick Schauer's suggestion that the Court used a categorization approach in *Ferber* to avoid diluting the *Brandenburg* test. *See* Schauer, *supra* note 29 at 314.

64. *See* Holder v. Humanitarian Law Project, 561 U.S. 1 (2010).

65. *See e.g.*, Schenck v. United States, 249 U.S. 47 (1919) (draft resistance); Am. Booksellers Ass'n v. Hudnut, 771 F. 2d. 323 (7th Cir. 1985) (violence against women); Central Hudson Gas & Elec. Corp. v. Pub. Serv. Comm'n, 447 U.S. 557 (1980) (increased use of

electricity). The other type of audience-related harm that the government often invokes to justify content-based speech restriction is preventing offense to the audience. *See, e.g.*, Cohen v. California, 403 U.S. 15 (1971); Boos v. Barry, 485 U.S. 312 (1988).

66. Brief and Appendices for Petitioner at 33, New York v. Ferber, 458 U.S. 747 (1982) (No. 81-55).

67. The state also cited evidence that "materials showing children engaged in sexual conduct are sold to adults who use the materials to convince other children to engage in similar conduct." *Id.* In *Ashcroft v. Free Speech Coalition*, 535 U.S. 234, 252–54 (2002), the Court specifically rejected each of these rationales as sufficient grounds for banning virtual child pornography. Previously, however, in *Osborne v. Ohio*, 495 U.S. 103, 111 (1989), though relying primarily on the harm-in-the-production rationale, the Court mentioned the use of child pornography to convince children to engage in similar conduct as an added reason why banning the possession of pornography did not violate the First Amendment. Both of these cases are discussed below.

68. Brief and Appendix for Petitioner at 32–33, New York v. Ferber, 458 U.S. 747 (1982) (No. 81-55).

69. *Ferber*, 458 U.S. at 758. Indeed, because the harm-in-the-production rationale foreswears any reliance on the communicative impact of the material, this *justification* for the ban on the distribution of pornography can be fairly characterized as content neutral. Still, because the *description* of the proscribed material is based on its content, the Court correctly classified the law as content based. *Cf.* Renton v. Playtime Theatres, 475 U.S. 41, 47–49 (1986) (because a zoning regulation restricting the places in which theaters showing "adult" films could be located was "*justified* without reference to the content of the regulated speech," the Court classified this time, place, or manner regulation as content neutral even though the "ordinance treats theaters that specialize in adult films differently from other kinds of theaters"). In addition, though the harm-in-the-production rationale itself does not turn on the communicative impact of the speech, the subsidiary argument that the material creates a "permanent record" of child abuse that exacerbates that harm *does* depend on the communicative impact of the material. Unlike the other two communicative-related justifications offered by the state, however (which the Court ignored), the "permanent record" rationale does not implicate any significant free speech values. Nonetheless, it is technically a content-based justification, which is an additional reason why the Court properly did not try to classify the New York law as content neutral.

70. *E.g.*, C. Edwin Baker, *Autonomy and Free Speech*, 27 CONST. COMMENT 251 (2011).

71. There are, of course, those who believe that such expression should indeed be suppressed for precisely these reasons. *E.g.*, CATHERINE A. MACKINNON, ONLY WORDS (1995) (arguing for the suppression of pornography); Mari J. Matsuda, *Public Response to Racist Speech: Considering the Victim's Story*, 87 MICH. L. REV. 2320 (1989) (arguing for suppression of racist speech). While in my view such restrictions would be contrary to core First Amendment values, *see* JAMES WEINSTEIN, HATE SPEECH, PORNOGRAPHY, AND THE RADICAL ATTACK ON FREE SPEECH DOCTRINE (1999), the merits of the regulation of hate speech and pornography is beside the point that it was speech-protective for the Court in *Ferber* to have eschewed a rationale that would have created a basis for the suppression of such material.

72. The Court further limited this rationale by emphasizing both that the state had a "compelling" interest in preventing the harm to children caused in the production and

that the distribution of child pornography must be prohibited in order to effectively combat the harm in the production.

73. *See, e.g.*, Amy Adler, *Inverting the First Amendment*, 149 U. PA. L. REV. 921, 947–48 (2001) (hereafter "*Inverting*"); Amy Adler, *The Perverse Law of Child Pornography*, 101 COLUM. L. REV. 209, 238–40 (2001) (hereafter "*The Perverse Law*"); Carissa Byrne Hessick, *The Limits of Child Pornography*, 98 IND. L.J. 1437 (2014).

74. *See* chapter 2, Carissa Byrne Hessick, Setting Definitional Limits for the Child Pornography Exception; chapter 3, Amy Adler, The "*Dost* Test" in Child Pornography Law: "Trial by Rorschach Test."

75. 394 U.S. 557 (1969).

76. *Id.* at 565.

77. *See* Brief for Appellant at 46–51, Osborne v. Ohio, 495 U.S. 103 (1990) (No. 88-5986).

78. 495 U.S. 103 (1990).

79. *Id.* at 108–109. In this regard, it is interesting to note that Justice White did not join the majority opinion in *Stanley*, but instead joined a concurring opinion that rested exclusively on Fourth Amendment grounds for reversing the conviction. *See Stanley*, 394 U.S. at 565.

80. *Osborne*, 495 U.S. at 110–11.

81. *Id.* at 110 (quoting *Ferber*, 458 U.S. at 761–62). The Court in *Osborne* does not specify what these "weak interests" consisted of beyond the interest in preventing obscenity from "poisoning the mind of the viewer," which in light of the Court's condemnation as "paternalistic" suggest that this interest is not merely weak but constitutionally impermissible. The Court in *Stanley*, however, lists preventing obscenity from falling into the hands of children and offending the sensibilities of unwilling viewers as additional reasons for outlawing its distribution. *See* 394 U.S. at 567; *see also* Paris Adult Theatre I v. Slaton, 413 U.S. 49, 59 (1973) (ban on the distribution of obscenity protects "the tone of society").

82. *Osborne*, 495 U.S. at 109 (quoting *Ferber*, 458 U.S. at 756–58).

83. *Id.* at 111.

84. *Id.* at 141–42 (Brennan, J., dissenting). In light of his full-throated endorsement of *Stanley's* principles in this dissent, it is interesting to note that Justice Brennan, like Justice White, had not joined Justice Marshall's majority opinion in *Stanley*. Justice Stevens had not yet joined the Court at the time *Stanley* was decided.

85. Justice Brennan also denied that the two "other interests" were adequate grounds to sustain the ban on possession. With respect to the interest in encouraging destruction of the "permanen[t] record" of the child's abuse, he found the law was not "narrowly tailored to this end" because there was "no requirement that the State show that the child was abused in the production of the materials or even that the child knew that a photograph was taken." *Id.* at 143, n.18. With regards to the argument that pedophiles use child pornography to seduce other children into sexual activity, Brennan first noted that the evidence on which the Court relied showed that pedophiles used adult as well as child pornography for this purpose. More fundamentally, he objected that this rationale "ignores fundamental principles of our First Amendment jurisprudence." He pointed out that if even if "obscene material could be proved to create a . . . danger of illegal behavior, it would not follow that the expression should be suppressed. Rather, the basic principles of a system of freedom of expression would require that society deal directly

with the . . . action and leave the expression alone." *Id.* (quoting T. EMERSON, THE SYSTEM OF FREEDOM OF EXPRESSION 494 (1970)).

86. While theoretically this might include a painting or drawing of actual children engaged in sexual conduct, in "almost every imaginable case this will be a photographic portrayal." Schauer, *supra* note 29 at 294.

87. *Id.*; Adler, *Inverting*, *supra* note 73 at 936–37; Hessick, *supra* note 73 at 19. The only express statement the Court made about the meaning of "sexual conduct" is that unlike under the *Miller* test for obscenity it need not "appeal to the prurient interest of the average person" or be portrayed in "patently offensive manner." *Ferber*, 458 U.S. at 764.

88. For a criticism of this strategy see Adler, *The Perverse Law*, supra note 73, at 235 (arguing that this approach has led to "a sense of boundlessness in child pornography law"); see also Hessick, supra note 73 (describing failure of state legislatures and lower courts to limit restrictions to underlying rationales of the child pornography exception).

89. *See supra* note 74.

90. New York Penal Law, § 263.00(3).

91. *Ferber* also confirms that statutes limited to the prohibition of those visual depictions of activities within New York's definition of "sexual conduct" will not be vulnerable to attack for substantial overbreadth.

92. Schauer, *supra* note 29 at 295. Indeed, though not focusing in this part of its opinion on the question of photographs of nude children, the Court in *Ferber* acknowledged that "nudity, without more is protected expression." 458 at 765, n.18 (citing *Erznoznik v. City of Jacksonville*, 422 U.S. 205, 213 (1975)).

93. 491 U.S. 576 (1989).

94. *Id.* at 580.

95. Mass. Gen. Laws § 272:31 (1986). The law provided that it was a defense to prosecution if the child was posed in a state of nudity "for a bona fide scientific or medical purpose, or for an educational or cultural purpose for a bona fide school, museum or library."

96. After the Supreme Court had agreed to review the case, the Massachusetts legislature amended the law to require that the posing of nude children to be done with "lascivious intent." *Oakes*, 491 U.S. at 483. Justice O'Connor, in an opinion joined by Chief Justice Rehnquist and Justices White and Anthony Kennedy, held that this amendment rendered the overbreadth challenge moot. *Id.* at 581–84. Justice Antonin Scalia, in an opinion joined by Justices Brennan, Marshall, Stevens, and Blackmun, disagreed that the amendment rendered the overbreadth claim moot. *Id.* at 585–88 (Scalia, J., concurring in the judgment in part and dissenting in part). However, since Scalia and Blackmun thought the law was not unconstitutionally overbroad, they concurred in the judgment of O'Connor's plurality opinion vacating the decision of the Supreme Judicial Court of Massachusetts. *Id.* at 588–90.

97. *Id.* at 590–99 (Brennan, J., dissenting).

98. *Id.* at 588–90 (Scalia, J., concurring in the judgment in part and dissenting in part). This was particularly true in Scalia's view since the scope of the statute was narrowed by the availability of the defense that the material was produced for scientific, medical, and educational purposes. *See supra* note 95. The statute at issue in *Osborne v. Ohio*, 495 U.S. 103 (1990), discussed above in text, also broadly banned visual depic-

tions of minors "in a state of nudity" subject to an exception similar to the defense provided by the Massachusetts law. A majority of the Court in *Osborne* summarily rebuffed an overbreadth claim because the Ohio Supreme Court had construed the ban to apply only when the nudity constituted "a lewd exhibition or involves a graphic focus on the genitals." *Id.* at 113. Justice Brennan, joined by Justices Marshall and Stevens, disagreed, finding the limiting construction ambiguous and in any event not sufficient to cure what was in his view the statute's substantial overbreadth. *Id.* at 126–39 (Brennan, J., dissenting).

99. Supporting the view that a ban on possession approached the limits of the harm-in-the-production rationale is that the Court felt it necessary to invoke an additional rationale—use of child pornography by pedophiles to seduce children. *See supra* text accompanying note 83.

100. *See* 18 U.S.C. § 2252 (1994 ed.).

101. 18 U.S.C. § 2256(8)(B). The statute specified that "visual depiction" included "any photograph, film, video, picture, or computer or computer-generated image or picture." *Id.* It defined "sexually explicit conduct" as "actual or simulated- . . . sexual intercourse . . . bestiality; . . . masturbation; . . . sadistic or masochistic abuse; or . . . lascivious exhibition of the genitals or pubic area of any person." 18 U.S.C. § 2256(2).

102. The law also prohibited the possession or distribution of images of actual children not engaged in sexual conduct altered or "morphed" to appear to be engaging in such conduct. Section 2256(8)(C). This provision, however, was not challenged in this case.

103. 535 U.S. 234 (2002).

104. Justices Stevens, David Souter, Ruth Bader Ginsburg, and Stephen Breyer joined Justice Kennedy's opinion. Justice Clarence Thomas filed an opinion concurring in the judgment. Justice O'Connor, joined in part by Chief Justice Rehnquist and Justice Scalia, filed an opinion concurring in part and dissenting in part. Chief Justice Rehnquist filed a dissenting opinion, which Justice Scalia joined except for the paragraph discussing legislative history.

105. *Free Speech Coalition*, 535 U.S. at 241.

106. *Id.* at 244.

107. *Id.* at 254.

108. *Id.* at 255. The Court further held that this problem was not cured by the availability of an affirmative defense by those charged with nonpossessory offenses that materials were produced using only adults and were not otherwise distributed in a manner conveying the impression that they depicted real children. Noting that imposing on a defendant the burden of proving his speech is not unlawful raises "serious constitutional difficulties," the Court declined to decide this difficult question because the defense was in any event "incomplete and insufficient" in not applying to possessory offenses. *Id.* at 255–56.

109. See *supra* note 67 and text accompanying note 83.

110. *Free Speech Coalition*, 535 U.S. at 252 (citing Sable Commc'ns of Cal., Inc. v. FCC, 492 U.S. 115 (1989)). Curiously, in rejecting the sufficiency of this rationale the Court makes no attempt to distinguish *Osborne*'s reliance on it. In an earlier section of the opinion, however, in rebuffing the government's argument that virtual child pornography can be constitutionally banned because it is "virtually indistinguishable" from pornography depicting actual children, the Court explained that although *Osborne* "noted

the State's interest in preventing child pornography from being used as an aid in the solicitation of minors," that decision "did not suggest that, absent this concern, other governmental interests would suffice." 535 U.S. at 250.

111. *Id.* at 253–54. The Court also struck down as unconstitutionally overbroad the CPPA's pandering provision, 18 U.S.C. § 2256(8)(D), which prohibited depictions of sexually explicit material "advertised, promoted, presented, described, or distributed in such a manner that conveys the impression that the material is or contains a visual depiction of a minor engaging in sexually explicit conduct," even if in fact the material did not contain images of children.

112. *Free Speech Coalition*, 535 U.S. at 259 (Thomas, J., concurring).

113. *Id.* at 260–61 (O'Connor, J., concurring). O'Connor also agreed that the pandering provision was unconstitutionally overbroad.

114. *Id.* at 263–64.

115. *Id.* at 267–68 (Rehnquist, C.J., dissenting).

116. Except for the discussion of the legislative history.

117. *Id.* at 268. Rehnquist also argued that the pandering provision could be narrowly construed to avoid constitutional difficulties. *Id.* at 271–73. In response to the Court's holding in *Free Speech Coalition*, Congress enacted the Prosecutorial Remedies and Other Tools to end the Exploitation of Children Today ("PROTECT") Act of 2003, 117 Stat. 650. Section 503 of the Act, 18 U.S.C. § 2252A(a)(3)(B), replaces the pandering provision struck down in *Free Speech Coalition* with a narrower pandering prohibition. In *United States v. Williams*, 553 U.S. 285 (2008), the Court, in a 7-2 decision, upheld this provision against a claim of substantial overbreadth. Another provision of the PROTECT Act, § 502, 18 USC § 2256(8)(B), prohibits receiving, distributing, or possessing any "digital image, computer image, or computer-generated image that is, or is indistinguishable from," an image of an actual minor engaging in sexually explicit conduct. This prohibition is subject to an affirmative defense that that the image in question is of an adult or did not involve an actual minor. *Cf.* United States v. Peel, 595 F.3d 763, 770–71 (7th Cir. 2010) (recognizing affirmative defense under § 2256(8)(B) where pornography was made with adult rather than child models but declining to extend it to case where legally created pornography was subsequently criminalized). For a discussion and criticism of this provision, see Rosalind E. Bell, Note, *Reconciling the PROTECT Act with the First Amendment*, 87 N.Y.U. L. REV. 1878 (2012). A third provision of the Act, § 504, 18 U.S.C. § 1466A, outlaws any sexually explicit visual depiction of minors, including a cartoon, sculpture, or painting, that is either obscene, 1466A(a)(1) and (b)(1), or "is, or appears to be, of a minor engaging in graphic bestiality, sadistic or masochistic abuse, or sexual intercourse, including genital-genital, oral-genital, anal-genital, or oral-anal, whether between persons of the same or opposite sex" and "lacks serious literary, artistic, political, or scientific value." 18 U.S.C. § 1466A(a)(2) and (b)(2). Since obscenity is categorically without First Amendment protection, the first part of this provision would appear to be constitutional since it applies only to legally obscene material. The second part of this prohibition, however, seems to include material that is neither obscene nor involves the depiction of actual children and thus is likely unconstitutional. *See* United States v. Handley, 564 F. Supp. 2d 996, 1005–07 (S.D. Iowa 2008) (finding 1466A(a)(2) and (b)(2) unconstitutionally overbroad); *see also* United States v. Dean, 635 F.3d 1200, 1204–08 (11th Cir. 2011) (finding that § 1466A(a)(2) undoubtedly criminalizes some protected speech, but holding that it is not substantially overbroad). Finally, § 504 may

be unconstitutional to the extent it criminalizes mere possession of obscene material. 18 U.S.C. § 1466A(b). *But see Handley*, *supra*, 564 F. Supp. at 1001 (holding the right to possess obscene material in the privacy of one's home recognized in *Stanley v. Georgia*, 394 U.S. 557 (1969) (see *supra* text accompanying notes 75–76), does not extend to material that has moved in interstate commerce); United States v. Mees, No. 4:09-cr-00145-ERW, 2009 WL 1657420, at *4 (E.D. Mo. June 10, 2009) (unpublished) (same).

118. *Ferber*, 458 U.S. at 759.

119. Hessick, *supra* note 73, at 8.

120. *Ferber*, 458 U.S. at 759.

121. *Id.*, n.16 (quoting Shouvlin, *Preventing Sexual Exploitation of Children: A Model Act*, 17 WAKE FOREST L. REV. 535, 545 (1981)).

122. Hessick, *supra* note 73, at 27–31.

123. Chapter 2, Carissa Byrne Hessick, *Setting Definitional Limits for the Child Pornography Exception*.

124. Hessick, *supra* note 123, at 71. As discussed above at note 102, a provision of the CPPA bans such material. Because this provision was not challenged in *Free Speech Coalition*, however, the Court did not rule on its constitutionality.

125. Hessick, *supra* note 123, at 70–71.

126. Thus Hessick notes that "a federal defendant found guilty of possessing twenty images of child pornography will receive a longer prison sentence than federal defendants who committed arson, burglary, robbery, or sexual abuse of a minor." Hessick, *supra* note 73, at 1438.

127. The Court, however, can be fairly faulted for not making clear in *Ferber* that this is not a justification independent of the harm in production.

128. 18 U.S.C. § 48. Specifically, the law applied to depictions "in which a living animal is intentionally maimed, mutilated, tortured, wounded, or killed," if the conduct depicted violates federal or state law where "the creation, sale, or possession takes place." The law contained an exemption for "serious religious, political, scientific, educational, journalistic, historical, or artistic value."

129. "[A]s the Court recognized with respect to child pornography, permitting the distribution of these materials encourages the very unlawful acts they record. The commercial market for depictions of animal cruelty 'provide[s] an economic motive for' production of these materials—and the abuse that is inherent in this production." Brief of Appellant-Petitioner at 36, United States v. Stevens, 559 U.S. 460 (2010) (No. 08-769) (quoting *Ferber*, 458 U.S. at 766). The government primarily relied on *Ferber*, however, not for its use of the harm-in-the-production rationale but rather for the decision's methodology in finding child pornography categorically unprotected because "'the evil to be restricted so overwhelmingly outweighs the expressive interests, if any, at stake' that the entire category may be prohibited." *Id.* at 12, quoting *Ferber*, 458 U.S. at 763–64. The Court in *Stevens* distinguished *Ferber* by explaining that the Court in *Ferber* had relied on the compelling interest in protecting children from sexual abuse as well as the *de minimis* First Amendment value of using actual children to create the material at issue in that case. *Id.* at 471. In addition, the Court emphasized that *Ferber* found that the market for child pornography was "intrinsically related" to the underlying abuse and was therefore "an integral part" of an illegal activity, 559 U.S. at 471, which would not be the case with respect to a substantial amount of expression prohibited by the law, such

as hunting magazines and videos. *Id.* at 481. Having thus rebuffed the government's reliance on *Ferber* as grounds for categorically excluding depictions of animal cruelty from the First Amendment, the Court evidently did not feel it necessary to respond specifically to the government's harm-in-the-production argument.

130. *Stevens*, 559 U.S. at 468–72.

131. *Free Speech Coalition,* 535 U.S. 234, 244 (2002).

2 | Setting Definitional Limits for the Child Pornography Exception

Carissa Byrne Hessick

Although the First Amendment ordinarily protects the creation, distribution, and possession of visual images, those protections do not apply to child pornography. But in exempting child pornography from First Amendment protection, the Supreme Court has failed to clearly define child pornography as a category of speech. Providing a precise definition of the child pornography exception to the First Amendment has become increasingly important because, in recent years, prosecutors across the country have used child pornography laws expansively to reach broader and broader sets of behavior.

Most visibly, some prosecutors have elected to charge teenagers with child pornography offenses for creating and sharing sexually explicit images of themselves—a practice that is often referred to as "sexting."[1] For example, when school district officials in Pennsylvania discovered photographs of "scantily clad, semi-nude and nude teenage girls" on several students' cell phones, the officials turned the photographs over to the local district attorney. The district attorney threatened to prosecute the minors depicted in the photographs and the minors who possessed the cell phones on which the images were stored with possession and/or dissemination of child pornography.[2]

Prosecutors have also filed charges in cases where adults have used technology to alter innocent images of children to make them appear sexually explicit. For example, prosecutors convicted a defendant on child pornography charges based on photographs that he had taken of children playing on the beach. Although the prosecutors conceded that the pictures the defendant had originally taken were not improper, they successfully argued that the defendant's subsequent "cropping" of those photographs to focus on the children's genitalia transformed the images into illegal child pornography.[3] Similarly, prosecutors obtained a child pornography conviction of a man based on his creation of morphed computer images. That is to say, the man digitally superimposed the faces of minor females from nonpornographic photographs onto images of adult females engaged in sexually explicit conduct.[4] Unlike sexting prosecutions, these cases involving alterations of innocent images have not received significant media attention, nor have these prosecutions been the subject of much criticism.[5]

There is an important similarity between these image alteration cases and the sexting cases: namely, that no children were harmed in the creation of the images. The idea that child pornography could be defined to include images that were created without harming children should give us pause. That is because the harm suffered by children in the creation of child pornography is one of the major reasons that judges and other public officials have offered to justify the exemption of child pornography from ordinary First Amendment protections. That harm is also what has driven up the punishments associated with child pornography crimes. When the state prosecutes and punishes people based on images that were created without harming children and instead based only on the content of the image, then child pornography law ceases to be a source of protection for children. Instead the law becomes a method of policing the acceptability of individuals' sexual fantasies.

This chapter makes the case for limiting the definition of child pornography—and by extension the child pornography exception to the First Amendment—to those images created through the sexual abuse or exploitation of a child. In making that case, the chapter considers and rejects another definition found in cases and academic literature: a definition created to minimize the harm caused to children by the circulation of images.

The chapter begins by noting that the Supreme Court created the child pornography exception to the First Amendment in order to protect children against two harms: the harm of creation and the harm of circulation. It then explains why limiting the definition of child pornography to images created through the sexual abuse or exploitation of a child is the best way to prevent unique harms to children without intruding on the First Amendment. The chapter concludes by briefly outlining how this more limited definition would restrict child pornography prosecutions in a number of different situations.

Child Pornography's Harm to Children, As Viewed by the Supreme Court

Ordinarily, the First Amendment protects sexually explicit speech and images. But there are some exceptions. The amendment does not protect images that are "obscene,"[6] although it does protect the private possession of obscene pornographic images.[7] Beginning with its 1982 decision in *New York v. Ferber*, the Supreme Court recognized a new categorical exception to the First Amendment: child pornography. Since that time, the Court has decided a series of cases developing and refining that exception.

Although the Court has not provided a clear definition of child pornography, the Court has consistently invoked two concerns in these cases: (1) the state's interest in preventing harm to children inflicted during the creation of the images, and (2) the state's interest in preventing harm to children caused by the circulation of the images. According to the Court, the first of these interests is sufficient to prohibit creating, distributing, and possessing child pornography. But the Court has yet to decide whether the harm of circulation, standing alone, is enough to justify the exception for child pornography.

New York v. Ferber

Much of the Court's guidance regarding the limits of child pornography can be drawn from the case that first recognized the First Amendment exception for child pornography, *New York v. Ferber*.[8] Paul Ferber, a bookstore owner, had been convicted under a New York statute that prohibited the knowing promotion of a sexual performance by a child under the age of sixteen.[9] Ferber was convicted for selling two films "depicting two young boys masturbating."[10] Ferber argued that the film was protected by the First Amendment because a jury had found that the films were not obscene. The Court rejected the argument, concluding that child pornography falls outside the First Amendment regardless whether it is obscene.

The Court identified the two major harms to children caused by child pornography: the harm of creation and the harm of circulation. The first harm is the physical and psychological harm that a child experiences in the process of creating child pornography. In discussing this harm of creation, the *Ferber* Court stressed that creating child pornography involved "exploitation"[11] and often involved "sexual molestation" of children by adults.[12]

The importance of protecting children from the sexual exploitation and abuse of creation can be seen throughout the opinion. For example, the Court framed the harms of child pornography in terms of an "intrinsic relationship" between the distribution of child pornography and child sex exploitation and abuse. This relationship led the Court to conclude that the only effective way to end the harm of creation was to shut down the distribution network of child pornography.[13]

The harm of creation also led the Court to reject the argument that the child pornography exception should be limited to images that are obscene. The Court observed that whether an image is obscene does not necessarily indicate "whether a child has been physically or psychologically harmed in the production of the work," whether an image "required the sexual exploitation of a child for its production."[14]

The second harm identified in *Ferber* is the harm children suffer by the circulation of pornographic images. The Court noted that "the materials produced are a permanent record of the children's participation [in sexual activity] and the harm to the child is exacerbated by their circulation."[15] The Court suggested this interest was as important as, if not more important, than the interest in preventing sexual abuse and exploitation during creation.[16]

Osborne v. Ohio

The Supreme Court's next child pornography case, *Osborne v. Ohio*, also highlighted both the harm of creation and the harm of circulation.[17] Osborne had been convicted under a state statute that prohibited the private possession of child pornography.[18] Osborne argued that the statute was unconstitutional because it conflicted with the Supreme Court's decision in *Stanley v. Georgia*.[19] *Stanley* had struck down a state law outlawing the private possession of obscene material—that is, pornography that did not depict children.

The Supreme Court rejected Osborne's argument. As in *Ferber*, the Court explained that the process of creating child pornography harmed the child. It also explained that prohibiting possession would dry up the market, which would result in fewer images being created and thus less sexual exploitation and abuse of children.[20] In addition to the harm of creation, the Court discussed the harm caused by circulation.[21] It explained that prohibiting private possession would "encourage[] possessors of these materials to destroy them."[22]

In the Court's view, the interest in preventing these harms to children justified different treatment for private possession of child pornography and private possession of obscenity. The Court explained that the state has only "weak interests" in prohibiting the private possession of ordinary obscenity, but that the interests of the State in prohibiting child pornography are much stronger.[23]

The *Osborne* Court also identified a third harm that was not mentioned in *Ferber*. It stated that prohibiting possession of child pornography could help to protect *future* victims of child sex abuse, not just those children depicted in child pornography. The Court based this conclusion on sources suggesting that "pedophiles use child pornography to seduce other children into sexual activity."[24] This new argument in favor of the exemption of child pornography from First Amendment protection was significant because it suggested that the compelling interest in protecting children is not limited to the abuse and exploitation in the *creation* of such images; it also includes the abuse and exploitation can also arise at a later date from the mere existence of such images.

Ashcroft v. Free Speech Coalition

In *Ashcroft v. Free Speech Coalition*,[25] the Supreme Court made clear that either the harm of creation or the harm of circulation must exist in order to trigger the First Amendment exception. It also indicated that the harm of creation—that is, the sexual exploitation and abuse of children to produce child pornography—plays a principal role in its child pornography doctrine. *Ashcroft* involved a First Amendment challenge to the Child Pornography Prevention Act of 1996, which outlawed virtual child pornography—that is, pornographic images created wholly by technological means—and any other "visual depiction" that "is, or appears to be, of a minor engaging in sexually explicit conduct."[26] The Court concluded that the statute was unconstitutional, explaining that virtual child pornography fell outside the constitutional category of child pornography.

In so holding, the *Ashcroft* Court explicitly rejected the new harm identified in *Osborne*—protecting *future* victims of child sex abuse, not just those children victimized by the creation of child pornography—as a government interest that outweighed the individual interests at stake.[27] The *Ashcroft* Court also left no doubt that the harm of creation is the touchstone of its child pornography doctrine. It noted that its analysis in previous cases about state interests outweighing private interests "was based on how [an image] was made, not on what it communicated."[28] Thus, *Ashcroft* leaves no doubt that the harm of *creation*, standing alone, is sufficient to overcome the individual interests at stake.

At the same time, however, *Ashcroft* did not resolve whether the harm of *circulation*, standing alone, justifies the child pornography exception. The harm of circulation arose in the Court's discussion of computer morphing, which is the process of creating sexually explicit images of children by "alter[ing] innocent pictures of real children so that the children appear to be engaged in sexual activity."[29] Because the litigants had not challenged the portion of the statute prohibiting morphed computer images, the Court explicitly declined to address whether such images fell within the category of child pornography. The Court did, however, note that morphed images "implicate the interests of real children and are in that sense closer to the images in *Ferber*."[30] A child who is the subject of a morphed computer image cannot demonstrate that he or she suffered the harm of sex abuse or exploitation in the creation of the image. He or she could, however, suffer mental or emotional anguish from the knowledge or fear that such images have been circulated. By declining to address this section of the law, and by noting that those images were "closer" to the images in *Ferber* than were virtual images, the Court left open the possibility that the harm of circulation, standing alone, might be sufficient to deprive an image of First Amendment protection.

Ashcroft does not tell us whether child pornography includes any sexually explicit depiction of real children, or only those sexually explicit images created through exploiting or abusing children. To be sure, parts of the opinion describe child pornography as any sexually explicit images produced using real children.[31] But, at other times, the opinion describes child pornography as those images created by harming (i.e., sexually exploiting or abusing) children in the production of the images.[32] Indeed, the opinion sometimes uses these alternative descriptions in the same sentence.[33]

Ashcroft did, however, establish that either the harm of creation or the harm of circulation is a necessary component of its child pornography definition. Where neither harm exists—such as when youthful looking adult actors are used or when an image is created by purely technological means—then the First Amendment still applies.

Paroline v. United States

The Supreme Court's most recent child pornography case, *Paroline v. United States*, involved victim restitution.[34] The particular question at issue in *Paroline* was how much restitution a child pornography possessor had to pay a victim of child pornography under a federal restitution statute. In deciding that question, the Court observed that a number of individuals were responsible for the harm to the victim—the person who created the images, the people who distributed the images, and the people who viewed the images. And because the restitution statute required child pornography defendants to pay restitution for only the amount of damages for which they were responsible, the Supreme Court had to analyze what amount of harm is attributable to an individual child pornography possessor.

Paroline was one of many individuals who possessed the victim's image, which made him a relatively minor cause of harm to the victim. The Court noted this fact in its analysis, and it also observed that he, as a mere possessor of child pornography, caused far less harm that the individuals who created and distributed the image.[35] In making this observation, the Court appears to confirm that the harm of creation is far worse than the harm of viewing an image at a later date—that is, the harm of circulation. At the same time, however, the Court confirmed that it does not perceive the harm of circulation to be negligible. It instructed district courts to use their discretion when applying the criteria the Court set forth for calculating restitution to ensure that possessors are not required to pay only "trivial restitution."[36]

Proposing a New Definition of Child Pornography

Although the Supreme Court has not decided whether the harm of circulation, standing alone, justifies the child pornography exception, many lower courts have held that the harm of circulation is significant enough to warrant exempting sexually explicit images from First Amendment protection. These courts have permitted child pornography prosecutions to proceed even when an image was created without any harm to children.

I believe that these courts have gone too far. The First Amendment ought to protect a visual depiction of a child unless the child suffered sexual abuse or exploitation in the creation of the image. Only when an image is created under circumstances that harm a child is the harm significant enough to justify exempting an image from First Amendment protection. To understand why the harm of circulation, standing alone, should be insufficient, it is first necessary to fully develop a definition of child pornography based on the harm at creation. This section articulates such a definition, making it easier to understand why that harm is much graver than the harms associated with circulation, as well as to understand why a definition that includes all sexual images whose circulation could harm a child is inappropriate.

Given that I am proposing that we limit child pornography to the primary harm it inflicts on children, one might ask why it is necessary to limit the definition of child pornography at all. I think it is important to limit the child pornography definition because child pornography is a categorical exception to the First Amendment. As Professor Weinstein tells us in chapter 1, categorical exceptions to the Free Speech Clause were already disfavored when *Ferber* was decided, and the Supreme Court has refused to recognize any new categorical exceptions since.[37] If the state were free to punish categories of speech whenever it perceived the speech as harmful, then we should expect to see a proliferation of criminal laws aimed at speech. In light of this, the child pornography exception is, in my opinion, best justified on grounds that make child pornography entirely different than other categories of speech. Sexual harm to children fits that bill.

My Proposed Definition

I propose that child pornography be defined to include only those images that were created through the sexual exploitation or abuse of children. Sexual exploitation or abuse contains two distinct components: (1) sexual activity and (2) the circumstance that renders that activity exploitative or abusive. Child pornography laws define sexual activity to include sexual molestation—that is, so-called "contact offenses" where there is physical, sexual contact between a minor and an adult. Contact offenses include both forcible contact (i.e., sexual assaults) and nonforcible contact to which a minor cannot legally consent. Many child pornography laws also define the sexual activity to include certain activity where there is no contact between the victim and another person, such as bestiality, masturbation, and at least some depictions of child nudity. As Amy Adler notes in chapter 3, the law has struggled in developing a standard that distinguishes between those instances of child nudity that constitute sexual activity and those that do not.[38] I do not take up that challenge here. Instead I adopt this common legislative definition of sexual activity for my proposed definition with the knowledge that it does not satisfactorily distinguish among images of child nudity.

The circumstance that renders an activity exploitative or abusive is more difficult to define than sexual activity. I propose that abuse and exploitation include force, coercion, or lack of consent. Some have defined the term "exploitation" to include any situation where a child could suffer emotional injury[39] or where the audience derives sexual gratification[40] These alternative definitions assess the abusive or exploitative circumstances after the fact—that is, after the image has already been created and is being viewed. In my definition, the exploitation or abuse must occur at the same time the image is created. If the sexual gratification of the viewer is our only criteria, then it could include wholly innocent images—such as pictures from the Sears catalog—which are apparently considered sexually titillating by some individuals.[41] And if emotional injury were the only criteria, then it could include, for example, written descriptions rather than visual depictions—which *Ferber* explicitly rejected.[42]

What is more, in my definition the exploitation or abuse must exist independently of the actual filming or photographing itself. That is to say, the mere fact that an image was created is not enough to demonstrate that the child in the image was abused or exploited. One must demonstrate that the child would have been abused or exploited even if no image had been captured—for example, because he or she had been subject to sexual contact or because he or she engaged in noncontact sexual activity that was not the product of his or her own free will.

It is important to note that my definition of the term "exploitation" is narrower than its common usage. Exploitation is a broad term, generally defined as "taking advantage of something" or "taking unjust advantage of another for one's own benefit."[43] This broad common understanding of the term has doubtlessly led many to define sexual exploitation to include any sexual depiction of a child. In adopting a more narrow definition of exploitation—the presence of an abusive condition such as force, coercion, or lack of consent—I am attempting to define exploitation in a manner that meaningfully distinguishes between adults and children. It is important to distinguish between children and adults when defining child pornography, because the legal classification of an image has dramatically different consequences depending on whether the person depicted is a child or an adult.

In sum, my definition of child pornography includes only those images created through sexual exploitation or abuse. Sexual exploitation or abuse is defined to include (a) sexual contact or noncontact sexual activity, which is (b) the result of force, coercion, or lack of consent. Of course, because children are legally incapable of consenting to sexual activity, one might argue that lack of consent does not place any meaningful limits on the term sexual exploitation or abuse. That is not accurate.

The phrase "lack of consent" suggests at least two limitations. First, it limits abuse or exploitation to situations involving another participant in addition to the minor depicted. The concept of consent assumes two actors: the person seeking consent and the person giving consent. Thus, it is best to understand a noncontact instance of sexual exploitation or abuse as a minor engaging in sexual activity at the prompting of another individual (e.g., based on a request or a threat).

Second, framing exploitation as a question of consent excludes a number of contact and noncontact activities by minors above the age of consent. Although child pornography laws prohibit images of minors below the age of eighteen, most American jurisdictions set the age of consent for sexual activity below that age.[44] Images that depict sexual activity of minors above the age of consent do not depict exploitation or abuse, as defined in this chapter, unless the image depicts forcible sexual contact or if it was the product of coercion. Without physical force or coercion, images depicting minors above the age of consent are not the product of exploitation or abuse and thus ought not be deemed child pornography.

Comparing the Harm of Creation to the Harm of Circulation

In addition to the harm of sexual exploitation and abuse in the creation of images, the harm most often discussed in the child pornography cases and academic literature is the harm of circulation.[45] The harm of circulation is often characterized as a "continuing harm," because the images "permanently record the victim's abuse" and "haunt[] the children in years to come."[46] There is ample evidence that this harm can have lasting effects on child pornography victims, necessitating years of therapy and negatively affecting their ability to work and socialize.[47]

The harm of circulation is distinct from the harm of creation. The harm of creation is the harm suffered by the child depicted at the time the image is created. The child suffers that harm because she is exploited or abused, and she suffers that harm independently from the creation of the image. Put differently, a child who is sexually assaulted or a child who is seduced into removing her clothes and posing in a sexually explicit manner is harmed regardless whether the moment is captured by a photograph.

In contrast, the harm of circulation is the reputational and privacy harm suffered by the child when the image is viewed at a later time. As the *Ferber* Court tells us, the distribution of child pornography "violates 'the individual interest in avoiding disclosure of personal matters.'"[48] The fact that a child was sexually assaulted is a highly private matter. What a child looks like without her clothes is also highly personal. A child whose sexual exploitation or abuse was captured on film or in a photograph has her privacy violated each time that image is viewed by another individual, much as the publication of a defamatory statement causes harm each time it is published.

If child pornography were defined to include any sexually explicit image that causes harm through circulation, that definition would presume not only that the harm inflicted on a child at the time of creation is exacerbated by the existence of the image, but also that a child suffers significant harm *even if* the child suffered no abuse or exploitation in the creation of the image. For example, a minor who creates a sexually suggestive image of herself, without any prompting or suggestion by a third party, could nonetheless suffer harm if that image were subsequently distributed to others.[49] The important question is whether the harms associated with circulation are unique and severe enough that the image should not be protected by the First Amendment. I do not believe they are. Others disagree with me; they believe that any depiction of sexual activity that involves a real child should be classified as child pornography, even if the image was created without exploitation or abuse.[50]

A definition that limits child pornography to images created through sexual exploitation or abuse is sensible because it limits child pornography according to the principal harm of such images. Although circulating a sexually explicit image of a child that was created without exploitation or abuse can result in harm to that child, the harm of circulation is both lesser than and derivative of the harm of the sexual exploitation and abuse in creating child pornography images. Therefore, the harm of circulation, standing alone, should be insufficient to classify an image as child pornography.

The relative severity of the harm of creation and the harm of circulation is apparent from a simple thought experiment: Given the choice between suffering a sexual assault or having a convincing but fraudulent pornographic image of oneself being assaulted circulated (i.e., an image created through digital manipulation), it is inconceivable that a person would chose the sexual assault. The reputational and psychological harm caused by the circulation of the image is significantly less than the physical and psychological harm caused by a sexual assault.

Of course, not all child pornography is the product of sexual assault. A person who, for example, convinces a child to remove her clothing and pose for photographs has not sexually assaulted the child. That individual has, however, sexually *abused* the child.[51] It is more difficult to construct a thought experiment for an adult involving a fraudulent pornographic image and an image created through noncontact sexual abuse. That is because it is more difficult to imagine a situation where a sexually explicit image of an adult has been created without an assault—that is, without force or threat of force—but under circumstances that are considered abusive. To return to the previous example, if one adult convinced another adult to remove her clothing and pose for photographs, we would generally conclude that the resulting pictures were the result of a consensual encounter rather than an abusive situation. And although the subsequent nonconsensual distribution of those images would likely result in many of the harms associated with circulation of child pornography images, the subsequent distribution would not render the *creation* of those images abusive.

Perhaps if the individual who took the photograph took advantage of a position of power—such as a supervisor who requests that a subordinate employee remove her clothes and who makes an explicit or implicit threat that the adult will lose her job if she does not comply—then we might say that those photographs were the product of an abusive situation. The result of the modified thought experiment is not nearly as certain: While I do not doubt that most everyone would choose to have a convincing but fraudulent pornographic image of oneself circulated rather than suffering a sexual assault, some might elect to remove their clothing under abusive circumstances rather than have the fraudulent photograph circulated.

But even if some of us might prefer the momentary humiliation of being coerced to remove our clothing for a supervisor over the ongoing embarrassment of the dissemination of a fraudulent image, that personal preference is not supported by substantive law. American criminal justice systems routinely punish sex offenses generally (and the sexual abuse of children specifically) far more severely than crimes that protect against privacy and reputational harm.[52] Indeed, even those who have recently advocated the criminalization of so-called revenge porn—sexually explicit images of adults that have been distributed without consent[53]—have sought criminal penalties that pale in comparison to the penalties imposed for child sex abuse.[54] There are a number of reasons that law assigns different penalties for different crimes, but one of the main reasons is differences in the seriousness of the crime. Thus, the relatively lenient penalties associated with crimes that protect against privacy and reputational harm are a reflection of the fact that they cause relatively less harm and that child sex abuse causes more harm to its victims.

The harm of circulation is not only less severe than the harm of creation, it is also derivative. This is illustrated by the fact that the harm-of-circulation argument is ordinarily framed as a concern that images remind victims of the abuse they suffered,[55] not the possibility that a person might be mistakenly identified as a child abuse victim.

Indeed, most of the arguments about the harmfulness of child pornography consist essentially of second-order arguments about the harm of child sex abuse. Those arguments include the idea that punishment is necessary either to stop the production of the pornographic materials[56] or it is necessary to prevent the consumers of child pornography (who are assumed to be sexually attracted to children) from sexually assaulting children later in time.[57] These discussions of the prohibition of circulation in terms of preventing the harms associated with creation confirm that sexual abuse and exploitation are the primary concerns of child pornography.

In addition to the fact that the harm of circulation is both less severe than and derivative of the harm of creation, the harm of circulation is both too broad and too narrow to use as the basis of a definition for child pornography. It is too broad because a definition based only on reputational harm would not be limited to "visual depictions" of minors engaged in sexual activity. If a written account of the sexual abuse of a child identified an actual minor—by name or physical description—that account would also cause reputational or emotional harm. Reputational and emotional harm also occur upon the disclosure of facts surrounding all sexual activity, not simply those that are abusive or exploitative.[58]

A definition based on the harm of circulation would also be too narrow because many child pornography prosecutions could not be justified on the basis of that harm. Children who are depicted but not identifiable—for example because their faces are not included in the image—do not suffer the reputational or privacy harm associated with circulation. Yet there is little doubt that such pictures fall within the core of what has traditionally been considered child pornography.

Prosecutions for private possession also cannot be justified based on the harm of circulation. The harm of circulation supports the prohibition of the production and distribution of child pornography because, as with defamatory statements, every distribution of a child pornography image causes new emotional and reputational harm to the child depicted.[59] But the harm of circulation is not present in cases involving only private possession. The private possession of child pornography causes no new privacy or reputational harm to the victim, just as a person repeating a defamatory statement in an empty room causes no new reputational harm. One could argue, of course, that the private possessor poses a *risk* of new reputational harm because he or should could distribute the image in the future. But if the mere risk of harm to children were enough to remove First Amendment protection, then significant amounts of speech would be in peril. That is why, for example, ordinary First Amendment principles protect even those individuals advocating force or violence unless their speech "is directed to inciting or producing imminent lawless action and is likely to incite or produce such action."[60] It is also why, in the child pornography context, the Supreme Court held that virtual child pornography cannot be prohibited even though it might result in certain thoughts or impulses in viewers; instead there must be a more direct connection between those images and the sexual abuse of children.[61]

Of course, one could respond to the objection that this definition is too narrow by noting that a child pornography definition need not be based *exclusively* on the harm in circulation. Child pornography could be defined as an image that causes harm in creation *or* in circulation. Indeed, the Court's repeated references to both the harm of creation and the harm of circulation could be read as endorsing such an alternative definition. But that dual definition sweeps too broadly because it extends the definition of child pornography beyond any salient differences between adults and children. First Amendment doctrine treats pornographic images very differently depending on whether those images depict adults or children. Adults and children do not have significantly different privacy or reputational concerns; they do, however, have very different concerns in the context of sexual activity.

Imagine, for example, a thirteen-year-old girl and a thirty-year-old woman who live in the same house across the street from a peeping Tom. The peeping Tom secretly watches the thirteen-year-old and the thirty-year-old through binoculars while they shower. Both the thirteen-year-old and the thirty-year-old have suffered a privacy invasion, and that harm is no different based on their age. Now imagine that instead of simply watching the thirteen-year-old and the thirty-year-old while they are in the shower, the peeping Tom decides to ask them to take off their clothes in front of him and pose for photos. If the thirteen-year-old agrees, she has been sexually exploited. If the thirty-year-old agrees, we would not say that she has suffered the same harm, even if she later regrets that decision. Imagine the same scenario, but without the camera. Again, we would say that the thirteen-year-old suffered a more significant harm than the thirty-year-old. The distinction here is not the reputational harm; it is the ability to consent to sexual activity and the inherent vulnerability of children in sexual situations.

The Practical Effect of a Limited Definition

One can easily see how sexting cases fall outside the proposed definition. Consider the following example: In 2009, a fourteen-year-old New Jersey girl posted nude pictures of herself on MySpace.com.[62] She did so because she wanted her boyfriend to see them. News accounts indicate that the girl posed for and created the photos without prompting by a third party, and so the photographs do not appear to have been created under circumstances that rendered that activity exploitative or abusive. And even if the girl was too young to consent to sexual activity, the concept of consent (like any agreement) assumes two actors: the person seeking consent and the person giving consent. As explained above, a noncontact instance of sexual exploitation or abuse arises only when a minor engages in sexual activity because of a threat, request, or encouragement by another individual. It was the girl's own idea to take these photos, thus there was no exploitation or abuse.

Teen sexting is not the only category of cases in which prosecutors have obtained child pornography convictions for images that are neither the product of child sex abuse nor child sex exploitation. Prosecutors have also successfully prosecuted individuals based on images that are the result of computer morphing,[63] images that depict an adolescent above the age of consent,[64] and images that were created through surreptitious filming.[65] In none of these categories of cases would my proposed definition permit prosecution of those individuals for child pornography crimes.

When innocent images—i.e., images no one would claim are child pornography, such as images of a fully clothed child riding a bicycle—are altered to make it appear as though children are naked or engaged in a sex act, no child is sexually exploited or abused. Thus those images would fall outside the proposed definition.[66]

The limited definition would also prevent prosecutions in cases involving images that depict a minor above the age of consent. Although federal law (and many state laws) set the age of consent for sexual activity below eighteen, most child pornography laws, including the federal laws, criminalize sexually explicit images of an individual under the age of eighteen. If the adolescent depicted in an image is above the age of consent, and if there is no indication that the sexual activity in which he or she engaged was the product of force or coercion, then the minor did not suffer abuse or exploitation. Criminalizing pornographic images of adolescents who are above the age of consent but below the age of eighteen does not further the state's interest in preventing exploitation and abuse. It only furthers the lesser and derivative interest in protecting those adolescents from the reputational harms associated with circulation.

Finally, the limited definition would also prevent prosecutions in cases involving images that are the result of surreptitious filming or photographing. Under the proposed definition, the manner in which an image is produced is essential in assessing whether it is appropriately classified as child pornography.[67] A case involving surreptitious photographing or filming is a case in which an image depicts a minor engaging in sexual activity and that image was created without the minor's knowledge and without the producer's manipulation of the minor's activities.

One might argue that these children have been exploited because these images were created without the children's consent. As noted above, lack of consent is one feature of sexual exploitation. If a child is photographed or filmed without her knowledge, then the image was necessarily created without her consent. But under my proposed definition, the lack of consent must be related not only to the creation of the image, but also to the activity depicted. Sexual exploitation would exist if, for example, an adult requested or encouraged a boy to masturbate in front of him and then filmed the boy without his knowledge.[68] That factual scenario would fall within the proposed definition because the producer would have manipulated the victim into engaging in sexual activity—activity to which the boy could not consent. In contrast, where the producer acts as "a sort of 'peeping Tom' catching children at intimate moments and exposing them for the world to see,"[69] the resulting image is not a record of abuse or exploitation.[70]

Excluding images from the definition of child pornography does not mean that individuals may create those images with impunity. That is because First Amendment protection is not absolute. There is no doubt, for example, that a child who is surreptitiously filmed while showering or masturbating has suffered a serious invasion of privacy. In recognition of this harm, some jurisdictions criminalize so-called "video voyeurism," which includes surreptitious photographing or filming both children and adults.[71] Similarly, many jurisdictions recognize the invasion of privacy tort, which would allow victims to recover damages when such a surreptitious image is created.[72] But an invasion of privacy is a harm that is different in kind from sexual abuse or exploitation. And the First Amendment analysis surrounding invasions of privacy is different in kind than the analysis involving child pornography.[73] Thus it is more appropriate to address cases of surreptitious filming or photographing of children using laws designed for that harm rather than child pornography laws.

Concluding Thoughts

Providing meaningful limits on child pornography is important not only because of the occasional prosecutorial abuse that makes headlines—such as teen sexting cases—but also because child pornography laws are intended to combat child sex abuse.[74] Judges repeatedly state that they are putting child pornography offenders in prison to protect children,[75] and law enforcement tout their child pornography arrests and convictions as success in their efforts to prevent child sex abuse.[76] Looking at the Supreme Court's child pornography cases, there is little doubt that the First Amendment leeway legislators and law enforcement have enjoyed with respect to child pornography is founded on the compelling interest of protecting children from child sex abuse and exploitation.

In bringing child pornography charges based on images that were created without sexual abuse or exploitation, prosecutors have shifted child pornography laws away from protecting children from this unique harm. Prosecuting individuals for images that are created without abusing or exploiting a child transforms child pornography law into a system for enforcing popular morality—specifically, popular disgust at the sexualization of children[77]—rather than a system for protecting children.

Limiting the definition of child pornography to those images created through the sexual abuse or exploitation of a child ensures that child pornography laws are directed at the unique harms to children caused by exploitation and abuse. A definition based on the harm of circulation does not focus on the unique harm to children; the privacy and reputational harms caused by circulation are no different for adults than for children. Reputational and privacy concerns not only fail to distinguish between children and adults, but they also fail to distinguish child pornography from several other categories of speech.

Limiting the definition of child pornography to those images created through the sexual exploitation or abuse of children ensures that law enforcement resources are directed only at those images that are the product of unique harms to children caused by sexual exploitation and abuse. And it also ensures that the severe penalties associated with child pornography are imposed only on those offenders whose conduct contributed to the sexual exploitation or abuse of children, whether as creators, distributors, or downstream consumers.

NOTES

1. As Wendy Walsh, Melissa Wells, and Janis Wolak note in chapter 8, 36 percent of prosecutors in their study sample reported having filed charges in at least one sexting case.

2. The prosecutor's behavior prompted widespread criticism, and a federal court ultimately enjoined the district attorney from bringing child pornography charges against

the children. *See* Miller v. Skumanick, 605 F. Supp. 2d 634 (M.D. Pa. 2009), *aff'd* 598 F.3d 139 (3d Cir. 2010).

3. United States v. Stewart, 839 F. Supp. 2d 914 (E.D. Mich. 2012).

4. United States v. Hotaling, 634 F.3d 725 (2d Cir. 2011).

5. *But see* Carissa Byrne Hessick, *The Limits of Child Pornography*, 98 IND. L.J. 1437 (2014) (criticizing these prosecutions).

6. *E.g.*, Miller v. California, 413 U.S. 15 (1973).

7. *See* Stanley v. Georgia, 394 U.S. 557 (1969).

8. 458 U.S. 747 (1982).

9. *Id.* at 749.

10. *Id.* at 752.

11. *Id.* at 758 (citing New York Legislature).

12. *Id.* at 758 n.9.

13. *Id.* at 759.

14. *Id.* at 761.

15. *Id.* at 759.

16. "[P]ornography poses an even greater threat to the child victim than does sexual abuse or prostitution." *Id.* at 760 n.10 (quoting Shouvlin, *Preventing the Sexual Exploitation of Children: A Model Act*, 17 WAKE FOREST L. REV. 535, 545 (1981)).

17. 495 U.S. 103 (1990).

18. *Id.* at 107.

19. 394 U.S. 557 (1969)

20. 495 U.S. at 109.

21. *Id.* at 111 ("the materials produced by child pornographers permanently record the victim's abuse," which "causes the child victims continuing harm by haunting the children in years to come." (citing *Ferber*, 458 U.S. at 759)).

22. *Id.*

23. *Id.* at 108.

24. *Id.* at 111.

25. 535 U.S. 234 (2002).

26. *Id.* at 241.

27. *Id.* at 250.

28. *Id.* at 250–51.

29. *Id.* at 242.

30. *Id.*

31. *See id.* at 245–46 ("The freedom of speech has its limits; it does not embrace certain categories of speech, including . . . pornography produced with real children."); *id.* at 241 ("Before 1996, Congress defined child pornography as the type of depictions at issue in *Ferber*, images made using actual minors.")

32. *See id.* at 251 (characterizing *Ferber* as "reaffirm[ing] that where the speech is neither obscene nor the product of sexual abuse, it does not fall outside the protection of the First Amendment."); *id.* at 249 ("Where the images are themselves the product of child sexual abuse, *Ferber* recognized that the State had an interest in stamping it out without regard to any judgment about its content. The production of the work, not its content, was the target of the statute."); *id.* at 250–51 ("*Ferber*'s judgment about child pornography was based upon how it was made, not on what it communicated."); *id.* at 250 ("In contrast to the speech in *Ferber*, speech that itself is the record of sexual abuse, the CPPA prohibits speech that records no crime and creates no victims by its produc-

tion."); *id.* at 249 ("*Ferber* upheld a prohibition on the distribution and sale of child pornography, as well as its production, because these acts were "intrinsically related" to the sexual abuse of children in two ways."); *id.* at 250 ("Virtual child pornography is not "intrinsically related" to the sexual abuse of children, as were the materials in *Ferber.* While the Government asserts that the images can lead to actual instances of child abuse, the causal link is contingent and indirect. The harm does not necessarily follow from the speech, but depends upon some unquantified potential for subsequent criminal acts."); *id.* at 254 ("In the case of the material covered by *Ferber,* the creation of the speech is itself the crime of child abuse; the prohibition deters the crime by removing the profit motive."); *see also id.* at 244 ("The sexual abuse of a child is a most serious crime and an act repugnant to the moral instincts of a decent people.").

33. *See id.* at 240 ("By prohibiting child pornography that does not depict an actual child, the statute goes beyond *New York v. Ferber,* which distinguished child pornography from other sexually explicit speech because of the State's interest in protecting the children exploited by the production process.").

34. 134 S. Ct. 1710 (2014).

35. *Id.* at 1725 ("Paroline's contribution to the causal process underlying the victim's losses was very minor, both compared to the combined acts of all other relevant offenders, and in comparison to the contributions of other individual offenders, particularly distributors (who may have caused hundreds or thousands of further viewings) and the initial producer of the child pornography.").

36. *Id.* at 1728.

37. Chapter 1, James Weinstein, *The Context and Content of* New York v. Ferber.

38. Child pornography statutes often identify prohibited images of child nudity as "lewd or lascivious exhibition of the genitals." It is difficult to articulate which depictions of child nudity ought to be prohibited and which should not. Using the terms "lewd or lascivious exhibition of the genitals" does not resolve the difficulty because, unlike the other commonly identified sexual activities, the terms "lewd" and "lascivious" do not have an accepted meaning. *See* Amy Adler, *The Perverse Law of Child Pornography,* 101 COLUM. L. REV. 209, 238–41 (2001) (discussing the problems in defining the term and noting that it has expanded steadily).

39. *See, e.g.,* COLO. REV. STAT. ANN. § 18-6-403 (West 2009); BLACK'S LAW DICTIONARY 1407 (8th ed. 2004).

40. *See, e.g.,* United States v. Dost, 636 F. Supp. 828, 832 (S.D. Cal. 1986), *aff'd* 813 F.2d 1231 (9th Cir. 1987).

41. *See* Amy Adler, *Inverting the First Amendment,* 149 U. PA. L. REV. 921, 943–44 (2001); Adler, *supra* note 38 at 259–61.

42. Ferber v. United States, 458 U.S. 747, 764 (1982) (stating that the exception for child pornography is limited to visual depictions).

43. BLACK'S LAW DICTIONARY 619 (8th ed. 2004).

44. *See* W. ESKRIDGE & N. HUNTER, SEXUALITY, GENDER, AND THE LAW 1021–1022 (1997) (noting that thirty-nine States and the District of Columbia set the age of consent at or below sixteen).

45. *See, e.g.,* Ferber, 458 U.S. 747, 760 n.10; Mary Graw Leary, *Sexting or Self-Produced Child Pornography? The Dialog Continues—Structured Prosecutorial Discretion Within a Multidisciplinary Response,* 17 VIRGINIA J. OF SOCIAL POLICY & THE LAW 486, 528 (2010); Audrey Rogers, *Child Pornography's Forgotten Victims,* 28 PACE L. REV. 847, 853–54 (2008).

46. *Osborne*, 495 U.S. 103, 111 (1990); Child Pornography Prevention Act of 1996, Pub. L. 104–208, § 7, 110 Stat. 3009–26 (1996), *codified at* 18 U.S.C. § 2251 *et seq.*

47. Paul G. Cassell, James R. Marsh, and Jeremy M. Christiansen detail these harms in chapter 7.

48. 458 U.S. at 759 n.10 (quoting Whalen v. Roe, 429 U.S. 589, 599 (1977)).

49. *See* Leary, *Sexting or Self-Produced Child Pornography?*, *supra* note 45, at 539–42.

50. *See, e.g.*, A.H. v. State, 949 So. 2d 234 (Fla. Dist. Ct. App. 2007); Leary, *Sexting or Self-Produced Child Pornography?*, *supra* note 45.

51. The concept of child abuse includes not only instances of physical contact between the offender and the victim, but also a number of other situations where the offender is responsible for harm to the child. For example, Black's Law Dictionary defines the verb "abuse" as "to injure (a person) physically or mentally," and it specifies that "a finding of [child] abuse is generally limited to maltreatment that causes or threatens to cause lasting harm to the child." BLACK'S LAW DICTIONARY 12 (10th ed. 2014).

52. For example, Florida classifies video voyeurism—a person who, without consent, records another person who is disrobing or otherwise not clothed—as a third-degree felony, FLA. STAT. ANN. § 810.145. In contrast, it classifies forcible sexual conduct with minors as a first-degree felony, FLA. STAT. ANN. § 794.05, and it classifies nonforcible conduct as a second-degree felony, FLA. STAT. ANN. § 794.011.

53. *See* Danielle Keats Citron & Mary Anne Franks, *Criminalizing Revenge Porn*, 49 WAKE FOREST L. REV. 345, 346 (2014).

54. As Danielle Citron and Mary Anne Franks report, several states have criminalized revenge porn. The maximum penalties adopted by the states vary from six months (California) to five years (New Jersey). *Id.* at 371–74.

55. *Ferber*, 458 U.S. at 759; *see also* Rosalind E. Bell, Note, *Reconciling the PROTECT Act with the First Amendment*, 87 N.Y.U. L. REV. 1878, 1887 (2012) ("Pornographic materials comprise permanent records of sexual exploitation, exacerbating a child's original injury through their circulation.").

56. *See, e.g.*, *Osborne*, 495 U.S. at 108–10; *Ferber*, 458 U.S. at 759–760, 761.

57. *See, e.g.*, *Osborne*, 495 U.S. at 111; *see also* Carissa Byrne Hessick, *Disentangling Child Pornography from Child Sex Abuse*, 88 WASH. U. L. REV. 853, 871–72 (2011) (collecting sources).

58. *See, e.g.*, RESTATEMENT OF TORTS 2d § 652 cmt. (b) ("Sexual relations . . . are normally entirely private matters.").

59. *See Ashcroft*, 535 U.S. 234, 250; United States v. Klug, 670 F.3d 797, 800 (7th Cir. 2012).

60. Brandenburg v. Ohio, 395 U.S. 444, 447 (1969).

61. *Ashcroft*, 535 U.S. 234, 253–254 (2002) ("The Government has shown no more than a remote connection between speech that might encourage thoughts or impulses and any resulting child abuse. Without a significantly stronger, more direct connection, the Government may not prohibit speech.").

62. Associated Press, *Girl Posts Nude Pics, Is Charged With Kid Porn*, MSNBC, Mar. 27, 2009, http://www.msnbc.msn.com/id/29912729.

63. *See, e.g.*, United States v. Ramos, 685 F.3d 120 (2d Cir. 2012); United States v. Hotaling, 634 F.3d 725 (2d Cir. 2011).

64. *See, e.g.*, United States v. Bach, 400 F.3d 622 (8th Cir. 2005); United States v. Freeman, 808 F.2d 1290, 1292–93 (8th Cir. 1987); United States v. Crane, 07-CR-408, 2008 WL 5075906 (N.D. Ga. Nov. 25, 2008); United States v. Shreck, No. 03CR0043, 2006 WL

2945368, at *2 (N.D. Okla. Oct 13, 2006); United States v. Sherr, 400 F. Supp. 2d 843, 849–50 (D. Md. 2005); United States v. Ortiz-Graulau, 397 F. Supp. 2d 345 (D. Puerto Rico 2005); Illinois v. Hollins, 971 N.E.2d 504 (Ill. 2012); Cochran v. Alabama,— So.3d—, 2012 WL 2481649 (Ala. Crim. App. June 29, 2012); Nevada v. Hughes, 261 P.3d 1067, 1070 (Nev. 2011); Nebraska v. Senters, 699 N.W.2d 810, 816–18 (Neb. 2005); Colorado v. Campbell, 94 P.3d 1186, 1189–90 (Colo. App. 2004).

65. *See, e.g.*, United States v. Klug, 670 F.3d 797 (7th Cir. 2012); United States v. Johnson, 639 F.3d 433 (8th Cir. 2011); United States v. Stewart, 839 F. Supp. 2d 914 (E.D. Mich. 2012).

66. A number of commenters have argued in favor of criminalization of such images, so long as the images depict an actual child. *E.g.*, SUZANNE OST, CHILD PORNOGRAPHY AND SEXUAL GROOMING: LEGAL AND SOCIETAL RESPONSES 127–31 (2009).

67. *Cf.* Ashcroft v. Free Speech Coalition, 535 U.S. 234, 250–51 (2002) ("*Ferber*'s judgment about child pornography was based on how it was made, not on what it communicated.").

68. The facts in *United States v. Johnson*, 639 F.3d 433 (8th Cir. 2011), present a close case under this standard. There, the defendant, a weightlifting coach, moved a scale into a small examining room and then hid a video camera in a position that would capture the actions of the young women he coached when they would weigh themselves. Johnson then proceeded to instruct the young women (some of whom were minors) to go into the examination room, take off all of their clothes, and weigh themselves. *Id.* at 436.

69. *Klug*, 670 F.3d at 802 (Cudahy, J., concurring).

70. *Cf. Ashcroft*, 535 U.S. at 250 (stating that "as a permanent record of a child's abuse, the continued circulation itself would harm the child who had participated").

71. *See, e.g.*, 18 U.S.C. § 1801; ARK. CODE ANN. § 5-16-101; FLA. STAT. ANN. § 810.145; HAWAII REV. STAT. § 711-1110.9; IDAHO CODE ANN. § 18-6609; KENTUCKY REV. STAT. § 531.100; LA. REV. STAT. ANN. § 14:283; R.I. GEN. LAWS 1956 § 11-64-2.

72. For examples of courts recognizing that surreptitious filming constitutes an intrusion of privacy, see *In re* Marriage of Tigges, 752 N.W.2d 452 (Iowa Ct. App. 2008); Lewis v. LeGrow, 670 N.W.2d 675 (Mich. Ct. App. 2003); Miller v. Brooks, 472 S.E.2d 350 (N.C. Ct. App. 1996).

73. A full explanation of those differences is beyond the scope of this chapter. For a trenchant overview of how categorical exceptions to the First Amendment operate differently than legal analysis involving a balancing of interests, see Joseph Blocher, *Categoricalism and Balancing in the First and Second Amendment Analysis*, 84 NYU L. REV. 375, 381–98 (2009).

74. Hessick, *supra* note 57 at 880–82.

75. *See, e.g.*, United States v. Crandon, 216 Fed. Appx. 613, 614 (8th Cir. 2007).

76. *See, e.g.*, Remarks of Assistant Attorney General Deborah J. Daniels at the Conference on Child and Family Maltreatment, January 28, 2004, *available at* http://www.ojp.usdoj.gov/archives/speeches/2004/confonchildabuse.htm (last visited Aug. 10, 2012) (reporting arrest rates for "Internet-based child sexual exploitation" and noting that every "such arrest means that untold numbers of innocent children will be protected from abuse" at the hands of "pedophiles").

77. *See* Hessick, supra note 57, at 865; *see also* Louis Henkin, *Morals and the Constitution: The Sin of Obscenity*, 63 COLUM. L. REV. 391 (1963) (positing that obscenity laws are principally motivated by traditional notions of decency and morality).

Part I (B) | Defining Child Pornography Crimes

Consequences of the Legal Definition

3 | The "*Dost* Test" in Child Pornography Law

"Trial by Rorschach Test"[1]

Amy Adler

This chapter considers a pivotal but deeply problematic aspect of the definition of "child pornography": the six factor "*Dost* test."[2] Although never considered by the Supreme Court, the *Dost* test, developed by a California district court, has become a key feature of child pornography law, adopted by virtually all state and lower federal courts as part of the definition of child pornography. Despite the near universal adherence to *Dost*, however, I argue that deep and unrecognized problems plague the test. Through a close reading of decisions applying the *Dost* factors, I show that these cases reveal startling uncertainties at the core of the test. Ultimately, these uncertainties pose severe and unrecognized First Amendment problems. In the final analysis, I argue that the *Dost* test poses not only constitutional problems, but also cultural ones. By requiring the viewer to evaluate suspected photos using the perspective of a pedophile, the test inadvertently replicates the very sexualized view of children that child pornography law seeks to fight.

Section I of this chapter sets forth an overview of child pornography law from the First Amendment perspective. Here I discuss the rationale for excluding child pornography from free speech protection: the harm caused to children in the production of the material. I also sketch the Supreme Court's definition of the constitutional bounds of the category and summarize the recent case law. Section II introduces the *Dost* test and explores both that test's remarkable predominance as well as the myriad disagreements it has generated in the lower courts. *Dost* governs a growing realm of proscribed child pornography: images that do not show children engaging in any sort of sexual conduct, but instead depict children in a way that may be perceived as "lascivious" by the viewer. My focus will be on two major controversies surrounding the test: (1) its fundamental unpredictability and (2) the debate over whether child pornography in this realm should be judged from the viewpoint of the average person or the pedophilic voyeur. As I will show, the current state of the law is surprisingly contested and complex. Section III evaluates the damage done by *Dost*. Here I show that *Dost* poses not only a significant threat of vagueness and overbreadth, but also a more fundamental First Amendment problem: In my view, many cases decided under *Dost* may be unconstitutional in light of Supreme Court precedent. Finally, I turn to the cultural risk of *Dost*: the test, designed to protect children from sexual abuse, may unwittingly further the sexualization of children that it fights.

I. Child Pornography Law and the First Amendment: An Overview

In 1982, a unanimous Supreme Court in *New York v. Ferber*[3] decided that "child pornography" was a new category of speech without constitutional protection.[4] Since *Ferber*, child pornography law has emerged as a complex, rapidly growing, and deeply anomalous area of First Amendment jurisprudence. The *Ferber* Court had encountered a novel First Amendment problem: whether nonobscene[5] sexual depictions of children—speech not falling into any previously defined First Amendment exception—could be constitutionally restricted. The Court's answer was yes. "Child pornography"—which has come to be defined as "visual depictions" of "sexual conduct involving a minor"[6]—thus joined a small and motley band of categories of expression that are excluded from constitutional protection by reason of their content. The Court has not created a new category since.[7]

Below I give an overview of the Court's rationale for banning child pornography from First Amendment protection and a brief introduction to the constitutional definition of child pornography. This sets the stage for section II, in which I explore the case law to illustrate the disconnect between the rationale for constitutional exclusion and the rapidly expanding definition of "child pornography." As I will show, this disconnect has grown considerably since the Court created child pornography law as a body of First Amendment law more than thirty years ago. Ultimately, this growing criminalization of material unconnected to the constitutional rationale for prohibiting child pornography means that a significant swath of recent cases may be unconstitutional under the First Amendment.

A. Rationale for Categorical Exclusion: Production Harm

Although the Supreme Court in *Ferber* announced five reasons that supported the exclusion of child pornography from First Amendment protection,[8] the fundamental focus of these rationales was this: child pornography must be prohibited because of the grievous harm done to children in the production of the material.[9] They key to the Court's reasoning was that the production of child pornography requires an act of child sexual abuse.[10]

Focusing on the trauma of child sexual abuse, the *Ferber* Court thus framed the issue as whether "a child has been physically or psychologically harmed in the production of the" material.[11] The Court wrote that the purpose of child pornography law was "to prevent the abuse of children who are made to engage in sexual conduct."[12] The opinion repeatedly emphasized the unspeakable harm caused to children who are abused in order to produce child pornography.[13] And once the abuse had occurred in the production of the images, the circulation of the resulting pictures compounded the harm by "haunting" the victims, forcing them to relive their molestation.[14] The Court concluded that because it was so difficult to prosecute the "low-profile, clandestine industry" of pornography production, the "most expeditious if not the only practical method of law enforcement" was to punish the speech that resulted from the underlying crime.[15] In short, the Court banned child pornography images because they were "intrinsically related" to the criminal child sexual abuse that was required to produce them.[16]

This urgent rationale behind child pornography law—to protect real children from abuse—explains why the Court's jurisprudence in this area departs so dramatically from obscenity law: obscenity law is premised on the worthlessness of certain expression,[17] whereas child pornography law excludes speech because of the horrible crime from which it stems. Thus, unlike obscenity law, child pornography law makes no exception for works of "serious literary, artistic, political or scientific value."[18] As the Court explained, even if a work possesses serious value, that "bears no connection to whether or not a child has been harmed in the production of the work."[19] Unlike obscenity law, child pornography law does not require us to evaluate works as a whole. And unlike obscenity law, child pornography law allows for the prosecution of mere possession, as opposed to distribution or production, of a suspect picture.[20] (Possession prosecutions have escalated dramatically since the early days of child pornography law because digital technology, unavailable then, has made it all too easy for perpetrators to download huge troves of images.)[21] As the Court explained, the underlying crime of child sexual abuse entitles the states to "greater leeway in the regulation" of child pornography than of obscenity.[22] This compelling rationale justifies the departure from traditional First Amendment strictures that child pornography law permits.

The Supreme Court's 2002 opinion in *Ashcroft v. Free Speech Coalition*[23] underscored that production harm is the key to understanding child pornography law. *Ashcroft* struck down as overbroad the "virtual child pornography" provisions of the Child Pornography Prevention Act of 1996 ("CPPA").[24] These provisions treated virtual child pornography—computer-generated materials produced without using any actual children—as if it were "real" child pornography. In holding these provisions unconstitutional, the Court found that these virtual child pornography images should not be legally proscribed under the category of "child pornography"—even though they were potentially indistinguishable in appearance—because virtual images lacked the distinguishing feature of child pornography: the abuse of children in the production of the material. Virtual child pornography can still be prosecuted as obscenity, as can textual pornography describing child abuse.[25] But these materials may not be prosecuted as child pornography and thus are exempt from the particularly harsh legal rules that have grown up around that doctrine.

The concept of production harm was pivotal to the *Ashcroft* Court's reasoning. The Court emphasized that Congress' prohibition on virtual child pornography was unconstitutional because it "does not depend at all on how the image is *produced*."[26] At another point the Court wrote that the law was overbroad because it targeted images that "do not involve, let alone harm, any children in the *production process*."[27] The Court explained that Congress' rationales for banning the material were constitutionally invalid because under those rationales, "harm flows from the content of the images, not from the means of their *production*."[28] As the Court concluded, "*Ferber*'s judgment about child pornography was based upon *how it was made*, not on what it communicated."[29] The case reaffirmed that "where the speech is neither obscene nor *the product of sexual abuse*, it does not fall outside the protection of the First Amendment."[30] In short, the Court made clear that "[t]he *production* of the work, not its content, was the target" of *Ferber*.[31]

In removing virtual child pornography from the category of real child pornography, the Court still acknowledged that virtual child pornography can be dangerous. Not only is virtual child pornography repugnant, but it might also be used by pedophiles to groom future victims. Indeed, it might "whet the appetites of pedophiles" and thus embolden them to commit crimes against children.[32] Nonetheless, the *Ashcroft* opinion (in line with other First Amendment cases) made clear that all of these reasons are insufficient as a matter of constitutional law to criminalize speech.[33] The Court repeatedly emphasized the distinction—as I had argued it should[34]—between criminal acts that occurred as a result of how people reacted to or used the material and criminal acts that were essential to produce the material in the first place. Only the latter could be the basis for criminalizing the material itself.[35] As the Court explained, "[t]he production of the work, not its content, was the target" of *Ferber*.[36]

In spite of the unqualified clarity of the *Ashcroft* decision, it left unsettled a number of pressing issues. Most prominently, *Ashcroft* did not address the legal status of morphed images—those that use digital technology to modify existing images to make it appear (falsely) that an identifiable child were engaging in sexual conduct. Like the virtual child pornography images in *Ashcroft*, such morphed photos are not the product of actual abuse. But unlike fully virtual images, morphed images cause harm to a real, identifiable child. Does harm that is caused by how a child is represented still count as harm for purposes of child pornography law, which has always depended on harm in production as its central rationale? The question of whether such images should be proscribable under the rubric of child pornography law is in my view unsettled.[37] Significant dignitary harms to our most vulnerable members of society are at stake. But so far, and in spite of a few court decisions to the contrary, I believe it is an open constitutional question whether child pornography law or some other body of law is the appropriate legal framework to address these concerns.

There are further open questions about the constitutional limits of child pornography law. These questions are multiplying for two reasons: one, changes in digital technology allow for new methods of creating images that, like morphed images, do not require production abuse; and two, lower courts have expanded the definition of child pornography since *Ferber* and *Ashcroft* in a way that makes the category less and less connected to the problem child abuse as the Supreme Court envisioned. I turn to the expanded definition below.

B. Defining Child Pornography: An Overview

Federal law defines "child pornography" as "visual depictions" of "sexual conduct involving a minor."[38] A minor is anyone under age eighteen.[39] The emphasis on visual depictions, which includes only photographic or filmic images made using real children (as opposed to drawings or textual descriptions which do not record actual abuse) has remained largely unchanged since *Ferber*, where the Court approved New York's statutory definition of the "child pornography." In line with *Ferber*, federal law defines "sexually explicit conduct" as "(A) sexual intercourse . . . ; (B) bestiality; (C) masturbation; (D) sadistic or masochistic abuse; or (E) lascivious exhibition of the genitals or pubic area of any person."[40]

The creation of this latter category—"lascivious exhibition of the genitals"—as part of the class of prohibited "sexually explicit conduct" introduced the most problematic aspect of defining child pornography. Determining whether a photo depicts a child being raped, for example, would appear to be a relatively straightforward (albeit repugnant) inquiry. But what exactly constitutes "lascivious exhibition of the genitals"? How does it differ from an innocent photograph of a naked child, such as a family photograph of a child in the bathtub? How does it differ from photographs used in mass market advertising, a realm that increasingly relies on highly sexualized images of teens?

The interpretive problems surrounding this category of "lascivious exhibition of the genitals" are compounded because the Court has made clear that nudity is *not* the dividing line between protected speech and child pornography. Indeed, the *Ferber* Court emphasized that child "nudity, without more is protected expression."[41] Conversely, and surprisingly, a picture can be criminalized as "lascivious" even if it contains *no* nudity. Although the Supreme Court has never directly approved this interpretation, several influential circuit court opinions have held that a picture can be a lascivious exhibition of a child's genitals—and thus child pornography—even if the child's genitals are not discernible and even if the child is wearing clothes.[42]

Further complicating the inquiry is that no identifiable sexual conduct is required in order for a photograph to constitute a "lascivious display of the genitals" and thus child pornography. This is peculiar, given that lascivious exhibition is included as one subcategory of the general category of "sexually explicit conduct" that the child pornography statute prohibits. How can an image with no sexual conduct be deemed "sexually explicit conduct"? For reasons we will see, it is common for the government to pursue images that "certainly [contain] no sexual activity" as a prosecutor conceded in a recent and successful case.[43] As the Eighth Circuit recently made clear, "even images of children acting innocently can be considered lascivious if they are intended to be sexual."[44]

Thus an image may be categorized as a criminal lascivious exhibition of the genitals and a type of "sexually explicit conduct" even if it contains no display of the genitals and no sexual conduct. As a result, the meaning of the term "lascivious" has acquired great constitutional and practical import. For a defendant, the boundaries of this term mark the distinction between freedom and jail. Yet other than to assert that lasciviousness and nudity are not identical, the Supreme Court has offered no guidance on the question of what constitutes a "lascivious exhibition of the genitals" or what differentiates such an image from constitutionally protected images of children, nude or otherwise. In the absence of any guidance, lower courts have been busily filling the gap left open by the Supreme Court. The result is a growing and troubling body of case law.

II. The *Dost* Test

The leading case on the meaning of "lascivious exhibition" is *United States v. Dost*, a 1986 California federal district court case that announced a six-part test for analyzing images.[45] Although courts routinely criticize the "*Dost* test," it is the reigning—and indeed the only—definition of "lascivious exhibition" in child pornography law. Virtually all state and federal courts follow the *Dost* test; even those courts that criticize the test apply it nonetheless.[46] As the Second Circuit recently stated in a case applying *Dost*, the factors may be "imperfect" and "cannot bear the fully analytical weight that has at times been placed on them," but "they have not been much improved upon."[47]

The *Dost* test identifies six factors that are relevant to the determination of whether a picture constitutes a "lascivious exhibition":

(1) whether the focal point of the visual depiction is on the child's genitalia or pubic area;
(2) whether the setting of the visual depiction is sexually suggestive, i.e., in a place or pose generally associated with sexual activity;
(3) whether the child is depicted in an unnatural pose or in inappropriate attire, considering the age of the child;
(4) whether the child is fully or partially clothed, or nude;
(5) whether the visual depiction suggests coyness or willingness to engage in sexual activity;
(6) whether the visual depiction is intended or designed to elicit a sexual response in the viewer.[48]

The test does not require that all factors be met to find that a depiction is a lascivious exhibition, nor are the factors meant to be exhaustive.[49]

When I first wrote about the *Dost* test more than a decade ago, I argued that it had produced a profoundly incoherent and troubling body of case law.[50] In the years since, the case law has grown considerably and the problems have multiplied. I analyze some of the most salient problems below.

A. The Test's Fundamental Malleability

Although the *Dost* test is nearly universally accepted, there are "myriad disputes" swirling around it.[51] Perhaps the most fundamental problem is that the *Dost* test is extraordinarily malleable. One judge, dissenting in a recent case, compared the defendant's conviction under the *Dost* factors as "trial by Rorschach test."[52] One could consider this malleability of *Dost* either a feature or a bug of the test. Viewed as a feature, one could praise the test for its adaptability to a wide range of fact patterns and individual photographs. Viewed as a bug, one could questions the test for its unpredictability and its manipulability, problems of special concern for defendants accused of the heinous crime of child sexual abuse, who are likely to be regarded with disgust and outrage by juries.

The malleable quality of the *Dost* test stems from several sources. First, it is unclear how many *Dost* factors must be met for a photograph to be seen as lascivious. No court demands that all six factors be present. But is there a minimum number of factors that must be met in order to designate an image "child pornography"? There is no agreement on this question. The Tenth Circuit suggested that if a jury found merely one of the six factors satisfied, it would suffice to criminalize a photograph as child pornography.[53] The Third Circuit, noting the general rule that all six factors need not be met, held that at least more than one factor was required, suggesting a possible minimum of two.[54]

Second, the application of each factor can be remarkably subjective.[55] For example, Judge Kozinski, sitting by designation in a district court case, dismissed the *Dost* factors as so "malleable and subjective in their application" that the test was simply "not helpful."[56] As an example, Judge Kozinski noted that the prosecutors in that case had argued that photos showing girls in an "open shirt and socks, or wearing open robes in a public area such as the beach" met the third Dost factor, which asks whether a child is wearing "inappropriate attire." The government argued that "shirts or robes are [no] less sexually provocative than garters and high heels; it's a matter of taste."[57] Under this view, normal children's clothes such as shirts or robes become sexually inappropriate because such attire could appeal to the "taste" of a pedophile voyeur.

In my view, each factor of the *Dost* test has the potential for subjective and unpredictable application. Consider, for example, the second factor of the test, which probes whether the setting is "sexually suggestive." In a First Circuit case, the government argued, unsuccessfully (and in my view quite startlingly) that a beach was a sexually suggestive setting because "many honeymoons are planned around beach locations."[58] A newly emerging question that has divided courts is whether a bathroom is a sexually suggestive setting. The question arises with surprising frequency because of an alarming trend revealed by the case law: as the fact patterns of recent cases show, offenders frequently hide cameras in bathrooms to capture images of children or teenagers undressing. Such intrusion upon the privacy of children is abhorrent and deeply disturbing. But the question raised by the cases is this: are images of children engaged in such mundane private conduct as showering and changing or using the toilet to be considered lascivious and sexual for purposes of the law? The Tenth Circuit has held that a bathroom is a sexually suggestive setting under the second factor because "showers and bathtubs are frequent hosts to fantasy sexual encounters as portrayed on television and film. It is potentially as much of a setting for fantasy sexual activity as an adult's playroom."[59] In contrast, an Oklahoma district court found that a bathroom is "not necessarily a sexually suggestive location."[60]

Or consider a recent Massachusetts case in which the Court applied the third *Dost* factor to a photo of a girl on the beach.[61] The government argued that the girl was in a "sexually suggestive" pose under the third *Dost* factor because the position of her left hand suggested that she was "about to touch herself . . . or masturbate." The dissent interpreted the girl's hand placement as showing nothing more than a child playing on the beach and about to dig into the sand.[62] What looked to the government like abuse and pornography appeared to the dissent to be a vacation photograph of a girl happily playing on a seashore.

The highly subjective nature of the factors suggests the need for interpretive guidelines that will allow juries and courts to reliably divide protected speech from abusive criminal pornography. As I will explore in the following section, however, courts are deeply divided about what these interpretive guidelines should be. These divisions highlight and exacerbate the deep uncertainties that plague the *Dost* test.

B. The Pedophile's Perspective and The Dost *Factors*

Courts disagree about several key interpretive issues surrounding the *Dost* test. In this section, I address two of the most prominent subjects of disagreement. First, courts have disagreed about whether lasciviousness should be evaluated by an objective standard, or whether we should imagine a pedophile voyeur's subjective desires in determining whether a picture of a child qualifies as lascivious. Second, courts are divided about whether determinations about a picture's lasciviousness should be based on the four corners of the picture, or on extraneous evidence about how the picture was used.

1. Is the Test Objective or Subjective?

In deciding if a picture contains a "lascivious exhibition of the genitals," a threshold question presents itself: does "lascivious" describe the child depicted, the photographer, or the viewer? In the *Knox* case, Solicitor General Drew Days had argued that the term "lascivious" must mean that the child depicted is "lasciviously engaging in sexual conduct (as distinguished from lasciviousness on the part of the photographer or consumer)."[63] Otherwise, Days reasoned, there is no child "sexual conduct," which is what child pornography law combats. The Court in *Ferber* had been clear: "the nature of the harm to be combated requires that the . . . offense be limited to works that visually depict sexual conduct by children."[64]

But courts have routinely rejected that argument, insisting that because children are innocent victims, they obviously cannot behave in a lascivious manner. Rather, as the Ninth Circuit explained in the case affirming *Dost*, "lasciviousness is not a characteristic of the child photographed but of the exhibition" set up for the photographer and pedophilic viewers.[65]

Because the sexual content of a photograph cannot be found in the actions of the child pictured, it must be apparent in some other way to the viewer. But the contentious and crucial question is: which viewer? A "normal" viewer would not find any photograph of a child sexually appealing, while a pedophile viewer could have a lascivious reaction to even the most banal and innocent photographs of children.

Therefore the question of which viewer, the "normal or the pedophile" becomes determinative of a depiction's criminality. As I have argued elsewhere, it is relevant to the application of each and every *Dost* factor.[66] But the major debate about this issue has emerged in courts' analyses of the sixth factor of the test, which asks "whether the photograph is intended or designed to elicit a sexual response in the viewer." Courts have split on this fundamental question: Whose perspective matters here, the normal viewer or the pedophile viewer? Is the *Dost* test objective or subjective? It is because of this uncertainty that courts routinely term the sixth factor "the most confusing and contentious" of the *Dost* factors.

a. Subjective

Dost itself had suggested a rule that many but not all courts follow: the proper inquiry into whether a photograph is "intended . . . to elicit a sexual response in the viewer" should be into the subjective response of a pedophile viewer rather than the average viewer.[67] The Ninth, Sixth, and Second Circuits, for example, have explicitly endorsed this view.[68] As the Ninth Circuit explained, we must evaluate the lasciviousness of the photographer and an "audience that consists of *himself or like-minded pedophiles*."[69] We must focus on the photographer's "*peculiar* lust."[70] This focus on a deviant's reaction is dramatically different from obscenity law, which, for all its complications, at least rests on the viewpoint of the "average person" in asking whether the material "appeals to the prurient interest" or is "patently offensive."[71]

b. Objective

Some courts, however, express wariness about the dangers of the subjective approach and have argued instead that images must be analyzed objectively. The Eighth Circuit, although it appears recently to have moved toward a subjective standard,[72] formerly followed an objective standard, which it described as follows: "the relevant factual inquiry . . . is not whether the pictures in issue appealed or were intended to appeal to [the defendant's] sexual interests but whether, *on their face, they appear to be of a sexual character*."[73] In defending the objective approach, the First Circuit warned that under the subjective approach, "a sexual deviant's quirks could turn a Sears catalog into pornography."[74] Similarly, a district court in Hawaii recently cautioned that assessing a photograph from the subjective perspective of a pedophile viewer "would support a finding of child pornography in almost all cases."[75]

As Judge Higgenbotham wrote, concurring in a recent case, further problems present themselves with the subjective approach depending on whether we focus on the photographer's subjective reaction or on the reaction of the consumer of the images: "A pedophile may be aroused by photos of children at a bus stop wearing winter coats, but these are not pornographic. Conversely, a photographer may be guilty of child pornography even though he is not aroused by the photos he produces purely for financial gain."[76] And the subjective approach has a more fundamental flaw: it departs so completely from the statutory language. As the judge wrote, "The statute does not suggest that the definition of pornography is contingent upon what arouses the defendant, especially if the defendant is aroused by objectively asexual images."[77] As I will show in section III, the problem is not merely that the analysis departs from the statutory language. It also departs from the constitutional basis of child pornography law as articulated by the Supreme Court.

2. Four Corners or Extrinsic Evidence?

There is yet another complication to this analysis that only deepens the reliance on the pedophile's perspective under *Dost*.[78] Courts have once again divided on a question of great import under the sixth factor: should the "intended effect" of a picture for purposes of the sixth factor be based on the four corners of the image, or should we interpret the image in light of extrinsic evidence about a defendant's predilections? This inquiry overlaps with but is not identical to the subjective/objective inquiry described above. Most courts that take a subjective approach do allow such evidence, but differ on what should and should not be considered relevant. Conversely, most courts that take an objective approach to *Dost* ignore extrinsic evidence. Nonetheless, some courts purport to take an objective approach yet admit evidence of the defendant's predilections. In doing so, these courts push further toward an interpretation of *Dost* in which the pedophile's perspective becomes determinative.

The First Circuit has been the most vocal in support of the four corners approach. As a court explained, "the focus should be on the objective criteria of the photograph's design."[79] Another First Circuit decision had held, "We must . . . look at the photograph rather than the viewer."[80] Under this view, the intended effect of a picture must be evident in the picture itself. Evidence about how the defendant used the picture is irrelevant.

More frequently, however, courts allow extrinsic evidence about the creator or possessor of an image to assess whether the intended effect of a picture should be seen as sexual. In my view, this inquiry threatens to convert what seem to be innocent pictures into child pornography based on little more than the identity of a defendant. Consider a recent Eighth Circuit case from 2012.[81] There the defendant had hidden a camera to make "secretly filmed" footage of a girl undressing to take a shower. Presumably the contents of the video—though obviously not the circumstances of its making—were innocent and quotidian; it depicted nothing more than a girl getting ready to shower. What the defendant did to take the picture is repugnant. Most video voyeurism statutes would also make such behavior criminal.[82] But putting aside for a moment his abhorrent and presumably criminal invasion of the girl's dignity and privacy, is it right to call the video of her getting undressed sexual "child pornography"? The Eighth Circuit acknowledged that the material captured on video did not involve any "sexual activity." But it interpreted the images as sexual because the defendant was discovered to possess an extensive collection of other child pornography. In this scenario, a nonsexual image of a girl (taken by repugnant means) becomes sexual and contraband by association.[83]

Some courts have made the inquiry all the more confusing because they purport to take an objective approach to the sixth factor, but nonetheless allow extrinsic evidence of the defendant's intent. For example, in a recent Eighth Circuit decision involving a coach who used a hidden camera to secretly take images of fifteen-to-seventeen-year-old girls weighing themselves on a locker room scale, the court used what it called an objective standard but also looked at extrinsic evidence beyond the four corners of the image.[84] The court explicitly stated that the standard given to the jury was an objective one, focusing only on whether the images "appear to be of a sexual character."[85] Objectively speaking there would seem to be nothing inherently sexual about images of girls weighing themselves on a scale. Yet the images were indeed sexual to the defendant because he said so. When asked why he took the pictures the defendant replied that "[his] pervertedness got the best of [him]." Based on this extrinsic evidence, the Court found the images were sexual even under a purportedly objective inquiry.[86] In doing so, I think the court transformed an objective inquiry into a subjective one. This marks another way in which the pedophile's perspective once again becomes determinative of whether an image is child pornography.

III. The Damage Done by *Dost*

In spite of the problems detailed above, there are still many reasons we may want to retain the *Dost* test. First, as the Second Circuit remarked, although the test has many shortcomings, no court has found a better alternative; the factors have "not been much improved upon."[87] But in my view, the most compelling argument that could be made in favor of retaining *Dost* is this: *Dost* is extremely capacious and to limit it (and the category of lascivious exhibition that it delineates) would mean that some child abusers would go free and that some abusive, harmful images would be free to circulate. In short, it seems fair to argue that if we are going to err, there are strong reasons to err on the side of protecting more victims. (That said, it is possible that in some cases, other areas of law could achieve the same or similar goals: obscenity laws, video voyeurism laws, and privacy laws might provide alternative to child pornography law.)

In what follows I set forth the countervailing arguments and make the case for reconsidering the *Dost* test. I present three sets of harms caused by the test. I leave it for another day to evaluate whether these costs I present are sufficient to outweigh the benefits of *Dost*.

A. First Amendment Harms

1. Vagueness and Overbreadth

First, from my discussion above it should be clear that the *Dost* test raises a number of First Amendment concerns. Most fundamentally, the test is unpredictable and vague in its application and presents risks of overbreadth. In its attempt to ban lascivious pictures of children, it also threatens to send innocent people to jail and to ban valuable speech (such as family photographs of children, nude or clothed) that ought to be protected. The Court has made clear that the consequences of unpredictability and vagueness in the First Amendment context are severe because of the chilling effect they produce. As I have argued previously, *Dost* threatens to chill pictures of children that we might value and that deserve First Amendment protection.[88]

2. *Dost* May Be Unconstitutional Under the First Amendment as Interpreted by *Ferber* and *Ashcroft*

There is a second and deeper First Amendment problem with *Dost*: Some of the prosecutions currently proceeding under the test may be unconstitutional under the *Ferber* rationales as underscored by *Ashcroft*. It is simply not clear whether the harm done to children in cases of surreptitious filming, for example, entails the kind of production harm that *Ferber* and *Ashcroft* require before an image can be characterized as child pornography. Such images may implicate other rationales detailed in *Ferber* and not present in *Ashcroft*, such as the need to protect a child from being "haunted" by traumatic images. (This issue was not implicated in *Ashcroft* because it addressed only the issue of virtual child pornography which by definition does not depict real children). But the kinds of images I am discussing here, such as those produced through surreptitious filming, are traumatic not at the time they are produced, when a child is simply going through the rituals of her daily routine; instead they become traumatic once the child learns she has been recorded and viewed in a sexual manner. As I suggested in my discussion of morphing above, it is in my view an open constitutional question whether such harm standing alone would suffice to deem an image "child pornography" as a constitutional matter.[89] The Court's jurisprudence is simply unclear on this point and there are significant reasons to suspect that the kind of harm caused by these images is simply too far afield from the abuse-in-production harm that is the foundation of child pornography law. As the Court has made clear, child pornography law was designed "to prevent the abuse of children who are *made to engage in sexual conduct*."[90] Although the *Ashcroft* case did not involve the interests of actual children and may be distinguishable, it nonetheless reaffirmed that "where the speech is [not] *the product of sexual abuse*" it is protected by the First Amendment.[91] If child pornography law is inapplicable, as I suspect it may be to the kind of pictures I am considering, other avenues of law—such as privacy or video voyeurism statutes[92] for example—may be possible ways to prohibit these abuses while better conforming to the demands of the First Amendment.

Furthermore, to the extent *Dost* has been interpreted to incorporate the pedophile's perspective in evaluating images, it raises a further First Amendment concern: it threatens to turn child pornography law into a thought crime. Once our criminalization of speech depends on the pedophile's imagined response to an image rather than any harm in production, we have begun to police thoughts and fantasy, not actions. The harm of the pictures no longer turns on what happened to the child. It now occurs in the possibility of *seeing* a picture in a certain way, in how someone might *perceive* the child. The determination of whether a picture is child pornography has grown increasingly bound up in our projections of whether these pictures will permit pedophiles to fantasize about them. Thus, child pornography law has begun to police speech based on how people may respond to it. This is in direct contravention of traditional First Amendment tenets.[93]

B. Practical Concerns: Dilution of the Category of Child Pornography

The expansive reading of *Dost* detailed above may cause another harm. Including images of normal child activity within the category of child pornography because of the pedophile's perspective may dilute the category itself. Such dilution is worrisome because it could detract from the true horror that the category was designed to police, a horror that has only escalated in recent years. The prevalence of child pornography has increased dramatically because of digital and technological advances, which have made it far easier than it once was for offenders to produce and distribute child pornography and to evade detection as they do so. As a result, child pornography images, according to the government, have become not only more prevalent but also much more disturbingly hard core. For example, Attorney General Alberto Gonzales spoke in 2006 in dramatic and graphic terms about the growing threat: "I have seen pictures of older men forcing naked young girls to have anal sex. There are videos on the Internet of very young daughters forced to have intercourse and oral sex with their fathers. . . . There are images of graphic sexual and physical abuse of innocent children, even babies."[94]

This is a horrifying development. Does it make sense to lump photographs of teenagers taking showers into the same category as pictures of children being raped? This admixture might threaten to dilute the category of child pornography and in doing so to detract from and even potentially trivialize the terrible horror it protects against. Such dilution may also divert prosecutorial resources away from pursuing the most extreme cases of abuse.

C. *The Final Cost of* Dost *Is Cultural Not Constitutional*

As detailed above, *Dost*'s purview has expanded to cover an increasing range of images that do not involve any sexual conduct, images that are objectively asexual but become sexual when viewed from the perspective of the pedophile. As a result, the pedophilic gaze has become central to how many, if not most, courts interpret *Dost*.[95] It is relevant in the test's premise as well as in its application. First, the obligation to see the world from the eyes of a pedophile arises from the basic assumption underlying *Dost*. The process begins once we accept that prohibited depictions of "sexually explicit conduct" by children can include pictures in which there is no overt sexual conduct. The law presumes that pictures harbor secrets, that judicial tests must guide us in our seeing, and that we need factors and guidelines to see the "truth" of a picture. As a court explained, *Dost* rests on the notion that a photograph contains "subtleties which the jury must study."[96] That even a clothed child can be engaging in lascivious exhibition of his genitals only makes the process more urgent and more difficult. Once the law acknowledges that pedophiles like many pictures of children and that clothed children can be sexy children, then we have to redouble our efforts and to doubt our instinctive ways of seeing.

The mechanisms of applying the *Dost* test usher us step by step into a pedophilic world. As discussed above, many courts follow the suggestion of the *Dost* court and interpret the sixth factor of the test subjectively, through the lens of a pedophile voyeur. But it is not only this factor of the *Dost* test that requires us to take on the perspective of the pedophile. The application of each *Dost* factor demands a heightened awareness of the erotic appeal of children. We must search out whether the child's genitals are the focal point of the picture, whether the pubic area is prominent, if the child is in a setting normally associated with sex, if the child conveys an erotic acquiescence in his gaze, or if there is some suggestion of his "coyness or willingness to engage in sexual activity." If a videotape depicts a clothed child dancing in a public park, we must look closer. For example, in *Knox* the court asked whether the children depicted were innocently dancing in the park or if they were "gyrating in a fashion indicative of adult sexual relations?"[97]

Consider how *Dost* itself explained the scrutiny necessary to determine whether a picture suggests "sexual coyness or a willingness to engage in sexual activity." The court described a photograph of a ten-year-old girl sitting naked on the beach:

> Her pelvic area appears to be slightly raised or hyperextended and her legs are spread apart. Her right leg is fully extended at a slight outward angle. Her left leg is bent at the knee and extends almost perpendicularly away from the body. Her pubic area is completely exposed not obscured by any shadow or body part.[98]

The court then analyzes whether such a photograph is lascivious—in particular whether the girl expresses a sexual "willingness." The court concludes that the girl does seem sexually inviting. Why? Although "nothing else" about the child's attitude conveys this, the court nonetheless concludes that the girl's "open legs do imply such a willingness [to engage in sexual activity]."[99]

Or consider the argument made to the Supreme Court in *Knox* by amici:

> Because lasciviousness should be examined in the context of pedophile voyeurs, this Court should view visual images of young girls

> in playgrounds, schools and swimming pools as would a pedophile. Pedophiles associate these settings with children, who to pedophiles are highly sexualized objects. It therefore follows as a matter of course that viewing videocassettes of young girls in these settings permits the pedophiles to fantasize about sexual encounters with them.

This argument exhorts the Court to see children as "highly sexualized objects." The Third Circuit seems to have accepted this argument when the *Knox* case was remanded to it from the Supreme Court. In examining the videotapes of clothed girls, the court found significant that "[n]early all of these scenes were shot in an outdoor playground or park setting where children are normally found."[100] This aspect of the videotapes—that they were filmed in a setting where "children are normally found"—became one of the details that the court specifically, though not exclusively, relied on in concluding that the material in question qualified under *Dost* as child pornography that "would appeal to the lascivious interest of an audience of pedophiles."[101] According to this logic, a place "where children are normally found" is now suspiciously erotic.

But what does it do to children to protect them by looking at them as a pedophile would, to linger over depictions of their genitals? And what does it do to us as adults to ask these questions when we look at pictures of children? As we expand our gaze and bend it to the will of the *Dost* test, do we run the risk of transforming the way we see children? It is my view that the expanded reach of the test has unwittingly contributed to a world in which we increasingly look at normal images of children through a sexual lens. As everything becomes potential child pornography in the eyes of *Dost*—clothed children, coy children, children in settings where children are found—perhaps everything really does become pornographic.

Congress passed the 1996 Child Pornography Prevention Act in part because it feared that child pornography was changing our view of children. Congress found, "The sexualization and eroticization of minors through any form of child pornographic images has a deleterious effect on all children by encouraging a societal perception of children as sexual objects . . ."[102] Although it is an unconstitutional basis on which to ban speech, the fundamental insight of Congress was fair: one harm done by child pornography is that it changes the way we perceive children. What Congress failed to see is that child pornography law itself has also done that. Even more directly than child pornography, child pornography law, as it has expanded under *Dost*, explicitly requires us to take on a "perception of children as sexual objects," to see, for a moment, as a pedophile does.

Conclusion

As prosecutions of child pornography offenders continue to rise, the *Dost* test reigns over an expanded and constitutionally uncertain terrain. The test has vexed courts. It raises significant, unresolved, and remarkably untheorized First Amendment questions. Scholars have paid it no attention.

So far the Supreme Court has not considered *Dost*. In the absence of guidance from the Court, lower courts have been busily expanding the test, and they have done so in a way that I believe raises serious constitutional concerns. Quite simply, lower courts frequently interpret *Dost* to criminalize speech that does not implicate the rationales that the Supreme Court has so far relied on to justify the exclusion of "child pornography" from First Amendment protection. *Dost* in its application has thus become divorced from the Court's foundational assumptions of why we may ban child pornography consistent with the First Amendment. Many convictions obtained under the test may therefore be of doubtful constitutional validity, at least to the extent that they proceed under the rubric of child pornography law as the Supreme Court has so far envisioned it.

Ultimately, I have suggested that *Dost* poses not only constitutional but cultural problems. Courts increasingly interpret the test in a way that invites us to view objectively nonsexual pictures of children through the gaze of the pedophile, transforming these images into "child pornography." As such, the *Dost* test, meant to protect children from sexual predation, may unwittingly contribute to the sexualization of children that it fights.

NOTES

Many thanks to Dan Markel, Carissa Hessick, and Melissa Hamilton for comments. I am very grateful to Andrew Moore, Haley Anderson, and Michael Simeone for superb research assistance; I am also grateful for the support of the Filomen D'Agostino and Max E. Greenberg Research Fund. I dedicate this chapter to the memory of Dan Markel.

1. Commonwealth v. Sullivan, 82 Mass. App. Ct. 293, 320 (2012) (Milkey, J., dissenting).

2. United States v. Dost, 636 F. Supp. 828 (S.D. Cal. 1986), *aff'd sub nom* United States v. Wiegand, 812 F.2d 1239 (9th Cir. 1987).

3. 458 U.S. 747 (1982).

4. *Id.* The Court's exclusion of certain categories of expression from constitutional expression was most famously articulated in *Chaplinsky v. New Hampshire*, 315 U.S. 568 (1942).

5. The materials at issue in *Ferber* had been found not obscene by the jury, which was instructed to consider obscenity as well as child pornography charges against the defendant. *See Ferber*, 458 U.S. at 751. Thus the issue for the Court was sharply defined. *Miller v. California*, 413 U.S. 15 (1973), sets forth the Court's obscenity standard. The "*Miller* test" asks: (1) whether the "average person" would find that the speech, "taken as a whole, appeals to the prurient interest"; (2) whether it is "patently offensive"; and (3) "whether the work, taken as a whole, lacks serious literary, artistic, political, or scientific value." *Id.* at 24 (citations omitted).

6. 18 U.S.C. § 2252. In response to *Ferber*, Congress quickly passed legislation modeled on the New York statute upheld in that case. The result was the Child Protection Act of 1984 Pub. L. No. 98–292, 98 Stat. 204 (1984) (codified as amended at 18 U.S.C. §§ 2251–2253 (2008)). That and subsequent acts have closely followed the *Ferber* definition.

7. *See* United States v. Stevens, 130 S. Ct. 1577 (2010).

8. *Ferber*, 458 U.S. at 756. The five rationales set out in *Ferber* were as follows:

1. The State has a "compelling" interest in "safeguarding the physical and psychological well-being of a minor." *Id.* at 756–57 (citing Globe Newspaper Co. v. Superior Court, 457 U.S. 596, 607 (1982)).
2. Child pornography is "intrinsically related to the sexual abuse of children in at least two ways. First, the materials produced are a permanent record of the child's participation and the harm to the child is exacerbated by their circulation. Second, the distribution network for child pornography must be closed" in order to control the production of child pornography. *Id.* at 759 (citations omitted). The Court went on to explain that the production of child pornography is a "low-profile clandestine industry" and that the "most expeditious if not the only practical method of law enforcement may be to dry up the market for this material" by punishing its use. *Id.* at 760.
3. The advertising and selling of child pornography provide an economic motive for and are thus an integral part of the production of child pornography. *Id.* at 761 (citations omitted).
4. The possibility that there would be any material of value that would be prohibited under the category of child pornography is "exceedingly modest, if not de minimis." *Id.* at 762.
5. Banning full categories of speech is an accepted approach in First Amendment law and is therefore appropriate in this instance. *Id.* at 763–64.

9. The opinion repeatedly emphasizes this concern for the "welfare of children engaged in [the] production" of child pornography. *Ferber*, 458 U.S. at 764. Indeed, the Court framed the issue as whether "a child has been physically or psychologically harmed in the production of the work." *Id.* at 765. The first three rationales address this central harm. The fourth rationale goes to the assumption that the category of speech in question is "low value"; banning it therefore presents little First Amendment concern.

The fifth rationale recognizes the Court's precedent of having banned whole categories of speech before.

10. This conception of child pornography—that it is sexual abuse, that it is in fact the core of sexual abuse—was the foundation of the approach taken by courts, legislators, politicians, and the media. *See, e.g.*, ATTORNEY GENERAL'S COMMISSION ON PORNOGRAPHY, FINAL REPORT 406 (1986) ("Child pornography *is* child abuse.") (emphasis in original); 142 CONG. REC. S-11886-01, S-11900 (Sept. 30, 1996) (statement of Sen. Biden) ("At the heart of the analysis . . . is a very straightforward idea: Children who are used in the production of child pornography are victims of abuse, plain and simple. And the pornographers, also plainly and simply, are child abusers."); *see also* 132 CONG. REC. S-14225-01 (Sept. 29, 1986) (statement of Sen. Roth) ("[T]hose who advertise in order to receive or deal in child pornography and child prostitution are as guilty of child abuse as the actual child molester . . ."). The Attorney General's Commission on Pornography stated that "[c]hild pornography must be considered as substantially inseparable from the problem of sexual abuse of children. . . . There can be no understanding of the special problem of child pornography until there is understanding of the special way in which child pornography is child abuse." ATTORNEY GENERAL'S REPORT, *supra*, at 406 (emphasis in original). The abuse of an actual child is "[t]he distinguishing characteristic of child pornography." *Id.* at 405.

11. *Ferber*, 458 U.S. at 765.

12. *Id.* at 753.

13. *Id.* at 759.

14. *Id.*

15. *Id.* at 760. In addition to this fundamental rationale, the Court articulated other reasons why child pornography could be categorically excluded from First Amendment protection. First, the Court noted the state's "compelling" interest in "safeguarding the physical and psychological well-being of a minor." *Id.* at 756–57. Second, the Court noted that it was unlikely that any material of value would meet the definition of "child pornography." *Id.* at 762. Third, the Court reasoned that since advertising and selling child pornography were "an integral part of the production" of the material, these activities could also be prohibited to protect children harmed in the production. *Id.* at 747. Finally, the Court also noted its precedents in which it had accepted categorical bans on certain types of expression. *Id.* at 768–69.

16. From the start, the Court viewed child pornography as a child abuse problem. *See Ferber*, 458 U.S. at 758 (describing "intrinsic[] relation[ship] of child pornography and child abuse"). In *Ferber*, the Court approvingly quoted one scholar who categorized child pornography as "an even greater threat to the child victim than . . . [routine] sexual abuse." *Id.* at 759 (quoting David P. Shouvlin, *Preventing the Sexual Exploitation of Children: A Model Act*, 17 WAKE FOREST L. REV. 535, 545 (1981)); *see also* WILLIAM A. STANMEYER, THE SEDUCTION OF SOCIETY 88 (1984) ("Child pornography is the worst form of child abuse."). According to the Court, child pornography documents an underlying act of abuse—the sexual use of a child. *Ferber*, 458 U.S. at 759 n.10. The recording of the act also becomes a collateral violation against the child's dignity. The circulation of the pictures comes to "haunt" the child, so that the initial act of abuse takes on a life of its own, exposing the child to perpetual reinjury. *Id.* ("Because the child's actions are reduced to a recording, the pornography may haunt him in future years, long after the original

misdeed took place.") (quoting Shouvlin, *supra*, at 545). The Court wrote that "the materials produced are a permanent record of the children's *participation* and the harm to the child is exacerbated by their circulation." *Id.* at 759 (emphasis added). The Court went on to explain that the production of child pornography is a "low-profile clandestine industry" and that the "most expeditious if not the only practical method of law enforcement may be to dry up the market for this material" by punishing its use. *Id.* at 760.

17. This is the fundamental principle of *Roth v. United States*, 354 U.S. 476 (1957), the Court's first modern obscenity decision, in which it held that "obscenity" was a category of expression that lacked First Amendment protection.

18. Miller v. California, 413 U.S. 15, 23 (1973) (establishing exception in obscenity law for works that lack such value). Although the Court has never entertained a child pornography case in which serious value was raised as a defense, the Court's dicta in *Ferber* seems to reject the idea of an exception for value. *Ferber* held that the lack of an exception for serious value did not render the law so overbroad that it failed under the doctrine of "substantial overbreadth." *Id.* at 766–74. Nonetheless, the concurring opinions in *Ferber* suggest some discord on the question of serious value among the members of the court at the time of the 9-0 decision. For example, Justice O'Connor wrote to emphasize that artistic value was irrelevant to the harm of child abuse that child pornography law sought to eradicate. "[A] 12-year-old child photographed while masturbating surely suffers the same psychological harm whether the community labels the photograph 'edifying' or 'tasteless.' The audience's appreciation of the depiction is simply irrelevant to New York's asserted interest in protecting children from psychological, emotional, and mental harm." *Id.* at 774–75 (O'Connor, J., concurring). In contrast, Justice Brennan assumed that serious artistic value would be a valid defense in a case if it were raised. He wrote that harm to a child and value of a depiction bear an inverse relationship to one another: "[T]he Court's assumption of harm to the child resulting from the permanent record and circulation of the child's participation lacks much of its force where the depiction is a serious contribution to art or science." *Id.* at 776 (Brennan, J., concurring) (citations omitted).

19. *Ferber*, 458 U.S. at 764.

20. In *Osborne v. Ohio*, 495 U.S. 103 (1990), the Court extended the reach of child pornography law in its decision to uphold the criminalization of mere possession as opposed to distribution or production of child pornography. Once again, the Court relied on the unique rationale underlying child pornography law to justify the decision and its rejection of a basic tenet of obscenity law: that privacy rights protect the individual possessor of obscenity in his own home even though the material he possesses is illegal to make or sell. *See* Stanley v. Georgia, 394 U.S. 557 (1969) (holding that the government cannot prohibit mere possession of obscene material). *Cf. Osborne*, 495 U.S. at 109 ("The State does not rely on a paternalistic interest in regulating Osborne's mind. Rather, Ohio has enacted [its law prohibiting possession of child pornography] in order to protect the victims of child pornography. . . .").

21. Chapter 2, Carissa Byrne Hessick, Setting Definitional Limits for the Child Pornography Exception; Amy M. Adler, *All Porn All the Time*, 31 N.Y.U. REV. L. & SOC. CHANGE 695 (2007).

22. *Ferber*, 458 U.S. at 756.

23. 535 U.S. 234 (2002).

24. 18 U.S.C. § 2251 *et seq*. The Court struck down Section 2256(8)(B), which prohibited "any visual depiction, including any photograph, film, video, picture, or computer or computer-generated image or picture" that "is, or appears to be, of a minor engaging in sexually explicit conduct." It also struck down Section 2256(8)(D), which defined child pornography to include any sexually explicit image that was "advertised, promoted, presented, described, or distributed in such a manner that conveys the impression" it depicts "a minor engaging in sexually explicit conduct."

25. *See* The "Protect Act" (Prosecutorial Remedies and Other Tools to End the Exploitation of Children Today Act of 2003), Pub. L. No. 108–21, § 504, 117 Stat. 650, 678 (2003) (regarding "Obscene Child Pornography"); *see also* Theresa "Darklady" Reed, Child Torture Sex Stories Earn PA Woman Federal Obscenity Charges, YNOT (Sept. 27, 2006, 3:09 PM), http://www.ynot.com/modules.php?op=modload&name=News&file=news_article&sid=16172&mode=thread&order=0&thold=0 (describing prosecution of purely textual website involving stories of child sexual abuse); United States v. Whorley, 550 F.3d 326 (4th Cir. 2008) (finding that cartoons depicting minors in sexually explicit conduct could be obscene).

26. *Ashcroft*, 535 U.S. at 241 (emphasis added).

27. *Id.* (emphasis added).

28. *Id.* at 242 (emphasis added).

29. *Id.* at 250–51 (emphasis added); *see also* United States v. Williams, 553 U.S. 285, 289 (2008) ("[T]he child-protection rationale for speech restriction does not apply to materials produced without children.").

30. *Ashcroft*, 535 U.S. at 251 (emphasis added).

31. *Id.* at 249 (emphasis added).

32. *Id.* at 253.

33. *Id.*; *see also* Brown v. Entertainment Merchants Ass'n, 131 S.Ct. 2729, 2734 (2011) (striking down California law regulating "patently offensive" video games).

34. Amy M. Adler, *Inverting the First Amendment*, 149 U. PA. L. REV. 921, 990–91 (2001).

35. Thus the Court specifically rejected the government's argument that virtual child pornography should be banned because it "whets the appetites of pedophiles." *Ashcroft*, 535 U.S. at 253. The Court wrote that the "mere tendency of speech to encourage unlawful acts is not a sufficient reason for banning it. . . . the Government may not prohibit speech on the ground that it may encourage pedophiles to engage in illegal conduct." *Id.* Furthermore, the Court rejected the argument that the material could be banned because it can be used to seduce children. Here the Court wrote, "The evil in question depends upon the actor's unlawful conduct, conduct defined as criminal quite apart from any link to the speech in question." *Id.* at 252.

36. *Ashcroft*, 535 U.S. at 249.

37. I consider the law to be unsettled even though several courts have decided that morphed images should constitute child pornography. *See, e.g.*, United States v. Hotaling 634 F.3d 725, 729 (2d Cir. 2011); United States v. Bach, 400 F.3d 622 (8th Cir. 2005). *Cf.* Doe v. Boland, 630 F.3d 491 (6th Cir. 2011). In my view, this position is potentially wrong under *Ferber* and *Ashcroft* and requires clarification by the Supreme Court. The Court deliberately avoided the question of morphed images in *Ashcroft*.

38. *See supra* note 6.

39. 18 U.S.C. § 2256(1).

40. 18 U.S.C. § 2256(2)(A)-(E). Congress adopted this definition from *Ferber* but changed the word "lewd" to "lascivious" in order to clarify the distinction between child pornography law and obscenity law, in which the word "lewd" is a term of art. Child Protection Act of 1984, Pub. L. No. 98-292, 98 Stat. 204 (1984); *see also* United States v. Dost, 636 F. Supp. 828, 830–32 (S.D. Cal. 1986) (discussing the Act).

41. *Ferber*, 458 U.S. at 765 n.18 (citations omitted).

42. United States v. Knox, 32 F.3d 733 (3d Cir. 1994); *accord* United States v. Helton, 302 F. App'x. 842, 847 (10th Cir. 2008) (holding videotape defendant recorded of an eleven-year-old girl wearing opaque underpants qualified as child pornography because of the way it was framed); United States v. Grimes, 244 F.3d 375 (5th Cir. 2001) (finding nude images of minors with pixel boxes covering their genitals are still lascivious within the meaning of the federal child pornography statute, noting it is an easier determination than *Knox*); United States v. Horn, 187 F.3d 781, 790 (8th Cir. 1999) (holding that a "reasonable jury could conclude that the exhibition of pubic area was lascivious" in "beach scenes [of] girls wearing swimsuit bottoms"); People v. Spurlock, 114 Cal. App. 4th 1122, 1127 (2003) (holding child pornography and child exploitation statutes could apply to image depicting topless fifteen-year-old girl in her underwear with her legs spread); People v. Kongs, 30 Cal. App. 4th 1741, 1755–56 (1994) (following *Knox*, finding photographs that zoomed in on girls' pubic area were lascivious even though the girls were wearing underwear); *Cf.* U.S. v. McGlothlin, 391 Fed. App'x 542 (7th Cir. 2010) (finding probable cause existed regarding photographs of clothed boy in innocent activity, but photographs focused on pubic area).

43. Commonwealth v. Sullivan, 82 Mass. App. Ct. 293, 322–23 (2012) (Milkey, J., dissenting). *Cf.* United States v. Johnson, 639 F.3d 433 (8th Cir. 2011) ("Thus, even images of children acting innocently can be considered lascivious if they are intended to be sexual.").

44. United States v. Johnson, 639 F.3d 433, 440 (8th Cir. 2011).

45. 636 F. Supp. 828 (S.D. Cal. 1986) *aff'd sub nom* United States v. Wiegand, 812 F.2d 1239 (9th Cir. 1987). *Dost* has been relied on by virtually all circuits that have considered it. *See, e.g.*, United States v. Rivera, 546 F.3d 245, 250 (2d Cir. 2008); *Knox*, 32 F.3d at 747 (3d Cir. 1994); United States v. Wolf, 890 F.2d 241, 244–46 (10th Cir. 1989); United States v. Rubio, 834 F.2d 442, 448 (5th Cir. 1987) (affirming use of factors without specifically citing *Dost*); United States v. Amirault, 173 F.3d 28, 31 (1st Cir. 1999) (emphasizing that factors are "neither comprehensive nor necessarily applicable in every situation"); United States v. Horn, 187 F.3d 781, 789 (8th Cir. 1999) ("We find helpful the six criteria" in *Dost*); U.S. v. Brown, 579 F.3d 672, 680 (6th Cir. 2009) ("This Court, in line with other Circuit courts, has applied a six factor test for 'lasciviousness,' as set forth in [*Dost*].") Numerous district courts have followed *Dost*, as have state courts. *See, e.g.*, Nebraska v. Saulsbury, 498 N.W.2d 338 (Neb. 1993).

46. For cases directly criticizing *Dost*, *see* United States v. Hill, 322 F. Supp. 2d 1081, 1085 (C.D. Cal. 2004) (criticizing *Dost* test as "highly malleable and subjective"); United States v. Frabizio, 459 F.3d 80, 90 (1st Cir. 2006) (questioning whether *Dost* factors are overly generous to defendant and noting that they are not the "equivalent of the statutory standard of 'lascivious exhibition'"). *Cf.* Craft v. State, 252 Ga. App. 834 (2001) (not using *Dost* test because Court found it was not relevant to Georgia statute). For cases applying the *Dost* factors but noting criticism or emphasizing their limited utility, *see, e.g.*, United States v. Overton, 573 F.3d 679, 686 (9th Cir. 2009) ("*Dost* factors are neither exclusive nor conclusive but operate merely as a 'starting point'"); United States v.

Campbell, 81 F. App'x 532, 536 (6th Cir. 2003) (*Dost* factors "not exhaustive" but "provide a framework for analyzing" image).

For positive statements about the *Dost* test, *see, e.g., Villard*, 885 F.2d at 122 ("[T]he *Dost* factors provide specific, sensible meaning to the term 'lascivious,' a term which is less than crystal clear.").

47. United States v. Rivera, 546 F.3d at 252; *see also* Com. v. Sullivan, 82 Mass. App. Ct. 293, 318 (2012) (discussing *Rivera*) ("Rather than treating the *Dost* factors as providing the overarching doctrinal framework under which lewdness issues should be analyzed, it makes far more sense to treat them as helpful considerations.").

48. *Dost*, 636 F. Supp. at 831.

49. *See, e.g.*, United States v. Horn, 187 F.3d at 789.

50. Adler, *Inverting the First Amendment*, *supra* note 34.

51. United States v. Frabizio 459 F. 3d 80, 87 (1st Cir. 2006).

52. Commonwealth v. Sullivan, 82 Mass. App. Ct. 293, 320 (2012) (Milkey, J., dissenting).

53. The Court wrote, "We do not hold that more than one *Dost* factor must be present." United States v. Wolf, 890 F.2d 241, 245 n.6 (10th Cir. 1989).

54. United States v. Villard, 885 F.2d 117, 122 (3d Cir. 1989) ("Although more than one factor must be present in order to establish 'lasciviousness,' all six factors need not be present."). A recent case concluded that the Second Circuit imposes no minimum number of *Dost* factors be present for an image to constitute child pornography. United States v. Goodale, 831 F. Supp. 2d 804, 810 (D. Vt. 2011) (citations omitted).

55. For one example of how easily manipulated the first factor of the test is, see *State v. Vander Logt*, 583 N.W.2d 673, 675 (Wis. App. 1998), where the court considered a picture of defendant lying in bed with two sixteen-year-old girls. The court noted that although "neither of the girls [were] naked below the waist," the picture still constituted a "lewd exhibition of the victims' genitals." *Id.* Because the adult defendant was nude, the court concluded "the exhibition of [the defendant's] naked genitals necessarily draws attention to the genitals of the semi-nude females in bed with him," and thus constituted a "lewd exhibition of the victims' genitals." *Id.* For a view that child pornography law should not apply to images of female breasts, see *United States v. Gleich*, 397 F.3d 608, 614 (8th Cir. 2005).

56. United States v. Hill, 322 F.Supp.2d 1081 (C.D. Cal. 2004), *aff'd* 459 F.3d 966 (9th Cir. 2006) ("Although we appreciate the district court's careful analysis and critique of *Dost,* we do not think it necessary to adopt a new test or to deny the utility of *Dost* in the context of this case. The *Dost* factors can be a starting point for judges.").

57. *Id.* at 1085.

58. United States v. Amirault, 173 F.3d 28, 32 (1st Cir. 1999).

59. United States v. Larkin, 629 F.3d 177, 183 (3d Cir. 2010), *see also* United States v. Goodale, 831 F. Supp. 2d at 810.

60. United States v. Helton, CR-07-70-T, 2007 WL 1674196 (W.D. Okla. June 7, 2007) *aff'd*, 302 Fed. App'x 842 (10th Cir. 2008).

61. The photograph was not taken by the defendant. Instead he had downloaded it from a Flickr-type Russian photo-sharing site that included "a lot of vacation photographs." *Id.*

62. Commonwealth v. Sullivan, 82 Mass. App. Ct. 293, 320 (Mass. 2012) (Milkey, J., dissenting).

63. Brief for the United States at 9, *Knox*, 32 F.3d 733 (No. 92-1183).

64. *Ferber*, 458 U.S. at 764.

65. United States v. Wiegand, 812 F. 2d 1239, 1244 (9th Cir. 1987). Courts have wavered on the question of whether the focus must be on the consumer, the photographer, or both. This question is crucial since there is not necessarily any correspondence between the photographer's intent and the consumer's use of a photograph.

66. Adler, *Inverting the First Amendment*, *supra* note 34.

67. *See Dost*, 636 F. Supp. at 832 (The question is whether the image is "designed to elicit a sexual response in the viewer, albeit perhaps not the 'average viewer,' but perhaps in the pedophile viewer.").

68. For examples of decisions focusing on the subjective view of the pedophile voyeur, *see, e.g.*, *United States v. Goodale*, 2:11-CR-37, 2012 WL 733874 (D. Vt. Mar. 6, 2012) (finding that the defendant who surreptitiously filmed victim in a bathroom had "composed the images to elicit a sexual response for himself"); *United States v. Rivera*, 546 F.3d 245, 250 (2d Cir. 2008) (examining defendant's intent in creating images); *United States v. Brown*, 579 F.3d 672, 682 (6th Cir. 2009), *cert. denied*, 558 U.S. 1133 (2010) ("We, like our sister circuits, have adopted a test that considers whether a visual depiction is *intended* or designed to elicit a sexual response in the viewer. The use of the word 'intended' seems to establish that the subjective intent of the photographer is relevant.") (citations and quotations omitted); *Perkins v. Texas*, 394 S.W.3d 203, 209 (Tex. Ct. App. 2012) (jurors' "common sense" could allow them to conclude that these images of 16 year old girl dressing and undressing surreptitiously filmed by hidden camera in bathroom were created to appeal to deviant and voyeuristic interests of viewer").

69. United States v. Wiegand, 812 F. 2d 1239, 1244 (9th Cir. 1987) (emphasis added).

70. *Id.* (emphasis added).

71. This standard of the "average" or "normal" person began in *Roth*, 354 U.S. at 489–90 and has persisted in obscenity law. *But see* Mishkin v. New York, 383 U.S. 502, 508 (1966) (in case involving homosexual pornography, adjusting "prurient appeal" prong of obscenity test to focus on appeal to a "clearly defined deviant [*sic*] sexual group").

72. United States v. Ward, 686 F.3d 879 (8th Cir. 2012) (finding that even though video of girl getting out of the shower is not "overtly sexual activity," it is child pornography because defendant "composed the images in order to elicit a sexual response in a viewer—himself" (quoting U.S. v. Rivera, 546 F.3d at 250)). Perhaps the confusion that seems to characterize the Eighth Circuit's approach may be explained by its conflation of the objective/subjective inquiry with the overlapping but analytically separate issue of extrinsic evidence, discussed *infra*.

73. United States v Wallenfang, 568 F.3d 649, 658 (8th Cir. 2009) (emphasis added) (citations omitted); *see also* People v. Lamborn, 785 N.E.2d 350, 355–56 (Ill. 1999) (rejecting inquiry into "whether defendant was aroused by the photographs"); Tennessee v. Whitlock, E2010-00602-CCA-R3CD, 2011 WL 2184966 (Tenn. Crim. App. June 6, 2011) (In refusing to inquire into the subjective response of defendant who appeared to attain sexual pleasure from filming children swimming in an apartment complex pool, the Court held that "however creepy the defendant's behavior was" the images he produced showed nothing more than "children engaging in normal, everyday behavior."); United States v. Steen, 634 F.3d 822, 829 (5th Cir. 2011) (Higgenbotham, J., concurring) ("Congress did not make production of child pornography turn on whether the maker or viewer of an image was sexually aroused, and this *Dost* factor encourages both judges and juries to improperly consider a non-statutory element.").

74. *Amirault*, 173 F.3d at 34. Some courts that adhere to the subjective standard respond that these criticisms of the subjective approach can be diminished by recognizing a distinction between production and possession cases. *See Rivera*, 546 F.3d at 252 ("The sixth *Dost* factor is not easily adapted to a possession case."); *see also* United States v. Overton, 573 F.3d 679, 688 (9th Cir. 2009) ("We think the sixth *Dost* factor . . . is of particular utility where, as is the case here, the criminal conduct at issue relates to a defendant's role in the *production* of the exploitative images under review, and not merely the *possession* of illicit materials.") (emphasis in original).

75. United States v. McCarty, 672 F. Supp. 2d 1085, 1101 n.11 (D. Haw. 2009).

76. *Steen*, 634 F.3d at 829 (5th Cir. 2011) (Higgenbotham, J., concurring).

77. *Id.* at 829–30.

78. *See, e.g.*, United States v. Frabizio 459 F. 3d 80, 89 (1st Cir. 2006) ("The issue of the four corners rule, and even of what it means, has not been decided by this Circuit, and we do not decide it here. The issue is complicated, and there are arguments going different ways.").

79. *Amirault*, 173 F.3d 28 (finding photograph of young naked girl on beach did not contain a "lascivious exhibition of the genitals").

80. United States v. Villard, 885 F.2d at 126.

81. United States v. Ward, 686 F.3d 879, 883–84 (8th Cir. 2012).

82. See *infra* note 92 (federal video voyeurism statute).

83. Nonetheless, there is still a significant argument in favor of categorizing the images involved in Ward as child pornography. This is because the defendant took a further step beyond using a hidden camera to secretly film his victim: he also physically positioned her for the hidden camera. This kind of posing of the victim, even if it results in images that do not seem objectively sexual, may still implicate the harm in production rationale of *Ferber*.

For cases that also rely on extrinsic evidence to criminalize material, see *United States v. Goodale*, 2:11-CR-37, 2012 WL 733874 (D. Vt. Mar. 6, 2012) (Images of a seventeen-year-old in the bathroom were lascivious because defendant "admitted to masturbating to the videos, confessed his sexual desires for [the victim], and culled particular still frames from the videos to make a separate collection of his favorite images."); *see also* United States v. Muscemi, 307 Fed. App'x 473 (allowing defendant's statements about photographs including "his belief that those photographs would sexually arouse him" to inform jury's view of whether photographs were lascivious).

The Sixth Circuit has taken what is termed a "hybrid" approach to this inquiry. In *United States v. Brown*, 579 F.3d 672, 683 (6th Cir. 2009), the Court applied what it called a "limited context" test that permits consideration of the context in which the images were taken, but limits the consideration of contextual evidence to the circumstances directly related to the taking of the images. Thus, other evidence, such as a defendant's possession of other child pornography, would not be admitted.

84. United States v. Johnson, 639 F.3d 433, 440 (8th Cir. 2011).

85. *Id.* ("The jury was carefully instructed that it was not to decide 'whether the pictures appealed, or were intended to appeal, to the defendant's sexual interests, only whether they appear to be of a sexual character.'").

86. *Id.* For a case that raises similar concerns about blending an objective inquiry with extrinsic evidence, see *United States v. Russell*, 662 F. 3d 831, 843 (7th Cir. 2011) ("Although the primary focus in evaluating the legality of the charged photographs must

be on the images themselves . . . the cases reveal that the intent and motive of the photographer can be a relevant consideration in evaluating those images.").

87. *Rivera*, 546 F.3d at 252. The Court summarized its use of the *Dost* test by writing, "Rather than treating the *Dost* factors as providing the overarching doctrinal framework under which lewdness issues should be analyzed, it makes far more sense to treat them as helpful considerations." *Id.*

88. See generally Adler, *Inverting the First Amendment*, *supra* note 34.

89. *See supra* note 37.

90. *Ferber*, 458 U.S at 753 (emphasis added).

91. *Ashcroft*, 535 U.S. at 251 (emphasis added).

92. *See, e.g.*, Video Voyeurism Prevention Act of 2004, 18 U.S.C. § 1801.

93. My discussion of the *Ashcroft* case, *supra*, should clarify that these tenets still extend to child pornography law. *Dost* is thus in tension with *Ashcroft*. See also chapter 1, James Weinstein, The Context and Content of *New York v. Ferber*, for discussion of *Ferber*'s avoidance of this route.

94. Terry Freidan, *Gonzales Gives Child Porn 'Wake-Up Call'*, CNN (Apr. 20, 2006, 4:15 PM), http://www.cnn.com/2006/LAW/04/20/gonzales.porn/.

95. The argument that follows draws upon my previous work. See Amy M. Adler, *The Perverse Law of Child Pornography*, 101 COLUM. L. REV. 209 (2001).

96. *Villard*, 885 F.2d at 811.

97. *Knox*, 32 F.3d at 747.

98. *Dost*, 636 F. Supp. at 833.

99. *Id.*

100. *Knox*, 32 F.3d at 747.

101. *Id.*

102. Pub. L. No. 110-358, title I, section 102(11)(A).

4 | The Language of Child Sexual Abuse and Exploitation

Mary Graw Leary

Language matters. Words matter. Labels, pedantic as they can be, matter. They matter because they convey not only meaning, but also tone, significance, and content. This is particularly true in the law, where definitions can represent the difference between a crime and a legal act, and where the wording of jury instructions can be the difference between acquittal and conviction. The need for precision takes on even more significance for subjects that implicate but are not exclusively limited to the law, such as child exploitation. The importance of such topics extends beyond the law, into fields such as medicine, social work, and juvenile development.

For child abuse and exploitation, precise language can help convey the particular gravity of harms against children and the seriousness with which society addresses such crimes. Unfortunately, however, this precision is absent from much of the modern discourse regarding these harms. Terminology surrounding child abuse and exploitation is often first produced by the media, which values sensational language to capture the viewer or reader over precise language. These terms can also be shaped by interest groups whose agendas do not include accurately labeling victimization. Such language then migrates not only into national policy dialogues but into discourse regarding crimes, laws, and legal sanctions. Here imprecision causes confusion and risks creating unintended legal and societal consequences.

This chapter explores some of the language of child exploitation and examines the implications of inadequate terminology across disciplines. Building on the work of other scholars, this chapter calls for an adoption and expansion of the "fair labeling" principle in the cross-disciplinary field of child abuse and exploitation. This chapter advocates for a two-pronged approach to the language of child abuse and exploitation. First, it seeks to import the fair labeling principle to child abuse and exploitation. Second, it calls for an expansion of this principle beyond its narrow use in statutory labels, but to the multidisciplinary landscape of child sexual abuse and exploitation. More generally, it calls for a more thoughtful approach to the labels used in this cross-disciplinary field to enhance precision. It therefore recommends using terms such as child sex trafficking victims, sexually abusive images of children, child-produced sexually abusive images of children, and first- and third-party traffickers.

Embracing the principle of fair labeling and applying it beyond the law to the terminology surrounding child sexual abuse and exploitation is a critical step for both improved dialogue and more effective responses. This approach is more than semantics. Society is struggling with these issues. This struggle is all the more difficult when terms are not used universally or those that are used have multiple meanings or are imprecise. Imprecise definitions of problems lead to solutions to perceived victimizations, but perhaps not victimizations as they actually exist. More precise descriptions of victimization leads to more precise responses, the effect of which should be more accurate prevention messaging and societal responses when prevention fails.

I. The Value of Precise Language

The need for language that clearly and precisely describes occurrences is not unique to child abuse and exploitation. A necessity for precision exists in many disciplines. At times this requirement is practical and at other times more conceptual. The following examples illustrate the value of precise language across disciplines.

In medicine, for example, accurate language is essential on a practical level. Imprecision in diagnosis may lead to incorrect treatment and disastrous outcomes. Medical professionals must speak with complete exactitude in complex matters such as naming the disease or injury, but also in more simple matters such as directing procedures to exact bodily location in need of care. There is also a more nuanced reason for exactitude in medicine: the need for informed patients. Doctor-patient communication must be precise, as it is the basis from which patients may make life-altering decisions. Medical professionals must choose their words carefully to avoid fear and panic, but also to convey seriousness and risk. A successful response to a medical emergency begins with a clear and shared understanding of the ailment by all parties.

A similar requirement to speak precisely and to choose words with special care exists in politics and government. The reasons for this are not only practical but value-laden as well. For example, in 2013 when the Egyptian military removed an unpopular but elected president from power, the executive branch of the United States government condemned the action in every manner short of labeling it a "coup d'état." The reason for stopping short of this label was quite practical. If the United States had deemed this event a military coup d'état, then Section 7008 of the Consolidated Appropriations Act of 2012 would have been triggered, which would have limited current foreign aid to this heavily relied upon ally.[1] Therefore, notwithstanding appearances, the executive branch tried to avoid a label that would trigger a statutory effect. Others both within the legislative branch and outside the government argued that the Egyptian military indeed engaged in a coup d'état and its actions should be labeled as such. They asserted that rather than giving the action an inaccurate label, it should be labeled accurately and the government response—whether applying the sanctions or amending the sanction regime—should be aimed at reality and not an inaccurate image of events.

Precise and accurate labels can also be critical in communicating social norms. This is exemplified in debates over language such as "ethnic cleansing" or "genocide." Genocide is a powerful and emotive term evoking images of the most depraved and systemic actions. It is also a label that carries with it specific components and consequences under international law. The definition of genocide advanced by the Convention on the Prevention and Punishment of the Crime of Genocide explicitly contains both a mental element (the intent to destroy in whole or in part, a national, ethnical, racial, or religious group) and a physical element (killing, causing serious bodily and mental harm, inflicting destructive life conditions, preventing births, or forcibly transferring children).[2] This label, therefore, conveys both the gravity of the offense as well as the mental state of the offender.[3] If a genocide occurs, then signatory nations to the Convention are in theory obligated to prevent and punish the acts.[4] In addition to this practical effect, labeling certain killings "genocide" sends a clear international message of the horrible and inexcusable nature of the acts, as well as the message that those who committed the acts did so with an intent to destroy a specific group. The definition of genocide, however, includes only four types of victim groups (national, ethnic, racial, or religious). The term "genocide," therefore, arguably communicates a value judgment regarding which groups are worthy of special protections.[5] The narrow definition, and the implicit judgment it communicates, has led some scholars to argue for an expansion of the word genocide to include more groups (such as political or gendered groups) as targets of genocide. In so doing they often make both practical and normative arguments. Expanding the definition would result in more international responses to such atrocities as well as universal condemnation of them. Normatively, these scholars assert that other labels fail to convey the seriousness of the conduct, the specific mental state of the offenders against a specific group, or the proper identity of the victim group necessary for the crime to be labeled genocide. Others oppose expansion of the term, arguing that blurring distinctions between genocide and other more generalized international crimes creates confusion and risks unsustainably triggering an international response for every conflict. As a result of this definitional disagreement, when atrocities occur, the international community cannot always agree whether to label such acts "ethnic cleansing," "genocide," or some other crime against humanity.[6]

The same definitional disputes and risks of imprecision exist domestically. For example, significant debate exists surrounding the use of the label "hate crime." This label is meant to distinguish certain crimes as motivated by prejudice. There is a lack of agreement regarding when the label "hate crime" is appropriate. Some believe the label should apply exclusively when the offender was *motivated* to select a victim based solely on the victim's race or other impermissible characteristic. Others assert that it should be used not to differentiate between offenders' motives, but instead to address the harm experienced by the victims.[7] Therefore, some have argued that the term should be used less often to avoid weakening its meaning and significance. Others have called for an expansion of the category of hate crimes to include a broader group of victims including female rape victims. Those who argue for the label to be used more often note that the term "hate crime" carries with it a certain stigma and that failure to use the label for all crimes motivated by prejudice minimizes the damage caused to the victims by the criminal activity.[8]

A. Labels Provide Insight

As a general matter, how a society refers to victimization provides important insight into the prevailing societal views of that behavior. How a society refers to conduct (criminal or not) may indicate whether the behavior is normalized, glorified, or condemned. For example, labeling the use of physical force to discipline a child as "corporal punishment" suggests an action by a parent or guardian within his or her authority to punish. Because most would agree that punishment is a necessary component of raising a child, this descriptive term suggests nothing nefarious. Labeling that same action "child abuse" evokes an entirely different understanding of the appropriateness of the force.

In addition to conveying a message about the appropriateness of an action, language can also serve as evidence of a shift of social concern and values. For example, a generation ago instances of physical abuse of a child or an elderly person were referred to as "assaults"—a term no different than what is used to label unlawful use of force against all persons. Today several states have specific crimes labeled "child abuse" or "elder abuse."[9] This new statutory language signifies a modern social awareness of these specific harms, as well as a legal shift that followed that change in social perception. Conversely, sometimes the law leads the national narrative. Acts such as the Violence Against Women Act not only changed the law but also shifted the general understanding of intimate partner violence and other forms of harm committed toward women because they are women. It made clear that this type of interaction is a form of *violence* and nothing else: not love, not a relationship gone out of control, not a temporary loss of judgment, but simply violence. Consequently, domestic violence has come out of the shadows as more victims are reporting the crime, more police are responding, and more victims are receiving services.[10]

B. Legal Insight

Because the manner in which a society refers to victimization can affect public perception of that victimization, special care should be taken to select the appropriate words to refer to crime and the harms those crimes cause. It is not enough to label a particular activity illegal. Rather, crimes must be understood within a wider setting of societal norms and political realities. They should also be described in such a way as to convey the serious nature of those activities. Ensuring that everyone understands the gravity of an act or crime and the specific harms caused by that action is more than just semantics. Such labels can also affect how society will target efforts to prevent those crimes or how it will target a response. Having a complete understanding of the victimization will inform a society's substantive approach to potentially harmful conduct.[11] For example, understanding "domestic disputes" as intimate partner violence is an important critical step to responding to a previously misunderstood victimization.

Assessing whether a term or a definition is sufficiently descriptive—

that is, not only whether the term is accurate but also whether it fully captures the seriousness of a crime and the harm it causes—must take account of how terms are used in ordinary language. To the extent that an otherwise descriptive term has become a euphemism in colloquial discussions, using that term as part of the public discourse on crime and victimization can minimize harms caused, normalize them, or even glorify them.[12] For example, much has been written about the mainstreaming of the term "pimp." The term "pimp" was first used to refer to an individual who uses manipulation, threats, or intimidation to control and force victims of prostitution to sell sex and then profits from that income.[13] Yet the term has been co-opted by elements of popular culture to depict a lifestyle which is to be exulted, not criminalized.[14] Thus the term's use in colloquial conversation minimizes the actual violence and harm inflicted by one who violently controls victims and forces them into commercial sex.

Labels minimizing the perceived harm appear often with media coverage of sensational cases. For example, this occurred regarding the case of Roman Polanski, a rape case in which he pled guilty to drugging and raping a thirteen-year-old-girl when he was forty-seven years old. Notwithstanding these facts, the case has since been referred to as a "sex scandal" as opposed to a sexual assault.[15] Similarly, when Jerry Sandusky was accused of raping multiple boys over several years, the media reframed it as the "Sandusky scandal."[16] When the media refers to a child abuse case or sexual assault as a "sex scandal" as opposed to a "sexual assault," such labels fail to appropriately describe the sexual violence experienced by the victim, as well as the rights and dignity of the victim.[17]

The principle function of labeling, then, is expression. The label addresses both the offender and the larger community, stigmatizing the offender for his culpable conduct and conveying the nature of his transgression to the public. It expresses society's revulsion to the violation of important norms and values.[18] Descriptors for child sexual abuse must convey the nature of these victimizations, and precise labels are critical to capture the gravity of the offense and condemnation of the perpetrator.

II. Labels in Criminal Victimization Discourse

A. Criminal Victimization Has a Particular Need for Sufficiently Descriptive Language

While precise language and definitions are important in many disciplines, they are particularly important when describing criminal victimization.

This is true not only for the labels given to the crimes themselves, but also for the corollary terms used surrounding criminal victimization. Crimes garner discussion. Modern criminal law encompasses many other disciplines including medicine, social work, and mental health. All these corollary discussions, as well as those originating in the law, must be precise.

An effective criminal justice system must not only achieve justice, but society must also perceive it to be a just system. Language plays an important role in this respect. Because a criminal conviction, as Henry Hart suggests, reflects the "solemn pronouncement" of the moral condemnation of society, the language surrounding a criminal act takes on added importance.[19] The language used as a label for each offense can convey meaning: "The unique labels associated with different crimes express varying degrees of social condemnation for the conduct."[20] Therefore, when crimes are poorly described or labeled, this may reflect, or affect, society's reaction to the conduct.[21]

Consequently, the language of criminal behavior must be sufficiently descriptive to be effective. To be adequately descriptive the language used in general criminal discourse, and the language that labels crimes more specifically, should convey both the nature of the crime and the appropriate level of social condemnation to it. The nature of the harm encompasses not only the injury but the mental state of the offender. Language that is not sufficiently descriptive can thwart the goals of criminal law and societal systems in a variety of ways. Too general or sanitized descriptors can minimize a harm or normalize it. Inflammatory language can miss the mark and condemn behaviors outside the culpable behavior. Criminal victimization is often very complex. Labels that are too general can encompass activities that are quite diverse from each other and that demand different treatment. Labels too precise can lead to loopholes for escaping liability. The words of criminal victimization, therefore, must be thoroughly considered.

On a practical level, statutes—the written laws themselves—require precision, because antecedent events can trigger legal sanctions. For example, labeling a child sold for sex as a victim of a "severe form of trafficking" triggers access to government services.[22] Labeling that same child a "juvenile prostitute" triggers access to juvenile detention. Therefore, the choice of label determines how future events will unfold.

This extends not only to the *titles* of specific crimes, but to general criminal legislation as well. Some scholars note the troubling trend of labeling legislation for the purpose of sensationalizing it to ensure its passage.[23] For example, a large criminal bill addressing various forms of crimes against children was labeled the PROTECT Act of 2013 for "Prosecutorial Remedy and Other Tools to End the Exploitation of Children Today." This trend continues today with bills proposed with titles, such as Big Oil Welfare Repeal Act of 2013 (HR 1426), Reducing Barack Obama's Unsustainable Deficit Act (HR 3140 2009), or Stop the FEDS Act (HR 118) (112th Cong) (Stop the Federal Exchanges from Destroying States Act). Such labels sacrifice precision for dramatics. Uelman convincingly challenges the use of those hyperbolic labels that disguise "the criminal justice system's complexity behind simplistic labels that actually impedes in our quest for justice."[24] The purpose of legislation is to respond and rectify a social problem. Imprecise and dramatic language does not further societal understanding of the problem or appropriate responses.

B. The Fair Labeling Principle

Some criminal law scholars have called for the adoption of what Andrew Ashworth articulated as a "fair labeling" principle. This principle focuses on the need for criminal labels to fairly represent the nature and magnitude of the defendant's criminal conduct.[25] Originally conceived of to address reforms of the English criminal law, the fair labeling principle requires a conscious effort to ensure that a label describing criminal conduct precisely reflects both its wrongfulness and its severity:

> A proper label reflects both the essence and the totality of the criminal conduct at issue. It is an amalgam of the interest invaded (bodily integrity or property interests), the gravity of the harm (taking of human life or destroying a shed), the mechanism of injury (stealing vs. swindling or arson vs. vandalism) and the offender's mental state. . . .[26]

That is to say, a label ought to explain the culpability of the defendant and the harmfulness of his actions.[27]

Adoption of the fair labeling principle facilitates a stronger social and criminal justice system. It has both descriptive and normative qualities. In a descriptive sense, it pushes the language of sexual victimization to sufficiently describe all the victimizing conduct. This is not limited to precision regarding the statutory name for the crime, but demands precision in describing any relevant surrounding conduct. In addition to precision, while not explicitly a component of fair labeling, this language must also indicate the level of condemnation by society. Such an approach not only increases understanding but also can reflect the complexities of criminal events and work toward more targeted and responsive initiatives within the criminal justice system.

There are two fundamental aspects of fair labeling: description and fairness. The descriptive component of fair labeling contains at least two subfeatures. The label of the offense must (1) sufficiently describe the conduct and (2) sufficiently reflect the "social harm" of that conduct.[28] This latter element requires the label to communicate the judgment of society.[29] Labels serve both a "symbolic" and "declaratory" function to "symbolize the degree of condemnation that should be attributed to the offender and signals to society how that particular offense should be regarded."[30] This condemnation and description should be intelligible to the general public.[31] For example, "assault" is technically accurate, but "elder abuse" more precisely conveys the particular offense and the specific enhanced condemnation of victimization of the vulnerable.

Labels must also be fair. This fairness is to the defendant, the victim, and the public. For the defendant, the label must precisely reflect the nature of conduct. For the victim, the label should indicate the way in which the victim was wronged and how he is affected by the wrongdoing.[32] Both of these are linked to fairness to the public. If the label of a crime is neutral regarding the gravity of the conduct, it is fair to neither the offender nor the victim, because the true nature of the conduct will not be shared with the general public.[33] The public must be able to understand from the label the nature of the transgression.[34]

III. The Language of Child Abuse and Exploitation

The fair labeling principle arose in Britain regarding a discussion of revising the English criminal laws. Ashworth and others invoked it as a principled method for the code to be reworked. This chapter advocates adopting this approach more broadly than statutory language. The aforementioned components of fair labeling would provide clarity and precision to many fields, including child abuse and exploitation. This chapter proposes consciously utilizing fair labeling for all aspects of child abuse and exploitation, not just criminal code terms. This is a multidisciplinary field, and clarity across disciplines in the media is needed.

In child sexual abuse and exploitation, language and labels are used inconsistently and inaccurately, resulting in a lack of fairness to the defendants, victims, and public. Not only do shortcomings exist in formal legal terms, but the terminology in public discussion is also insufficiently descriptive. Because the media is a main source of public information on criminal issues, the manner in which it uses problematic terms to describe crimes of child exploitation and abuse can contribute to the harms caused by the insufficiently descriptive terms discussed above.[35]

Within criminal law, nowhere is the need for accurate language as great as in the area of child abuse and exploitation. The United Nations NGO group for the Convention of the Rights of the Child (the "UN NGO CRC") recognized that the need for fair, agreed-upon terms was more than symbolic.[36] It discussed the tangible effects of failure when it noted that "unless we have clear and agreed definitions in relation to sexual harm against children, the data collected, the strategic response designed, the legislation implemented, and the protection interventions will most likely be impaired."[37] Accurate language is demanded at all phases of a criminal occurrence because without it, information gathered to more fully comprehend the victimization would be tainted. Phrased another way, the conclusions drawn from that data will be incorrect. The necessary response to the data will be misguided, and the prevention messaging sourced from that data will miss its mark entirely. This describes a criminal justice system which fails at all levels: investigation, response, and prevention. Those demanding accurate and consistent language underscore that effective collaboration from diverse stakeholders requires an agreed-upon understanding of the harms children experience and the distinction between different forms of abuse and exploitation.

For example, reference to all offenders against children as "child predators" is problematic. It evokes an image of an animalistic stranger waiting to violently kidnap an innocent child. In reality, most offenders are known to their victims and patiently groom him or her into harm. This label, however, can lead to prevention messaging aimed at a small minority of offenders, thus missing the opportunity to prevent more common abuses.[38]

Achieving fair labeling principles regarding child sexual abuse and exploitation is particularly complex. Child sexual abuse and exploitation can take many diverse forms, including intrafamilial abuse, child sex trafficking, production of sexually abusive images of children, and a number of other crimes. This section will address some reasons why fair labeling principles have yet to be achieved in these cases, and it will also discuss some of the results of the current insufficiently descriptive state of language in child sexual abuse and exploitation.

A. Causes of Mislabeling

Child sexual abuse and exploitation is an umbrella term for numerous distinct forms of victimization. On the one hand, the breadth of the victimization is profound. Its victims include a cross-section of children; one out of five girls and one out of twenty boys experience a sexual abuse event prior to their eighteenth birthday, and one out of seven youths is propositioned by a stranger online.[39] On the other hand, these types of victimizations have many subforms. Effective responses to each of these subforms require clear comprehension of the forms of victimization. In addition to the breadth of this problem, many obstacles exist that impair the understanding of these victimizations.

1. Social Silences

These victimizations are aptly described as occurring "in the shadows." However, certain other forces are at play in keeping the victimization secretive as well. These obstacles lead to underreporting or prevention of these cases from coming into the light, being accurately understood, and informing public policy.[40] Similarly, the secretive nature of the acts thwarts the effort to use precise language to describe all the distinct subcategories of child sexual abuse and exploitation.

Although these victimizations are significant, most people do not know the realities of many forms of child victimization, have not been trafficked, do not join peer-to-peer networks to trade sexually abusive images of children, or sexually assault others. Therefore, most people will need accurate information about the nature of these victimizations to understand them. However, due to the secretive nature of these forms of victimization, this information is not readily available. Thus labels are attached to aspects of it that are inadequate because not enough is known to make them more precise.

This secretive nature, therefore, can be a compounding cause of imprecise labeling. Labels are often put in place by the media. Then, when the public hears labels or terms, it brings its own perceptions, often inaccurate due to the lack of data available, to the issue. In this way the public can be misled by imprecise terms with ambiguous meanings or attribute imprecise labels to misunderstood victimization.

The silence is not only in the failure to openly discuss child sexual abuse and exploitation. It is also in the failure to report it. This allows for not only increased victimization, but also for hiding it more easily. Offenders often target marginalized victims who possess some vulnerability. Offenders with direct access to victims or their caregivers often can groom their victims not only to abuse or exploit them, but also to keep their silence after an abusive event or during an ongoing period of victimization.[41] These offenders target vulnerable victims and further groom caregivers, family members, and others for not only access to children but to prime them to disbelieve the child should a report be made.[42] Therefore, obtaining information about the details of the offense, how it is committed, and the experience of the victims is more challenging to accomplish.

An example of this interface between a lack of information and an imprecise label could be the labeling of sexually abusive images of children as "child porn" or "child pornography," which likely is caused by unfamiliarity of the actual content and fuels the misinformation about the content. The process begins with the premise that most people are not traders in these images nor have they been victimized in this way. They hear, however, these images labeled with such terms as "child porn" or "kiddie porn." To the layperson, "child porn" or "kiddie porn" do not convey the serious nature of the material; instead they are slang terms. Slang terms are by definition a "flippant, irreverent, or indecorous" form of language, not to be used in reference to images of exploitation and abuse.[43] Yet these terms are used by journalists,[44] scholars,[45] and even Supreme Court Justices.[46] "Child pornography," although certainly less problematic than "child porn," likely conjures up images of younger looking adults striking provocative poses, as opposed to the reality of an increasingly violent collections of photographs and video depicting younger and younger children being violently victimized.[47] Consequently, the public's impression of its content is influenced by such labels and is inaccurate.

Although one might argue that since the public has such a negative reaction to "child pornography," there is no confusion as to its understanding of the content of this material. This argument is flawed for a number of reasons. As a threshold matter, it is hard to imagine any person questioned about his or her views of child pornography answering anything that suggests tolerance. Second, concluding that such a response indicates that the public understands the *content* of this material because society is troubled by its existence is unwarranted. Many people when they hear terms such as "substance abuse," "child neglect," or others are disturbed by the concepts, but that does not mean they fully appreciate the experience of it. The reality is that most people do not trade in sexually abusive images of children. Most people have, however, been exposed to adult pornography.[48] Pornography, which is not obscene, can be legal. While the Supreme Court has described such material as including "adaptation" (as in writing or painting) of "licentiousness or lewdness: a portrayal of erotic behavior designed to cause sexual excitement,"[49] neither it nor any court of appeals has defined it.[50] Similarly, pornography is a legal industry in the United States with its own trade association and paid "performers," individuals who consent to staging sexual acts.[51] Accordingly, it is fair to conclude that adult pornography conveys a consensual and intentionally produced aspect to it, which is designed to entice and entertain. This is not the material traded among child pornography traders.

The "[t]ypical child pornography possessed and distributed by federal child pornography offenders today depict prepubescent children engaging in graphic sex acts, often with adult men," and half of the images depict children under six years old.[52] The National Center for Missing and Exploited Children ("NCMEC") reports that 76 percent of known victims of sexually abusive images of children are prepubescent and 10 percent are infants and toddlers.[53] Of the most frequently traded series of known victims, 84 percent of the series contained images depicting oral copulation, 76 percent contained images depicting anal and/or vaginal penetration, 52 percent contained images depicting the use of foreign objects or sexual devices, and 44 percent contained images depicting bondage and/or sadomasochism.[54] More than 81 percent of the sexually abusive images of children analyzed by the Internet Watch Foundation in 2012 involve victims less than ten years old, and more than half showed sexual activity between adults and children, including rape and sexual torture.[55] Therefore, putting together the words "child" (someone unable to consent to sexual activity or exploitation) and "pornography" (consensually produced erotic entertainment) is at best imprecise but more likely misleading. At best, while people no doubt are uncomfortable with the idea of trading these images, they are ignorant of its content, and the phrase "child pornography" does nothing to communicate it accurately *or* with precision. At worst, child pornography causes people to associate the content with their previously held understanding of pornography, thus leaving room for the incorrect view that the images are similar to adult pornography with consenting subjects—a legal impossibility.

Again, it is helpful to turn to trends in judicial sentencing to underscore the lack of understanding of the label of "child pornography." An active debate exists regarding the federal sentencing guidelines for child pornography offenders. Indeed many, including the Department of Justice, agree that the Sentencing Commission should revisit and update the guidelines to reflect the modern methods by which offenders are collecting these images, so the guidelines can "better calibrate the severity and culpability of defendants' criminal conduct."[56] That debate is outside the scope of this chapter. The lighter sentences being imposed by some judges cannot be entirely explained by a dispute with the federal sentencing guidelines, and similarly light sentences exist on the state level when no similar dispute exists.[57] Some observations of sentencing practices illustrate a fundamental lack of understanding of the harm the images cause and the gravity of the offense. Among child pornography offenders—producers, distributors, and possessors—possessors, while serious offenders, are likely regarded as the least egregious. Moreover, within this group of possessors, any sentencing court must consider many factors, including the nature and circumstances of the offense and the history and characteristics of the defendant to craft an appropriate sentence.[58]

Nonetheless, many sentences reflect a lack of understanding of child pornography for what it is. As noted by Hamilton and Rogers, trial courts have characterized the active collection of sexually abusive images of children as a result of "depression," as due to the "ease and addictive quality of internet searching," "passive," "harmless," the product of "boredom and stupidity," an outlet for attention, and some offenders as "upstanding" or "mainstays" in the community.[59] Some judges have characterized the defendants as the *victims* of harsh sentences, even analogizing their prosecution to witchcraft trials.[60] While some courts have rejected such characterizations of these defendants as "a terrible divergence between appearance and reality,"[61] these misconceptions of the images' contents and the victimization felt by its subjects speak to the inadequacy of that label criticized by researchers and scholars.[62]

The Guardian recently noted announced its refusal to use such terms: "'[C]hild pornography, child porn, and kiddie porn' are not acceptable terms. The use of such language acts to legitimize images which are not pornography, rather, they are permanent records of children being sexually exploited."[63] "Child pornography" undermines the victimization because the term suggests a relationship to pornography—conduct that may be legal, whose subject is voluntarily participating in, and whose subject is capable of consenting to the conduct.

The fact of the matter is that sexual abuse and exploitation are complex behaviors. Attempting to define its parameters as clearly as possible "must not result in minimizing the focus on all specifics and the significance those factors play."[64] It is, however, essential to accurately describe these behaviors.

2. Social Forces

There are a number of social forces that obfuscate the occurrence or the severity of child sexual abuse and exploitation beyond the aforementioned silence. These include social messages, financial influences, and characteristics of perpetrators.

The devastating trauma of child sexual abuse and exploitation exists in a world replete with social messages endorsing sexual objectification of children.[65] This is distinct from sexuality of teens or emerging adults—a natural part of development and maturity. This is the specific objectification suggesting that children are sex objects for sexual use by adults.[66] These messages are not without social effect. Sending such messages affects both victims and offenders. Sending the message that children are commodities to be used and objectified contributes to injuring victims by laying the groundwork for grooming.[67] It also affects offenders by validating the abusive and exploitative inclinations of offenders and normalizes some forms of objectification.

A second social force contributing to obfuscating reality could be the profit generated from many commercial aspects of child sexual abuse and exploitation. The severity of the child sexual victimization can be clouded due to the financial immensity of the industry. The role that so-called "legitimate businesses" play in some of these crimes, such as production of sexually abusive images of children and sex trafficking, can blur the victimization. The child exploitation and human trafficking industries are estimated to be valued in the billions of dollars in revenue per year.[68] These profits go not only to traffickers but also to the ancillary businesses that facilitate the victimization. For example, some advertisers, hotels, and cab drivers can profit from sex trafficking.[69] Similarly, prior to the development of the Financial Coalition Against Child Pornography, some financial institutions were profiting from the trading of sexually abusive images of children.[70] Anonymous alternative currencies, such as Bitcoin, are valued by these same offenders.[71] When the line between legitimate business and criminal conduct is blurred, this relationship (a) strengthens the criminal entrepreneur by infusing the illegal activity with capital and (b) normalizes the criminal acts by legitimizing certain aspects.

The fact that many offenders do not conform to commonly held, if not accurate, criminal stereotypes may also cloud the frequency and harmfulness of child sexual abuse and exploitation. For example, possessors of sexually abusive images of children are reported to be overwhelmingly Caucasian males, a majority of whom are higher educated and more often employed than criminal defendants of other races.[72] Although much has been written regarding sentencing ranges authorized by the federal sentencing guidelines for nonproduction offenders, federal judges often treat this group of defendants more leniently than other groups of offenders. Relative to the sentencing guidelines, judges impose lighter sentences on possessors of sexually abusive images of children than many other groups of federal offenders.[73] Four out of five such possessors benefit from this practice used by prosecutors or judges to limit their sentencing exposure.[74]

These sentencing practices disproportionately benefit a group of offenders who are more white, more wealthy, and more educated than other offenders. It also sends a message to the public that conflicts with the experience articulated by the victims: that the possession of sexually abusive images of children is a serious offense that victimizes those children.[75] The Department of Justice has argued that federal judges and the media emphasize the outward appearance of those who trade in sexually abusive images of children rather than the seriousness of their crimes.[76] One reason for this divergence could be the reality that child pornography offenders as a group resemble the demographics of the bench, more so than other segments of offenders. Hamilton notes that many judges describe offenders "in ways that conceptualized them as ordinary, even upstanding men (there were few female defendants) whose only flaw appeared to be an interest in child pornography."[77] As will be discussed below, this conceptualization of child pornography trading as a "flaw" risks using an offender's social status as an educated, higher-income, Caucasian males to divorce the offender from the harm caused to victims of his crime.

B. Effects of Mislabeling

1. Confusion

Mislabeling affects the manner in which society conceptualizes child sexual abuse and exploitation. How society conceptualizes a crime directly frames society's efforts to respond and prevent further victimization. Distinct words are often used to describe child sexual abuse or exploitation. Those words have different connotations, and using the words interchangeably can cause confusion.[78] If the abuse and exploitation is labeled with insufficiently descriptive terms, then the response is likely to be misplaced as well. This confusion can lead to minimization or even normalization of harmful behavior.

For example, identifying a child involved in "pimp-controlled" commercial sex acts as a "juvenile prostitute" evokes one image of the child. Identifying him or her as a "victim of child sex trafficking" evokes an entirely different image. While the first term connotes only the illegality of exchanging money for sex, the second term explicitly identifies the child as a victim, and it suggests the more widespread nature of the sex trafficking industry.

2. Alarmism or Underreaction

The effects of mislabeling extend far beyond confusion. It also can lead to alarmism or underreaction; neither response allows society to correctly assess a social problem. For example, national attention to teen "sexting" accelerated after the release of initial anecdotal or survey-based claims regarding the frequency of the behavior. Unfortunately, the media applied the label "sexting" imprecisely, using it to refer to a wide range of activities including, on one end of the spectrum, sexually explicit texts, nude pictures, sexually explicit pictures, and, on the other end of the spectrum, the recording of sexual assaults.[79] The resulting claim that a large percentage of the youth population was producing pictures caused great alarm among various segments of the media. An overly general use of an undefined term drove this alarmist reaction and resulted in an incorrect and oversimplified conclusion.[80]

Conversely, some labels contribute to minimizing or normalizing other forms of exploitation. An example of this is outlined by a prostitution researcher:

> Sexual exploitation as strip club prostitution has been reframed as sexual expression and freedom to express one's sensuality by dancing. Brothels are referred to as short-time hotels, massage parlors, saunas, health clubs, or sexual encounter establishments. Older men who buy teenagers for sex in Seoul call prostitution compensated dating. In Tokyo prostitution is described as assisted intercourse.[81]

Although referencing adult prostitution, the example speaks to a concerted effort to relabel a form of exploitation and reconceptualize it as legitimate.

The National Academy of Sciences discussed the inconsistent use of terms in sex trafficking and child sexual exploitation and noted that "clarity and consistency in the use of these key terms are vital for a variety of purposes, including developing an in-depth understanding of these crimes; conducting, evaluating, and comparing relevant research;

and developing appropriate laws, policies, and programs aimed at preventing, identifying, and responding to these abuses of children."[82] Only by truly understanding the facets of the exploitation can stakeholders form effective policies targeting actual aspects of it instead of exaggerated or nonexistent problems. Similarly, reframing illegal behavior in a way that legitimizes it may have similar effects. Regarding the aforementioned panic over teen "sexting," inconsistent use of the term to refer to many different types of images and behaviors led to somewhat of a panic in the general population. Many understood the term to refer to self-produced sexually abusive images, while some media reports used the term to include less troubling behavior, such as teens sending sexually explicit text messages. This confusion in terminology likely led many people to overestimate the number of children creating sexually explicit images of themselves, which in turn aided in creating a panic that exploded until later research indicated the behavior was far from normative.[83] Furthermore, the use of this same inconsistent term failed to call attention to the significant subproblem of those who forward or distribute images of others.[84] In short, the term "sexting" tended to confuse an already poorly understood phenomenon.[85]

3. Legal Implications

Another effect of insufficiently descriptive labels concerns the legal implications of certain labels: labels matter as they relate to statutes. If an action meets a legal definition, it can fall within the proscriptions of a criminal statute. For example, "child sex tourism" is understood by most stakeholders to occur when an individual travels from one place to another and engages in sexual acts with children. But because of confusion in the field of exactly what triggers sanctions for this behavior, clarification must be made. The UN NGO CRC felt the need to explicitly clarify that this behavior is not limited to the person who travels *with the purpose* of having sex with a child (preferential child sex offenders), but also applies to the traveler who forms the intent while on location (situational child sex offenders).[86] Without this change a group of offenders were unintentionally excluded from laws targeting them. Such confusion results from an inadequate label. Therefore, descriptive labels of activity must be consistent with statutory definitions so when the infractions are measured, there is a common understanding of the significance of the actions and the data collected about them.

The UN NGO CRC outline why this definitional clarity matters. Ultimately, the goal of society is to limit and end child sexual abuse and exploitation. The first step to achieving this goal is articulating a clear and precise understanding of the victimization and all its nuances. Based on that understanding, society can develop prevention programs and multidisciplinary responses when prevention fails. The success or failure of these ventures turns on whether that conceptualization is precise and accurate. As the UN CRC NGO noted, "unless we have clear and agreed definitions in relation to sexual harm against children the data collected, the strategic responses designed, the legislation implemented, and the protection interventions developed will most likely be impaired."[87] This same NGO group understood that the importance of shared understanding in specific terminology was cross-disciplinary. Effective counteraction by society, both in prevention and disruption, requires that all sectors of society fully understand the realities of the complex sexual harm.[88]

The consequences of mislabeling are not limited to negatively affecting prevention efforts or law enforcement but extend to the courtroom as well. If behaviors are mislabeled, crimes insufficiently defined, or the language surrounding child sexual abuse and exploitation inconsistent and insufficient, then an incomplete picture of the actions develops. If that lack of a complete picture sanitizes the crime, as in the crime labeled "child pornography," courts and society undervalue these matters. As discussed above, judicial commentary and sentences for nonproduction child sexual abuse images offenses depart from the sentencing guidelines at a higher rate than any other crime.[89] The language of many trial courts reflects a viewpoint that sees nonproduction child pornography offenses are less serious crimes.

Consider *United States v. Reingold*, a case in which the Second Circuit Court of Appeals vacated the district court's sentence.[90] The district court failed to apply the mandatory minimum sentence for distribution of child pornography to a defendant who not only pled guilty to the charge of distribution, but also admitted to hands-on sexually offending his minor half sister.[91] The Second Circuit reiterated to the district court that the distribution of child sexual abuse images is "a serious crime that threatens real and frequently violent harm to vulnerable victims."[92] This point appeared lost on the district court, which actually described the defendant's distribution as "mere peer-to-peer file sharing."[93] Similarly, a district court judge in *United States v. Campbell* initially acknowledged that such images harm children, but stated that the images he observed in this case, in which apparently trafficked girls from Eastern Europe (ages thirteen to fifteen) were depicted in a sexually explicit manner, were "relatively tame."[94] The district court judge reasoned that the girls were not prepubescent or engaged in sexual penetration with an adult. Although less severe than a filmed sexual assault, the lack of penetration of two girls who are exploited is not "tame." Again, such a view of the sexually explicit images suggests a conceptualization consistent with the voluntary or consensual aspect often attributed to adult pornography. Such descriptions reflect the concerns articulated by the prominent NGO Save the Children when addressing revisions to the Council of Europe's definitional scheme: "The term 'child pornography' undermines the seriousness of the offence because it associates child abuse with conduct which, while pornographic, may be legal in an adult environment. 'Child pornography' always involves sexual abuse and exploitation of a child, and therefore constitutes evidence of a crime committed against a child."[95] Because the label "child pornography" can create such an association, it should be eliminated.

IV. Fair Labeling in Child Sexual Abuse and Exploitation

It is within this cauldron of victimization, conflicting social messaging, normalization, and cultural confusion that the language of child sexual abuse and exploitation becomes clouded. Distinctions between appropriate and inappropriate behaviors become blurred. Distinct activities become grouped together under general terms. This can have two equally unappealing effects. First, activities can be overgeneralized and minimize the victimization. For example, the term "commercial sexual exploitation of children" has been criticized as being too sanitized, failing to capture the violence often inflicted and failing to focus on the child.[96] Second, terms can become too inflammatory. The term "sexual predator" has been used to refer to a broad range of persons who commit sexual offenses equating disparate behaviors, such as indecent exposure and aggravated rape.[97]

As discussed in the previous sections, there is a need for fair labeling in the dialogue of child sexual abuse and exploitation. More is needed, however, than accurate labeling of relevant statutes. Because child sexual abuse and exploitation affects so many other disciplines, this effort must transcend simple statutory labels and include clear definitions within the academic, professional, and child abuse communities. What follows is a discussion of terms that have been particularly problematic. Employing the fair labeling principle to these concepts justifies the elimination of certain terms and the adoption of those proposed terms.

A. *"Child"*

The term "child" does not have a universally understood meaning. Within the United States, different jurisdictions define "child" or "minor" to include individuals of different ages. Moreover, within a given jurisdiction, an individual can be a "child" for one purpose, such as voting, but an adult for other purposes, such as marriage. Most but not all federal statutes treat a person less than eighteen years old as a minor, but this is not universal.[98] Internationally, when childhood begins and ends varies among countries and cultures. Some nations allow an individual to marry as young as thirteen years of age for girls or labor for children of all ages, while other countries limit complete legal adulthood until eighteen years of age.

This state of confusion exists notwithstanding the fact that several influential international documents define "children" as people who have not yet attained the age of eighteen. The Convention of the Rights of the Child, Palermo Protocol, and ILO # 182 all agree that people under the age of eighteen should be thought of as children.[99] The UN NGO CRC finds the deviation from this universal rule "deeply concerning," and "walking away from a straight commitment that determines all children to be anyone aged under [eighteen] years has seriously increased the vulnerability of children to violence and exploitation."[100]

In the context of child sexual abuse and exploitation, the term "child" should be understood to include all people under the age of eighteen. Support for this understanding can be found in several recent Supreme Court decisions. For more than a decade, many in the juvenile justice field advocated for a distinctly different treatment of youthful offenders under the age of eighteen. In *Roper v. Simmons*, the Court held that the death penalty was unconstitutional when applied to an offender who had not reached eighteen years of age. The Court expanded this reasoning in *Graham v. Florida*, which prohibited states from sentencing such juveniles convicted of nonhomicide crimes to incarceration for life without the possibility of parole. This logic was further affirmed in *Miller v. Alabama*, which found unconstitutional the mandatory sentencing of life without parole for juveniles convicted of any crime. These cases outlined three "general differences between juveniles under [eighteen] and adults."[101] These differences formed the basis of understanding the "diminished capacity" of a minor, including (1) a lack of maturity and an underdeveloped sense of responsibility, (2) a heightened susceptibility to negative influences and outside pressures, and (3) the fact that the character of a juvenile is "more transitory" and "less fixed" than that of an adult.[102] The Court based this conclusion on the emerging evidence of the juvenile brain, which does not reach full formation until between the ages of twenty-one to twenty-five.[103] Last to form are the sections of the brain that address risk assessment, impulse control, and judgment. Therefore, the Court reasoned that the person under eighteen should be recognized as one with a somewhat diminished capacity that will be eliminated with growth and maturity.

Categorically, the law understands that child offenders under eighteen years old have different brain functionality than adults. It should do the same for victims, as research suggests that the juveniles, not only juvenile offenders, differ from adults in their neurological, intellectual, emotional, and psychosocial development.[104] This means that juvenile victims have the same limits regarding judgment, impulse control, and risk taking and thus demand increased protection. Juveniles also are uniquely vulnerable to victimization, and the effects of victimization on children are compounded and enduring. Research specifically regarding victimization indicates that the devastating effects of experiencing victimization as a child can be magnified due to the still developing brain of a juvenile. Maltreatment "is considered more detrimental if it occurs during childhood and adolescence."[105] Victims of child sexual abuse and exploitation can experience "a substantial range of psychological problems . . . throughout [their] lives . . . [including] depression, anxiety, psychosis, posttraumatic stress disorder (PTSD), guilt, fear, sexual dysfunction, substance abuse, and acting out."[106] Victimization not only has long-term psychological and developmental effects when it occurs as this vulnerable age, but permanent neural development can be affected.[107]

Because of the increased vulnerability and increased harm experienced by juvenile victims, the laws implicating criminal victimization should consistently recognized as children those under eighteen years of age. This recognition of brain development would alleviate any suggestions of "consent" of victims to exploitation or abuse, underscore the vulnerabilities of children's undeveloped minds often exploited by offenders, and put into context the devastating impact of trauma on children.

Having a universal term for children is not to say that children have no rights vis-à-vis adults. Nor is it to say that there must be one universal age for all legal issues regarding children that applies to education, medical care, emancipation, and voting. It should, however, be uniform within specific fields, such as the field of child sexual abuse and exploitation. Therefore, in criminal law just as child offenders under the age of eighteen must be treated as distinct from adults due to their brain development, so too should victims under eighteen. Failure to do so creates a structure in which juvenile offenders are held less culpable for their actions but victims—who possess the same characteristics—are viewed as adults with completely formed and matured intellect and self-possession.

The fair labeling principle supports this label. Consistent with international law and Supreme Court jurisprudence, victims under eighteen years of age should be considered children in a legal sense. This "goes to the heart of societal interpretations regarding the way in which a child is perceived. . . . Within communities if a child is seen as no different than an adult things such as child marriage and child pornography become acceptable."[108]

B. "Sexually Abusive Images of Children"

The dominant American term for "sexually abusive images of children" is "child pornography." The latter term is understood generally to refer to "representations of a child engaged in real or simulated explicit sexual activities or representation of sexual parts of a child, the dominant characteristic of which is depiction for a sexual purpose."[109] In the United States, this term is often defined as images of actual children engaged in "sexually explicit conduct." Sexually explicit conduct in most jurisdictions is specifically defined as including "actual or simulated—(i) sexual intercourse, including genital-genital, oral-genital, anal-genital, or oral-anal, whether between persons of the same or opposite sex; (ii) bestiality; (iii) masturbation; (iv) sadistic or masochistic abuse; or (v) lascivious exhibition of the genitals or pubic area of any person."[110]

These activities are severe, so the international and domestic communities have moved away from the use of "child pornography" to label such egregious images. They have adopted various terms, such as "child sexual abuse images,"[111] "child abuse material,"[112] "child abuse imagery,"[113] or "sexually exploitive material."[114] They have done so because they have recognized that the term "child pornography" "does not accurately reflect its content, and implicitly implies consensual activity."[115] Many researchers have followed suit, noting that "[m]any professionals working in the area have expressed the belief that such terminology ["child pornography"] allows us to distance ourselves from the true nature of the material. A preferred term is abuse images."[116] The term "child sexual abuse images" is being used increasingly in both the courts[117] and state statutes.[118] The migration from the term "child pornography" is attributable to the growing recognition that images of child sexual abuse are not younger versions of adult pornography.[119] Rather, the term is often more accurately described as "crime scene photos," which document the sexual abuse of a child[120] either by memorializing the sexual contact or by filming or photographing the child in such a context.

This more enlightened and descriptive label is also grounded in the recognition that the sexual abuse occurs not only in the production of the images, but also in the many additional harms the victim suffers from the creation of the images. The UN NGO CRC has compiled a partial list of the harms caused by these images: (1) the harm children suffer in production of the images; (2) the harm children suffer when the images are copied and/or circulated; (3) the harm suffered when possessors continue to exploit the children by their consumption of the images; (4) the harm possession causes children by maintaining the demand for the images; (5) the harm caused by the images' role in normalizing sexual abuse of children; (6) the harm caused by using the images to groom other victims; (7) the harm caused when such images are used to blackmail, intimidate, or coerce children; and (8) the harm caused by trading such images, which "works to rationalize and establish a sexual desire for children in the public realm."[121] These images harm children in a variety of profound ways.

Although the organizations that monitor sexually abusive images of children have all recorded that such images are becoming increasingly violent and are containing images of younger and younger children, it is true that the content of such images is not uniform. The legal definition includes images as severe as masochism and bestiality, and it also includes lascivious displays of genitals. This has led a minority group to object to the term "child abuse images," arguing that not all images depict abuse.

There are two flaws with this argument. First, it conflates "abuse" with "assault," incorrectly suggesting that a child must be assaulted for an image to meet the definition of child pornography or child abuse images. Second, it fails to understand what has been made clear by the law, courts, and research: the child in the image is abused and exploited both during the production and after the creation of the filmed or photographed "sexually explicit" event conduct."[122]

Children need not be assaulted on film in order to be victims of child pornography or sexually abusive images.[123] These images are defined by content. If an image depicts a child engaged in sexually explicit conduct, then the image is child pornography or a sexually abusive image of a child. The images themselves are harmful and *that* is one of the social harms the laws attempt to address. In *New York v. Ferber*, the Supreme Court first recognized this harm and held the First Amendment does not protect child pornography.[124] It did not extend First Amendment protection to child pornography not because of the assault suffered in production, but rather because any children photographed in the sexually explicit context suffered "psychological, emotional and mental harm."[125] The *Ferber* Court listed five reasons for its holding, including the psychological harm resulting from the creation of a "permanent record" of the children's "participation" in the images.[126]

In other words, the Court has always understood that the pictures *themselves* are harmful to children.[127] This was later underscored in *Osborne v. Ohio*, when the Court noted the psychological harm of children from the "continued existence" of the images.[128] Similarly, in dicta the Court has since indicated that even morphed images implicate the interests of real children and "[were] closer" to the images in *Ferber*, while virtual images, those with no actual children to be psychologically harmed, are not.[129]

Much of the confusion around the term "child sexual abuse images" focuses on the word "abuse." Although the images need not depict an assault to be abusive, one could still argue that the use of the word "abuse" suggests the images *do* have to display an assault to meet the definition. By using the noun "abuse," this label could lead to such confusion. But labeling the images as only "exploitive" is underinclusive, as a significant portion of the images traded depict assaults. The more precise word is perhaps not "abuse," because as used in this context, "abuse" is meant to *describe* the image itself, not necessarily what actually occurred in production. As such, the more precise label would be the adjective "*abusive*," not the noun "abuse." Therefore, the most precise label that sufficiently encompasses the harm caused by the images and their content is "sexually abusive images of children."

Fair labeling requires that these images be referred to as "sexually abusive images of children." This label more precisely describes the content and harm of the images. Furthermore, the term eliminates confusion between these materials and adult pornography. Finally, it remains a more precise description as to whether or not physical assault is committed in production. It is abundantly clear in the courts and the international community that these images harm children in many ways beyond harm in production, and this label indicates as much.

C. *"Child Sex Trafficking"*

Child sex trafficking is a form of organized child abuse.[130] The language surrounding prostitution has often been contentious for a number of reasons. A small but vocal group of activists support legitimizing prostitution. The sharp difference in views of commercial sex is reflected by a split between those who label prostitution as "sex work" and those who reject such a label. Regardless of the debate over adult prostitution, this label clearly has no place regarding children, who are unable to consent to exploitation. To label children caught up in sex trafficking as "sex workers" suggests that they are engaged in labor rather than suffering as victims. As others have noted, "when prostitution is defined as labor, the predatory, pedophiliac purchase of a human being by a john becomes a banal business transaction . . . the sexism, racism, and violent degradation of prostitution fade from sight."[131]

Many use the term "child prostitution." While that term is preferable to the term "sex worker," it is also problematic because it suggests equivalence between a child and an adult prostitute. Ordinarily, when an adult has sexual contact with a child, society recognizes that as child sexual abuse, and society recognizes the child as a victim. When money is exchanged, however, some perceive the child not as a victim but as a criminal. The phrase "child prostitute" has several flaws.

First, implicating the child as a criminal evokes the applicable framework of adult prostitution. It conveys that the child who is victimized is actually a willing participant in his or her exploitation.[132] This connection is inaccurate because it fails to reflect the reality of both children and commercial sex. The child is the victim because children are not capable of giving legal or, given what is known about the brain research, intellectual, consent to prostitution. Second, many children are driven to sex acts not only by force and coercion, but also by the need for survival. This "survival sex" occurs when a child engages in sexual contact or exploitation in exchange for a human need such as food, clothing, or shelter.[133] Such a child takes no freely chosen course but has had his or her economic vulnerability exploited further. Third, regarding commercial sexual exploitation, this concept of adult prostitution suggesting complicity in criminality is itself problematic. It reflects "an antiquated view that prostitution is a chosen profession," when in fact a majority of prostitutes are "pimp controlled."[134] The social assumptions surrounding prostitution are also problematic because child victims of prostitution can then be assumed to be adult-like:

> [T]hese constructions, on their own, fail to make it clear that children cannot be expected to make an informed choice to prostitute themselves. . . . These terms do not adequately express the child's

experience of force, exploitation, and physical and psychological harm inflicted through their engagement in prostitution.[135]

Finally, the term does not merely suggest the child is a criminal, but a particular kind of criminal "unworthy of sympathy because they engage in conduct perceived to be degrading and objectionable."[136]

Because of these concerns about the term "child prostitution," the fair labeling principle indicates that "child sex trafficking victim" should be used to reference this form of victimization. Such a label conveys both the gravity of the harm and the condemnation of society.

Concerns about language within the context of child sex trafficking are not limited to victims. The transformation of the understanding of prostitution of minors to child sex trafficking appropriately readjusts the focus from the child to the offender. Both "purchasers" and "sellers" are perpetrators of child sex trafficking, but neither term adequately label the role played by the offender.

Traditionally, the term "pimp" refers to a person who controls the child and obtains profits from her exploitation.[137] While originally a technical term, it has moved into the mainstream vernacular and has been given a glamorous quality signifying money and power. Yet, far from being glamorous, "pimp controlled prostitution is characterized by extreme violence to break victims and establish total dominance over them."[138] Because "pimp" has become associated with glamor instead with this violence, it has become an inappropriate label for a human trafficker. Fair labeling would suggest that such individuals be referred to as "traffickers."

Even more confusion exists regarding purchasers of children for sex. A "purchaser" of a child for sex has been given many labels: customer, client, or john. Such terms, while not necessarily glorifying, are indeed sanitizing and inaccurate. The terms "customer" or "client" are insufficient because they merely reaffirm the commercial nature of the exchange but eliminate from the description the exploitation. "John" simply is an innocuous label for the purchase of a victimized person by another. In fact, under the TVPA, one who obtains a child for a commercial sex act is a trafficker.[139]

Although both "purchaser" and "seller" of children for sex are "traffickers," they can play very different roles in the crime of child sex trafficking, and equating the terms by giving them the same label seems to violate fair labeling. A main feature of the fair labeling principle is to have the language encompass both the severity of the crime as well as a mental state of the wrongdoing. Therefore, distinctions need be made between these two forms of traffickers. Thus, "third-party trafficker" has been recommended to replace the term "pimp." This denotes that a third party is facilitating the purchase of a human being and profiting from the action. However, a third party is not necessary for trafficking to take place.[140] When one obtains or entices a child into a commercial sex act, one engages in human trafficking as a first party. In such a case the purchaser could be labeled a "first-party trafficker."

Although these suggested labels are more precise that "pimp" and "purchaser," they suffer from another attribute: they sanitize the reality. Such terms are improvements, but they still have limitations: namely, they require explanation. Some use the term "sex purchaser" to more vividly elucidate the nature of purchaser's actions, but this label conveys the impression that the trafficker is purchasing only sex when, in reality, he is purchasing a person. Therefore, the label somewhat depersonalizes a very personal form of victimization, equating it almost with arms or narcotics trafficking. Therefore the most appropriate, if not ideal, labels are "first-party sex trafficker" for purchasers and "third-party sex traffickers" for "pimps." These terms more precisely describe the activity and convey what is being trafficked, placing the activity squarely within the realm of human trafficking.

D. "Sexting"—"Child-Produced Child Pornography"— "Sexualized Images of Children"

In the mid-2000s, when mobile technology became more advanced and widely available, some children began taking sexualized pictures of themselves and other children and some children distributed them. The content of the images and the circumstances surrounding the production of these images were very diverse. Some of these pictures were sexual but not explicit, while others were graphic and met the legal definition of child pornography, that is, they were visual depictions of a child or children engaged in sexually explicit conduct. Some of these pictures were of the person taking the picture, some were not. Some of the pictures were taken with the permission of the subject, some were not. Some of the pictures were taken of a consensual sexual act, while others were essentially videos or still images of a sexual assault. Some of these pictures were taken without any coercion; others were the product of a range of coercive tactics from peer pressure to blackmail to threats.[141]

Despite significant distinctions in these images—differences in the content of the images and differences in the role that juveniles played in creating these images—a number of media outlets decided to label all these diverse activities with one all-encompassing and glorifying label: "sexting."[142] This term is problematic for several reasons, including its overgeneralization, imprecision, and glorification of an act which, because of the perpetuity of the images, can cause "uniquely pernicious harm."[143]

The term "sexting" does not conform to the fair labeling principle. In particular, it fails to distinguish images both in terms of content and the circumstances surrounding their production. The content of an image provides important information about the legal status of that image, most importantly whether it depicts sexually explicit conduct and, therefore, falls within the legal definition of child pornography or sexually abusive images of children. The circumstances surrounding its creation convey important information about the mental state of the individual who created or distributed the image or important information about the level of harm caused by the image. Images that meet the definition of child pornography or sexually abusive images of children should retain a label that indicates that fact.

That is not to say that the images' producers should always be prosecuted. Rather, that determination should be made on a separate basis.[144] Several images that do not meet the legal definition should be labeled as "sexualized images of children." What is clear is that if there is an adult involved at all in the production, either in the grooming for its production or the taking of the images, these are not child-produced images but are the products of a sexually abusive or exploitive act by an adult with the child as a victim.

In recent years, some efforts have been made to define these acts more precisely. For example, Wolak and Finkelhor have used the label "youth-produced sexual images" and have made further distinctions between images, labeling some images "aggravated images" and others "experimental images." The label "aggravated images" refers to images that possess a criminal or abusive aspect, such as the involvement of adults, the presence of extortion, or the distribution of these images without the subject's knowledge. The label "experimental images" applies only to pictures taken by the subject and sent to an established partner or the target of a romantic interest.[145]

The typology suggested by Wolak and Finkelhor is consistent with the author's previous writing in this area. In the first law review article on the subject, the author suggested the term "self-produced" or "child-produced child pornography" for those images that meet the legal definition of child pornography, but called for a detailed system called "structured prosecutorial discretion in a multidisciplinary context" to distinguish those youths whose actions do not deserve a legal response from those engaging in coercive or malicious actions.[146] However, in light of the aforementioned discussion surrounding "abuse," "child-produced sexually abusive images of children" may be more accurate.[147]

These efforts are positive movements toward fair labeling. They do not overgeneralize and they capture the harm caused. For images that meet the definition of child pornography, or sexually abusive images of children, child-produced sexually abusive images "more accurately describes the conduct of concern because 'sexting' may encompass material that fails to meet the narrower legal definitions of child pornography."[148]

Conclusion

The fair labeling principle furthers the idea that labels play a significant role in the law. It requires that labels of criminal wrongdoing communicate the gravity of the offense, the mental state of the offender, and the harm experienced by the victim. This principle can play an important role in the realm of child sexual abuse and exploitation. Given the complicated nature of this conduct and society's reaction to it, careful and precise labels are needed. Therefore, stakeholders should endeavor to ensure that the labels in this field reflect the true nature of the victimization. Consequently, prevention efforts and responsive programs will become more effective as they target more specific conduct and harm.

NOTES

1. Consolidated Appropriations Act, 2012, Pub. L. No. 112-74, § 7008, 125 Stat. 786, 1195–96 (2011).
2. Convention on the Prevention and Punishment of the Crime of Genocide, art II, Dec. 9, 1948, S. Exec. Doc. O, 81-1 (1949), 78 U.N.T.S. 277.
3. David Nersessian, *Comparative Approaches to Punishing Hate: The Intersection of Genocide and Crimes Against Humanity*, 43 STAN. J. OF INT'L L. 221, 221 (2007).
4. Faustin Ntoubandi, *When to Act: A State's Obligations & Responsibilities Regarding Genocide*, THE SENTINEL PROJECT (June 14, 2013), http://thesentinelproject.org/when-to-act-a-states-obligations-and-responsibilities-regarding-genocide/.
5. Nersessian, *supra* note 3, at 221–22.
6. Linnea Manoshow, Comment, *Genocide and Ethnic Cleansing: Why the Distinction? A Discussion in the Context of the Atrocities Occurring in the Southern Sudan*, 35 CAL. W. INT'L. L.J. 303, 304, 309 (2005).
7. James B. Jacobs & Kimberly A. Potter, *Hate Crimes: A Critical Perspective*, 22 CRIME & JUST. 1, 30–32 (1997).

8. Jacobs & Potter, *supra* note 7, at 30; Kathryn Carny, Note, *Rape: The Paradigmatic Hate Crime*, 75 ST. JOHN'S L. REV. 315, 340 (2001).

9. *E.g.*, ALA. CODE § 38-9E-4 (West, Westlaw through Act 2014-09) (elder abuse and neglect); 13 CAL. PENAL CODE §368 (West 2004) (crimes against elder adults); S.C. CODE ANN. §16-3-85 (2003) (homicide by child abuse); UTAH CODE ANN. §76-5-208 (LexisNexis 2008) (child abuse homicide).

10. *White House Fact Sheet: The Violence Against Women Act*, WHITE HOUSE, www.whitehouse.gov/sites/default/files/docs/vawa_factsheet.pdf (last visited Feb. 23, 2014) (documenting improvements made since passage of VAWA); SENATE JUDICIARY COMM. MAJORITY STAFF, WHY THE VIOLENCE AGAINST WOMEN ACT MATTERS (2012) *available at* http://www.leahy.senate.gov/imo/media/doc/042612VAWA-WhyVAWAMatters-OnePager.pdf (same).

11. SUBGROUP AGAINST THE EXPLOITATION OF CHILDREN, NGO GROUP FOR THE CONVENTION ON THE RIGHTS OF THE CHILD, SEMANTICS OR SUBSTANCE? TOWARDS A SHARED UNDERSTANDING OF TERMINOLOGY REFERRING TO THE SEXUAL ABUSE AND EXPLOITATION OF CHILDREN 89 (2005).

12. Lisa Thompson, *Preferred Terminology for Sex Trafficking and Prostitution*, 39 SOC. WORK & CHRISTIANITY 481, 482 (2012).

13. Toko Serita, *In Our Own Backyards: The Need for a Coordinated Judicial Response to Human Trafficking*, 36 N.Y.U. REV. L. & SOC. CHANGE 635, 641 n.41 (2012).

14. *Id.* at 642.

15. *E.g.*, Mary Elizabeth Williams, *Polanski's Victim Is Not a "Sex Scandal Teen,"* SALON (Oct. 10, 2012, 12:20 PM), http://www.salon.com/2012/10/10/polanskis_victim_isnt_a_sex_scandal_teen/.

16. *See Jerry Sandusky Scandal*, CENTRE DAILY TIMES, www.centredaily.com/sandusky-scandal (last visited Feb. 24, 2014).

17. Thompson, *supra* note 12, at 482.

18. Nersessian, *supra* note 3, at 224.

19. Henry Hart, *The Aims of the Criminal Law*, 23 LAW & CONTEMP. PROBS. 401, 405 (1958).

20. Nersessian, *supra* note 3, at 225.

21. *Id.* at 224.

22. 28 CFR § 1100.27 (2011).

23. Gerald Uelman, *Victim Rights in California*, 8 ST. JOHN'S J. LEGAL COMMENT. 197 (1972).

24. *Id.* at 199.

25. ANDREW ASHWORTH, PRINCIPLES OF CRIMINAL LAW 86 (7th ed. 2013); James Chalmers & Fiona Leverick, *Fair Labelling in Criminal Law*, 71 MOD. L. REV. 218, 237–39 (2008); Sandeep Gopalan, *Skilling's Martyrdom: The Case for Criminalization Without Incarceration*, 44 U.S.F. L. REV. 459, 467 (2010).

26. Nersessian, *supra* note 3, at 255–56.

27. Dennis Baker, *Complicity, Proportionality, and the Serious Crime Act*, 14 NEW CRIM. L. REV. 403, 405 (2011).

28. Alice Ristroph, *Criminal Law in the Shadow of Violence*, 62 ALA. L. REV. 571, 578 (2011).

29. Chalmers & Leverick, *supra* note 25, at 226, 240.

30. *Id.* at 226.

31. *Id.*

32. Barry Mitchell, *Multiple Wrongdoing and Offense Structure: A Plea for Consistency and Fair Labelling*, 63 MOD. L. REV. 393, 399 (2001).

33. Chalmers & Leverick, *supra* note 25, at 225 (2008) (quoting Jeremy Horder, *Rethinking Non-fatal Offenses Against the Person*, 14 OXFORD J. LEGAL STUD. 335, 351 (1994)).

34. A. P. SIMESTER & G. R. SULLIVAN, CRIMINAL LAW THEORY AND DOCTRINE 45 (2d ed. 2003).

35. Chalmers & Leverick, *supra* note 25, at 226.

36. SUBGROUP AGAINST THE EXPLOITATION OF CHILDREN, *supra* note 11, at 7.

37. *Id.*

38. David Finkelhor, *Five Myths About Missing Children*, WASH. POST, May 12, 2013, at B3.

39. U.S. DEP'T OF HEALTH & HUMAN SERVS., CHILD MALTREATMENT 22 (2011); JANIS WOLAK, ET AL., ONLINE VICTIMIZATION OF YOUTH: FIVE YEARS LATER, 1–2 (2006); *Child Sexual Abuse Services*, NAT'L CENTER FOR VICTIMS OF CRIME, www.victimsofcrime.org/media/reporting-on-child-sexual-abuse/child-sexual-abuse-statistics (last visited Feb. 26, 2014).

40. Serita, *supra* note 13, at 639.

41. JAMES H. FARROW, PSYCHOLOGICAL CONTEXT LEADING JUVENILES TO PROSTITUTION AND SEXUAL EXPLOITATION, MEDIA, LEGAL AND SOCIAL ASPECTS OF CHILD SEXUAL EXPLOITATION 337–41 (2005).

42. KEN LANNING, CHILD MOLESTERS: A BEHAVIORAL ANALYSIS 27 (5th ed. 2010).

43. Mary Graw Leary, *Worth a Few Appalled Words*, LEGAL TIMES, Dec. 17, 2007.

44. *E.g.*, Karen Duffin, *New Frontiers in Child Porn Law*, ON THE MEDIA (January 24, 2014), http://www.onthemedia.org/story/new-frontiers-child-porn-law/; Jessica Gresko, *Ex Teacher Writes Judge Overseeing Child Porn Case*, HUFFINGTON POST (Feb. 25, 2014, 2:03 PM), http://www.huffingtonpost.com/huff-wires/20140225/us-teacher-child-pornography/?utm_hp_ref=politics&ir=politics; *Supreme Court to Decide on Child Porn Victim Restitution*, N.Y. DAILY NEWS (Jan. 20, 2014, 10:11 AM), http://www.nydailynews.com/news/politics/supreme-court-decide-child-porn-victim-restitution-article-1.1585302.

45. Craig Bradley, *With Narrow Reading of Child Porn Law, Court Dodges a Dilemma*, TRIAL MAG. Aug. 2008, at 52; Russell Weaver, *Speech & Technology*, 110 PENN ST. L. REV. 703, 704, 715 (2006); David L. Hudson, *Reflecting on the Virtual Child Porn Decision*, 36 J. MARSH. L. REV. 211 (2002).

46. Transcript of Oral Argument at 12, 44, 20, 25, United States v. Williams, 553 U.S. 285 (2007) (No. 06-694) (statements of Justices Scalia, Ginsburg, and Souter).

47. *Human Trafficking: Organized Crime and the Multi-Billion Dollar Sale of People*, UNODC (July 19, 2012), www.unodc.org/unodc/en/frontpage/2012/July/human-trafficking-oranigzed-crime-sale-of-people.html.

48. Jason S. Carroll, et al., *Generation XXX, Pornography Acceptance and Use Among Emerging Adults*, 23 J. ADOLESCENT RES. 6, 7 (2008).

49. Miller v. California, 413 U.S. 15, 18 n.2 (1973).

50. United States v. Loy, 237 F.3d 251, 263–65 (3rd Cir. 2001).

51. FREE SPEECH COALITION, INC., www.freespeechcoalition.org (last visited Feb. 26, 2014).

52. U.S. SENTENCING COMM'N, FEDERAL CHILD PORNOGRAPHY OFFENSES vi, 86–87 (2012) [hereinafter CHILD PORNOGRAPHY REPORT].

53. *Id.* at 89.

54. Testimony of Michelle Collins, Vice President, Exploited Children Div. & Assistant to the President of Nat'l Ctr. for Missing and Exploited Children, to the U.S. Sentencing Commission, at 5 (February 15, 2012).

55. INTERNET WATCH FOUNDATION, INTERNET WATCH FOUNDATION ANNUAL & CHARITY REPORT 11 (2011).

56. Letter from Jonathan J. Wroblewski, Dir., Office of Policy and Legislation, Dep't of Justice, to Hon. William K. Sessions, III, U.S. Sentencing Comm'n at 6 (June 28, 2010).

57. Audrey Rogers, *Child Pornography's Forgotten Victims*, 28 PACE L. REV. 847, 851 (2008).

58. 18 U.S.C. § 3553(a) (2012).

59. Melissa Hamilton, *The Efficacy of Severe Child Pornography Sentencing: Empirical Validity of Political Rhetoric*, 22 STAN. L. & POL'Y REV. 545, 562–67 (2011); Rogers, *supra* note 57, at 848–52; *see also* United States v. Grinbergs, No. 8:05CR232, 2008 WL 419 1145, at *2, *11 (D. Neb. Sept. 8, 2008).

60. United States v. Paull, 551 F.3d 516, 533 (6th Cir. 2009) (Merritt, J., dissenting), *cert. denied*, 558 U.S. 827 (2009).

61. United States v. Goff, 501 F.3d 250, 251 (3rd Cir. 2007).

62. *E.g.* Paul Cassell, James Marsh, & Jeremy Christiansen, *The Case for Full Restitution for Child Pornography Victims*, 82 GEO. WASH. L. REV. 61 (2013); Rogers, *supra* note 57.

63. Chris Elliot, *Open Door: Why the Term 'Child Porn' Should Not Be Used*, THE GUARDIAN (June 5, 2011), http://www.theguardian.com/commentisfree/2011/jun/06/open-door-term-child-porn (quoting Internet Watch Foundation).

64. SUBGROUP AGAINST THE EXPLOITATION OF CHILDREN, *supra* note 11, at 58.

65. AM. PSYCHOLOGICAL ASSOC., REPORT OF THE APA TASK FORCE ON THE SEXUALIZATION OF GIRLS (2010).

66. *Id.* at 2.

67. *Grooming Dynamic*, NAT'L CTR. FOR VICTIMS OF CRIME, http://www.victimsofcrime.org/media/reporting-on-child-sexual-abuse/grooming-dynamic-of-csa (last visited Feb. 26, 2014).

68. Joseph Bova Conti & William Carson, *An Investigation of Victim Dynamics in Prostitutes and Incarcerated Pedophiles*, *in* MEDICAL LEGAL AND SOCIAL SCIENCE ASPECTS OF CHILD SEXUAL EXPLOITATION 728–29 (Sharon Cooper et al. ed., 2005).

69. Anna Williams Shavers, *Human Trafficking, The Rule of Law, and Corporate Social Responsibility*, 9 S.C. J. INT'L L. & BUS. 39, 84–85 (2012).

70. Ron Scherer, *A Siege on the Child-Porn Market*, CHRISTIAN SCIENCE MONITOR (March 16, 2006), http://www.csmonitor.com/2006/0316/p01s03-ussc.html.

71. Timothy Lee, *Here's How Bitcoin Charmed Washington*, WASH. POST (Nov. 21, 2013, 2:52 PM), http://www.washingtonpost.com/blogs/the-switch/wp/2013/11/21/heres-how-bitcoin-charmed-washington/.

72. CHILD PORNOGRAPHY REPORT, *supra* note 52, at 232; U.S. SENTENCING COMM'N, 2012 SOURCEBOOK OF FEDERAL SENTENCING STATISTICS tbl. 4, 8 (2013). This is not dissimilar from the federal bench, which is also overwhelmingly Caucasian and majority male as well. RUSSELL WHEELER, GOVERNANCE STUDIES AT BROOKINGS, THE CHANGING

FACE OF THE FEDERAL JUDICIARY app. at 11 tbl. 1 (2009); Jonathan Stubbs, *A Demographic Snapshot of the Federal Judiciary: A Case for Change*, NAACA NEWS, Feb. 2011, at 4.

73. CHILD PORNOGRAPHY REPORT, *supra* note 52, at ii, 224; U.S. SENTENCING COMM'N, REPORT OF THE CONTINUING IMPACT OF *United States v. Booker* ON FEDERAL SENTENCING 3, 68 (2012) [hereinafter BOOKER REPORT].

74. CHILD PORNOGRAPHY REPORT, *supra* note 52, at 225.

75. Testimony of Michelle Collins, *supra* note 54, at 5.

76. ALEXANDRA GELBER, U.S. DEPT. OF JUSTICE, RESPONSE TO "A RELUCTANT REBELLION" 8 (July 1, 2009).

77. Hamilton, *supra* note 59, at 561.

78. SUBGROUP AGAINST THE EXPLOITATION OF CHILDREN, *supra* note 11, at 6.

79. Mary Graw Leary, *Sexting or Self-Produced Child Pornography—The Dialog Continues: Structured Prosecutorial Discretional in a Multidisciplinary Context*, 17 VA. J. SOC. POL'Y & LAW 487, 505 (2009); ANDREW HARRIS ET AL., DEP'T OF JUSTICE, BUILDING A PREVENTION FRAMEWORK TO ADDRESS TEEN "SEXTING" BEHAVIORS 3 (2013).

80. HARRIS, *supra* note 79, at 3.

81. Melissa Farley, *Prostitution, Trafficking, and Cultural Amnesia: What We Must Not Know in Order To Keep the Business of Sexual Exploitation Running Smoothly*, 18 YALE J.L. & FEMINISM 109, 132 (2006).

82. ELLEN WRIGHT CLAYTON, ET AL., INST. OF MED. OF THE NAT'L ACADEMS., CONFRONTING COMMERCIAL SEXUAL EXPLOITATION OF MINORS IN THE UNITED STATES 401 (2013).

83. Abigail Judge, *"'Sexting' Among Adolescents: Psychological and Legal Perspectives*, 20 HARV. REV. PSYCHIATRY 86, 89 (2012).

84. HARRIS, *supra* note 79, at 3.

85. Judge, *supra* note 83, at 87.

86. SUBGROUP AGAINST THE EXPLOITATION OF CHILDREN, *supra* note 11, at 18–19.

87. *Id.* at 7.

88. *Id.* at 56–57.

89. CHILD PORNOGRAPHY REPORT, *supra* note 52, at ii, 224; BOOKER REPORT, *supra* note 73, at 3, 68.

90. United States v. Reingold, 731 F.3d 204 (2d Cir. 2013).

91. *Id.* at 206–8.

92. *Id.* at 217.

93. United States v. C.R., 792 F. Supp. 2d 343, 510 (E.D.N.Y. 2011) *reversed sub nom.* United States v. Reingold, 731 F.3d 204 (2d Cir. 2013).

94. 738 F. Supp. 960, 962 (D. Neb. 2010).

95. SAVE THE CHILDREN, CHILD SEXUAL ABUSE AND EXPLOITATION: PROPOSAL FOR A NEW EU LEGAL FRAMEWORK 5 (2009).

96. SUBGROUP AGAINST THE EXPLOITATION OF CHILDREN, *supra* note 11, at 58.

97. LANNING, *supra* note 42, at 112; Linnea Smith, et al., *Commercial Sexual Exploitation of Children in Advertising*, *in* MEDICAL, LEGAL AND SOCIAL ASPECTS OF CHILD SEXUAL EXPLOITATION, *supra* note 68, at 25–59.

98. Mary Graw Leary, *Death to Child Erotica: How Mislabeling the Evidence Can Risk Inaccuracy in the Courtroom*, 16 CARDOZO J. L. AND GENDER 1, 8 n. 40–41 (2009).

99. Protocol to Prevent, Suppress, and Punish Trafficking in Persons, Especially Women & Children, supplementing the United Nations Convention against Transnational Organized Crime, art. 3(d), *adopted* Nov. 15, 2000, T.I.A.S. No. 13127, 2237 U.N.T.S. 319; Convention of the Rights of the Child, art. 1, *adopted* Nov. 20, 1989, 1577 U.N.T.S. 3; International Labour Organization (no. 182) Convention Concerning the Prohibition and Immediate Elimination of the Worst Forms of Child Labor, art. 2, *adopted* June 17, 1999, 2133 U.N.T.S. 161.

100. SUBGROUP AGAINST THE EXPLOITATION OF CHILDREN, *supra* note 12, at 62.

101. Roper v. Simmons, 543 U.S. 551, 569 (2008); Graham v. Florida, 560 U.S. 48 (2010).

102. Graham v. Florida, 560 U.S. 48, 89 (2010) (Roberts, J., concurring) (citing *Roper*, 543 U.S. at 569–71).

103. Given this research, some have criticized the cutoff age of eighteen as too low. Presumably, the Court accepted eighteen because the research supports at a minimum, the previously adopted, if not universal age of eighteen as the latest possible age between childhood and adulthood. While arguments could be made for older ages, such would be a position outside any previously adopted legal conceptualization of children.

104. Elizabeth Scott and Thomas Grisso, *Developmental Incompetence, Due Process, and Juvenile Justice Policy*, 83 N.C. L. REV. 793, 811–817 (2005).

105. Joan Reid and Christopher Sullivan, *A Latent Class Typology of Juvenile Victims and Exploration of Risk Factors and Outcomes of Victimization*, CRIMINAL JUSTICE AND BEHAVIOR (2009).

106. Eileen Vizard, *Practitioner Review: The Victims and Juvenile Perpetrators of Child Sexual Abuse—Assessment and Intervention*. JOURNAL OF CHILD PSYCHOLOGY AND PSYCHIATRY 54: 503–15 (2013). http://dx.doi.org/10.1111/jcpp.12047.

107. *Id.*

108. SUBGROUP AGAINST THE EXPLOITATION OF CHILDREN, *supra* note 11, 62.

109. Optional Protocol to the Convention on the Rights of the Child on the Sale of Children, Child Prostitution and Child Pornography, art. 2(c), *adopted* May 25, 2000, 2171 U.N.T.S. 227.

110. 18 U.S.C. 2256(2)(a) (2012).

111. *E.g.*, WOLAK, ET AL. *supra* note 39.

112. MARY AIKEN ET AL., CHILD ABUSE MATERIAL AND THE INTERNET: CYBERPSYCHOLOGY OF ONLINE CHILD RELATED SEX OFFENDING 2 (2011).

113. Google uses this term when warning a user that his search may lead to questionable images. *Protecting Children from Sexual Abuse*, GOOGLE, www.google.com/landing/protectchildren/ (last visited Feb. 22, 2014).

114. People v. Renander, 151 P.3d 657, 661 (Colo. App. 2006).

115. AIKEN, *supra* note 112, at 2.

116. ETHEL QUAYLE & MAX TAYLOR, CHILD PORNOGRAPHY: AN INTERNET CRIME (2003); JANIS WOLAK, DAVID FINKELHOR & KIMBERLY J. MITCHELL, NAT'L CTR. FOR MISSING & EXPLOITED CHILDREN, CHILD-PORNOGRAPHY POSSESSORS ARRESTED IN INTERNET-RELATED CRIMES: FINDINGS FROM THE NATIONAL JUVENILE ONLINE VICTIMIZATION STUDY vii n.1 (2005).

117. *See, e.g.*, United State v. Aguirre, 448 F. App'x 670, 673 (9th Cir. 2011); United States v. Christman, 607 F.3d 1110,1113 (6th Cir. 2010); State v. Barger, 247 P.3d 309, 310 (Or. 2011); State v. Hess, 178 N.C. App. 742 (N.C. Ct. App. 2006).

118. Mich. Comp. Laws Ann. § 750.145c(o) (West 2000); N.H. REV. STAT. ANN. § 649-A:3-b (2009).

119. INT'L CTR. FOR MISSING AND EXPLOITED CHILDREN, CHILD PORNOGRAPHY: MODEL LEGISLATION & GLOBAL REVIEW 7 (6th ed. 2010).

120. *Protecting Children from Internet Pornographers Act of 2011: Hearing on H.R. 1981 Before the Subcomm. on Crime, Terrorism & Homeland Sec. of the Comm. on the Judiciary*, 112th Cong. 68 (2011) (statement of Ernie Allen, President and CEO, National Center for Missing & Exploited Children).

121. SUBGROUP AGAINST THE EXPLOITATION OF CHILDREN, *supra* note 11, at 27–28.

122. SAVE THE CHILDREN, *supra* note 95, at 5.

123. *Id.*

124. 458 U.S. 747 (1982).

125. *Id.* at 756–58; *Id.* at 774–75 (O'Connor, J., concurring).

126. *Id.* at 759 (majority opinion).

127. Leary, *supra* note 79, at 523–27.

128. 495 U.S. 103, 111 (1990).

129. Ashcroft v. Free Speech Coalition, 535 U.S. 234, 241–42 (2002).

130. CLAYTON, ET AL., *supra* note 82, at xi.

131. Farley, *supra* note 81, at 111–12.

132. CLAYTON, ET AL., *supra* note 82, at 34.

133. *Id.* at 402.

134. Serita, *supra* note 13, at 642–43; Press Release, N.Y. State United Court Sys., NY Judiciary Launches Nations First Statewide Human Trafficking Intervention Initiative (Sept. 25, 2013) *available at* http://www.nycourts.gov/press/PR13_11.pdf.

135. SUBGROUP AGAINST THE EXPLOITATION OF CHILDREN, *supra* note 11, at 14.

136. Serita, *supra* note 13, at 658.

137. *See id.* at 641.

138. CLAYTON, ET AL., *supra* note 82, at 643.

139. 22 U.S.C. § 7802 (2012).

140. United States v. Jungers, 702 F.3d 1066 (8th Cir. 2013).

141. Leary, *supra* note 79 at 492–93; NAT'L CTR. FOR MISSING AND EXPLOITED CHILDREN, POSITION PAPER ON SEXTING (2010).

142. *Id.*; Judge, *supra* note 83, at 87.

143. Judge, *supra* note 83, at 89.

144. Leary, *supra* note 79.

145. JANIS WOLAK AND DAVID FINKELHOR, CRIMES AGAINST CHILDREN RESEARCH CTR., SEXTING: A TYPOLOGY 3 (2011).

146. Leary, *supra* note 79, at 488.

147. *Id.*

148. Susan Hanley Duncan, *A Legal Response Is Necessary for Self-Produced Child Pornography: A Legislator's Checklist for Drafting a Bill*, 89 OR. L. REV. 645, 648 (2010).

Part II (A) | Refining Child Pornography Law

The Special Case of Possession

5 | Questioning the Modern Criminal Justice Focus on Child Pornography Possession

Carissa Byrne Hessick

Recent years have seen a significant increase in the number of prosecutions for possessing child pornography, as well as an increase in the criminal penalties for that crime. The decisions to increase the number of prosecutions and the length of sentences are, at bottom, decisions to invest more criminal justice resources in the detection, prosecution, and punishment of those who possess child pornography. Although these decisions are often touted as decisions that protect children, this chapter questions whether the American criminal justice system ought to prioritize child pornography possession over other crimes in the fight to eliminate child sexual abuse and exploitation.

Instead of being a critical tool to protect children, the focus on possession crimes may be evidence that current law and law enforcement practices are misdirecting criminal justice resources. In focusing resources on those who possess child pornography instead of other crimes against children, many American jurisdictions do not sufficiently take into account that possessing child pornography is one of the least serious crimes involving the sexual abuse of children. The prevailing focus on child pornography possession may have the unintended consequence of leaving children less safe than a system that spends fewer resources on detecting, prosecuting, and punishing those who possess child pornography.

The chapter begins by identifying the modern criminal justice focus on child pornography possession. It then explains why those who possess child pornography pose less of a threat and cause less harm than those who create or distribute child pornography. In doing so, it questions the arguments that are generally given in support of the focus on child pornography possessors. Drawing an analogy to the war on drugs, the chapter explains why focusing criminal justice resources on possession cases not only seems less fair but also does not seem calculated to sensibly reduce the availability of child pornography.

The chapter concludes by setting forth the unintended consequences of a criminal justice strategy that targets possessors of child pornography. It explains that the strategy creates incentives for law enforcement to spend fewer resources on cases involving direct sexual abuse of children. By cloaking child pornography cases in the rhetoric of protecting children, the strategy prevents the public from being able to accurately assess whether the focus on possession is an effective method for protecting children.

A. The High Number of Prosecutions and Penalties for Possession

As a general matter, the number of child pornography prosecutions has increased in recent years.[1] And within the category of child pornography offenses, the number of possession cases far exceeds the number of production or distribution cases. In the federal system, for example, the number of defendants sentenced and a breakdown of the proportions is shown in table 1.[2] In addition to increasing the number of prosecutions for possessing child pornography, many American jurisdictions have significantly increased the criminal penalties associated with possessing child pornography.[3] For example, in 1990 federal law punished the possession of child pornography by up to ten years of imprisonment.[4] In 1996, the maximum penalty was increased to fifteen years.[5] In 2003 a mandatory minimum five-year sentence was added and the statutory maximum sentence was raised from fifteen years to twenty.[6] One recent report notes that

TABLE 1. Federal Child Pornography Offenders

Type of CP offense[a]	Number of cases in 2005	% of CP cases in 2005	Number of cases in 2007	% of CP cases in 2007	Number of cases in 2011	% of CP cases in 2011
Production	238	20.7%	292	20.2%	481	22.3%
Distribution	450	39.1%	385	26.7%	618	28.7%
Possession	463	40.2%	765	53.1%	1,061	49.1%
Total	1,151		1,442		2,160	

[a]The distribution of offenders into the categories of "possession" and "distribution" was accomplished by categorizing those offenders who were sentenced only for "simple receipt" as possessors rather than distributors. *See* U.S. SENTENCING COMMISSION, THE HISTORY OF THE CHILD PORNOGRAPHY GUIDELINES 48 (2009).

the average sentence for child pornography defendants increased by 350 percent in the ten years from 1997 to 2007.[7]

The federal government is not alone in increasing the penalties for possession. Thirty states have increased the penalties available for possession of child pornography since criminalizing it, and four states have increased the penalties for possession of child pornography multiple times in the last twenty years.[8]

Some of the state sentencing increases have been particularly dramatic. For example, in 1995 Montana increased the maximum penalty for possessing child pornography from six months to ten years in prison.[9] And in 2003 Georgia reclassified possession of child pornography from a misdemeanor to a felony with a mandatory minimum sentence of five years imprisonment and a maximum sentence of twenty years.[10]

In some jurisdictions, sentencing severity can be traced to statutory schemes that treat the possession of child pornography as equivalent to other child pornography crimes. For example, Arizona, Kansas, Mississippi, Oklahoma, South Dakota, and Utah all punish the possession of child pornography as harshly as they do the production of child pornography.[11] In other words, these jurisdictions punish those who abuse or exploit children to create child pornography the same amount as those who merely possess it. Arkansas, Louisiana, and the federal government punish possession of child pornography as harshly as distribution.[12]

Although some states explicitly equate the seriousness of possessing child pornography with the seriousness of producing or distributing child pornography, not all lengthy possession sentences can be traced to a conscious legislative choice. The fact that some child pornography possession defendants receive long sentences is attributable to the piling on of various sentencing enhancements. Most notably, a number of jurisdictions increase sentences based on the number of images a child pornography offender possesses,[13] and several states treat each image possessed as a separate criminal offense.[14]

Charging and plea bargaining practices also contribute to possession defendants receiving lengthy sentences. There is evidence that many defendants convicted of possession end up serving significantly longer sentences than defendants who sexually abused children. For example, an Arizona defendant was sentenced to two hundred years' imprisonment for the possession of child pornography; the sentence was the result of a statutory mandatory minimum sentence of ten years[15] in connection with a statutory mandate that requires a consecutive sentence for each image possessed.[16] (The defendant was charged with possessing twenty images.)[17]

The same Arizona state sentencing regime that sent a defendant to jail for two hundred years for possession also imposed a fifteen-year sentence on another defendant who twice molested a six-year-old girl; imposed a twenty-two-month sentence on a priest who molested an altar boy; and imposed a *one-year* sentence on a man who kidnapped and sexually assaulted a fourteen-year-old girl who was selling candy door to door.[18]

The Arizona case is not an isolated example. Troy Stabenow's recent study of federal sentencing practices documents that a typical possessor of child pornography will receive a significantly longer sentence under the federal sentencing guidelines than will a defendant who engages in repeated sex with a twelve-year-old girl.[19]

In sum, those who possess child pornography are currently subject to high levels of enforcement and punishment. Certain jurisdictions explicitly classify child pornography possessors as deserving the same punishment as those who produce or distribute child pornography. And even in those jurisdictions that do not explicitly provide for similar treatment, defendants charged with possession will sometimes serve longer sentences than defendants charged with creation or distribution of child pornography because of statutory enhancements and plea bargaining practices. Those plea bargaining practices also sometimes result in sentences for child pornography possession that are longer than sentences for sexually abusing a child.

B. Examining the Relative Seriousness of Possession

That some jurisdictions classify child pornography possessors the same as producers or distributors reflects a legislative determination that possession is as serious as producing or distributing child pornography. And when child pornography possessors spend more time in prison than those who sexually abuse children, it suggests that child pornography offenders are more deserving of punishment than child molesters. Both of these conclusions are difficult to accept.

It may be useful to draw analogy to drug policy to understand why these conclusions about child pornography possession are troubling. In the late 1980s, the federal government changed its enforcement strategy with respect to illegal drugs, focusing not only on drug traffickers, but also on drug users.[20] The decision to target users has since been subject to significant criticism; in particular, critics question why resources are being used to arrest and incarcerate possessors and low-level dealers rather than focusing on trafficking "kingpins."[21] Focusing on drug possessors rather than major suppliers is inefficient because the money used to detect, arrest, and imprison a possessor results only in getting one "customer" off the street, rather than disrupting a supply chain to many customers.[22] Perhaps because of this criticism, state and federal governments occasionally protest that they rarely target low-level drug users for prosecution.[23]

In contrast, the states and the Department of Justice have vigorously defended their strategy of prosecuting and imprisoning child pornography possessors.[24] Government officials have offered a number of reasons why aggressive enforcement and severe punishment are appropriate in child pornography possession cases. Each of those reasons is addressed below.

Before discussing these three arguments in favor of targeting child pornography possessors, it is worth noting that the analogy between child pornography possessors and drug possessors is far from perfect. One obvious difference is that drugs can be produced, distributed, and consumed without harm to anyone except the consumer. The violence associated with the drug trade is a result of the illegal status of drugs, not an inherent aspect of the drugs themselves. In contrast, child pornography is created through the sexual exploitation or abuse of a child. Because the salient harms associated with drugs are internalized by drug possessors but the harms associated with creating child pornography are not internalized by possessors, one might argue that the arguments against pursuing a law enforcement strategy against drug possessors are not persuasive in the child pornography context.

The lack of external harm caused by drug possessors is certainly a good reason for punishing child pornography offenders more harshly than drug offenders. But it does not suggest that many of the criticisms about the incarceration of drug possessors and low-level dealers do not apply to child pornography crimes. In both the drug and the child pornography context, focusing on possessors and low-level distributors is not only less effective than targeting trafficking "kingpins," but it also fails to target those individuals who are more blameworthy—that is to say, those who have committed a more serious crime.

Now let us turn to the major arguments that law enforcement has offered in defense of their policies of actively targeting child pornography offenders: (1) that focusing on possession helps dry up the market for child pornography, which will ultimately reduce the creation of such images; (2) that child pornography possessors pose a significant risk of molesting children, and thus focusing on their arrest and prosecution will help protect children; and (3) that because child pornography possession is as serious or worse than other child exploitation crimes, it is appropriate to focus significant law enforcement resources on possession cases.

1. The Market Theory

The first reason for aggressive enforcement against possessors is that they drive the market for the creation of child pornography.[25] If people did not want to view these images, so the argument goes, there would be no incentive for other individuals to create these images and the market for these images would dry up. And because the creation of child pornography involves the sexual exploitation or abuse of children, those individuals who possess child pornography are arguably responsible for the abuse and exploitation of the children in the images. Essentially, this market theory argument is a claim that targeting child pornography possessors is an effective way to end the creation and distribution of child pornography. More fundamentally, the market theory argument rests on the assumption that creation and distribution are the more serious crimes, and that the focus on possession offenders is not justified simply in order to end possession itself, but rather to stop production and distribution.

There is significant reason to doubt the market theory argument. In particular, the market theory is problematic because the so-called child pornography market does not function as a commercial market. Many individuals who create and distribute child pornography do not make a profit, but instead appear to be motivated by a desire for status.[26] Because those who produce child pornography are not motivated by economic gain, the standard market theory that eliminating demand will eventually reduce the supply does not necessarily apply. Indeed, those who champion the market theory do not rely on any empirical evidence that arresting and prosecuting possessors has affected the production of child pornography; instead they simply rely on the logical appeal of the standard economic argument.[27]

2. Possessors Have Molested or Will Molest Children

Another argument often raised in favor of targeting child pornography possessors is that the possessors themselves pose a risk to children. The risk is sometimes framed as "inflaming" those who look at the images, making them more likely to molest a child in the future.[28] Sometimes the risk is framed as an argument that those who possess child pornography have already molested children, but that those crimes have gone undetected.[29] A recent Department of Justice memorandum, for example, stated that the lack of previous convictions for possession offenders often "hides years of systemic criminal behavior. The defendants simply had never been caught—the anonymous nature of internet-based crimes and the silent and secret nature of sex crimes in general (particularly with a vulnerable population such as children) protect defendants from detection by law enforcement whether they are collectors or molesters."[30]

Like the market theory, the risk theory rests on shaky ground. A number of critics have explained in detail that the supposed risk posed by child pornography possessors to children is not supported by reliable evidence.[31] In justifying lengthy punishments for child pornography possessors, legislators, courts, prosecutors, and interest groups regularly rely on two studies from the Butner Federal Prison.[32] The Butner studies rely on self-reporting by inmates incarcerated for various crimes, including child pornography possession. Based on admissions made by the inmates, the studies report that most of the child pornography offenders had also committed sexual assaults, and that they, on average, victimized large numbers of individuals.[33] It is not surprising that government officials regularly rely on the Butner studies to justify the modern criminal justice focus on possessors. That is because these studies suggest that it is much more likely that someone convicted of child pornography possession also molested a child than do other studies of child pornography offenders.[34]

But there are significant reasons to doubt whether the Butner studies actually demonstrate that child pornography possessors pose a risk of molesting children.[35] A recent article in the *New Yorker* magazine reports that the inmates participating in the Butner studies were under significant pressure to admit to having sexually assaulted numerous victims, and that a number of inmates have since stated that their self-reports were fabricated.[36] Notably, one of the Butner study authors has expressed concern that the results of the study have been "misused" to support a claim that the majority of child pornography offenders are also child molesters, a claim that the author characterizes as "not supported by the scientific evidence."[37]

In addition to the Butner studies, government officials repeatedly rely on the "general view" among law enforcement that "possessors of child pornography are invariably actual or potential child sex abusers."[38] A recent memorandum from the Department of Justice stated that "you can talk to any prosecutor or investigator in this area and they will tell you in no uncertain terms that with frightening frequency, investigations of offenders for possession, receipt or distribution offenses ultimately uncover evidence that the offender was also abusing children."[39]

There are reasons to be skeptical of these general impressions from law enforcement about the link between child pornography possession and child molestation. A 2005 study of child pornography possession investigations revealed that in 84 percent of cases investigators did not detect either child sex abuse or attempted child sex abuse.[40] One might wonder why law enforcement's general impressions diverge from the social science evidence; perhaps it is because situations involving both child pornography possession and child molestation are more salient to law enforcement than situations involving possession alone. That is to say, officers are more likely to recall situations involving possession and molestation and thus overestimate the frequency with which it occurs. The difference between these general impressions and the actual rate of possessors engaging in abuse may also be attributable to the fact that officers may have "strong suspicions" about whether a possessor is also victimizing children but are unable to locate evidence to support those suspicions.[41]

3. Possession Is as Bad As or Worse Than Abuse

The third argument in favor of focusing criminal justice resources on child pornography possessors is that child pornography possession is as serious as or worse than other child exploitation crimes. Unlike the market theory argument and the risk argument, this argument does not target criminal justice resources at possession cases as a way to indirectly reduce the creation of child pornography, nor as a way to prevent child molestation. Instead this argument justifies the focus on child pornography possession on its own terms, often by repeating statements from victims that suggest that those who possess child pornography images inflict greater harm on them than did the people who created the images.[42] A recent memorandum from the Department of Justice's Child Exploitation and Obscenity Section, for example, quoted one child pornography victim as saying, "I'm more upset about the pictures on the Internet than I am about what [the defendant] did to me physically." It quoted another as saying "thinking about all those sick perverts viewing my body being ravished and hurt like that makes me feel like I was raped by each and every one of them."[43]

That some victims of child pornography believe that the viewing of child pornography is more harmful than the sexual abuse they suffered when the images were created is a powerful, emotional argument in favor of focusing child pornography resources on child pornography possession, even at the expense of pursuing those who create and distribute such images. After all, criminal justice resources should be focused on the most serious crimes, and the amount of harm a crime inflicts on the victim is a primary measure of serious a crime is.

But we should hesitate before we allow the statements of these victims to dictate criminal justice policy. For one thing, the harm of child pornography possession described by the victims is often framed in terms of the psychological harm to the victim that these images have been widely circulated and viewed by many individuals.[44] If it is the widespread circulation that harms child pornography victims the most, then instead of targeting possessors it would be more effective to target those who *distribute* these images to large numbers of individuals.[45]

For another, although individual victims may perceive the crime of child pornography possession as being equivalent to or worse than child sex abuse, that does not appear to be a widely held belief. As noted above, there are several jurisdictions that classify the possession of child pornography as deserving the same punishment as the creation of child pornography. But those jurisdictions are outliers. Most states classify the creation and distribution of child pornography as more serious crimes than possession. And many states treat the sexual assault of a child as one of the most serious crimes possible. Indeed, although the Supreme Court has since declared the practice unconstitutional, a number of states historically imposed the death penalty for the rape of a child.[46] Although these criminal laws are the result of representative governments rather than public referenda, they are much more reliable indicators of the public perception of crime seriousness than are statements by an individual crime victim.

Finally, this argument may have the unintended consequence of perpetuating the underreporting of sex crimes. That is because the harm of child pornography is often described as exacerbating the harm to victims of child sex abuse because the images of that abuse may haunt them for years to come.[47] There is little doubt that having images of sexual abuse circulated and viewed by others is a serious invasion of privacy and an affront to personal dignity; Paul G. Cassell, James R. Marsh, and Jeremy M. Christiansen detail the lasting and serious harms associated with repeated viewings of child pornography in chapter 7. But the idea that these images haunt their child victims may ultimately reinforce the pernicious secrecy associated with child sex abuse. Child sex abuse victims are often subject to repeated abuse at the hands of their abusers. The abuse continues because offenders are able to manipulate their victims into keeping the abuse secret.[48] The claim that viewing child pornography causes more harm to the victims than the sexual abuse when the images were created taps into this pernicious culture of secrecy by perpetuating the idea that allowing others to see pictures of the abuse—that is, revealing the secret of the abuse—is as bad as or worse than the abuse itself.[49]

C. Unintended Consequences of Targeting Possessors

Just as targeting drug users is not the most effective way to combat illegal drugs, focusing criminal justice resources on child pornography possessors is not the best way to protect children from sexual abuse and stop the proliferation of child pornography. Aside from concerns about efficiency, there are two additional arguments that counsel against focusing law enforcement resources on the possession of child pornography. First, because child pornography possession is easier to detect and to prosecute than child sex abuse, law enforcement agencies and prosecutors' offices may already have disproportionately strong incentives to devote more energy to child pornography cases than to child sex abuse cases. Second, because the modern rhetoric surrounding the criminalization and punishment of child pornography crimes conflates child pornography possession and child sex abuse, the public may not be able to accurately assess how law enforcement is focusing its resources, that is, whether they are spending sufficient time and attention on child molestation cases as compared to child pornography cases.

1. *Ease of Enforcement and Prosecution*

There are a number of reasons that child sex abuse cases are more difficult to prosecute than possession of child pornography cases. First, child molestation is, as a general matter, difficult to detect.[50] Law enforcement offices largely rely on reports from individuals to pursue sex abuse cases.[51] There is significant evidence that sex abuse cases are underreported,[52] often because offenders threaten their victims into silence.[53] In contrast, law enforcement can detect those who possess child pornography by tracing IP addresses of those who visit pornographic sites or by engaging in sting operations.[54] In other words, law enforcement need not wait for victims or third parties to report a child pornography crime, but instead they can proactively seek and identify child pornography offenders.

Second, once child sex abuse is detected, there are evidentiary problems associated with pursuing many child molestation cases. Lack of physical evidence, problems with the credibility of child witnesses, or the unwillingness of the victim's family to have their child suffer through the trauma of a trial may convince a prosecutor either to offer a favorable plea bargain or even to dismiss the case altogether.[55] Similar issues rarely arise in possession cases because, once law enforcement obtains a warrant and seizes an offender's computer, the prosecution essentially has all the evidence it needs to obtain a conviction. Prosecutors in child pornography possession cases need not worry about victim credibility or about a victim's willingness to testify.

Because child pornography crimes are easier to detect and easier to prosecute, police and prosecutors have an incentive to devote more resources to child pornography cases than to child molestation cases. Put simply, pursuing child pornography crime results in "more bang" for the law enforcement "buck."[56] While it is difficult to prove that these incentives are actually resulting in law enforcement's prioritizing child pornography cases over child sex abuse cases, the fact that child pornography arrests have increased so dramatically in recent years may be evidence of such incentives.[57] This is especially troubling because the number of child pornography offenses appears to be much lower than other sex offenses involving children.[58] Thus, focusing on child pornography possession may result not only in the prioritization of less serious crime (child pornography possession), it may also result in too few resources for the more commonly committed crime (child sex abuse).

2. *The Role of Public Opinion*

One might think that law enforcement's incentives to prioritize child pornography cases would be overcome by public pressure to combat child molestation. That is because ease of enforcement is not the only issue that the public cares about; they also care about preventing and punishing more serious crimes. For example, while it may be far easier to prosecute traffic and parking violations than murder, public opinion would not permit law enforcement to prioritize traffic tickets above a murder investigation. Similarly, we would expect that public opinion would keep law enforcement from pursuing less serious child pornography cases at the expense of pursuing more serious child sex abuse cases.

Although public opinion ordinarily ensures that more serious crime receives significant law enforcement resources, there is reason to doubt that this is the case with child pornography. The current reporting methods for child pornography prosecutions may mislead the public into overestimating law enforcement's success combating child sex abuse. The public may believe that law enforcement is devoting a lot of resources to combating child sex abuse because reports about enforcement in this area often use the ambiguous term "child sexual exploitation." That term encompasses a wide range of activities, from the possession of child pornography to the sexual molestation of children.[59] Reporting arrest and prosecution statistics using the term "exploitation" obscures whether the offenses at issue are contact offenses, such as molestation, or noncontact offenses, such as the possession of child pornography. Examples of this ambiguity can be seen in reports from both federal and state agencies.[60]

Law enforcement creates further ambiguity when they refer to child pornography possessors as "predators" or "pedophiles."[61] Because those terms are generally understood to refer to individuals who molest children, the public might misunderstand such statements as reports about child molesters, rather than child pornography offenders.

If reporting methods and statements by law enforcement mislead the public into believing that the arrest and prosecution rates associated with child pornography possession are instead associated with child molestation, then public opinion will not act as a counterbalance to law enforcement incentives to pursue the easy child pornography cases. If the public were aware of law enforcement's relatively low success rate in detecting and prosecuting child sex abuse, then there would likely be political pressure on law enforcement to develop more effective techniques to detect and prevent those crimes. But if successes in child pornography cases are portrayed as successes in child sexual abuse cases, then such political pressure will never develop.

D. Conclusion

A large amount of criminal justice resources are currently focused on arresting, prosecuting, and punishing those who possess child pornography. Although campaigns against possession crimes have been criticized in other contexts—most notably in the war on drugs—government actors have been quick to defend the current policies of aggressive enforcement and severe punishment for child pornography possessors. But the arguments in favor of those policies are significantly flawed.

I do not mean to question whether the possession of child pornography ought to be illegal.[62] Because the creation of child pornography requires the sexual exploitation or abuse of children, there is ample reason to prohibit individuals from acquiring those images. My complaint is with the amount of criminal justices resources that are being focused on the possession of child pornography, as compared to the resources focused on the creation of child pornography, the widespread distribution of child pornography, and the many instances of child sex abuse that do not result in the creation of child pornography. Some legal regimes explicitly state that possessing child pornography ought to receive the same punishment as producing or distributing child pornography. And in other legal regimes, statutory sentencing enhancements and plea bargaining practices result in defendants who possess child pornography receiving longer sentences than defendants who sexually molest a child.

The physical, sexual abuse of a child, the creation of child pornography, and the distribution of child pornography are all more serious crimes than the possession of child pornography. Modern American criminal law and the focus of modern criminal justice resources should reflect that reality.

NOTES

1. For data on the increase in federal cases, see BUREAU OF JUSTICE STATISTICS, FEDERAL PROSECUTION OF CHILD SEX EXPLOITATION OFFENDERS, 2006 at 1 (2007) (reporting that the number of federal child pornography cases rose from 169 in 1994 to 2,539 in 2006). State prosecutions have also increased. *Compare* BUREAU OF JUSTICE STATISTICS, PROSECUTORS IN STATE COURTS, 2001 at 5 (2002) (reporting that 30 percent of state prosecutors' offices prosecuted cases involving the transmission of child pornography in the previous twelve months) *with* BUREAU OF JUSTICE STATISTICS, PROSECUTORS IN STATE COURTS, 2005 at 5, tbl. 6 (2006) (reporting that 67 percent of state prosecutors' offices prosecuted cases involving the transmission of child pornography in the previous twelve months).

2. This table was created from data reported in the following sources: U.S. SENTENCING COMMISSION, USE OF GUIDELINES AND SPECIFIC OFFENSE CHARACTERISTICS FISCAL YEAR 2011, at 40–42; U.S. SENTENCING COMMISSION, USE OF GUIDELINES AND SPECIFIC OFFENSE CHARACTERISTICS FISCAL YEAR 2007, at 35–37; U.S. SENTENCING COMMISSION, USE OF GUIDELINES AND SPECIFIC OFFENSE CHARACTERISTICS FISCAL YEAR 2005, at 34–36. Some percentages do not add to 100 percent because of rounding.

3. *See generally* Carissa Byrne Hessick, *Disentangling Child Pornography from Child Sex Abuse*, 88 WASH. U. L. REV. 853, 856–64 (2011) (documenting the modern trend of increasing criminal penalties for child pornography possession).

4. *See* 18 U.S.C. § 2252(b) (1990).

5. *See* Child Pornography Prevention Act of 1996, Pub. L. No. 104-208, § 121(5), 110 Stat. 3009-26, 3009-30, *invalidated by* Ashcroft v. Free Speech Coal., 535 U.S. 234 (2002).

6. *See* PROTECT Act, Pub. L. No. 108-21, § 103(a)(1)(B)(i), 117 Stat. 650, 652 (2003) (codified as amended at 18 U.S.C. § 2252(b)(1)). The maximum penalty was increased from fifteen to twenty years for "receiving" child pornography. The legislation also increased the maximum penalty for possession from five to ten years. PROTECT Act § 103(a)(1)(C)(i). Because receipt is a necessary component for possession, it is the

twenty-year maximum penalty that represents the true exposure for offenders who possess child pornography.

7. Mark Hansen, *A Reluctant Rebellion*, A.B.A. J., June 2009.

8. Hessick, *supra* note 3, at 857–59 (collecting sources).

9. H.R. 161, 54th Leg., Reg. Sess. (Mont. 1995) (codified as amended at MONT. CODE ANN. § 45-5-625(2)(c) (2009)).

10. H.R. 462, 2003 Gen. Assem., Reg. Sess. (Ga. 2003) (codified at GA. CODE ANN. § 16-12-100 (2003)).

11. ARIZ. REV. STAT. ANN. § 13-3553 (2010); KAN. STAT. ANN. § 21-3516(c) (2007); MISS. CODE ANN. §§ 97-5-33, 97-5-35 (2006); OKLA. STAT. tit. 21, § 1021.2 (2002); S.D. CODIFIED LAWS § 22-24A-3 (2006); UTAH CODE ANN. § 76-5a-3 (2010). Wyoming treats subsequent child pornography possession offenses the same as subsequent convictions for manufacture or distribution of child pornography, though it distinguishes between possession and manufacture and distribution for first offenses. WYO. STAT. ANN. § 6-4-303(d), (e) (2009).

12. ARK. CODE. ANN. § 5-27-602 (2006); LA. REV. STAT. ANN. § 14:81.1(A)(2), (E)(3) (2004).

The federal statutory scheme is complicated. 18 U.S.C. § 2252(a) (2006) prohibits four distinct categories of conduct: (1) transporting or shipping child pornography in interstate or foreign commerce; (2) receiving or distributing child pornography that has been mailed, shipped, or transported in interstate or foreign commerce; (3) selling, or possessing with intent to sell, child pornography that has been mailed or shipped in interstate or foreign commerce; and (4) knowingly possessing child pornography that has moved in interstate or foreign commerce. The statute appears to treat simple possession less harshly than other conduct, as it is punishable by a maximum sentence of ten years with no mandatory minimum, 18 U.S.C. § 2252(b)(2), while the other three categories are punishable by a minimum sentence of five years and a maximum sentence of twenty years, 18 U.S.C. § 2252(b)(1). But in reality most possessors of child pornography are subject to the five- to twenty-year sentence for "receiving" because most child pornography is found on the Internet and it "is generally necessary to receive pornography in order to possess it." United States v. Sudyka, No. 8:07CR383, 2008 WL 1766765, at *8 (D. Neb. Apr. 14, 2008).

13. For example, Connecticut differentiates between various degrees of possession based on the number of images an offender possesses. *See* CONN. GEN. STATS. § 53a-196f (possessing child pornography in the third degree; Class D felony; fewer than twenty images; minimum one year imprisonment); CONN. GEN. STATS. § 53a-196e (possessing child pornography in the second degree; Class C felony; between twenty and forty-nine images; minimum two years imprisonment); CONN. GEN. STATS. § 53a-196d (possessing child pornography in the first degree; Class B felony; fifty or more images; minimum five years imprisonment). And the federal sentencing scheme also provides for sentencing increases based on the number of images possessed. USSG §2G2.2(b)(7).

14. ALASKA STAT. §11.61.127(c); ARIZ. REV. STAT. §§ 13-3551(11), -3553(A)(2); FL. STAT. ANN. § 827.071(5); TENN. CODE ANN. § 39-17-1003(b), (d); UTAH CODE ANN. § 76-5a-3(3).

15. ARIZ. REV. STAT. ANN. § 13-705(D) (2010) (possession of child pornography that depicts a minor under the age of fifteen is subject to a mandatory minimum sentence of ten years' imprisonment). The state provides the same penalties for possession of child

pornography as it does for "molestation of a child, commercial sexual exploitation of a minor, . . . aggravated luring a minor for sexual exploitation, child abuse [and] kidnapping" of a child. *Id.*; State v. Berger, 134 P.3d 378 (Ariz. 2006).

16. ARIZ. REV. STAT. ANN. § 13-705(M) (2010) ("The sentence imposed on a person . . . shall be consecutive to any other sentence imposed on the person at any time. . . .").

17. *Berger*, 134 P.3d at 379.

18. Supplemental Brief for Appellant, State v. Berger, 134 P.3d 378 (Ariz. 2006) (No. CR-05-0101), 2006 WL 1002320 at *1–2.

19. TROY STABENOW, FED. PUB. DEFENDER OFFICE, DECONSTRUCTING THE MYTH OF CAREFUL STUDY: A PRIMER ON THE FLAWED PROGRESSION OF THE CHILD PORNOGRAPHY GUIDELINES 26–29 (rev. ed. 2009), *available at* http://www.fd.org/pdf_lib/childpornjulyrevision.pdf.

20. *See* MARK C. DONOVAN, TAKING AIM: TARGET POPULATIONS AND THE WARS ON AIDS AND DRUGS 36 (2001); Michael Schecter, *Fear and Loathing and the Forfeiture Laws*, 75 CORNELL L. REV. 1151, 1151 n.2 (1990).

21. *See, e.g.*, THE SENTENCING PROJECT, DISPARITY BY GEOGRAPHY: THE WAR ON DRUGS IN AMERICA'S CITIES 31 (2008); Michèle Alexandre, *Sex, Drugs, Rock & Roll and Moral Dirigisme: Toward a Reformation of Drug and Prostitution Regulations*, 78 UMKC L. REV. 101, 108 (2009); Alex Kreit, *Beyond the Prohibition Debate: Thoughts on Federal Drug Laws in an Age of State Reforms*, 13 CHAP. L. REV. 555, 579 (2010).

22. *See* Samuel R. Gross & Katherine Y. Barnes, *Road Work: Racial Profiling and Drug Interdiction on the Highway*, 101 MICH. L. REV. 651, 698 (2002).

23. *E.g.*, Kreit, *supra* note 21, at 579 (noting that the Office of National Drug Control Policy has made it a point to emphasize that the federal government rarely targets drug users); ARIZONA SENTENCING REPORT, Top 5 Myths About Arizona's Sentencing Laws, available at http://azsentencing.org/component/content/article/35-services/112-top-myths-about-arizona-sentencing-laws#myth3 (last visited Sept. 9, 2013) ("Fewer than 100 of the roughly 40,000 inmates in our prison system are there for possessing drugs—and most of these convicts pled their cases down from more serious offenses. All other drug offenders in our prisons are there for narcotics trafficking, a serious crime with enormous economic and societal costs.").

24. *See* ALEXANDRA GELBER, U.S. DEP'T OF JUSTICE, RESPONSE TO "A RELUCTANT REBELLION" (2009), *available at* http://www.justice.gov/criminal/ceos/downloads/ReluctantRebellionResponse.pdf; Daisy Flores, *Why Arizona Is Tough on Child Pornography*, ARIZONA SENTENCING REPORT, *available at* http://azsentencing.org/issues/118-arizona-is-tough-on-child-pornography (last visited Sept. 9, 2013).

25. *See, e.g.*, Osborne v. Ohio, 495 U.S. 103, 110 (1990); *see also* SUZANNE OST, CHILD PORNOGRAPHY AND SEXUAL GROOMING: LEGAL AND SOCIETAL RESPONSES 114–15 (2009) (collecting sources making this argument).

26. *See* PHILIP JENKINS, BEYOND TOLERANCE: CHILD PORNOGRAPHY ON THE INTERNET 91 (2001); OST, *supra* note 25, at 113.

27. *See* OST, *supra* note 25, at 116.

28. *E.g.*, GELBER, *supra* note 24, at 4 ("[W]hat is the point of any pornography if not to stoke the fires of sexual desire."); *see also* Hessick, *supra* note 3, at 871–72 (collecting sources making this argument).

29. *See* Hessick, *supra* note 3, at 882 (collecting sources making this argument).

30. GELBER, *supra* note 24, at 6.

31. *See, e.g.*, OST, *supra* note 25, at 108–13; Melissa Hamilton, *The Child Pornography Crusade and Its Net-Widening Effect*, 33 CARDOZO L. REV. 1679, 1694–1716 (2012); Hessick, *supra* note 3, at 873–80, 882–86; Neil Malamuth & Mark Huppin, *Drawing the Line on Virtual Child Pornography: Bringing the Law in Line with the Research Evidence*, 31 N.Y.U. REV. L. & SOC. CHANGE 773 (2007); Michael C. Seto & Angela W. Eke, *The Criminal Histories and Later Offending of Child Pornography Offenders*, 17 SEXUAL ABUSE 201 (2005).

32. *See* Hamilton, *supra* note 31, at 1699–1703 (collecting numerous examples of how these studies have been used to justify the modern criminal justice focus on child pornography possession as protecting children from child sex abuse). For two specific examples of such justifications, see GELBER, *supra* note 24, at 6; Flores, *supra* note 24.

33. The first study reported that 76 percent of offenders had molested children, with an average of 30.5 victims per offender; the second reported that 85 percent of offenders had molested children, with an average of 13.56 victims per offender. *See* ANDRES E. HERNANDEZ, FED. BUREAU OF PRISONS, SELF-REPORTED CONTACT SEXUAL OFFENSES BY PARTICIPANTS IN THE FEDERAL BUREAU OF PRISON'S SEX OFFENDER TREATMENT PROGRAM: IMPLICATIONS FOR INTERNET SEX OFFENDERS (2000), available at http://www.ccoso.org/library articles/Hernandez et al ATSA 2000.pdf; Michael L. Bourke & Andres E. Hernandez, *The "Butner Study" Redux: A Report on the Incidence of Hands-On Child Victimization by Child Pornography Offenders*, 24 J. FAM. VIOLENCE 183 (2009).

34. *See* Rachel Aviv, *The Science of Sex Abuse*, THE NEW YORKER (Jan. 14, 2013); Michael C. Seto, et al., *Contact Sexual Offending By Men Arrested for Child Pornography Offenses*, 23 SEXUAL ABUSE: A JOURNAL OF RESEARCH AND TREATMENT 124 (2011).

35. *See* Hamilton, *supra* note 31, at 1703–10 (cataloging a serious of shortcomings with the study).

36. *See* Aviv, *supra* note 34.

37. ANDRES E. HERNANDEZ, PSYCHOLOGICAL AND BEHAVIORAL CHARACTERISTICS OF CHILD PORNOGRAPHY OFFENDERS IN TREATMENT 4–5 (2009), available at http:// www.iprc.unc.edu/G8/Hernandez_position_paper_Global_Symposium.pdf.

38. OST, *supra* note 25, at 111 (collecting sources).

39. GELBER, *supra* note 24, at 7.

40. JANIS WOLAK ET AL., NAT'L CTR. FOR MISSING & EXPLOITED CHILDREN, CHILD-PORNOGRAPHY POSSESSORS ARRESTED IN INTERNET-RELATED CRIMES: FINDINGS FROM THE NATIONAL JUVENILE ONLINE VICTIMIZATION STUDY 17 (2005), *available at* http://www.missingkids. com/en_US/publications/NC144.pdf.

41. *See id.*

42. *See* Hessick, *supra* note 3, at 866 (collecting sources making this argument).

43. GELBER, *supra* note 24, at 3.

44. *E.g.*, GELBER, *supra* note 24, at 3, 18; Paul G. Cassell, James Marsh, and Jeremy M. Christiansen, *The Case for Full Restitution for Child Pornography Victims*, 82 GEO. WASH. L. REV. 61, 70–71 (2013).

45. *Cf.* United States v. Laraneta, 700 F.3d 983, 991–92 (7th Cir. 2012) (noting that in the context of restitution, unlike a distributor of child pornography, it is unclear what harm a child pornography possessor inflicts on the victim).

46. *See* Kennedy v. Louisiana, 554 U.S. 407, 422–23 *as modified* (Oct. 1, 2008), *opinion modified on denial of reh'g*, 554 U.S. 945 (2008).

47. *See, e.g.*, New York v. Ferber, 458 U.S. 747, 759–60 & n.10 (1982).

48. "Abused children are often told not to disclose [the sex abuse] to anyone. . . . Secrecy is usually reinforced by violence, threats of violence or punishment. Sometimes we find a mixture of threats and bribery where the secondary gain of bribes and of special treatment maintains the secrecy, which is nonetheless basically founded on threats." TILMAN FURNISS, THE MULTI-PROFESSIONAL HANDBOOK OF CHILD SEXUAL ABUSE 24 (1991); *see also* CARLA VAN DAM, THE SOCIALLY SKILLED CHILD MOLESTER: DIFFERENTIATING THE GUILTY FROM THE FALSELY ACCUSED 84 (2006); Amy Hammel-Zabin, *The Mind of a Child Molester*, PSYCHOL. TODAY, July 1, 2003, http://www.psychologytoday.com/articles/200306/the-mind-child-molester.

49. Corey Rayburn Yung has made a related observation with respect to the modern discussion of rape being a fate worse than death, that is, that "the rhetoric comparing death to rape contributes to a cultural norm built upon Victorian artifacts that elevates wom[e]n's chastity to the very essence of their identity." Corey Rayburn, *Better Dead than R(ap)ed?: The Patriarchal Rhetoric Driving Capital Rape Statutes*, 78 ST. JOHN'S L. REV. 1119, 1154 (2004).

50. *See* HOWARD N. SNYDER, BUREAU OF JUSTICE STATISTICS, SEXUAL ASSAULT OF YOUNG CHILDREN AS REPORTED TO LAW ENFORCEMENT: VICTIM, INCIDENT, AND OFFENDER CHARACTERISTICS 11 (2000), *available at* http://bjs.ojp.usdoj.gov/content/pub/pdf/saycrle.pdf [hereinafter SEXUAL ASSAULT OF YOUNG CHILDREN] (reporting a 27 percent arrest rate); TIM TATE, CHILD PORNOGRAPHY: AN INVESTIGATION 109–10 (1990) (suggesting that only 1 percent of all child sex abusers are "caught and sentenced").

51. *See* WOLAK ET AL., *supra* note 40, at 14 (reporting that 98 percent of sexual victimization cases originated as a report to law enforcement by an individual, as compared to 57 percent of child pornography possession cases).

52. *See* Catherine Rylyk, Note, *Lest We Regress to the Dark Ages: Holding Voluntary Surgical Castration Cruel and Unusual, Even for Child Molesters*, 16 WM. & MARY BILL RTS. J. 1305, 1305 n.5 (2008) (noting that "child molestation remains one of the most underreported crimes" and that one study reported that less than 11 percent of all incidents are ever disclosed).

53. *See, e.g.*, FURNISS, *supra* note 48, at 39.

54. *See* WOLAK ET AL., *supra* note 40, at 13–14 (reporting that 43 percent of U.S. child pornography possession cases in 2000 "originated with investigations by law enforcement" as compared to 2 percent of child sex abuse cases).

55. For example, in 2006, federal prosecutors declined to prosecute more than half of the child sex abuse cases that were referred to them, as opposed to only a 38 percent declination rate for child pornography referrals, FEDERAL PROSECUTION OF CHILD SEX EXPLOITATION OFFENDERS, *supra* note 1, at tbl.2, and the reasons given for declining prosecution were more likely to be concerns about weak evidence in child sex abuse cases than in child pornography cases, *id.* at 3 ("More than half of sex abuse declinations were due to weak evidence. In comparison, weak evidence was stated as the reason for 24 percent of declinations for child pornography.").

56. *See* William H. Stuntz, *Race, Class and Drugs*, 98 COLUM. L. REV. 1795, 1799, 1819–24 (1998) (explaining that the cost of different enforcement strategies and scarce resources is a factor that results in law enforcement targeting of the street-level crack trade instead of more upscale drug markets).

57. *Cf.* Hamilton, *supra* note 31, at 1691–92 (documenting dramatic increases in enforcement and noting that the "vast majority" of cases involve nonproduction child pornography offenses).

58. *See* DAVID FINKELHOR & RICHARD ORMROD, U.S. DEP'T OF JUSTICE, OFFICE OF JUVENILE JUSTICE AND DELINQUENCY PREVENTION, JUVENILE JUSTICE BULLETIN 6 (2004), *available at* http://www.ncjrs.gov/pdffiles1/ojjdp/204911.pdf ("Crimes involving pornography and juvenile victims . . . are relatively infrequent . . . . [T]he estimated 2,900 incidents in 2000 are dwarfed by reports of overall sex crimes against juveniles, which can be roughly estimated at 269,000 for the same period.").

59. *E.g.*, FEDERAL PROSECUTION OF CHILD SEX EXPLOITATION, *supra* note 1, at 1 (defining "[f]ederal child sex exploitation offenses" to include "child pornography, sex transportation, and sex abuse"); *FAQ: Child Sexual Exploitation*, NAT'L CTR. FOR MISSING & EXPLOITED CHILDREN, http://www.missingkids.com/missingkids/servlet/PageServlet?LanguageCountry=en_US&PageId=2815 (last visited Jan. 23, 2011) (defining term as including "Possession, Manufacture, and Distribution of Child Pornography; Enticement of Children for Sexual Acts; Child Prostitution; Child Sex Tourism; Child Sexual Molestation"). There appears to be a movement within the child advocacy community to use the term "child sexual exploitation" as a substitute for "child pornography" because the latter term is thought to insufficiently "describe the true nature and extent of sexually exploitive images of child victims." WOLAK ET AL., *supra* note 40, at vii n.1.

60. *See, e.g.*, DEP'T OF JUSTICE, FACT SHEET SUPPORTING STATE AND LOCAL LAW ENFORCEMENT ACCOMPLISHMENTS 2001–2008 (2008), *available at* http://www.ojp.usdoj.gov/newsroom/pressreleases/2008/psc08–993.htm (describing the Internet Crimes Against Children (ICAC) task force program, which "supports law enforcement's efforts to prevent, investigate, and stop computer-facilitated child sexual exploitation" and discussing arrest rates); DEP'T OF JUSTICE, FACT SHEET: PROJECT SAFE CHILDHOOD (2008), *available at* http://www.ojp.usdoj.gov/ newsroom/pressreleases/2008/doj08845.htm (describing arrest rates and funding amounts for the ICAC program in efforts to stop "sexual crimes against children"); Dan Miller, *Child Exploitation Units Apprehend Online Predators*, COUNTY NEWS (Wash., D.C.), Feb. 14, 2005, at 2, *available at* http://www.naco.org/newsroom/countynews/archives/ documents/2005/cnews-feb14–05.pdf.

61. *See, e.g.*, Deborah J. Daniels, Remarks at the Conference on Child and Family Maltreatment (Jan. 28, 2004) (transcript available at http://www.ojp.usdoj.gov/archives/speeches/2004/ confonchildabuse.htm) (reporting arrest rates for "Internet-based child sexual exploitation" and noting that every "such arrest means that untold numbers of innocent children will be protected from abuse" at the hands of "pedophiles"); *see also* Miller, *supra* note 60, at 2 (describing a person who distributes child pornography as a "predator").

62. When individuals questioned these aggressive policies in the past, the Department of Justice sought to undermine such criticism by stating that "[a]t its heart, the current criticism of child pornography sentences is not really about the sentence imposed on these defendants, but rather whether [this activity] . . . should be viewed as a crime at all." GELBER, *supra* note 24, at 15. This response is troubling because it suggests that one cannot question the severity of punishment specifically, or the allocation of criminal justice resources more generally, without being accused of possessing a decriminalization agenda.

6 | The Dignitary Harm of Child Pornography—From Producers to Possessors

Audrey Rogers

Human dignity is offended by the pornographer. American law does not protect all human dignity; legally, an adult can consent to its diminishment. When a child is made the target of the pornographer-photographer, the statute will not suffer the insult to the human spirit, that the child should be treated as a thing.[1]

This chapter addresses the harm inflicted by child pornographers on their victims. It discusses both the producers and nonproducers or downstream users of pornographic images, describing the different and similar harms their actions inflict. The chapter begins with definitions of the various actors involved in child pornography, because current law ties harm and punishment to these categories. It explains the historical development of the different categories of downstream actors in the child pornography market and their concomitant sentencing structure.

The chapter then identifies the ways technology has blurred the categories of pornographers so that different punishment among nonproducers has become difficult to support. In particular, it notes that child pornography possessors are no longer easily distinguished from those who receive or distribute child pornography. Thus while much scholarly and judicial criticism has been directed at sentences for possessors, this focus risks clouding a full discussion of appropriate punishment for nonproducing child pornographers. A better approach examines these downstream users as a whole and how they inflict injury on the child depicted in the images. Essentially, the thesis of this chapter is that harm is inherent in the images themselves since their very existence violates the privacy and dignity of the depicted child. Thus even if a downstream child pornographer does not inflict physical or emotional injuries in the creation of an image, he has nonetheless harmed the depicted child. The injury he causes by being an integral part of the image's circulation is what merits his punishment.

A. Categorizing Pornographers

The federal child pornography statutes divide participants in child pornography into two main groups: producers and nonproducers or downstream users. Downstream users are distributors (which cover transporters), receivers, and possessors.[2] Producers are punished the most severely, with a mandatory minimum of fifteen years imprisonment.[3] Distributors and receivers are subject to a mandatory five-year minimum; there is no mandatory minimum for possessors.[4]

Congress defines "producing" as "producing, directing, manufacturing, issuing, publishing, or advertising."[5] The statutes do not define the other participants, but the federal sentencing guidelines provide some assistance.[6] For example, its commentary defines "distribution" for the purpose of calculating sentences as any act "related to the transfer of material involving the sexual exploitation of a minor."[7] These acts include "posting material involving the sexual exploitation of a minor on a website for public viewing but does not include the mere solicitation of such material."[8]

With respect the definitions of "receipt" and "possession," we need some background history to understand what they mean. In 1977, Congress passed the first child pornography statutes to stop the trafficking of child pornography for commercial purposes by banning the producing, distributing, and receiving of obscene images.[9] The Sentencing Commission, charged with establishing guidelines for calculating sentences within the statutory mandates, labeled transporting, receiving, or distributing offenses as "trafficking" in child pornography.[10]

Congress later removed the obscenity and commercial purpose requirements because it found them to be unnecessary limitations on the reach of the law.[11] Congressional hearings also revealed that production of child pornography was so clandestine that between 1978 and 1984, only one person was convicted for producing child pornography.[12] Thus stopping the flow rather the production of child pornography became the focus of prosecutions.

Congress did not ban possession until 1990, after the Supreme Court ruled it was constitutionally permissible to prohibit private possession.[13] Accordingly, the Sentencing Commission created a sentencing guideline for possession with a lower sentencing range than the other offenses. It also aligned the receipt offense guideline with the lower possession guidelines because it determined that "receipt is a logical predicate to possession."[14] This move was rejected by Congress on the ground that receipt was more akin to distribution.[15] One member of Congress explained: "Virtually all enforcement of the child pornography laws is accomplished through sting operations through the mails. As a result, most offenders (even active distributors) are caught in the act of receiving child pornography out of their mail box. . . . Distributors who are apprehended are likely to be caught in the act of receipt."[16]

Despite congressional opposition, the perceived similarity between receipt and possession has continued. In its 1996 report to Congress, the Commission detailed that some courts were sentencing receipt cases as possession cases because there was little difference in the perceived seriousness of the offenses.[17] In its 2012 report, the Commission unanimously recommended that receipt and possession offenses be punished the same.[18] It explained that the law enforcement rationale was outmoded as most offenders are using the Internet and not the mail.[19]

The question remains: What does "possession" (and by extension "receipt") mean? Courts have used a plain meaning definition that covers both physical and constructive possession.[20] Constructive possession means typically to have "dominion and control" over an item.[21] For example, one can actually hold a picture of child pornography in his hand, or have it locked in a desk to which he has the key. He would be in possession of the image in either instance.[22] Similarly, one constructively possesses a computer image when he exerts dominion and control over it, as evidenced by acts such as saving it, sending it, or manipulating it.[23]

With the vast increase in computer use to obtain and view child pornography, new issues have emerged over what it means to be a possessor, receiver, or distributor. Computer technology has made file sharing and on-line discussions increasingly popular.[24] The number of computers that are networked has grown explosively, from one million in 1992[25] to more than two billion by 2011.[26] A large proportion of personal computers regularly connect to the Internet to communicate and receive information through no-cost, decentralized, peer-to-peer file sharing.[27] The ability to seek, download, and share files has completely changed the landscape for many industries, notably the legitimate entertainment world. It has had the same dramatic impact in the child pornography arena.[28] One file-sharing network alone reported receiving 116,000 requests for child pornography in 2010.[29]

As file-sharing networks have proliferated, participants in the child pornography industry can no longer be defined by terms more suited for a bricks-and-mortar world. Forty years ago, when investigative reporters first exposed the child pornography market, it was clear who fell into the categories of transporters, distributors, and receivers. For example, the defendant in *New York v. Ferber* was the owner of an adult bookstore who knowingly sold films of underage boys masturbating.[30] Once sold, those films were no longer available for Ferber to resell.[31] In contrast, consider the person today who uploads a child pornography video to a peer-to-peer network and then leaves his file open. The video is never depleted; even if someone downloads it, the original is still available for further downloads. The ramifications of this new technology are causing a collapse of easily definable offenses, and with it the rationale behind charging and sentencing differences.

Prosecutors who find child pornography on a person's computer often file receiving and possessing charges.[32] Defendants convicted of both have increasingly claimed violations of their Fifth Amendment double jeopardy right because the two statutory provisions proscribe the same conduct.[33] As one defendant claimed, "[i]t is impossible to 'receive' something without, at least at the very instant of 'receipt,' also 'possessing' it."[34] Some courts agree that the multiple charges are duplicitous,[35] but with defendants using computers to obtain quantities of images via the Internet, it appears quite easy for the government to fashion a case that avoids the prohibition on double jeopardy by basing the receipt count on different images than the possession count.[36]

Yet it is questionable whether filing separate charges is appropriate when the statutes themselves no longer reflect clear divisions of activity. It is outmoded to find, as some courts have, that those who traffic in child pornography by receiving it "are more directly tied to the market for such products" and the abuse of children necessary for that market than are possessors.[37] When a receiver and a possessor are one and the same person, and the actions he takes to obtain the images are also identical to the actions that constitute possession, this division is no longer appropriate.[38] A child is harmed because the image is circulated, but the offender who uses technology to both receive and possess the image cannot be said to be more entrenched in the market by his receipt than by his possession of the image.

Peer-to-peer networks are also blurring the distinction between distributing and receiving child pornography. In one case, a defendant downloaded images and videos from a peer-to-peer network and stored them in a shared folder on his computer that was accessible to others.[39] Arguing that he merely left open his shared file, defendant sought to have his conviction for distribution set aside. The court rejected his contention, holding the knowing passive distribution of child pornography from a shared network was sufficient to sustain the conviction.[40] It made an analogy to a self-serve gas station where the gas station owner who advertises his product need not actively pump gas to be in the business of distributing it.

Other courts have begun to recognize the overlap between offenses caused by technology. The Third Circuit affirmed a sentence that substantially deviated from the guidelines in a case where the defendant traded via the Internet a number of images of child pornography.[41] Rejecting the government's appeal of the sentence, the court found the deviation was appropriate because it agreed that the case "center[ed] on personal possession of illicit images obtained online, and involving no production or distribution other than noncommercial bartering," notwithstanding the defendant's guilty plea on the transporting and receiving counts.[42] Most recently, the Sentencing Commission has reported that not all distributors are the same; it distinguished those who traded images through active participation in child pornography communities via chats, e-mails and closed peer-to-peer networks from those who traded passively through open peer-to peer networks.[43] Finding the former more culpable that the latter, the Commission recommended a new enhancement based on an offender's "community involvement."[44]

This area of the law is in a great state of flux and controversy. The once-clear divisions between distribution, transportation, and receipt are blurred in cyberspace. Whereas many courts and scholars have criticized sentences for possession of child pornography, it is no longer clear what differentiates a possessor from a receiver or distributor. Further complicating the issue over the appropriate punishment for possessors is that multicount indictments often result in plea agreements solely for possession when the conduct included knowing receipt or distribution.[45] Statistics show that more than 92 percent of offenders convicted only of possession also knowingly received the materials, and more than 65 percent distributed child pornography.[46] Receipt by peer-to-peer networks was 56 percent in 2010, while distribution using this technology was more than 73 percent; by early 2012 these numbers rose to 54.3 percent and 85.3 percent respectively.[47] Thus, even without technological changes, critics of possession sentences may be focusing too narrowly on end results rather than looking at the offender's conduct in total. How nonproduction offenders should be punished, and whether they should be punished differently, needs to be tied to something more than their labels and final dispositions.[48] We must ground meaningful scrutiny in the rationale for the ban on child pornography: the harm to the children depicted.

B. The Harm of Child Pornography

1. *Producers*

Child pornography producers harm children by inflicting physical or psychological injury. In *New York v. Ferber*, the seminal case banning child pornography, the Supreme Court stated that the "use of children as subjects of pornographic materials is harmful to the physiological, emotional, and mental health of the child."[49] It stressed that the government interest in preventing the "sexual abuse and exploitation of children" is of the highest importance. In a counterfactual scenario, the Supreme Court ruled in *Ashcroft v. Free Speech Coalition* that the ban on child pornography did not extend to computer-generated images because there were no real children harmed in its creation. As more fully discussed below, in addition to the physical or psychological injury a child suffers at the time of the making of the image, the *Ferber* Court explained that disseminating child pornography was "intrinsically related to the sexual abuse of children . . . the materials produced are a permanent record of the children's participation and the harm to the child is exacerbated by their circulation."[50]

Studies of victimized children support the rationale behind the ban on child pornography to stop sexual abuse and exploitation.[51] As to sexual abuse, some children incur physical injuries such as genital bruising, cuts, lacerations, and sexually transmitted diseases.[52] The children may suffer psychological injuries including depression, anger, withdrawal, low self-esteem, and feelings of worthlessness.[53] As detailed below, they often engage in self-destructive behavior including substance abuse, prostitution, depression, and suicide.[54] The 2012 Sentencing Commission report reaffirmed the harm child pornography inflicts on its victims at all stages. Some images are of children clearly in pain or distress as they are being violently sexually abused.

However, many depictions do not show children in distress because the producers exploit the children to appear willing and happy to participate in the sexual abuse.[55] The groomer shows images of children apparently "enjoying" themselves to coax other children into engaging in sex. Producers use a variety of methods to get children to participate in the production of pornographic images including threats, coercion, and payment of drugs, money, or alcohol.[56] These means can cause psychological harm, because the children can feel guilty that they appear to be willing participants.[57] This harm, however, may only appear later when the child realizes he has been manipulated. No one suggests, of course, that grooming a child somehow makes the child less of a victim of abuse or exploitation. A child cannot legally consent to participating in the creation of child pornography; therefore, using trickery, grooming, deception or threats to obtain consent falls within the plain meaning of the word "exploitation."

This leads to the issue of whether surreptitiously recorded images or images created by manipulating a picture of a child to make him or her appear to be engaging in sexually explicit conduct constitute child pornography. The *Ashcroft* Court left open the issue of whether "morphed" images created by combining real and computer-generated children was subject to the ban on producing child pornography, although it noted that "they implicate the interests of real children and are in that sense closer to the images in *Ferber*."[58] Lower courts have held that both constitute child pornography.[59]

Morphed or surreptitiously made images may not be the product of physical child abuse, but they are the product of sexual exploitation. The producer is using the child and the child is participating, albeit unknowingly, in creating child pornography. Nevertheless, some of this book's contributors suggest that such images should fall outside the definition of child pornography because they do not memorialize an act of sexual abuse.[60] This stance would improperly limit protections against exploitation. Consider the images banned in *Ferber*, that of boys masturbating. Why should it matter whether the boys were acting at the prompting of the producer or were taped without their knowledge? Their injury manifests later in the form of harm to their emotional and psychological health when they realize they have been used, even if the victim does not suffer either physical or psychological injury *at the time of production*.

Moreover, if we exclude surreptitious taping as not constituting exploitation because of lack of immediate psychological injury, could we not say the same for victims groomed by candy? They, too, are not aware they are being victimized at the time, although they are engaging in the act at the behest of the producer. Some judicial language suggests that the ban is meant to protect children from being "made to engage in sexual conduct."[61] That language could imply some awareness by the child of the abuse. But it could equally mean protecting the child from being used in any sexually explicit image. For example, a child who is sexually molested while asleep is not "made to engage" in the conduct since he or she is unaware it is occurring; we would not say images of such molestation falls outside the definition of child pornography simply because the child was asleep. Thus we have a continuum from explicit threats and use of force, to grooming, to sleeping, to surreptitious taping. If the images meet the legal definition of child pornography,[62] the producers' methods of getting the images should be irrelevant since the child has been abused or exploited.

Professor Hessick suggests the term "exploitation" be limited to "force, coercion, or lack of consent."[63] She further limits lack of consent to scenarios where the child is prompted by another to engage in the activity, thereby excluding surreptitiously or self-created child pornography. Moreover, she requires that the exploitation or abuse exist independently of the recording itself. In other words, abusing or exploiting a child for the purpose of creating child pornography falls outside her definition of exploitation or abuse. This "independent purpose" limitation does not appear in any Supreme Court child pornography cases. More importantly, it leaves unprotected the multitude of children abused and exploited specifically created to meet the commercial and noncommercial market of child pornography.

The sexual abuse or exploitation inflicted by a producer is a traumatic event that is a "psychosocial stressor."[64] The effects of the trauma include "(1) a clustering of disturbing psychological phenomena of intrusive and repetitive imagery associated with memories of the traumatic event and (2) avoidance strategies employed to keep associations to the trauma out of awareness."[65] Furthermore "when the event is remembered, the attendant feelings are neutralized, and the anxiety generated by the event is controlled."[66] In addition, "[w]hen a traumatic event is not resolved and either remains in active memory or becomes defended by a cognitive mechanism such as denial, dissociation, or splitting," the diagnosis is generally post traumatic stress disorder (PTSD).[67] A child who has symptoms of PTSD, may re-experience the event with "intrusive thoughts, nightmares, flashbacks and vivid memories, and might engage in repetitive play."[68]

In one report of sixty-six children and adolescents who had been sexually abused and exploited, it was found that the children exhibited symptomatic behavior and were "troubled by feelings of anxiety, depression, guilt, and blame, and are vulnerable to further exploitation and victimization."[69] The data from the sixty-six victims "indicate that clear symptoms of distress are present during the period of sexual exploitation, at the time of disclosure, and in the posttraumatic phase."[70] Parents who discussed their observations of their children in the studies noted that while the sexual abuse was taking place, "the children complained of urinary infection, genital soreness, or anal irritation" as well as "headaches, loss of appetite, stomachaches, short vomiting spells, difficulty sleeping, marked daydreaming and fantasizing."[71] Furthermore, the parents noticed changes in school behavior such as declining grades, withdrawal from peer activities, arguments with siblings, parents, and peers, mood swings, edginess, and refusal to participate in activities such as church functions.[72] In addition, the parents stated the children acted out by stealing, setting fires, and having "sexually focused behaviors."[73] The study found that the children "essentially had no control over the intrusive imagery" and "reported recurrent memories and dreams of a frightening nature . . . increased tension, and general malaise."[74] Many children withdrew from their normal activities; one child was even unable to walk down the street where her offender lived.[75] Furthermore, the children experienced recurring feelings of guilt and hopelessness for the future.[76]

Experts report difficulties in treating sex abuse victims because of barriers put up the victims, their parents, lack of resources, and professional bias.[77] Since children do not generally talk directly or explicitly about their sexual abuse or subsequent sexual exploitation, the most significant barrier is from the guilt and secrecy surrounding the victimization and exploitation.[78] The secrecy that has been demanded of them from the child's abuser increases the child's sense of guilt to the point that "[a]s they reach adolescence, the increased understanding of the nature of their activities provokes guilt." Furthermore, as "[c]hildren often try to make sense of their experiences by deciding that they were acceptable and inevitable [they are] . . . entirely trapped and exiled by silence and secrecy."[79]

Others have reported that "the psychological scarring and emotional stress deriving from the sexual exploitation of children in many cases leads to other significant problems including the child turning to illicit drugs and alcohol to deaden memories and desensitize present experiences."[80] One study further found that child victims share the common feelings of "betrayal, guilt, rage, and worthlessness" and exhibit self-destructive or "aberrant social behavior" such as withdrawal, isolation, drug or alcohol abuse, juvenile delinquency, promiscuity, prostitution, and violence.[81]

Studies have also shown that there is a relationship between prior sexual abuse and prostitution. One study found that "9 out of 10 female prostitutes have been sexually assaulted during childhood."[82] In an investigation of a conspiracy to produce and distribute international films and other visual material of sexually explicit conduct of thirty young boys, twenty-five of whom were interviewed in depth, the majority of children were "permanently affected by these activities" and were still prostituting themselves or continuing in some errant behavior.[83] Furthermore, a report of twenty-eight young male prostitutes found that twenty-four of them reported "coercive sexual experience . . . prior to hustling."[84]

2. *Nonproduction Offenders*

A 2011 study of child pornography possessors conducted by the National Center for Missing and Exploited Children found more than 80 percent of arrested child pornography possessors had images of prepubescent children.[85] In addition, 80 percent had images of children being sexually penetrated.[86] Twenty percent of the defendants had images of children enduring sadistic sex and bondage[87] and 39 percent had videos of children being abused.[88] Thus the vast majority of possessors of child pornography are viewing hard-core child pornography involving young children. Accordingly, there can be few legitimate claims that the possessor did not know he was viewing a child.[89]

Downstream users of child pornography inflict harm because it is traumatic for a child to know his image is being recirculated.[90] The *Ferber* Court stated that:

> *[P]ornography poses an even greater threat to the child victim than does sexual abuse or prostitution.* Because the child's actions are reduced to a recording, the pornography may haunt him in future years, long after the original misdeed took place. A child who has posed for a camera must go through life knowing that the recording is circulating within the mass distribution system for child pornography.[91]

The Supreme Court repeatedly has stressed that victims of child pornography suffer as "pornography's continued existence causes the child victims continuing harm by haunting the children in years to come."[92] It has also repeated that the harm child pornography causes to children is both in its creation *and* its circulation.[93] We can prove the importance of both rationales by reconsidering the following example first raised above: A producer convinces a young child to pose in a manner that meets the legal standard of a lewd and lascivious image. The child is given candy or treats and thus is not traumatized by the production, particularly if the producer is known to the child, as is often the case. Yet she has been exploited and she may later suffer emotionally and psychologically thinking of how she was manipulated to create the image. Then, when the child learns of the image's circulation, she suffers new emotional and psychological pain.

As one circuit court described, the victim (who discovered her images were on the Internet by a notification by the NCMEC) was able to "'function [ ] pretty well normally' until she learned that her image was being traded on the internet, after which she experienced a fear 'of being at parties, fear of being in public gatherings,' and had difficulty coping 'with her life because of her sense of pervasive helplessness' about the fact that people were viewing her image."[94] Furthermore, the expert in the case concluded that knowing that the victim's images were being viewed by the defendant directly "caused emotional and psychological problems: she bit her nails to the point of bleeding, took to alcohol, and could not finish college."[95]

The Eleventh Circuit stated in stark terms that "possessors of child pornography can constitute a 'slow acid drip' of trauma, which may be exacerbated 'each time an individual views an image depicting her abuse.'"[96] The court added that "[t]his slow drip resulted from the 'extraordinarily distressing and emotionally painful' reaction suffered by the victim 'each time an individual views an image depicting her abuse.'"[97]

The victimization lasts forever since the pictures can resurface at any time.[98] As one expert explained, "The victim's knowledge of publication of the visual material increases the emotional and psychic harm suffered by the child."[99] This humiliation is exacerbated by the Internet. As one court described, "The child victims suffer not only from the initial physical sexual abuse of their tormentors, but also from the knowledge that their degradation will be repeatedly viewed electronically into near perpetuity by a large audience."[100] When adult abuse survivors become aware that the images of them as children are circulating on the Internet they become even more mistrustful of people and have more of a sense of helplessness and hopelessness.[101] As one psychologist explained, "In childhood, they knew that they were physically invaded and they couldn't stop it. As adults, they know they're visually invaded and they can't stop it. . . . So, knowing that [the images] are out there just deepens the pathology that they're already suffering from."[102]

The *Ferber* Court declared that child pornography market inflicts harm on their victims both in its creation and circulation. Nevertheless, some scholars sharply criticize the punishment of possessors by questioning whether possession inflicts its own, independent harm.[103] They assert supporters of punishment fail to recognize the derivative nature of nonproduction child pornography offenses which, they claim, make the images unlawful only because they memorialize actual abuse.[104] These scholars state the harm in circulation is not an independent harm, and if there is no abuse or exploitation in the image's creation, the injury suffered by the victim when the image is circulated should not be covered by child pornography laws.[105] Yet to get to the circulation alone argument, they seem to conflate the two separate mental harms that child pornographers may inflict: first in creating the image and second in disseminating it. Much like the producer who tricks a victim into posing for images or surreptitiously records the victim, the child is harmed psychologically when she learns she has been manipulated to create the image, and then again when it is circulated.[106]

Critics further claim that part of the increase is based on an unproven preventative rationale that possessors of child pornography are more likely to abuse children.[107] The link between downstream users of child pornography and prior child sex abuse has been the focus of a number of studies, with conflicting results.[108] The Sentencing Commission reviewed these studies and then conducted its own analysis on the danger that downstream users have or will abuse children. It made the following findings:

1. The rate of prior "criminally sexual dangerous behavior" [CSDB][109] for downstream users is approximately 33 percent, although the Commission believes the percentage is greater based on studies that indicate underreporting of the actual rate.
2. The offenders who engaged in "personal" distribution, such as through e-mails or closed peer-to-peer networks had a higher rate of prior CSDB (38.4 percent) than that of "impersonal" distribution via open peer-to-peer networks (26.2 percent), though similar to those who did not distribute (37.2 percent).

This finding supports the thesis of this chapter that technology has blurred the categories of offenders. Passive distributors are much more like receivers/possessors than like other distributors.

3. Rates of known general recidivism of downstream offenders was 30 percent, and of known sexual recidivism was 7.4 percent, of

> which a little less than half (3.6 percent) was for contact offenses.[110] The general recidivism rate was comparable to the known rate for a comparable portion of all federal offenders.[111]

Thus, there appears to be a link between downstream child pornography use and prior sex crimes against children, although the rate of recidivism for sexual offenses is comparable to other offenders. In response to the proxy argument, the Commission noted that whether a downstream user has or will engage in sexual abuse of a child is a primary factor in imposing sentences.[112]

3. Harm Inherent in the Images

Beyond physical and psychological injury, the depicted child suffers a more fundamental harm. Even if the child was unaware the image was made or circulated, those who create, trade, and view child pornography harm the child's inherent right of human dignity not to be viewed in this fashion. This right is violated each and every time an image is made and circulated. The Supreme Court recognized these human dignity and privacy concerns from the outset of its child pornography jurisprudence. In *Ferber*, the Court stated that distribution of the material violates "the individual interest in avoiding disclosure of personal matters."[113] Other courts agree; as one court noted "the mere existence of child pornography represents an invasion of the privacy of the child depicted."[114] Another court stated the images were an "affront to the dignity and privacy of the child and the exploitation of the child's vulnerability."[115]

The right of human dignity not to be depicted in a degrading fashion is recognized far beyond the child pornography arena. It is the harm in the image itself, separate from the portrayed act. Images are so powerful that in diverse settings, special rules apply to them. For example, the Geneva Convention requires prisoners of war be treated humanely, and this includes banning photographs of them that subject them to humiliation or public curiosity.[116] Under Articles 13 and 14 of the 1949 Geneva Conventions III Relative to the Treatment of Prisoners of War, POWs are also "are entitled in all circumstances to respect for their persons and their honor."[117] Even non-POWs or so-called enemy combatants are entitled to protection against "outrages on personal dignity, in particular humiliating and degrading treatment."[118] One need only think of the disgrace over the Abu Ghraib incident to see the impact of photographs. It was not just the humiliating treatment itself; it was the taking and dissemination of photographs of the humiliation that was contemptible.[119] The same criticism was made following the release of photographs of Saddam Hussein after his capture.[120]

Death scene and autopsy photographs are also subject to dissemination restrictions. In *National Archives and Records Admin. v. Favish*, the Supreme Court ruled there is a "familial right of privacy over the death-scene images of a loved one."[121] The case involved death-scene photographs of Vincent Foster, Jr., deputy counsel to President Clinton, and respondent's Freedom of Information Act (FOIA) request for the photos. In denying the FOIA request, the Court noted that FOIA exemption 7(C) excuses from disclosure information compiled by law enforcement if their production "could reasonably be expected to constitute an unwarranted invasion of personal privacy."[122] Foster's sister opposed the disclosure of the disputed pictures because "[u]ndoubtedly, the photographs would be placed on the Internet for world consumption" and would renew media interest in her brother's death.[123]

The Court agreed that FOIA exemption 7(C) extended beyond the person depicted to his family members, and it banned release of the images unless the person requesting the information establishes a significant public interest in the information sufficient to override the family's privacy interest in the images.[124] It found the respondent failed to meet this burden.[125] The Court stated that Congress "intended to permit family members to assert their own privacy rights against public intrusions long deemed impermissible under the common law and in our cultural traditions."[126]

Tort law also limits dissemination of non-newsworthy death and autopsy images.[127] Courts have ruled that these images are inherently humiliating and distressful for the family, and thus those who release the images may be subject to damages.[128] Other courts ban the release of private information even if identities are protected. For example, in *Northwestern Memorial Hospital v. Ashcroft*,[129] the government sought medical records of patients who received late-term abortions to aid the government's constitutional challenge to the Partial-Birth Abortion Act of 2003.[130] In rejecting the government's demand, the Seventh Circuit ruled it was an invasion of privacy even if there was no possibility that a patient's identity might be learned from a redacted medical record.[131] In doing so, the court made the following apt analogy:

> Imagine if nude photos of a woman, uploaded to the Internet without her consent though without identifying her by name, were downloaded in a foreign country by people who will never meet

her. She would still feel that her privacy had been invaded. The revelation of the intimate details contained in the record of a late-term abortion may inflict a similar wound."[132]

The common thread in the above cases is that dissemination of certain images for no worthy purpose inflicts harm on the depicted person. The absolute lack of any worthy reason to trade in child pornography establishes the inherent harm to the dignity of the child depicted. The person inflicting the abuse captured in a pornographic image is obviously deserving of substantial punishment as a child molester. The producer of the image is guilty of documenting the infliction of sexual abuse. The harm by possessors and other downstream users lacks physicality, but they too inflict distinct, actual harm on the child whose image is disseminated and collected.

Conclusion

The ban on child pornography is meant to stop sexual abuse and exploitation. Sexual abuse is apparent when the images show children in pain and incurring physical injuries such as genital bruising, cuts, and lacerations. Yet even depictions that do not show children in physical pain are the product of exploitation. Pornographers may groom children to participate in the production of pornographic images through trickery, threats, coercion, or gifts. This exploitation may cause psychological harm because the children can feel guilty that they appear to be willing participants. Since a child cannot legally consent to participating in the creation of child pornography, using trickery, grooming, deception, or threats to obtain consent falls within the plain meaning of the word "exploitation."

Nonproducers, such as possessors, victimize children because "pornography's continued existence causes the child victims continuing harm by haunting the children in years to come."[133] The psychological injury caused by the circulation of the images is independent and separate from the physical or psychological harm often caused in the creation of the image. The Internet has exacerbated this harm as millions of images are permanently circulating in cyberspace.

More essentially, producers and nonproducers alike inflict dignitary harm upon the children whose images are depicted in pornography. Plainly said, children have a right not to be seen in pornographic images, and offenders who get these images are an essential part of the pornography network that inflicts dignitary harm. As technology continues to advance the ways in which these nonproduction offenders get their images, the label "possessor" is losing its distinctiveness; as this trend continues, we should not single out the possessor for special consideration or treatment. Instead, the focus needs to be on the manners in which victims are harmed.

NOTES

1. United States v. Eigand, 812 F.2d 1239 (9th Cir. 1987).
2. 18 U.S.C. § 2251 prohibits the production of sexually explicit images of children. 18 U.S.C. § 2252A covers the downstream participants in the child pornography market.
3. 18 U.S.C. § 2251.
4. 18 U.S.C. § 2252A
5. *See* 18 U.S.C. § 2256 (3).
6. The sentencing guidelines contain definitions of "distribution" for the purposes of assessing sentences. *See* USSG § 2G2.2, Commentary, Application notes. The guidelines further distinguish distributing for pecuniary and nonpecuniary gain. *Id.*
7. *Id.*
8. *Id.*
9. Child Protection Act of 1977, Pub. L. No. 95-225, 92 Stat. 7 (1977) (codified at 18 U.S.C. §§ 2251–2253) (1978)).
10. Initially, there were only two offense characteristics increase triggers: minor under twelve and distribution based on retail value. U.S. SENTENCING COMMISSION, THE HISTORY OF THE CHILD PORNOGRAPHY GUIDELINES 54 (2009), *available at* http://www.ussc.gov/Research/Research_Projects/Sex_Offenses/20091030_History_Child_Pornography_Guidelines.pdf [hereinafter "2009 Comm'n Report"] at 12, 17. *See generally,* Audrey Rogers, *From Peer-to-Peer Networks to Cloud Computing: How Technology Is Redefining Child Pornography Laws*, 87 ST. JOHN'S L. REV. 1013 (2013), *available at* papers.ssrn.com/sol3/papers.cfm?abstract_id=2006664.
11. Child Protection Act of 1984, Pub. L. No. 99–292, 98 Stat. 204 (1984) (codified at 18 U.S.C. §§ 2251–2253).
12. *See* ATTORNEY GENERAL'S COMMISSION ON PORNOGRAPHY, FINAL REPORT 599–603, 604 (1986).
13. The lack of a federal ban on possessing child pornography was in large part because the Supreme Court had previously ruled possession of obscene materials was protected by the First Amendment. The Court distinguished private possession of obscene material from that of child pornography in Osborne v Ohio, 495 U.S. 103 (1989). For more on the history, see Audrey Rogers, *Protecting Children on the Internet, Mission Impossible?*, 61 BAYLOR L. REV. 323, 326–28 (2009).
14. 2009 Comm'n Report, *supra* note 10 at 19.
15. U.S. Sentencing Commission, Federal Child Pornography Offenses, *available at* http://www.ussc.gov/Legislative_and_Public_Affairs/Congressional_Testimony_and_Reports/Sex_Offense_Topics/201212_Federal_Child_Pornography_Offenses [hereinafter "2012 Comm'n Report"] at 29.

16. *Id.* at 30, n.58.

17. 2009 Comm'n Report, *supra* note 10 at 29–30.

18. 2012 Comm'n Report, *supra* note 15 at 329.

19. Since law enforcement can now catch distributors more easily, the need to catch them in the act of receiving via the mail is obsolete. 2012 Comm'n Report, *supra* note 15 at 328.

20. *See, e.g.*, United States v. Tucker, 305 F.3d 1193 (10th Cir. 2002).

21. *See, e.g.*, United States v. Woerner, 709 F.3d 527 (5th Cir.), *cert. denied*, ___ U.S. __, 134 S. Ct. 146 (2013); United States v. Romm, 455 F.3d 990, 999 (9th Cir. 2006).

22. When images are found on a person's computer screen, some issues over possession have arisen. In the past, the lack of a definition has caused some defendants to argue that they did not possess images on their computer screen if they appeared or were saved automatically. *See generally*, Ty E. Howard, *Don't Cache Out your Case: Prosecuting Possession Laws Based on Images Located in Temporary Cache Files*, 19 BERKELEY TECH. L.J. 1227 (2004). This issue was resolved by Congress in 2008 when it added a ban on "accessing with intent to view" child pornography. 18 U.S.C. §2252A (a)(5).

23. *See, e.g.*, United States v. Ramos, 685 F.3d 120 (2d Cir. 2012); United States v. Winkler, 639 F.3d 692 (5th Cir. 2011).

24. In the 1990s the tandem spread of applications like e-mail and the World Wide Web, and the development of fast networking technologies like Ethernet. John E. George & Paul F. Kolesar, *10-Gigabit Ethernet Development for LAN Cabling Systems Well Underway*, LIGHTWAVE (1999), *available at* http://www.lightwaveonline.com/articles/print/volume-16/issue-13/special-report/10-gigabit-ethernet-development-for-lan-cabling-systems-well-underway-53490282.html. Ethernet is computer connectivity hardware that was developed by Xerox Parc (a research and development company). Edward L. Rubin, *Computer Languages as Networks and Power Structures: Governing the Development of XML*, 53 SMU L. REV. 1447, 1450 (2000).

25. COMPUTER HISTORY MUSEUM, http://www.computerhistory.org/internet_history/internet_history_90s.html.

26. *Usage and Population Statistics*, INTERNET WORLD STATS, http://www.internetworldstats.com; George & Kolesar, *supra* note 24.

27. United States v. C.R., 792 F. Supp. 2d 343, 352 (E.D.N.Y. 2011). *See generally*, Rogers, *supra* note 10.

28. *See* U.S. Gov't Gen. Accounting Office, GAO-03-351, File-Sharing Programs: Peer-to-Peer Networks Provide Ready Access to Child Pornography 6 (2003), available at http://www.gao.gov/new.items/d03351.pdf at 11, 13. See ALSO U.S. DEP'T OF JUSTICE, THE NATIONAL STRATEGY FOR CHILD EXPLOITATION PREVENTION AND INTERDICTION: A REPORT TO CONGRESS 11 (2010), available at http://www.justice.gov/psc/docs/natstrategyreport.pdf (listing Internet distribution channels).

29. *Pornography Industry Is Larger than the Revenues of the Top Technology*, Cy Talk Blog (Jan. 1, 2010) http://blog.cytalk.com/2010/01/web-porn-revenue/; Jelani Jefferson Exum, *Making the Punishment Fit the (Computer) Crime: Rebooting Notions of Possession for the Federal Sentencing of Child Pornography Offenses*, 16 RICH. J.L. & TECH. 1, 6 (2010).

30. 458 U.S. 747, 751–52 (1982).

31. *See id.*

32. United States v. Davenport, 519 F.3d 940 (9th Cir. 2008). The Sentencing Com-

mission also noted the reverse—only charging a possession offense despite evidence of other trafficking, often times as a result of a plea agreement. 2012 Comm'n Report, *supra* note 15 at 219–22.

33. *Davenport*, 519 F.3d at 942–43. The Fifth Amendment's double jeopardy clause guarantees that no person shall "be subject for the same offence to be twice put in jeopardy of life or limb." U.S. Const., amend. V.

34. *Davenport*, 519 F.3d at 943.

35. *See, e.g., id.*

36. *See, e.g.*, United States v. Polouizzi, 564 F.3d 142, 147–48 (2d Cir. 2009); United States v. Burgess, No. 1:09CR17, 2010 WL 2219335, at * 1 (W.D.N.C. May 28, 2010).

37. *See* United States v. Myers, 355 F.3d 1040, 1042–43 (7th Cir. 2004). *Accord* United States v. Grosenheider, 200 F.3d 321, 332–33 (5th Cir. 2000); United States v. Davenport, 519 F.3d 940, 950 (9th Cir. 2008) (Graber, J., dissenting) ("[T]he statutory provisions are directed toward different harms."). The Sentencing Commission recommended unanimously that Congress align the receipt and possession offenses. 2012 Comm'n Report, *supra* note 15 at 326–32. The Commission did not have a recommendation on the sentence or whether it should be mandatory other than to state that if it were mandatory, it should be less than five years. *Id.* at 329.

38. The Sentencing Commission agrees with this conclusion. *See* 2012 Comm'n Report, *supra* note 15 at 326–29. It is, of course possible to inadvertently receive child pornography, and then consciously choose to keep it. In that instance, the person would be guilty only of possession. *See* United States v. Watzman, 486 F.3d 1004, 1009 (7th Cir. 2007).

39. United States v. Schaffer, 472 F.3d 1219 (10th Cir. 2007). *See generally*, Rogers, *supra* note 10.

40. *Id.* at 1223–24; *accord* United States v. Collins, 642 F.3d 654, 656–57 (8th Cir. 2011); United States v. Layton, 564 F.3d 330, 335 (4th Cir. 2009); United States v. Geiner, 498 F.3d 1104, 1109–10 (10th Cir. 2007); United States v. Carani, 492 F.3d 867, 875–76 (7th Cir. 2007); United States v. Griffin, 482 F.3d 1008, 1011–12 (8th Cir. 2007); United States v. Mathenia, 409 F.3d 1289, 1290 (11th Cir. 2005).

41. United States v. Grober, 624 F.3d 592 (3d Cir. 2010).

42. *Id.* at 598.

43. 2012 Comm'n Report, *supra* note 15 at 94–99, 313, 323–24.

44. *Id.* at 324. A "closed" peer-to-peer network allows a person to create a private network to which he can invite participants and choose what information to share among them. 2012 Comm'n Report, *supra* note 15 at 52–53. An "open" network allows for passive sharing. It is the default setting for most peer-to-peer software and the user has no control over who accesses his files. *Id.* at 52.

45. *See supra* note 37.

46. 2012 Comm'n Report, *supra* note 15 at 147–50.

47. *Id.* at 153–54.

48. The Sentencing Commission has acknowledged that technological changes have made some of its sentencing factors obsolete. For example, it found the existing enhancement for use of a computer applied in "virtually every case" and thus was no longer a relevant way to differentiate sentences. *Id.* at 323–24. Similarly, it found the number of images alone as a sentencing enhancement needs revision to more fully account for different offender behavior and more finely calibrated enhancements. *Id.* at 322–24.

Although the Commission did not go so far as to collapse all divisions between downstream users, as previously noted, it recommended sentences between receivers and possessors be aligned. *Id.* at 329; *see supra* note 38.

49. 458 U.S. 747, 756–57 (1982).

50. *Id.*

51. R. BARRI FLOWERS, THE VICTIMIZATION AND EXPLOITATION OF WOMEN AND CHILDREN 177 (1994).

52. Eva J. Klain, Heather J. Davies, Molly A. Hicks, *Child Pornography: The Criminal Justice Response* at 10 (National Center For Missing and Exploited Children 2001) (http://www.missingkids.com/en_US/publications/NC81.pdf).

53. *Id.*

54. *Id.* at 1–11.

55. 2012 Comm'n Report, *supra* note 15 at 110.

56. *Id.* at 109.

57. Approximately 25 percent of the time, children are unaware they are being depicted; at least 10 percent of victims are babies or toddlers. Others are sexually abused while drugged or asleep. Some producers covertly produce images with hidden cameras in bathrooms or locker rooms. While this last group of producers do not directly inflict physical harm on the victims, as discussed below there is psychological and inherent damage to the victims.

58. *Ashcroft*, 535 U.S. at 242. *See* notes 60–62 and accompanying text *infra*.

59. See, e.g., United States v. Hotaling, 634 F.3d 72 (2d Cir. 2011); United States v. Bach, 400 F.3d 622 (8th Cir. 2005).

60. See, e.g., chapter 3, Amy Adler, "The 'Dost Test' in Child Pornography Law: Trial by Rorschach Test," at n. 37; chapter 2, Carissa Byrne Hessick, "Setting Definitional Limits for the Child Pornography Exception"; chapter 1, James Weinstein, "The Context and Content of *New York v. Ferber*," at note 109.

61. *Ferber*, 458 U.S. 747, 753.

62. The question of how to measure what is "lewd and lascivious" is outside the scope of this chapter. For a thorough analysis, see Adler, *supra* note 60.

63. See Hessick, *supra* note 60.

64. ANN WOLBERT BURGESS, CHILD TRAUMA: ISSUES AND RESEARCH 64 (1992).

65. *Id.* at 65–65.

66. *Id.*

67. *Id.* at 65.

68. TALI GAL, CHILD VICTIMS AND RESTORATIVE JUSTICE 63 (2011). As of May 2013 the American Psychiatric Association (APA) moved PTSD out of a general anxiety disorder class into a new category titled, "trauma and stressor-related disorders," from an anxiety disorder. The new class requires "exposure to actual or threatened death, serious injury or sexual violation." American Psychiatric Association, Diagnostic and Statistical Manual of Mental Disorders [hereinafter DSM], Rev.5th Ed. (Washington, DC: APA, 2013), available at http://www.ptsd.va.gov/professional/pages/diagnostic_criteria_dsm-5.asp.

69. ANNE WOLBERT BURGESS, CHILD PORNOGRAPHY AND SEX RINGS 111,112 (Marieanne Lineqvist Clark, ed., 1984) [hereinafter BURGESS, CHILD PORNOGRAPHY].

70. *Id.*

71. *Id.* at 113.

72. *Id.*
73. *Id.*
74. *Id.* at 114.
75. *Id.*
76. *Id.* at 118.
77. *Id.* at 16.
78. *Id.* at 16–17.
79. *Id.* at 17.
80. RONALD B. FLOWERS, CHILDREN AND CRIMINALITY: THE CHILD AS VICTIM AND PERPETRATOR 97 (1986).
81. *Id.*
82. FLOWERS, *supra* note 51, at 177.
83. BURGESS, *supra* note 64, at 38.
84. *Id.* at 135.
85. The ages of the victims in possessors collections were as follows: under three years old, 28 percent; three to five years old, 46 percent; six to twelve years old, 86 percent; older than twelve, 67 percent. 2012 Comm'n Report, *supra* note 15 at 108.
86. Janis Wolak, David Finkelhor, & Kimbery J. Mitchell, *Child-Pornography Possessors: Arrested in Internet-Related Crimes: Findings from the National Juvenile Online Victimization Study* 5 (Nat'l Ctr for Missing and Exploited Children, 2005).
87. *Id.* at vii.
88. *Id.*
89. In *United States v. X-citement Video, Inc.*, 513 U.S. 64 (1994), the Supreme Court ruled that section 2252 requires knowledge that pornographic images portrayed minors. This case involved a seventen-year-old who was a pornography star. It led Congress to impose stringent record-keeping and labeling requirements on producers of adult pornography to ensure that minors are not used in their productions.
90. New York v. Ferber, 458 U.S. 747, 761 (1982).
91. *Id.* at 760, n.10 (quoting David P. Shouvlin, *Preventing the Sexual Exploitation of Children: A Model Act*, 17 WAKE FOREST L. REV. 535, 545 (1981)) (emphasis added).
92. Osborne v. Ohio, 495 U.S. 103, 111 (1990); *see also* Ashcroft v. Free Speech Coalition, 535 U.S. 234, 249–250 (2002); United States v. Williams, 553 U.S. 285 (2008).
93. Ashcroft v. Free Speech Coalition, 535 U.S. 234 (2002); Osborne v. Ohio, 495 U.S. 103 (1990); New York v. Ferber, 458 U.S. 747 (1982).
94. United States v. Aumais, 656 F.3d 147, 150 (2d Cir. 2011).
95. *Id.*
96. *Id.*
97. *Id.*
98. *See* Janis Wolak, Kimberly Mitchell & David Finkelhor, *Internet Sex Crimes Against Children* (National Center For Missing and Exploited Children, 2003) (http://www. ncmec.org/en_US/publications/NC132.pdf); *see also, Hearing Before the Subcommittee on Crime, Terrorism, and Homeland Security, Committee on the Judiciary United States House of Representatives* 107th Cong. (2002) (testimony of Michael J. Heimbach, Crimes Against Children Unit, Criminal Investigative Division, FBI) at http://www.fbi.gov/congress/congress02/heimbach050102.htm.
99. Note, *Protection of Children from Use in Pornography: Toward Constitutional and Enforceable Legislation*, 12 U. MICH. J. LAW REFORM 295, 301 (1979) (interview with

child psychiatrist), *quoted in* United States v. Clayton, 2008 U.S. App. LEXIS 2077 * 11 (January 31, 2008).

100. E.D. v. C.R., 792 F. Supp. 2d 343 (E.D.N.Y. 2011). *See also* New York v. Ferber, 458 U.S. 747 (1982); Ashcroft v. Free Speech Coalition, 535 U.S. 234 (2002).

101. E.D. v. C.R., 792 F. Supp. 2d 343 (E.D.N.Y. 2011).

102. *Id.*

103. *See, e.g.*, Amy Adler, *Inverting the First Amendment*, 149 U. PA. L. REV. 921, 985 (2001) ("Child pornography law conflates act and image[s]."); Carissa Byrne Hessick, *Disentangling Child Pornography From Child Sex Abuse*, 88 WASH. U. L. REV. 853, 864–65 (2011); Weinstein, *supra* note 60.

104. *See, e.g.*, Hessick, *supra* note 103, at 865, 867–68. The Sentencing Commission has stated in no uncertain terms that the harm inflicted on child pornography victims extends beyond, and is separate from, its production. *See* 2012 Comm'n Report, *supra* note 15 at 112–14, 311–12.

105. *See, e.g.*, Adler, *supra* note 60 at n.37 and accompanying text; Hessick, *supra* note 60.

106. *See supra* notes 53, 57, 90 and accompanying text.

107. *See* Hessick, *supra* note 103, at 870–71.

108. 2012 Comm'n Report, *supra* note 15 at 172, n.12.

109. The Commission divided its CSDB into three categories: (1) contact offenses such as rape and sexual assault, (2) non-contact offenses, such as enticing a minor to engage in cybersex, and (3) prior nonproduction child pornography offenses. *Id.* at 414, and n.20.

110. The Commission noted its results comported with other studies on recidivism rates. 2102 Comm'n Report, *supra* note 15 at 306–08.

111. *Id.* at 310.

112. 2012 Comm'n Report, *supra* note 15 at 169–71, 320.

113. *Ferber*, 458 U.S. at 756 n.10.

114. United States v. Norris, 159 F.3d 126, 130 (5th Cir. 1998); *see also* United States. v. Cunningham, 680 F. Supp. 2d 844 (N.D.Ohio 2010).

115. United States v. Knox, 32 F.3d 733 (3d Cir. 1994).

116. Article 13 of the Third Geneva Convention in relation to the Treatment of Prisoners of War 1949 and Article 27 of the Fourth Geneva Convention in relation to the Protection of Civilian Persons in Time of War 1949. *See generally* Noel Whitty, *Soldier Photography of Detainee Abuse In Iraq: Digital Technology, Human Rights and the Death Of Baha Mousa*, 10 HUM. RTS. L. REV. 689 (2010); Robert Cryer, *The Fine Art of Friendship: Jus In Bello In Afghanistan*, 7 J. CONFLICT & SECURITY L. 37, 73–76 (2002). *See also* Rogers, *supra* note 10.

117. Articles 13 and 14 of the Third Geneva Convention in relation to the Treatment of Prisoners of War 1949.

118. Additional Protocol I, art. 75(2)(b). *See generally* Cryer, *supra* note 116.

119. *See* Cryer, *supra* note 116, n.200 ("the reference is, strictly speaking to the customary concomitant of art. 75, as the US is not bound by the Protocol, having signed, but not ratified it."); http://www.upi.com/Business_News/Security-Industry/2003/03/23/Geneva-Convention-prohibits-filming-POWs/UPI-80261048460384/http://www.upi.com/Business_News/Security-Industry/2003/03/23/Geneva-Convention-prohibits-filming-POWs/UPI-80261048460384/.

120. http://www.washingtonpost.com/wp-dyn/content/article/2005/05/20/AR2005052000197.html.

121. National Archives and Records Admin. v. Favish, 541 U.S. 157 (2004). *See generally*, Rogers, *supra* note 10.

122. *Id.* at 160.

123. *Id.* at 167.

124. *Id.* at 172.

125. *Id. See generally,* Clay Calvert, *Salvaging Privacy & Tranquility From the Wreckage: Images of Death, Emotions of Distress & Remedies of Tort In the Age of the Internet,* 2010 MICH. ST. L. REV. 311.

126. *Favish,* 541 U.S. 157, 167.

127. *Id.*

128. *See, e.g.,* Catsouras v. Dep't of Cal. Highway Patrol, 104 Cal. Rptr. 3d 352, 357 (Cal. Ct. App. 2010).

129. 362 F.3d 923 (7th Cir. 2004).

130. 18 U.S.C. § 1531.

131. 362 F.3d at 929.

132. *Id.*

133. 495 U.S. 103, 111 (1990); *see also* Ashcroft v. Free Speech Coalition, 535 U.S. 234, 249–50 (2002); United States v. Williams, 553 U.S. 285 (2008).

7 | Not Just "Kiddie Porn"

The Significant Harms from Child Pornography Possession

Paul G. Cassell, James R. Marsh, and Jeremy M. Christiansen

The severity of criminal penalties for possessing child pornography has recently come under attack. Both judges and academic commentators have been heard to complain that the prison sentences for child pornography possessors are too long. Implicit in these criticisms is often the claim that possessing child pornography is not a serious crime—that while those who create (or perhaps distribute) child pornography inflict severe harms on their child victims, those who merely possess images are not significantly blameworthy. Indeed, in a case that recently attracted national attention, a man who was convicted of child pornography possession (possessing images of children as young as two years old being sodomized and performing oral sex on adult men) was allowed to keep his pension because his felony crime was not deemed to even rise to the level of "moral turpitude."[1]

In a series of federal cases involving restitution for child pornography victims, the authors of this chapter have encountered the misguided sentiment that possessors of child pornography cause little harm. We have represented such victims in many federal cases across the country, seeking to obtain restitution from those who commit child pornography crimes.[2] Much of that litigation has involved the proper interpretation of the Mandatory Restitution for Sex Crimes provision of the Violence Against Women Act[3] and specifically whether victims should receive full, some, or no restitution from convicted child pornography defendants. The authors' efforts culminated in the recent United States Supreme Court case, *Paroline v. United States*.[4] Unfortunately, a majority of the Court disagreed with the position of child pornography victims: that Congress passed the Mandatory Restitution for Sex Crimes provision to guarantee full restitution for child pornography victims. However, the *Paroline* decision contains a silver lining: All the opinions in the case agreed the crime of possession of child pornography results in significant suffering on the part of the victims.

Despite the Court's recognition of this suffering, the misguided view that child pornography possession is largely harmless persists. This chapter demonstrates otherwise. In reality, possession of such images causes significant trauma to the victims depicted. The endless collecting and viewing of a victim's child sex images subjects victims to continuous invasions of privacy, producing lasting psychological injury and significant economic losses.

This chapter will detail the significant harms that child pornography possession causes to the children depicted in the images of abuse. The crime of child pornography possession inflicts substantial harm on its victims, through continually reminding the victims of the initial sexual abuse. We illustrate this point with a discussion of two young victims of child pornography possession—two young women we will refer to as "Amy" and "Vicky." We then turn to the issue of quantifying those harms for purposes of restitution. Those who collect and view child pornography cause significant losses for which victims should receive significant compensation. Moreover, each individual defendant should be held jointly and severally liable for all of the harms that child pornography possession causes. This conclusion is consistent with basic principles of tort law, which identify all who contribute to a single harm as being responsible for paying for the entire harm.

I. The Harms Victims of Child Pornography Possession Endure

At the outset, a brief discussion of terminology is in order. The efforts to minimize the harm to child pornography victims begins even with the phrase used to describe the crime. Although the term "child pornography" is widely used,[5] it carries misleading connotations. The term "pornography" suggests that child pornography is akin to adult pornography,that is, erotic material appealing to the viewer's interest in normal sexual activities involving consenting adults. An even more deficient term is "kiddie porn," which some prominent and thoughtful commentators have used.[6]

"Pornography" and, worse yet, "porn" are neither the best nor the most accurate terms to describe, for example, images and videos which often graphically record prepubescent children (including toddlers) being raped by adults.[7] As one doctor who works closely with victims explained:

> In the context of children . . . there can be no question of consent, and use of the word pornography may effectively allow us to distance ourselves from the material's true nature. A preferred term is *abuse images*, and this term is increasingly gaining acceptance among professionals working in this area. Using the term abuse images accurately describes the process and product of taking indecent and sexualized pictures of children, and its use is, on the whole, to be supported.[8]

Other terms that have been suggested as suitable substitutes include "child abuse material," "child sexual abuse material," "documented child sexual abuse," and "depicted child sexual abuse."[9] Given the widespread use of the term "child pornography"—especially in the criminal context—we reluctantly bow to convention in this chapter and will use that term here.

In discussing the harms to the victims of "child pornography" possession crimes, it is also important to understand the vast criminal machinery that generates those harms. In enacting laws criminalizing all aspects of child pornography, Congress (for example) realized that it had to address every stage of this sordid joint enterprise—countless criminals who together create, distribute, and possess child pornography. As the Supreme Court explained, "it is difficult, if not impossible to halt" the sexual exploitation and abuse of children by pursuing only child pornography producers.[10] It was therefore reasonable for Congress to conclude that "the production of child pornography [will decrease] if it penalizes those who possess and view the product, thereby decreasing demand."[11] Indeed, the Court explained that "[t]he most expeditious if not the only practical method of law enforcement may be to dry up the market for this material by imposing severe criminal penalties" on all persons in the distribution chain.[12] Congress did just that by criminalizing child pornography possession.[13]

Congress properly recognized that child pornography possessors are inextricably linked to child pornography producers. Congressional findings concerning child pornography possession crimes explain that "prohibiting the possession and viewing of child pornography will . . . [help] to eliminate the market for the sexual exploitative use of children. . . ."[14] A recent Justice Department analysis reported that "the growing and thriving market for child pornographic images is responsible for fresh child sexual abuse—because the high demand for child pornography drives some individuals to sexually abuse children and some to 'commission' the abuse for profit or status."[15]

Once a child is sexually abused to produce digitized child pornography, the images can be disseminated exponentially. Peer-to-peer file sharing (commonly called "P2P") is "widely used to download child pornography."[16] Two recent law enforcement initiatives "identified over 20 million unique IP [Internet Protocol] addresses offering child pornography over P2P networks from 2006 to August 2010."[17] The ease with which child pornography can now be downloaded creates "an expanding market for child pornography [that] fuels greater demand for perverse sexual depictions of children, making it more difficult for authorities to prevent their sexual exploitation and abuse."[18] In other words, those who possess child pornography become a cog in the vast machinery that sexually abuses and exploits children through child pornography.[19]

The machinery of child pornography leaves in its wake horrific human suffering. *New York v. Ferber*,[20] the leading Supreme Court case on the subject, well articulates the serious long-term physiological, emotional, and mental harms to victims who are sexually exploited to produce such images. "[T]he use of children as . . . subjects of pornographic materials is very harmful to both the children and the society as a whole. It has been found that sexually exploited children are unable to develop healthy affectionate relationships in later life, have sexual dysfunctions, and have a tendency to become sexual abusers as adults."[21] The Court has also recognized that child pornography can pose "an even greater threat to the child victim than does sexual abuse or prostitution. Because the child's actions are reduced to a recording, the pornography may haunt [her] in future years, long after the original misdeed took place. A child who has posed for a camera must go through life knowing that the recording is circulating within the mass distribution system for child pornography."[22] And more recently, the Court has unanimously reaffirmed *Ferber*'s central premise: "[i]t is common ground that the victim suffers continuing and grievous harm as a result of her knowledge that a large, indeterminate number of individuals *have viewed and will in the future view* images of the sexual abuse she endured."[23]

Ferber elucidates an unfortunate reality for victims of child pornography crimes: the initial production of the videos and other images of their sexual abuse is only the beginning of a lifetime of trauma. Victims deal with intense physical and emotional anguish for decades as a direct result of the distribution and possession of their child sex abuse images. The following brief accounts are illustrative of the harms they suffer on a daily basis. Two of the victims who are most active in attempting to secure restitution, "Amy" and "Vicky,"[24] have detailed their experiences in their own words through victim impact statements and psychological reports.

A. The Harms Suffered By "Amy"[25]

Amy was just four years old when her uncle began sexually abusing her.[26] At a time when most girls her age were just learning about letters and numbers, Amy was forced to endure repeated rape, cunnilingus, fellatio, and digital penetration by her uncle, a trusted family member.[27] Her uncle perpetrated some of the sexual assaults in order to produce child pornography for a child molester living in the Seattle area. This illustrates what is often described as the "market creation" effect of child pornography possession—that those who want to possess child pornography often directly cause the sexual abuse of a child to produce those images.[28]

When Amy was nine years old, her uncle was apprehended, ending the direct sexual abuse. Amy then received psychological counseling to cope with the trauma caused by the abuse and the associated child pornography production. When her treatment concluded in 1999, Amy's therapist reported that Amy was "back to normal" and that she engaged in age-appropriate activities like dance.[29] Although Amy always suspected her child sex abuse images were probably somewhere on the Internet, at age seventeen Amy discovered that countless individuals were in fact trading and collecting a vast catalog of her images.[30] Amy's use of a pseudonym reflects a painful irony: she seeks anonymity, but hers is among the most widely trafficked child pornography series in the world.[31] Her own words describe her agony:

> Every day of my life I live in constant fear that someone will see my pictures and recognize me and that I will be humiliated all over again. It hurts me to know someone is looking at them—at me—when I was just a little girl being abused for the camera. I did not choose to be there, but now I am there forever in pictures that people are using to do sick things. I want it all erased. I want it all stopped. But I am powerless to stop it just like I was powerless to stop my uncle.[32]

This knowledge of the ongoing distribution and possession of Amy's child sex abuse images has had "long lasting and life changing impact[s] on her" that "are more resistant to treatment than those that would normally follow a time limited trauma, as her awareness of the continued existence of the pictures and their criminal use in a widespread way leads to an activation in [her posttraumatic] symptoms."[33] As a result, Amy will require counseling for the rest of her life—counseling that, of course, costs money.[34] Amy also has difficulty maintaining gainful employment in jobs that require even routine interaction with the public.[35] Thus, she experiences not only ongoing psychological trauma but also substantial financial losses.

B. The Harms Suffered By "Vicky"[36]

"Vicky" suffered fate similar to Amy's at the hands of her father when she was ten and eleven years old.[37] As with Amy's abuse, Vicky's abuse was made to order. She was forced to perform scripted videos of rape, sodomy, and bondage based on requests placed with her abuser by child molesters and pedophiles, who later downloaded and traded her videos.[38]

Vicky also first learned that her images were in circulation when she was seventeen years old.[39] As detailed in her victim impact statement, Vicky suffers ongoing serious psychological trauma because of the possession and distribution of her child sex abuse images and videos.[40] Indeed, her condition deteriorated markedly in the years following her discovery of the widespread proliferation of the images of her childhood sexual abuse.[41] When she became aware of how many people around the world are "entertained by [her] shame and pain," Vicky started having nightmares about strangers staring at images of her naked body on their computer screens.[42] She is further burdened by the thought that her images "might be used to groom another child for abuse," which is a seduction technique utilized by pedophiles that her own father used on her as a child.[43]

Here again, Vicky's own words best describe her harm:

> I had no idea the "Vicky" series, the child porn series taken of me, had been circulated at all, until I was 17. My world came crashing down that day, and now, two years later, not much has changed. These past years have only shown me the enormity of the circulation of these images and added to my grief and pain. This knowledge has given me a paranoia. I wonder if the people I know have seen these images. I wonder if the men I pass in the grocery store have seen them. Because the most intimate parts of me are being

> viewed by thousands of strangers and traded around, I feel out of control. They are trading my trauma around like treats at a party, but it is far from innocent. It feels like I am being raped by each and every one of them. What are they doing when they watch those videos anyway? They are gaining sexual gratification from images of me at ages 10 and 11. It sickens me to the core and terrifies me. Just thinking about it now, I feel myself stiffen and I want to cry. So many nights I have cried myself to sleep thinking of a stranger somewhere staring at their computer with images of a naked me on the screen. I have nightmares about it.
>
> My paranoia is not without just cause. Some of these perverts have tried to contact me. One tried to find me through my friends on MySpace. Another created a slide show of me on Youtube. I wish I could one day feel completely safe, but as long as these images are out there, I never will. Every time they are downloaded I am exploited again, my privacy is breeched, and my life feels less and less safe. I will never be able to have control over who sees me raped as a child. It's all out there for the world to see and it can never be removed from the internet.[44]

Vicky also suffers great anxiety that she will encounter individuals who have seen the worst moments of her life—a fear that, sadly, is not unjustified.[45] Multiple child pornography users have contacted Vicky, even sending her e-mails suggesting that she "mak[e] porn" with them.[46] One so-called "end user" of her images and videos actually stalked her through a social media page and harassed her with pointed sexual questions.[47] Unable to cope with the demands of college life while at the same time dealing with her immense emotional suffering, Vicky returned home for counseling.[48] Vicky also limits her employment to jobs that do not involve dealing with the public because of the difficulty she experiences when interacting with unknown male adults.[49] She left her job at an ice cream store, for example, because each encounter with a stranger, each smile from a man at the counter, struck at Vicky's deepest fear: has he seen me in the most humiliating moments of my life?[50]

C. Translating the Harms to Economic Losses

Unsurprisingly, the knowledge that thousands of individuals possess images and video of a child victim being raped can inflict deep, life-lasting trauma that extends well beyond the initial sexual abuse. The Supreme

Court's recent decision in *Paroline* agreed with this conclusion when it recognized that it was "common ground that the victim suffers continuing and grievous harm as a result of her knowledge that a large, indeterminate number of individuals have viewed and will in the future view images of the sexual abuse she endured."[51]

This emotional trauma results in economic burdens, particularly for psychological counseling costs and lost income.[52] Although each victim may suffer a baseline amount of harm as a result of such trauma, no two victims are exactly alike. Determining each victim's losses requires a careful analysis of how each victim's life is damaged by child pornography.

For victims like Amy and Vicky, the economic losses are substantial. Both Amy and Vicky have enlisted experts who calculated their losses using standard econometric tools based on their individual circumstances.[53] These calculations serve as the basis for the restitution requests that Amy and Vicky made under federal law from possessors and distributors of their images—restitution that is vitally important to their recovery. The restitution payments have helped them secure not only psychological counseling, but also vocational and educational training to move forward with their lives.[54]

Consider the restitution request Vicky recently filed in a federal criminal case in Washington.[55] In that request, Vicky documented "economic losses" totaling $1,327,166.[56] The losses were comprised of $106,900 in future psychological counseling expenses, $147,830 in educational and vocational counseling needs, $722,511 in lost earnings, $52,110 in expenses paid for such things as forensic evaluations and court costs, and $297,815 in attorneys' fees.[57] Supporting each request was an expert report or declaration.[58]

For example, concerning lost income—the largest item requested—Vicky submitted a forensic economic analysis by Stan V. Smith, an expert economist who isolated the lifetime loss to Vicky's earnings due to the trauma associated with the worldwide circulation of her images and videos.[59] In doing so, Dr. Smith quantified the losses attributable to Vicky's difficulties both in pursuing a college degree and in maintaining employment following her identification as a victim of child pornography. Vicky entered college, but then had to withdraw to focus on therapy.[60] While attempting to hold various jobs, she suffered panic attacks when interacting with men who could have viewed her images.[61] Dr. Smith calculated the economic consequences of a delayed completion of a college degree as well as the reduced employment opportunities that come from restricting her employment to situations where she does not have to interact with unknown men.[62] Accounting for these variables and limitations, Dr. Smith determined that Vicky's net loss of earnings capacity attributable to her ongoing "psychological injuries" related to the worldwide circulation of her images is $722,511.[63]

The goal of the Mandatory Restitution for Sex Crimes provision of the Violence Against Women Act is to restore to victims the losses they suffer as a result of the child pornography crimes. In other words, its purpose is restorative, not punitive.[64] Yet there often seems to be a misunderstanding about the nature of the losses sought by child pornography victims like Amy and Vicky. For example, one academic commentator, Professor Cortney Lollar, recently argued that restitution in such cases is being imposed "not as disgorgement of unlawful economic gains, but as a punitive mechanism of compensation for emotional, psychological, and hedonic losses in a manner resembling civil damages."[65] Professor Lollar then paradoxically argues that such restitution is actually harmful to child pornography victims.[66]

Describing Amy's and Vicky's restitution requests as involving emotional or hedonic losses is inaccurate. Amy and Vicky are only seeking restitution for the kinds of out-of-pocket pecuniary losses that are typically recoverable from convicted criminals in restitution actions.[67] Indeed, Professor Lollar is ultimately forced to concede that "the restitution being requested and ordered is technically for future therapy and mental health treatment and sometimes future lost wages."[68] This is entirely consistent with federal law, which specifically enumerates *pecuniary* losses related to "psychological care" and "lost income" as those that are compensable in restitution.[69]

II. Allocating the Harms Caused by Child Pornography Crimes

Courts have tended to generally agree with the point that child pornography possession crimes cause harm to their victims. The courts have varied widely, however, on the question of how much harm such crimes cause. Indeed, a number of courts have minimized the harm to the point where restitution awards become vanishingly small. In this section we critique these efforts at minimization. We advance the thesis that the proper way to assess the magnitude of harm is not to attempt to disaggregate the harms child pornography victims suffer, but rather to view them in the aggregate. On this view, each criminal who contributes to a child pornography victim's indivisible harm becomes jointly and several liable for the full amount of that harm—the standard answer under conventional tort law principles. The Supreme Court's recent decision in *Paroline v. United States*, which requires disaggregation, misapprehends both the factual and legal predicates for full restitution.

A. The Problems from Disaggregation

Courts considering restitution requests from victims of child pornography crimes have almost uniformly agreed that some harm exists. The generally accepted view is that each act of viewing a victim's image is a gross invasion of privacy that causes additional suffering to a victim. The Ninth Circuit has articulated the conventional view of this point in a case involving restitution requests from both Amy and Vicky:

> Amy and Vicky presented ample evidence that the viewing of their images caused them emotional and psychic pain, violated their privacy interests, and injured their reputation and well-being. Amy, for example, stated that her "privacy ha[d] been invaded" and that she felt like she was "being exploited and used every day and every night." Vicky described having night terrors and panic attacks due to the knowledge that her images were being viewed online. Even without evidence that Amy and Vicky knew about [the defendant's] conduct, the district court could reasonably conclude that Amy and Vicky were "harmed as a result of" [the defendant's] participation in the audience of individuals who viewed the images.[70]

Because viewing those images harms the children depicted, the children are properly considered victims of those who possess the images. The U.S. Supreme Court has acknowledged that "[t]he full extent of [these victims'] suffering is hard to grasp."[71] Yet in a series of cases concerning the amount of restitution that child pornography victims may collect from child pornography possessors, federal courts have often struggled to determine how much harm possessors of child pornography cause their victims, sometimes minimizing the harm from each crime.

This minimization is especially visible in cases like Amy's and Vicky's, where the victim's image has been viewed by thousands (or even tens of thousands) of criminals. In those cases, some courts seem to suggest that the harm caused by any one defendant who possesses child pornography is minimal. For example, in one case involving Amy, the D.C. Circuit acknowledged that the "possession of child pornography causes harm to the minors depicted."[72] But the court concluded that one criminal defendant who possessed and viewed Amy's image only "added to her injuries"; "[s]he would have suffered tremendously from her sexual abuse regardless of what [he] did."[73] Similarly, in a case involving Vicky, the Fourth Circuit stated that one child pornography possessor was not responsible for the losses Vicky has suffered; indeed, the court went so far as to state that Vicky's financial losses are "wholly disproportionate to the harm inflicted by an individual defendant."[74]

Unfortunately the Supreme Court's recent *Paroline* decision went down this path. *Paroline* reversed the Fifth Circuit's award of full restitution to Amy on the grounds that Mr. Paroline's "contribution to the causal process underlying [Amy's] losses was very minor, both compared to the combined acts of all other relevant offenders, and in comparison to the contributions of other individual offenders, particularly distributors (who may have caused hundreds or thousands of further viewings) and the initial producer of the child pornography."[75] *Paroline* ultimately concluded that any one defendant's restitution obligation was to be based on "the significance of the individual defendant's conduct in light of the broader causal process that produced the victim's losses."[76]

Paroline and similar lower court opinions are troubling because they almost seem to cavalierly invite additional victimization. Under such opinions, the larger the number of criminals who view a victim's images, the less responsible any particular criminal is for the harm caused to the victim. In other words, "the more, the merrier." This problem has been aptly named by one of the nation's leading tort law scholars, Professor Richard Wright, as a "tortfest": each criminal can reduce his restitution liability by encouraging other men to join in and abuse the victim.[77] For example, if a rapist would cause a victim to suffer $10,000 in medical bills (a physical examination, etc.), a gang rapist who gets four of his friends to join in attacking the victim might be responsible for only $2,000, his "fair share" of the bill for the medical examination. Of course, such an approach unfairly and even perversely invites greater victimization. It also might leave the victim with uncompensated losses if the four friends are never apprehended or are insolvent.

Amy raised this point in her arguments to the Supreme Court in *Paroline*. The Court, however, found the point unpersuasive because unlike gang rapists, child pornography possessors do not act in concert.[78] The Court, however, never explained why this should make a difference. The goal of restitution is to compensate victims, regardless of whether they suffered harm from defendants actually individually or in concert. Moreover, as explained in the introduction to section I above, although child pornography defendants may not formally agree to act in concert, as a practical matter they are all part of a de facto joint criminal enterprise.

The obvious and conventional solution to concerns about how to allocate responsibility is to bar a criminal from debating what fraction of the single loss he has caused a victim. A standard illustration is offered by Professors Harper and James, who give the example of "several ruffians [who] set upon a man and beat him, each inflicting separate wounds." Under traditional tort doctrine, the ruffians—intentional tortfeasors—are each "liable for the whole injury."[79] Child pornography victims are the twenty-first-century victims of these hypothetical attackers. A victim like Amy, for instance, is essentially "set upon" by digital "ruffians" who are all harming her. Even if her psychological wounds can somehow be viewed as "separate," conventional tort law demands that liability for her "whole injury" be imposed on each and every one of the ruffians, that is, each and every child pornography distributor and possessor.

B. Child Pornography Possessors Contribute to All of a Victim's Losses

Some courts—including the Supreme Court in *Paroline*—have taken the position that the losses suffered by child pornography victims should be allocated across countless defendants. Using what it described as "traditional principles" of tort law, an influential D.C. Circuit opinion, *United States v. Monzel*, rejected Amy's argument that a child pornography possessor should be held jointly and severally liable for all of her losses.[80] Because Monzel's possession of a "single image" was not independently sufficient to cause the entirety of Amy's injury, the Circuit reasoned that he did not create a single, "indivisible" injury.[81] Thus, because Amy suffered separate injuries each time someone viewed her images, Monzel was obligated to pay restitution only for the separate injury for which he was individually responsible.[82] With less extended analysis, *Paroline* reached essentially the same conclusion, limiting a defendant's responsibility to pay restitution to his "relative role in the causal process that underlies the victim's general losses."[83]

Paroline and similar opinions conveniently duck the fundamental question left by this approach: Just exactly how much restitution should a defendant pay for injuring Amy? In *Monzel*, for example, the D.C. Circuit remanded to the district court for such a calculation. And the district court judge then threw up her hands, awarding Amy no restitution whatsoever because she was unable to determine what fraction of Amy's substantial losses could be specifically assigned to Monzel. In the wake of the *Paroline* decision, some district courts have had great difficulty in applying the Supreme Court's instructions. A few months after the decision, one frustrated district court judge wrote, "It appears to this Court that some of the factors the Supreme Court suggests be considered are at best difficult, and at worst impossible to calculate in this case as in most similar cases."[84]

But the more fundamental problem with this disaggregation approach is that it fails to recognize that the crime of one child pornography defendant combines with that of other criminals to produce an aggregated harm to Amy. When these crimes are all combined, the collective conduct overdetermines, or is more than sufficient to cause the harm (i.e., the costs of counseling), because Amy will presumably need the same amount of counseling regardless of whether the number of defendants possessing her images was 69,999 (without a particular defendant) or 70,000 (with him).[85] In such situations, the standard answer in tort law is *not* the one reached by the Supreme Court; instead, the standard answer is to hold all defendants jointly and severally liable for the entire injury.

The problem described by *Paroline* is a conundrum about factual causation that modern tort theory resolved long ago.[86] As the *Restatement (Third) of Torts* describes the problem, "[i]n some cases, tortious conduct by one actor is insufficient, even with other background causes, to cause the plaintiff's harm. Nevertheless, when combined with conduct by other persons, the conduct overdetermines the harm, i.e., is more than sufficient to cause the harm."[87] The standard solution not to award the victims nothing in such circumstances. Instead, the standard answer, as recounted in the *Restatement (Third) of Torts*, is to treat each wrongdoer as being a contributing cause to the entirety of the loss that is created.

The *Restatement* aptly recognizes that it is never possible to identify a single "cause" for an event. For example, an arsonist who uses a match to light a house ablaze is the cause of the house burning down only because of the existence of other conditions as well, such as a lack of rain at the time, the existence of oxygen in the atmosphere, the delay in the fire department responding to the fire, and so forth. It is all of the things—a causal set—that contributes to the ultimate harm.[88]

Reasoning from this insight, it is then possible to consider examples such as five people beating a sixth, who dies from the blows, any three of which would have been sufficient to kill the victim.[89] This is an illustration of an overdetermined causal set causing harm; none of the five attackers is the but-for cause of death, as it is possible to eliminate one of the five attackers and death still results. But this would produce the anomalous and counterintuitive conclusion that the victim died from *none* of the attackers! Instead of this bizarre result, at least for purposes of tort law,[90] the solution is that all five of the attackers are responsible for the death. It is possible to construct a causal set of three of the attackers, which produces the death. And the mere fact that other causal sets could be constructed is no defense to tort liability. Under the *Restatement*, "[w]hen an actor's tortious conduct is not a factual cause of harm under the standard in § 26 [i.e., independently sufficient or but-for causation] only because one or more other causal sets exist that are also sufficient to cause the harm at the same time, the actor's tortious conduct is a factual cause of the harm."[91]

The *Restatement* notes that well-established tort precedent (predating Congress' 1994 enactment of the restitution statute) underlies this contributing cause approach. The *Restatement* reporter explains that, for example, "[s]ince the first asbestos case in which a plaintiff was successful, courts have allowed plaintiffs to recover from all defendants to whose asbestos products the plaintiff was exposed."[92] While numerous toxic tort cases illustrate the contributing cause approach, the *Restatement* identifies much deeper roots: "Nuisance cases were the pre-toxic-substances equivalent of asbestos and other such cases, and courts resolved them similarly."[93] In other words, traditionally in American tort law, an "independent-sufficiency requirement is not followed by the courts. . . . [Instead], courts have allowed the plaintiff to recover from each defendant who contributed to the . . . injury, even though none of the defendants' individual contributions were either necessary or sufficient by itself for the occurrence of the injury."[94]

In their restitution applications, Amy and Vicky are seeking recovery for a single "injury," their psychological counseling costs. Those counseling costs do not increase or decrease with the addition or subtraction of an additional criminal from the estimated tens of thousands of men who have viewed their rapes. In other words, the psychological counseling costs are "indivisible," because the evidence fails to provide "a reasonable basis for the factfinder to determine . . . the amount of [those costs] separately caused" by any particular child pornography possessor or distributor.[95] Against that backdrop, it is not surprising the Congress directed that each convicted child pornography criminal who contributed to a victim's psychological counseling costs must pay for the "full amount" of those costs in the child pornography restitution statute.

The Sixth Circuit's decision in *Michie v. Great Lakes Steel Division, National Steel Corp.*[96] offers a good illustration of this point. In that case, several air polluters argued that plaintiffs could not proceed with a nuisance action against them when their pollutants "mix[ed] in the air so that their separate effects in creating the individual injuries [were] impossible to analyze."[97] The Sixth Circuit rejected this approach, holding that Michigan tort law allowed the polluters to be held liable as joint tortfeasors for the indivisible injuries caused.[98] The court noted that "it is clear that there is a manifest unfairness in putting on the injured party the impossible burden of proving the specific shares of harm done by each."[99] The rule in such cases is that "[w]hen the triers of the facts decide that they cannot make a division of injuries we have, by their own finding, nothing more or less than an indivisible injury, and the precedents as to indivisible injuries will control."[100]

The application of this principle to child pornography possession cases is obvious. Although it is possible that an individual tortfeasor's action—such as polluting the air or possessing child pornography—is neither "necessary" nor "sufficient" by itself to cause all the injuries, the general approach in American tort law is to hold each tortfeasor fully liable for the entire injury caused.[101] The injury to victims of child pornography due to possession or distribution manifests itself in the same way as other harms caused by multiple tortfeasors. And although some injuries may be theoretically divisible, where it is practically impossible to divide up the injury by causation, "the modern approach has been to hold each defendant . . . jointly and severally liable for all the injuries."[102] Thus, the appellate courts should have paid closer attention to one of the most compelling reasons to apply joint and several liability in analogous tort situations—that is, joint and several liability is applicable where "there is no reasonable basis for division" of the injury suffered.[103]

To this conclusion, it might be objected that each child pornography possessor contributes only a trivial amount to a victims' ultimate harm and thus liability is improper. In support of such a conclusion, one could cite tort theory that there is no liability "where one defendant has made a clearly proved but quite insignificant contribution to the result, as where he throws a lighted match into a forest fire."[104] The *Restatement*, for example, recognizes that a trivial cause can be excluded from tort liability.[105] The *Restatement*, however, specifically notes that this triviality limitation "is not applicable if the trivial contributing cause is necessary for the outcome . . . ,"[106] with a cross-reference back to the contributing cause cases that involve constructing a sufficient causal set. Put another way, if all causes would be regarded as trivial causes, then none of them can be regarded as trivial causes. Of course, child pornography possessors are part of a causal set sufficient to produce Amy's psychological harm. Thus, their crimes are not like tossing a match into an already raging fire. Instead, conceptually the proper hypothetical would be thousands of arsonists all collectively tossing matches into a forest to start the fire or, alternatively, sequentially tossing matches to keep a fire burning. Rather than allowing all of the wrongdoers to escape liability through an exercise in blame shifting and finger pointing, standard tort principles hold all of them liable.

In any event, Congress itself has answered what is considered "trivial" in the context of restitution. Section 2259 mandates imposition of a restitution award for the "full amount" of Amy's losses in every case of a criminal conviction for child pornography possession.[107] By operation of law, the serious felony of possessing child pornography is never trivial.

Amy presented all these arguments to the Supreme Court in *Paroline*. And the majority acknowledged that tort law had, in some areas, applied the principle of "aggregate causation."[108] The majority, however, tersely held that such principles "can be taken too far."[109] Curiously, the majority seemed to agree that the "strict logic" of the recognized tort principles supported Amy.[110] But the majority was simply unwilling to proceed logically because of the "the striking outcome of this reasoning—that each possessor of the victim's images would bear the consequences of the acts of the many thousands who possessed those images."[111]

"Striking" outcome or not, the Court should have simply followed the generally recognized tort principles. Criminal defendants like Paroline have a choice about whether to commit their crimes. The fact that they are part of a vast enterprise with thousands of other similar actors should be an aggravating factor, not a mitigating one. As Justice Sotomayor explained in her dissent, restitution statutes should offer "no safety-in-numbers exception for defendants who possess images of a child's abuse in common with other offenders."[112] Justice Sotomayor went on to explain that "the injuries caused by child pornography possessors are impossible to apportion in any practical sense. It cannot be said, for example, that Paroline's offense alone required Amy to attend five additional minutes of therapy, or that it caused some discrete portion of her lost income."[113] She concluded that the restitution statute should be interpreted to mandate "full restitution," which "dispenses with this guesswork . . . and in doing so it harmonizes with the settled tort law tradition concerning indivisible injuries."[114]

Fortunately the Supreme Court does not have the last word on restitution in this country. The decision about how much restitution to award victims of child pornography crimes belongs to Congress. Congress should amend the statute to ensure that child pornography victims receive "full" restitution. And Congress has a bill pending before it that would exactly that. Known as the Amy and Vicky Act,[115] the bill should be enacted as soon as possible to ensure that victims will not be left without restitution for losses inflicted by criminals too numerous to count.

Conclusion

In this chapter, we have attempted to provide some insight into the serious harms suffered by the victims of child pornography possession crimes. Possessing child pornography is not just looking at "kiddie porn." Instead, such criminal acts scar real-world victims, who live in constant fear of being exposed and humiliated by those who are obtaining sexual gratification through viewing images of their childhood rape. We have tried to illustrate this point in describing the experience of two young victims of child pornography crimes, Amy and Vicky. Against the backdrop of the suffering of victims such as these, stiff criminal penalties unsurprisingly address, as one court aptly put it, "a tide of depravity that Congress, expressing the will of our nation, has condemned in the strongest terms."[116] Without trying to identify the exact quantum of punishment appropriate for child pornography possession, it is clear that the crime produces real and quantifiable harms on its victims that should be reflected in significant prison terms.

But in addition to punishing those who possess child pornography, it is equally important to compensate their victims. When awarding restitution for such aggregated crimes, some courts have minimized each defendant's culpability to the vanishing point. This concern is ironically most acute in cases (like Amy's and Vicky's) where the victim's images have been most widely viewed. Trying to apportion the amount of financial loss among tens of thousands of criminals invariably neglects the very significant psychological harm each crime causes. Those viewings represent continuous invasions of privacy that cause lasting psychological injury.

Traditional tort principles instruct instead that each defendant should be viewed as a contributing cause to the entirety of a victim's injury. This approach properly recognizes that a defendant is part of a group of criminals who cause harm—a harm that is aggravated by the presence of many others working together. Acknowledging the seriousness of harm caused by each possessor is important not only for determining how to compensate victims under federal restitution law, but also for calibrating the criminal penalties imposed for and the enforcement resources devoted to the possession of child pornography. Child pornography possessors should not be able to hide in a crowd. Instead, they are all jointly responsible for seriously harming victims—and should be held fully accountable through both appropriate criminal penalties and awards of full restitution.

NOTES

1. http://cnsnews.com/news/article/michael-w-chapman/san-francisco-s-gay-icon-larry-brinkin-guilty-felony-child-porn.

2. Paul Cassell and James Marsh have represented child pornography victims at every level of the federal court system in their efforts to obtain restitution, including Amy and Vicky, two child pornography victims whose plight is discussed in this chapter. Jeremy Christiansen has assisted in preparing briefs filed for Amy through the University of Utah Appellate Clinic.

3. 18 U.S.C. § 2259.

4. Paroline v. United States, 134 S. Ct. 1710 (2014).

5. Federal law criminalizes possession of "child pornography," 18 U.S.C. § 2252A, although in other places it is referred to as "material involving the sexual exploitation of minors," 18 U.S.C. § 2252.

6. *See, e.g.*, Douglas A. Berman, *If "Most Egregious and Horrific" Kiddie Porn Offender Gets 15 Years, What Should Mere Downloaders Get?*, SENT'G L. & POL'Y BLOG (May 13, 2011, 10:01 AM), http://sentencing.typepad.com/sentencing_law_and_policy/2011/05/if-most-egregious-and-horrific-kiddie-porn-offender-gets-15-years-what-should-mere-downloaders-get.html; *cf.* Carissa Byrne Hessick, *Disentangling Child Pornography from Child Sex Abuse*, 88 WASH. U. L. REV. 853, 864 (2011) (contending that sentences for child pornography crimes have become entangled with the sentences for the underlying sex abuse).

7. NCMEC quite accurately refers to these images as "crime scene photos." Brief of the National Center for Missing and Exploited Children, United States v. Paroline, No. 12-8561 at 18. NCMEC also reports that "[a]pproximately 6% of identified children were infants or toddlers; 39% were prepubescent; and 55% were pubescent when the images were created. The files depict several types of sexually exploitative activity, including oral copulation (84%), anal and/or vaginal penetration (76%), use of foreign objects or sexual devices (52%), bondage and/or sado-masochism (44%), urination and/or defecation (20%), and bestiality (4%)." *Id.* at 4–5.

8. Motion for Leave to Participate as Amicus Curiae and Brief of the National Crime Victim Law Institute as Amicus Curiae in Support of Petitioners at 1–2 n.1, Amy & Vicky v. Kennedy, No. 12-651 (2012) (quoting 1 SHARON W. COOPER ET AL., MEDICAL, LEGAL, & SOCIAL SCIENCE ASPECTS OF CHILD SEXUAL EXPLOITATION 258 (2005)).

9. http://en.wikipedia.org/wiki/Child_pornography (visited on Feb. 28, 2014).

10. *Ferber*, 458 U.S. at 759–60.

11. *Osborne v. Ohio*, 495 U.S. 103, 109–10 (1990).

12. *Ferber*, 458 U.S. at 760.

13. *See, e.g.*, 18 U.S.C. 2252(a)(4).

14. Pub. L. No. 104-208, § 121(12), 110 Stat. 3009–27 (1996); *see also* 132 Cong. Rec.

33781 (1986) (statement of Sen. Roth) ("[M]y subcommittee's investigation disclosed the existence of a seamy underground network of child molesters . . . and it showed that the very lifeblood of this loosely organized underground society is child pornography.").

15. Department of Justice, *National Strategy for Child Exploitation Prevention* 17 (2001).

16. U.S. Sentencing Commission, *Report to the Congress: Federal Child Pornography Offenses* 51 (2012) (hereinafter "*Sentencing Comm'n Report to Congress*").

17. *Id.* at 51–52.

18. *United States v. Reingold*, 731 F.3d 204, 217 (2d Cir. 2013).

19. *See* Rachel O'Connell, *Paedophiles Networking on the Internet*, in CHILD ABUSE ON THE INTERNET: ENDING THE SILENCE 65, 77 (Carlos A. Arnaldo, ed., 2001) (networks for sharing child pornography are "an example of a complex criminal conspiracy").

20. New York v. Ferber, 458 U.S. 747 (1982).

21. *Id.* at 758 n.9 (internal quotation marks and citations omitted).

22. *Id.* at 759 n.10 (internal quotation marks omitted) (quoting David P. Shouvlin, *Preventing the Sexual Exploitation of Children: A Model Act*, 17 WAKE FOREST L. REV. 535 (1981)).

23. *Paroline*, 134 S. Ct. at 1226 (emphasis added); *see also id.* at 1732 (Roberts, J., dissenting) (noting that child pornography victims suffer a "qualitatively different injury" from other types of victims, an injury that is "a result of the collective actions of a huge number of people—beginning with [the initial abuser], to the distributors who make those images more widely available, *to the possessors* . . . who view [those] images" (emphasis added)); *id.* at 1741 (Sotomayor, J., dissenting) ("Child pornography possessors are jointly liable . . . for they act in concert as part of a global network of possessors, distributors, and producers who pursue the common purpose of trafficking in images of child sexual abuse. . . . By communally browsing and downloading Internet child pornography, offenders . . . fuel the process that allows the industry to flourish.").

24. These names are pseudonyms used in all court hearings to protect the victims' privacy.

25. The harms Amy suffers from child pornography are detailed in the expert evaluations and her own victim impact statements that accompany her restitution requests in various cases. This part relies specifically on the reports and statements contained as attachments to one of Amy's recent restitution requests, submitted in March 2013. *See* Letter from James R. Marsh, Counsel for "Amy," Marsh Law Firm PLLC, to Camil Skipper, Appellate Chief, E.D. Cal. U.S. Attorney's Office (Mar. 22, 2013) [hereinafter "Amy's Restitution Request"] (on file with authors). Attachment 1 of this request contains Amy's victim impact statement, hereinafter referred to as "Amy's 2013 Impact Statement"; Attachment 2 contains Dr. Joyanna Silberg's November 21, 2008, report of her psychological evaluation of Amy, hereinafter referred to as "Amy's Psychological Evaluation", and Attachment 6 contains Dr. Stan V. Smith's September 15, 2008, report that calculates Amy's lost income and other economic losses attributable to the distribution of her child sex abuse images, hereinafter referred to as "Amy's Economic Loss Report."

26. Amy's 2013 Impact Statement, *supra* note 25, at 1.

27. *See* Amy's Psychological Evaluation, *supra* note 25, at 2.

28. *See id.*; *see also* Bazelon, *The Price of a Stolen Childhood,* http://www.nytimes.com/2013/01/27/magazine/how-much-can-restitution-help-victims-of-child-pornography.html?pagewanted=all&_r=0 at 25 (describing how Amy's uncle forced her to per-

form sexual poses for photographs in response to specific requests from anonymous Internet users).

29. Amy's Psychological Evaluation, *supra* note 25, at 2–3 (quoting notes of Amy's original therapist, Dr. Ruby Salazar).

30. *Id.* at 3; Amy's 2013 Impact Statement, *supra* note 25, at 1.

31. Amy is the victim portrayed in what law enforcement officials have identified as the "Misty" series. As of July 2009, analysts at NCMEC had encountered more than 35,570 separate images associated with the "Misty" series, received from law enforcement officials around the world. NCMEC Brief, *supra* note 7, at 5.

32. Amy's 2013 Impact Statement, *supra* note 25, at 2.

33. Amy's Psychological Evaluation, *supra* note 25, at 8. Dr. Silberg explains that the feelings of shame and humiliation that are typically felt by victims of sexual abuse are "multiplied exponentially for victims of internet child pornography." *Id.* at 9. With typical sexual abuse victims, therapists can offer "anonymity" along with the "acknowledgment that they deserve this protection of privacy." *Id.* Dr. Silberg explains, however, that "knowing one's image is out there at all times is an invasion of privacy of the highest degree which makes the victim feel known, revealed and publically shamed, rather than anonymous." *Id.* The course of treatment for these victims must account for the unique harms involved, as certain therapeutic techniques useful to survivors of sexual abuse might actually be "ineffective and potentially harmful" to victims of child pornography. *See id.* The "imagery technique," for example, is used to help victims cope with flashbacks of abuse and requires the victim to imagine herself "going back in time and standing up to the abuser to undo the experience of victimization in their imagination." *Id.* But, as Dr. Silberg explains, "[f]or victims like Amy, such a technique would actually be harmful as she has to face [that] she can never erase the ongoing 'evidence' and 'proof' of what she was forced to do. Such an exercise would add to her feelings [of] helplessness." *Id.*

34. *See* Amy's Economic Loss Report, *supra* note 25, at 3.

35. *See* Amy's 2013 Impact Statement, *supra* note 25, at 3.

36. The facts about the harms Vicky suffers from child pornography come from the reports and statements contained within one of Vicky's recent restitution requests, which is included as an unsealed exhibit (Exhibit B) to a government sentencing memorandum, which itself is still sealed. *See* Government's Resentencing Memorandum Regarding Restitution at Exhibit B, United States v. Kennedy, No. 2:08-CR-00354-RAJ-1 (W.D. Wash. Aug. 21, 2012) [hereinafter "Vicky's Restitution Request"]. The restitution request itself contains several relevant exhibits: Exhibit 1 contains an August 2012 letter from Vicky to a district court judge in Washington State regarding the sentencing of a defendant convicted of possessing her images, hereinafter referred to as "Vicky's Letter to Sentencing Judge;" Exhibit 2 contains two victim impact statements written by Vicky, hereinafter referred to as "Vicky's 2008 Impact Statement" and "Vicky's 2011 Impact Statement," respectively; Exhibit 4 contains two reports of her psychological evaluations conducted by Dr. Randall L. Green, which will be referred to hereinafter as "Vicky's May 2009 Psychological Evaluation" and "Vicky's Dec. 2009 Psychological Evaluation" respectively; and Exhibit 9 contains Dr. Stan V. Smith's November 10, 2010, report calculating Vicky's lost income and other economic losses attributable to the distribution of her child sex abuse images, hereinafter referred to as "Vicky's Economic Loss Report."

37. *See* Vicky's May 2009 Psychological Evaluation, *supra* note 36, at 18–21; *see also* Vicky's 2008 Impact Statement, *supra* note 36, at 1.

38. Vicky's May 2009 Psychological Evaluation, *supra* note 36, at 20.

39. Vicky's 2008 Impact Statement, *supra* note 36, at 1.

40. *See* Vicky's 2011 Impact Statement, *supra* note 36, at 1 ("My world came crashing down the day I learned that pictures of me being sexually abused had been circulated on the internet. Since then, little has changed except my understanding that the distribution of these pictures grows bigger and bigger by the day and there is nothing I can do about it."); *see also* Vicky's May 2009 Psychological Evaluation, *supra* note 36, at 24–29 (detailing Vicky's experiences following her discovery of the worldwide distribution of her images).

41. *See* Vicky's Dec. 2009 Psychological Evaluation, *supra* note 36, at 2–8 (describing Vicky's deteriorating emotional state in the wake of learning about the circulation of her images online). Dr. Green categorized the "knowledge of the dissemination and proliferation of the images of [Vicky] at her times of greatest humiliation and degradation" as a Type II trauma, which represents a "chronic, toxic condition, the knowledge of which continuously works like corrosive acid on the psyche of the individual." Vicky's May 2009 Psychological Evaluation, *supra* note 36, at 6. Other examples of stressors that constitute Type II traumas include the "challenges endured by those who live near Chernobyl, Three Mile Island or the Love Canal or a war zone." *Id.* at 6–7.

42. Vicky's 2011 Impact Statement, *supra* note 36, at 1.

43. Vicky's Letter to Sentencing Judge, *supra* note 36, at 2.

44. Vicky's 2011 Impact Statement, *supra* note 36, at 1.

45. *Id.* at 1–2.

46. *Id.*

47. *Id.*; *see* Press Release, U.S. Dep't of Justice, Man Who Harassed and Stalked Victim of Child Pornography Series Sentenced to 25 Years in Prison (April 28, 2010), *available at* http://www.justice.gov/usao/nv/news/2010/04282010.html.

48. Vicky's 2011 Impact Statement, *supra* note 36, at 3; *see also* Vicky's Dec. 2009 Psychological Evaluation, *supra* note 36, at 4–5 ("[Vicky] says that if there had been a way to afford to stay in college and seek therapy rather than return to her home town, she would have much preferred doing so. [Vicky] says, 'Coming home is difficult because so many know and ask about [her depiction in child pornography].' However, she says that she has learned that she can't escape her issues by changing her geographical location, in view of the impact of the universal reach of the Internet. She explains, 'They follow me.'").

49. Vicky's Letter to Sentencing Judge, *supra* note 36, at 2.

50. Vicky's Dec. 2009 Psychological Evaluation, *supra* note 36, at 2, 4–5, 8. Vicky offered insight into this fear in a statement she wrote for the recent sentencing of defendant Joshua Kennedy:

> I understand that [Kennedy] had a good job, and that many people who are looked up to in the community came to make statements on his behalf at his first sentencing. This tells me that he blended into society and would have previously been seen as someone who was law-abiding and not someone who enjoyed looking at pictures of children being raped. This feeds my paranoia even more,

> and confirms for me that I do need to be afraid of people that I see on an everyday basis, because anyone I see is suspect of being a consumer of child pornography. I could have walked past Joshua Kennedy on the street any time and he might have recognized me from those pictures he had of my sexual abuse. This chills me to the bone.

Vicky's Letter to Sentencing Judge, *supra* note 36, at 2.

51. *Paroline v. United States*, 134 W. Ct. 1710, 1726 (2014).

52. 18 U.S.C. § 2259(b)(3)(A)–(F) (2012).

53. *See* Amy's Economic Loss Report, *supra* note 25; Vicky's Economic Loss Report, *supra* note 36.

54. *See* Bazelon, *supra* note 28, at 45–47.

55. *See* Vicky's Restitution Request, *supra* note 36.

56. *Id.* at 1.

57. *Id.* at 1–2.

58. *See id.* at Exhibit 4 (original and updated psychological evaluation reports); *id.* at Exhibit 7 (vocational evaluation report); *id.* at Exhibit 9 (forensic economic analysis report); *id.* at Exhibit 13 (declaration of attorneys' fees and costs).

59. *See* Vicky's Economic Loss Report, *supra* note 36, at 2–5. To assess her specific situation, Dr. Smith relied on the victim impact statements of Vicky and her mother, the reports of vocational and psychological experts who evaluated Vicky, and his own interview of Vicky. *Id.* at 1.

60. *Id.* Although she returned to school after taking a year off, her psychologist has recommended that due to her "reduced tolerance for stress," she should take a reduced course load each semester, which will further delay her career. *Id.* at 4.

61. *Id.*; *see supra* notes 49–50 and accompanying text.

62. Specifically, Dr. Smith determined that her net loss of earnings capacity is $722,511 to age sixty-seven for full-time employment, assuming a three-year delay of entry into the workforce and a 20 percent reduction in worklife, as she will likely experience more frequent job changes and time off from work than her peers. Vicky's Economic Loss Report, *supra* note 36, at 5.

63. *Id.* at 1.

64. Most federal courts have agreed that restitution is remedial in nature and therefore not subject to Eighth Amendment punishment or "excessive fine" limitations, but a circuit split exists on this issue. *Compare, e.g., In re* Amy Unknown, 701 F.3d 749, 771–72 (5th Cir. 2012) (en banc) (holding Eighth Amendment not applicable to § 2259 because the purpose of restitution "is remedial, not punitive"), *with* United States v. Dubose, 146 F.3d 1141, 1144 (9th Cir. 1998) ("[R]estitution under the [Mandatory Victim Restitution Act ("MVRA")] is punishment" and subject to Eighth Amendment limitations "because the MVRA has not only remedial, but also deterrent, rehabilitative, and retributive purposes." (citation omitted)). We believe that restitution is nonpunitive for the reasons articulated in *United States v. Visinaiz*, 344 F. Supp. 2d 1310, 1318–23 (D. Utah 2004) (Cassell, J.). *See also* Amicus Brief of Vicky and Andy, *U.S. v. Paroline*, No. 12-8561 (explaining why restitution is not punitive).

65. Cortney Lollar, *Child Pornography and the Restitution Revolution*, 103 J. CRIM. L. & CRIMINOLOGY 343, 346 (2013).

66. *Id.* at 382. Federal law affords child pornography victims the right to receive (and

to opt out of receiving) notifications when a defendant is arrested or charged in connection with their images or videos. *See* Crime Victims' Rights Act of 2004, 18 U.S.C. § 3771(a) (2012); Crime Control Act of 1990, 42 U.S.C. § 10607(b)–(c) (2006); *see also* DEP'T OF JUSTICE, CHILD PORNOGRAPHY VICTIMS ASSISTANCE (CPVA) PROGRAM: A REFERENCE FOR VICTIMS AND PARENT/GUARDIAN OF VICTIMS, *available at* http://www.fbi.gov/stats-services/victim_assistance/brochures-handouts/cpva.pdf (describing victims' opt-out rights). According to Professor Lollar, victims would be better off not being notified about the circulation of their images and not receiving restitution for the losses associated with their injuries because:

> Money is not going to make the young women depicted in child pornography emotionally whole or restore what was lost. Yet by notifying child pornography victims of all known uses of their images and then ordering compensation, legislators and courts are reinforcing the message that a young woman's worth is in her body and is linked to the sexual acts in which she participates. . . . Notification and restitution reaffirm the damaging messages the young women learned during their abuse.

Lollar, *supra* note 65, at 382. Vicky herself has pointedly responded to such criticism in her victim impact statement, however, explaining:

> I have a right to know who has my pictures and who is trading them. While it hurts to know, not knowing makes me feel more in danger. To be criticized for wanting to know what is going on with the humiliating pictures of me, to exercise the few rights I have under the law, only makes the hurt that much worse. How can such people not understand, or care?

Vicky's 2011 Impact Statement, *supra* note 36, at 1.

67. In fact, Dr. Smith calculated hedonic damages (reduction in the value of life) for Vicky to be an additional $2,615,542 on top of the economic losses he calculated in light of her lost earnings. *See* Vicky's Economic Loss Report, *supra* note 36, at 7. Vicky, however, has never requested restitution in a criminal case on the basis of such losses.

68. Lollar, *supra* note 65, at 348 n.10. Notably, although they deny responsibility, even the defendants in these cases have not challenged the calculation of the losses. *See, e.g.*, United States v. Laraneta, 700 F.3d 983, 989 (7th Cir. 2012) (noting defendant did not challenge the district judge's calculation of Amy's and Vicky's losses, which were $3,367,854 and $1,224,697.04 respectively).

69. *See* 18 U.S.C. § 2259(b)(3)(A)–(F) (2012) (specifying economic-based losses available to victims of child pornography).

70. United States v. Kennedy, 643 F.3d 1251, 1263 (9th Cir. 2011) (citation omitted).

71. *Paroline v. United States*, 134 S. Ct. 1710, 1717 (2014).

72. United States v. Monzel, 641 F.3d 528, 537 (D.C. Cir. 2011).

73. *Id.* at 538.

74. United States v. Burgess, 684 F.3d 445, 458 (4th Cir. 2012).

75. *Paroline*, 134 S. Ct. at 1725.

76. *Id.* at 1727–28.

77. *See* Richard W. Wright, *The Logic and Fairness of Joint and Several Liability*, 23 MEMPHIS U.L. REV. 45, 57 (1992).

78. *Paroline*, 134 S. Ct. at 1725.

79. 2 FOWLER HARPER & FLEMING JAMES, THE LAW OF TORTS 1124 (1956) (hereinafter *Harper & James*).

80. United States v. Monzel, 641 F.3d 528, 538 (D.C. Cir. 2011).

81. *Id.* at 538–39.

82. *Id.* at 538.

83. *Paroline*, 134 S. Ct. at 1727.

84. United States v. Crisostomi, CR 12-166-M, 2014 WL 3510215 (D.R.I. July 16, 2014).

85. In Amy's brief to the U.S. Supreme Court, she estimated that approximately 70,000 men around the world had viewed her sexual abuse images, relying on 2009 data from NCMEC and the U.S. Justice Department. Brief for Respondent Amy, *United States v. Paroline*, No. 12-8561, at 65. More current data from NCMEC would place the number of men at around 140,000. *See* Brief for Amicus National Center for Missing and Exploited Children, *United States v. Paroline*, No. 12-8561, at 11 (noting doubling of Amy's images found at American crime scenes from 35,000 to 70,000 over the period 2009 to 2013).

86. *See generally* Eric A. Johnson, *Criminal Liability for Loss of a Chance*, 91 IOWA L. REV. 59, 88–92 (2005) (explaining development of the "multiple sufficient causal sets" rule which emerged as the "dominant theory of causation among tort scholars").

87. THE AMERICAN LAW INSTITUTE, RESTATEMENT (THIRD) OF TORTS: LIABILITY FOR PHYSICAL AND EMOTIONAL HARM § 27 cmt. f (2000) (hereinafter cited as *Restatement*).

88. *See id., Restatement* § 27 cmt. f, Rptrs. Note at 391 (collecting authorities discussing this point).

89. *See* W. PAGE KEETON ET AL., PROSSER AND KEETON ON THE LAW OF TORTS 267 n.25 (5th ed. 1984).

90. *Cf. Burrage v. United States*, No. 12-7515 (U.S. Jan. 27, 2014) (concluding that for purposes of a mandatory minimum statute, death does not "result" from illegal distribution of heroin to a victim unless that death was the but-for cause of death).

91. *Restatement, supra* note 87 at § 27 cmt. f at 381.

92. *Restatement, supra* note 87 at § 27, cmt. g, Rptrs. Note at 392 (*citing, e.g.*, Borel v. Fibreboard Paper Prods., 493 F.2d 1076, 1094 (5th Cir. 1973); Ingram v. ACandS, Inc., 977 F.2d 1332, 1340 (9th Cir. 1992); Richard W. Wright, *Causation, Responsibility, Risk, Probability, Naked Statistics, and Proof: Pruning the Bramble Bush by Clarifying the Concepts*, 73 IOWA L. REV. 1001, 1073 & n.384 (1988) (collecting authorities)).

93. *Restatement* § 27 cmt. g, Rptrs. Note at 393 (*citing* Bollinger v. Am. Asphalt Roof Corp., 19 S.W.2d 544, 552 (Mo. Ct. App. 1929) ("If there was enough of smoke and fumes definitely found to have come from defendant's plant to cause perceptible injury to plaintiffs, then the fact that another person or persons also joined in causing the injury would be no defense; and it was not necessary for the jury to find how much smoke and fumes came from each place.")); *see also* Phillips Petroleum Co. v. Hardee, 189 F.2d 205, 212 (5th Cir. 1951) ("According to the great weight of authority where the concurrent or successive acts or omissions of two or more persons, although acting independently of each other, are in combination, the direct or proximate cause of a single injury to a third person, and it is impossible to determine in what proportion each contributed to the injury, either is responsible for the whole injury, even though his act alone might not have caused the entire injury, or the same damage might have resulted from the act

of the other tortfeasor." (*quoting* AMERICAN JURISPRUDENCE)); Northrup v. Eakes, 178 P. 266, 268 (Okla. 1918) (where "separate and independent acts or negligence of several combine to produce directly a single injury, each is responsible for the entire result, even though his act or neglect alone might not have caused it"); The "Atlas," 93 U.S. 302, 315 (1876) ("Nothing is more clear than the right of a plaintiff, having suffered . . . a loss, to sue in a common-law action all the wrong-doers, or any one of them, at his election; and it is equally clear, that, if he did not contribute to the disaster, he is entitled to judgment in either case for the full amount of his loss.").

94. Richard W. Wright, *Causation in Tort Law*, 73 CAL. L. REV. 1735, 1792 (1985) (discussing various cases).

95. RESTATEMENT (THIRD) OF TORTS: APPORTIONMENT OF LIABILITY § 26.

96. Michie v. Great Lakes Steel Div., Nat'l Steel Corp., 495 F.2d 213 (6th Cir. 1974); *see also* Wright, *supra* note 94, at 1792 & n.239 (explaining that courts have allowed plaintiffs in pollution cases, including *Michie*, to recover from "each defendant who contributed to the pollution that caused the injury, even though none of the defendants' individual contributions was either necessary or sufficient by itself for the occurrence of the injury").

97. *Michie*, 495 F.2d at 215.

98. *Id.* at 217.

99. *Id.* at 216 (quoting Maddux v. Donaldson, 108 N.W.2d 33, 36 (Mich. 1961)) (internal quotation marks omitted).

100. *Maddux*, 108 N.W.2d at 37; *accord* John Henry Wigmore, *Joint-Tortfeasors and Severance of Damages*, 17 ILL. L. REV. 458, 459 (1923) ("Wherever two or more persons by culpable acts, whether concerted or not, cause a single general harm, not obviously assignable in parts to the respective wrongdoers, the injured party may recover from each *for the whole*." (emphasis removed)).

101. In his Seventh Circuit opinion, Judge Posner curiously recognized that this principle applied to child pornography cases, but only if the defendant was convicted of *distributing* child pornography, not just possessing it. He explained:

> The number of pornographic images of a child that are propagated across the Internet may be independent of the number of distributors. A recipient of the image may upload it to the Internet; dozens or hundreds of consumers of child pornography on the Internet may download the uploaded image and many of them may then upload it to their favorite child-pornography web sites; and the chain of downloading and uploading and thus distributing might continue indefinitely. That would be like the [indivisible injury] case.
>
> United States v. Laraneta, 700 F.3d 983, 992 (7th Cir. 2012).

Judge Posner distinguished distribution from possession, explaining that if Laraneta did not upload any of Amy and Vicky's images to the Internet, "then he didn't contribute to those images 'going viral.'" *Id.* at 991. He continued, "If we consider only [Laraneta] having seen those images, and imagine his being the only person to have seen them, Amy's and Vicky's losses would not have been as great as they were." *Id.* But this logic does not provide any clear reason to distinguish between distributors and possessors, especially because it is each act of possession that creates the harm to a child pornography victim.

Further, this misses the implication of what it means to "go viral." A video, for example, can be "distributed" by being put on YouTube where the general public can view it, but it only "goes viral" once many people *actually view* it.

102. Brief of American Law Professors as Amici Curiae Supporting Respondents at 17, Norfolk & W. Ry. Co. v. Ayers, 538 U.S. 135 (2003) (No. 01-963), 2002 WL 1964118 [hereinafter Brief of American Law Professors].

103. 74 AM. JUR., 2D TORTS § 65 (2013).

104. W. Page Keeton et al., *supra* note 89, at 267–68.

105. RESTATEMENT (THIRD) OF TORTS: LIABILITY FOR PHYSICAL AND EMOTIONAL HARM § 36.

106. *Id.* cmt. b at 599.

107. 18 U.S.C. 2259(b)(4).

108. *Paroline*, 134 S. Ct. at 1723.

109. *Id.* at 1724.

110. *Id.*

111. *Id.*

112. *Id.* at 1737 (Sotomayor, J., dissenting).

113. *Id.* at 1740 (Sotomayor, J., dissenting).

114. *Id.* (Sotomayor, J., dissenting).

115. S. 2301 (113th Cong., 2014).

116. United States v. Goff, 501 F.3d 250, 259 (3d Cir. 2007).

Part II (B) | Refining Child Pornography Law

Child Pornography Definitions at Work

8 | Challenges in Investigations and Prosecutions of Child Pornography Crimes

Wendy Walsh, Melissa Wells, and Janis Wolak

The prosecution of child pornography possession and production has increased in recent years, as the Internet has enhanced its availability and law enforcement has refined its techniques for its detection. Given the growth and complexity of child pornography crimes, it is critical to better understand the nature of these crimes as well as dilemmas and challenges law enforcement investigators and prosecutors encounter. Those dilemmas include the consistency of legal standards, problems with statutory frameworks, and the suitability of the punishments being sought. Law enforcement and prosecutors have also faced challenges related to the legal definition of child pornography. In particular, they have sometimes faced difficulty proving that a child depicted in a child pornography image is an actual child (rather than a computer-generated image) or that the child depicted is young enough for a specific law to apply. They have also struggled with how to resolve cases involving sexting—sexually explicit images that minors create of themselves—given that those images fall within most legal definitions of child pornography.

This chapter will first explore the growth and complexity of child pornography possession and production crimes and will then explore changes and challenges faced by law enforcement investigators and prosecutors of child pornography crimes. The data presented here come from three waves of the National Juvenile Online Victimization (N-JOV) study, conducted by the Crimes against Children Research Center at the University of New Hampshire. The N-JOV study collected information from a national sample of law enforcement agencies about the prevalence of arrests for and characteristics of technology-facilitated child sexual exploitation crimes and a convenience sample[1] of state prosecutors about challenges associated with such crimes.

The purpose of this chapter is to use the N-JOV study data to highlight important aspects of these investigations for law enforcement officers and prosecutors and to incorporate findings from other research studies in order to broaden our understanding of investigating and prosecuting these crimes. Specifically, we examine the nature of the law enforcement response, explore the tactics used to investigate these crimes, and explore the extent to which law enforcement investigations that begin as child pornography crimes identify offenders who commit child sexual assaults, that is, dual offenders. Understanding the law enforcement response to this type of crime relates to a number of important policy issues for law enforcement agencies. One issue is how much time and how many resources should be allocated to this particular type of crime compared to other types of crimes against children. On one hand, given the hard evidence available in these crimes, these cases could be considered relatively easy to investigate and prosecute. On the other hand, perhaps resources and investigations are focused on "easy offenders" compared to other types of offenders.

The issue of resources also extends to the nature of the prosecution response. Given the resources required to perform the necessary computer forensics analysis, we examine the extent to which this causes difficulties for prosecutors. Another area of concern for prosecutors is the extent to which to involve victims with the investigation and how to display images during a trial. Given the strict federal sentences for these crimes, we next explore prosecutors' experience deciding whether to refer a case for federal prosecution. Lastly, we explore how prosecutors are handling a relatively new type of child pornography case: youth-produced sexual images.

National Juvenile Online Victimization (N-JOV) Study

The N-JOV study is the first research to systematically collect data about the number and characteristics of offenders arrested for Internet-related sex crimes against minors, the dynamics of the crimes they commit, and changes over time. The study collected data pertaining to arrests for technology-facilitated crimes in 2000, 2006, and 2009. In each year of the study, mail surveys were sent to the same national sample of more than 2,500 law enforcement agencies asking if they had made arrests for specific types of online child sexual exploitation crimes during the study year. Then telephone interviews were conducted with law enforcement investigators to collect details about a random sample of arrest cases.[2] For the third N-JOV study, in addition to the interviews with law enforcement investigators, researchers also conducted telephone interviews with prosecutors involved with technology-facilitated child sexual exploitation crimes.[3] The study collected data on both child pornography possession and production crimes. The N-JOV study is the most comprehensive study to date on Internet-related sex crimes against minors.

Growth and Complexity of Child Pornography Crimes

Child pornography possession crimes involving the Internet often involve multiple child pornography images, which may be stored on individual computers, may be located on peer-to-peer file-sharing networks, and sometimes involve offenders who also commit contact child sexual abuse crimes. Not only is there tremendous variation in the characteristics of these crimes, but there has also been substantial growth in arrests for child pornography crimes involving the Internet[4] that has likely impacted both the law enforcement investigation and prosecution of these crimes. Arrests for crimes involving child pornography possession grew significantly between 2000 and 2006 and again in 2009.[5] In 2009, U.S. law enforcement agencies made an estimated 4,901 arrests that included child pornography possession, almost three times as many as in 2000 and a 33 percent increase over 2006 arrests. It is not possible to determine whether this is an increase in child pornography or an increase in the effectiveness of law enforcement mobilization. Some of these arrested offenders committed other sexual offenses against minors, such as child molestation, in addition to possessing child pornography. Others were arrested for child pornography possession only. Arrests that involved only child pornography possession increased almost fourfold between 2000 and 2009 and grew by about 50 percent between 2006 and 2009. In 2009, there were 3,719 arrests for child pornography possession only. In 2009, more arrested offenders had child pornography videos and a higher percentage of child pornography possessors arrested also distributed child pornography compared to earlier years. There has also been a dramatic increase in arrests for crimes involving child pornography production, which more than quadrupled between 2000 and 2009.[6] In 2009, U.S. law enforcement agencies made an estimated 1,910 arrests for crimes that included child pornography production. Growth in arrests likely impacts investigator and prosecutor decisions about which cases to prioritize, how best to proceed, and issues related to having access to training and adequate resources.

Given the increase in these crimes, it is critical to understand changes and challenges that law enforcement officers and prosecutors encounter. The next section highlights ways in which the law enforcement response has changed over time, how changing definitions of child pornography impact the law enforcement response, and how the issue of dual offenders (offenders who access child pornography and have sexual contact offenses against children) has impacted law enforcement arrests. The Internet has also allowed law enforcement investigators to enhance investigations, such as by using novel technological investigative approaches as described in the following section.

Law Enforcement Response

The N-JOV1 study collected data in 2001 on challenges related to defining child pornography in a sample of cases where there was *no arrest*.[7] Those findings identified four primary categories of dilemmas for law enforcement agencies: (1) definitional challenges, (2) difficulty identifying offenders, (3) training and/or resource gaps, and (4) lack of collaboration with other agencies.[8] While there continue to be investigative dilemmas in these child pornography possession cases, several innovations have facilitated arrests in the past decade. These include increased volume and sophistication in law enforcement agencies' proactive or undercover investigations. These proactive investigations include law enforcement agents posing online as traders, tracing suspects who transact business related to child pornography, and monitoring file-sharing or peer-to-peer (P2P) networks where a larger volume of images may be shared.[9] The use of P2P file-sharing networks has dramatically changed the nature of these investigations. P2P file-sharing networks allow users to search for and download electronic files directly from other computers. Participants download software that connects them to a network of users and they may upload files for sharing with others in the network. Media attention has focused on copyright violations when music and videos are exchanged in file-sharing networks, but users also share pornography, legal and illegal. Investigations revolving around these P2P file-sharing networks may allow law enforcement agents opportunities to target offenders considered to be trading images with more graphic content.[10] In 2000, only 4 percent of arrested child pornography possessors used P2P sharing networks, compared to 28 percent in 2006 and 61 percent in 2009.

Law enforcement agencies are actively engaging in these and other proactive online child pornography investigations, and arrests that began as proactive investigations more than doubled between 2006 and 2009. Moreover, in 2009, for the first time, more child pornography arrests began with proactive child pornography investigations than with individuals reporting child pornography possession or other sexual offenses to police. Thus the nature of how these investigations begin has dramatically changed over time.

Definitions of Child Pornography

Information collected in N-JOV1 illustrated that defining child pornography could be challenging because law enforcement agencies were required to prove that images fit statutory definitions of child pornography and that they depicted minors.[11] The content of child pornography images in cases ending in arrest has consistently included sexual penetration of a child, generally of girls aged six to twelve.[12]

Since 2000, however, a new type of child pornography producer emerged, youths who create sexual images that meet the legal definition of child pornography. Law enforcement officers saw a dramatic increase in these youth-produced types of cases in 2009. For example, the largest part of the increase in child pornography production arrests involved youth-produced sexual images, from an estimated 233 in 2006 to 1,198 in 2009. These cases are diverse, but many involved adult offenders who solicited sexual images from their underage victims.[13] Youth-only incidents made up almost one-quarter of 2009 child pornography producer arrests, most of these for crimes involving serious criminal activity that included sexual abuse or blackmail or other malicious acts (16 percent of arrests). It was much more typical in cases ending in arrest, however, to have adults entice minors to produce the images (39 percent of arrests) or for adults to create images of minors (37 percent of arrests).

One definitional issue still in flux involves these sexual images that youth produce.[14] Research suggests that youth-produced images can be classified into two categories: aggravated and experimental. Aggravated youth-produced incidents typically involve "adult-involved" situations where adults solicited sexual images from underage adolescent victims.[15] However, some of the arrests involved images that could be categorized as "sexting," which is the commonly used term for images created by minors in the context of romantic relationships or for sexual attention seeking among adolescents (7 percent of arrests).[16]

Dual Offenders

N-JOV1 identified a group of cases in which challenges in identifying offenders made it impossible for law enforcement agencies to make an arrest.[17] In those cases where law enforcement agencies were not able to make an arrest, there was not enough information to identify an offender, there could have been multiple users on the same computer system, or too much time might have passed to retrieve digital evidence related to a specific allegation.[18] In the past decade, there has been tremendous advancement in the ability of law enforcement to detect and apprehend offenders. This is evidenced, in part, by the dramatic increase in arrests for child pornography possession and production cases between 2000 and 2009.

Currently, there is emphasis on assessing which child pornography offenders can be identified as both accessing child pornography and sexually exploiting children. It is important to law enforcement agencies to identify these "dual offenders."[19] This term describes offenders who use the Internet to access child pornography and are also likely to commit, or have committed, conventional or online child sexual assaults. Between 2000 and 2009, there was a decrease in the proportion of arrested child pornography possessors whose cases started with possession who were also dual offenders.[20] Even though the proportion of dual offenders was smaller in 2009 than in previous years, the estimated number of arrests was similar to 2006 because there were more arrests overall. In 2000 and 2006, about one in six cases that started with child pornography possession identified a dual offender, compared to one in ten cases in 2009. Additional research is needed to explain this decrease, which may be related to law enforcement success in arresting known offenders, to challenges in identifying victims in images, or to other factors.

There has also been a decrease in the proportion of child pornography producers who also commit contact sexual offenses.[21] In 2000, 63 percent of arrested child pornography producers committed contact sexual offenses, in 2006 it was 69 percent of cases, and in 2009 53 percent of cases. Across all waves of the study, approximately half of the contact sexual offenses were penetrative.

Produced child pornography continues to play an important role in the disclosure of child sexual exploitation crimes. In both 2006 and 2009, 40 percent of cases started when someone found sexual pictures that child pornography producers had taken of victims. A family member, for example, found the pictures and reported offenders to police or police investigating possession of child pornography or other crimes found images of an offender abusing a child. Thus, the images themselves can be a critical type of evidence for investigators

Additional research is needed to assist in identifying these dual offenders, with current research suggesting that online offenders were more likely to be Caucasian, young, more likely to be unemployed, and more likely to have greater sexual deviancy than offline offenders.[22] Both online and offline child pornography offenders have been found to be more likely to report histories of childhood physical and sexual abuse than nonoffenders.[23] Other research has been less definitive; there are mixed results related to whether or not the quantity of child pornography images an offender possesses is a clear predictor of being a dual offender.[24] If child pornography cases do not begin with an allegation of sexual abuse, it may be challenging to assess whether or not the offender perpetuated such abuse in addition to possessing child pornography.[25]

Assets for Law Enforcement Investigations

Expert witness testimony, centralized databases of images, and Internet Crimes Against Children Task Forces are all assets in these investigations. Expert witnesses may be used in an effort to identify children in cases involving dual offenders, as well as to ascertain the age of children who appear in pornographic images. Additionally, expert witness testimony can be a valuable resource to assist in building subjective and objective data to determine the age of children in images if those ages are ambiguous.[26] For instance, expert witness testimony may assist in a determination that a child is under age twelve if there is no evidence of pubic hair or breast development in girls or pubic hair in boys.[27] If the child has begun puberty, the experts can examine tooth development and presence of adult teeth.[28] However, there is also evidence that medical expert witness testimony of developmental level may underestimate the age of individuals depicted in pornographic images.[29] There is some indication that expert witnesses may vary in their predictions of girls' ages once puberty has begun, especially given the inconsistent age of the onset of puberty.[30]

An additional resource for law enforcement agencies are centralized databases of images. Many of the images in these investigations are shared among child pornography offenders or are "known" to law enforcement agencies. Identification of known images, such as through the U.S. Immigration and Customs Enforcement's National Child Victim Identification System (NCVIS) or the National Center for Missing and Exploited Children's Child Victim Identification program (CVIP), have likely facilitated the identification of some images. These databases are intended to help identify the victims of child pornography and include images of child pornography submitted by federal, local, state, and international law enforcement agencies.

N-JOV1 identified a final category of law enforcement dilemmas in cases in which there was no arrest, which was related to challenges in multijurisdictional cooperation.[31] These challenges may include differences in resources, training needs across jurisdictions, or differing protocols for specific types of cases. Existing protocols and best practice generally lead to collaborations with jurisdictions or task force units with specialization in child pornography. Formal affiliations with Internet Crimes Against Children (ICAC) Task Forces are likely also associated with increased likelihood of arrest in child pornography possession cases. Increasingly, state and local law enforcement agencies have such affiliations, and arrests by ICAC Task Forces increased from 14 percent in 2000 to 39 percent in 2006 and 59 percent in 2009.[32]

Prosecution Response

Like law enforcement officers, prosecutors have enormous discretion about whether to prosecute a particular case, and both legal and extralegal factors are used when making decisions about sexual assault cases.[33] Legal factors have to do with the extent of evidence available and extralegal factors have to do perceptions of victim credibility and whether the victim was engaged in risk-taking behaviors as well as suspect characteristics.

Prosecuting child pornography possession and production crimes has some advantage compared to other child sexual abuse crimes in that evidence of a crime is readily available. Given that the crime of sexual abuse is often committed in private, there are rarely eyewitnesses, and the child's testimony usually provides most of the information about the crime. Having concrete evidence, such as child pornography images, can dramatically change the nature of the investigation. For example, previous research has found child sexual abuse cases resulting in charges filed tended to have at least two types of evidence, such as a corroborating witness or an additional report of abuse, compared to those without charges filed, regardless of whether there was a child disclosure or not.[34] The most common reason for not filing charges in these conventional child sexual abuse crimes was insufficient evidence. Obviously, child pornography crimes differ dramatically from conventional child abuse crimes in that hard evidence of a crime is readily available.

Even though prosecutors may have evidence of a crime with child pornography cases, prosecutors need to make decisions regarding whether or not a conviction is likely given the legal and policy changes in the prosecution of computer child pornography.[35] Prosecutors encounter a number of dilemmas and issues regarding what types of images are graphic or explicit enough to fit existing definitions of child pornography.[36] Investigations of Internet child pornography possession also require specific resources such as computer forensics experts with specialized training to retrieve evidence.[37] It is critical to better understand how prosecutors are handling some of these issues because child pornography is a common type of computer crime prosecuted by local prosecutors. For example, the 2005 National Prosecutors Survey[38] found that 67 percent of all offices that reported prosecution of a computer crime in the previous year prosecuted child pornography cases. Full-time offices that served large (one million or more) or medium-sized populations were more likely to prosecute cases (90 percent and 82 percent respectively) compared to full-time offices that served smaller populations (250,000 or less population, 69 percent). Only 22 percent of part-time offices prosecuted these cases.

Not only does it appear that most offices are prosecuting these types of crimes, but the great majority of child pornography possession and production cases end in conviction, with few cases dropped or dismissed.[39] Despite the likelihood of conviction, prosecutors may encounter a number of issues when prosecuting child pornography possession and production cases. The following sections highlight some of these issues: handling computer forensic examinations and technology-related defenses, taking these cases to trial, deciding whether to file federal charges, and prosecuting sexting cases. The findings are based upon telephone interviews with state prosecutors involved with technology-facilitated child sexual exploitation crimes as part of the third N-JOV study (N-JOV3).

Computer Forensics

The detection and prosecution of child pornography requires technological expertise, such as the ability to examine temporary Internet files and find secondary storage devices, as well as the continual training in the handling of electronic evidence.[40] Prosecutors must continually develop cases based on evidence that may be hidden and stored in microchips that are mobile and easily altered.[41] Furthermore, given rapid technological advances, such as how images are created and stored, laws about computer crime may also change, which may result in legal challenges about the seizure of evidence in child pornography cases. There is also the possibility of legal challenges regarding definitions about what constitutes possession and viewing of child pornography online.[42] Given the nature of computer forensics and the need to secure digital evidence for child pornography cases, some legal scholars have expressed concerns about the preparedness of local prosecutors to handle this type of evidence.[43]

In order to explore some of these issues, N-JOV3 examined the extent to which prosecutors encountered difficulties with computer forensics, the police investigation, and formally raised defenses. Nearly two-thirds of prosecutors in the sample (62 percent) reported encountering difficulties with computer forensics or the police investigation.[44] These difficulties had to do with:

- Timeliness of the forensic exam (33 percent)
- Lack of equipment or training of officers (24 percent)
- Search warrant issues (23 percent)
- Chain of custody issues (8 percent)
- P2P investigations (5 percent)
- Credentials of forensic examination or lab (5 percent)

Yet when prosecutors reported having any of these difficulties, only 16 percent reported that charges against the defendant were ultimately dismissed because of problems with the police investigation or computer forensic exam. And when this occurred, the vast majority of prosecutors (79 percent) reported that this occurred in only one case. This suggests that although some difficulties exist with computer forensics or police investigation, the consequences of these difficulties are not significant.

About half of prosecutors (56 percent) reported handling a case where the defense formally raised technology-related issues that required the prosecutor to explain technical details to a judge or jury. These types of cases include describing the computer search history, examining the time in which events took place, and describing the ways in which computer files are set up. Yet when this happened, 75 percent of prosecutors reported being mostly or very satisfied with resources their office had to explain technical evidence or rebutting technical defenses.

As ways to store images expand and technology continues to change, child pornography crimes can become more difficult to prosecute because of the need to prove that the defendant knowingly possessed the images. The N-JOV3 study found that 77 percent of prosecutors had handled cases in which the defendant claimed to have downloaded child pornography unknowingly or claimed that someone else with physical access to the computer downloaded child pornography. Other types of formally raised defenses were much less common: 44 percent of prosecutors had handled a case in which the defendant claimed addiction or mental illness, 40 percent of prosecutors had dealt with cases in which the defendant claimed the images were not child pornography, and 16 percent of prosecutors had cases in which the defendant claimed the child pornography was downloaded for research.

Although many prosecutors mentioned handling cases with these formally raised defenses, only one-third of prosecutors reported that these defenses created real difficulty for them and resulted in a plea to significantly reduced charges, dismissal of charges, or losing the case. Prosecutors reported that the most effective strategy for countering formally raised defenses was to use computer forensics, such as using experts to show that the images did not unknowingly or unintentionally get on computer because of a computer virus or using forensics to track actual searches or search history. Clearly having access to well-trained experts and adequate resources is essential when prosecuting these cases.

Trial Cases

Due to the nature of child pornography images, there are a number of special issues that can develop when child pornography cases are resolved at trial. One is the extent to which child pornography cases are resolved in front of juries, who may have difficulties viewing child pornography images. Another is the extent to which the defense objects to introducing child pornography images into evidence and whether the defense is successful in keeping images away from the jury. Both of these issues could affect how child pornography cases are prosecuted. Another issue is the extent to which child pornography cases are resolved with reduced case outcomes, such as allowing a defendant to plea to a misdemeanor rather than a felony or not requiring sex offender registration when a defendant pleads guilty. In the interest of resolving as many cases as possible, prosecutors may be accepting these reduced case outcomes. The extent to which this occurs or in what types of circumstances it occurs are not known.

Another important issue is the methods used during trial to prove that the child pornography images depicted actual children.

Before examining these issues, it is first important to recognize that a very small percentage of child pornography cases are resolved at trial. According to data from the N-JOV3 law enforcement study in 2009, only 5 percent of cases in which outcomes were known ended with convictions after trial.[45] The vast majority (84 percent) of cases with an arrest ended with a guilty plea. Charges were dropped or dismissed in 7 percent of cases. There was some other outcome, such as the suspect died, or an unknown outcome in 4 percent of cases. No cases ended in acquittals after trial.

N-JOV3 prosecutor data also found that a minority of prosecutors in the sample had a child pornography case go to trial: 33 percent of prosecutors had a child pornography case go to trial in the past two years and 26 percent of prosecutors in the sample had a child pornography case in front of a jury in the past two years.[46] There was no predominant method of displaying images to the jury; instead images were displayed to the jury in a variety of ways.

- Displayed on a large screen/TV that only the jury and judge could see (35 percent)
- Displayed on a large screen/TV that the whole courtroom could see (30 percent)
- Still images that were passed to the jury or described by experts (18 percent)

About half of prosecutors (55 percent) had the defense object to displaying the images to the jury (claiming for example that the images were inflammatory). Although the majority of prosecutors (70 percent) said that defense attorneys were not successful in keeping images out of evidence, 30 percent of prosecutors noted that this defense tactic succeeded. Another critical aspect of child pornography trial cases is the process used to prove that images depicted actual, not computer-generated, children. In 2002, the Supreme Court ruled that the constitutional definition of child pornography includes only images depicting "real" children and that virtual or computer-generated images were not considered "real" children.[47] The burden is on the government, therefore, to prove that an image of child pornography depicts actual children. The difficulty of determining the age of the victim often presents a problem for the prosecution, especially when the victim is postpubescent. Cattaneo et al. found that even the experts (pediatricians and gynecologists) were often unable to determine whether the victim was a juvenile or not.[48]

The N-JOV3 study found that prosecutors used multiple methods to prove the age of children. These included testimony that the identities of children were known (43 percent); testimony, such as from a pediatrician, that images were not virtual or computer-generated (24 percent); or allowing the jury or judge to decide for themselves if the images were actual (32 percent). A physician, for example, may be able to testify that characteristics such as the proportions, body fat distribution, and skin tone of the children depicted are consistent with those of real children. Perhaps because trial cases are not common, there does not appear to be a consistent way of displaying images to the jury or of proving the age of children in the images.

Deciding to Refer for Federal Investigation for Prosecution

Given the strict federal sentences, the global and complex nature of child pornography crimes, and that these crimes often require additional resources for experts, state and local prosecutors may seek federal assistance in these cases.[49] Additionally, federal law enforcement officers are more likely to be trained in the detection and arrest of child pornography trafficking than are state or local officers. Another reason state and local prosecutors may refer a case for federal prosecution is that federal penalties are sometimes more severe than state penalties. In federal cases, the mandatory minimum for downloading images is five years in prison without parole, and those who download particularly images of young children, download images of especially heinous activity, or possess a large number of images often get sentences of fifteen to twenty years.[50] Other issues may also affect the decision by local prosecutors whether to refer a case for federal prosecution. One is the extent to which particular courts make individualized assessments to arrive at sentences that diverge from the calculated guidelines.[51] If, for example, a prosecutor knew that a court or particular judge is known to reduce sentences, that prosecutor could be more likely to refer the case for federal prosecution.

Given that few studies have identified reasons local prosecutors do not pursue child pornography cases and the extent to which prosecutors seek federal assistance in the prosecution of these cases,[52] the N-JOV3 study explored some of these issues. N-JOV3 found that from 2009 to 2011, 48 percent of prosecutors in the sample had referred a child pornography case for federal prosecution.[53] Of those who had not referred a case, 24 percent of prosecutors said that their cases have not warranted it (e.g., the cases did not involve high number of images or multiple jurisdictions); 20 percent of prosecutors said that their state has equal or stricter sentencing levels, so they like to keep the cases and do not refer to federal prosecutors; 15 percent of prosecutors said that it generally works the other way around and the federal prosecutors will refer child pornography cases to them or federal prosecutors will take the child pornography cases they want to prosecute; 6 percent of prosecutors said it wouldn't be helpful (i.e., it takes too long, federal prosecutors would end up giving the case back); and 5 percent of prosecutors mentioned that they split cases (e.g., federal will take the child pornography portion and local prosecutors will take contact offenses) or use the option of referring to federal prosecutors in order to help get the offender to plea to state charges.

About half of prosecutors in the N-JOV3 sample (56 percent) reported that all their cases were accepted and not declined for federal prosecution, 28 percent of prosecutors reported a mix of cases accepted and declined, and 13 percent of prosecutors reported that all their cases had been declined for federal prosecution. Of those prosecutors with cases declined for federal prosecution ($n = 72$), only 29 percent ($n = 21$) reported that this caused real difficulty. The majority of prosecutors said the difficulty was that the federal prosecutors took too long with the case, with eighteen months or three years sometimes going by with nothing happening, and then state prosecutors would then have to start the case again.

In order to better understand referral for federal prosecution, the N-JOV3 study also examined whether prosecutors had a clear understanding of what types of child pornography cases would be accepted. A third of prosecutors (37 percent) reported that it was not at all clear which child pornography cases would be accepted for federal prosecution, 21 percent reported it was somewhat clear, 23 percent reported it was reasonably clear, and 19 percent reported that it was very clear which child pornography cases would be accepted. Just over half of prosecutors (52 percent) wished to see guidelines on which child pornography cases would be accepted for federal prosecution. When asked what type of guidelines prosecutors would like to see concerning federal prosecution, 57 percent of prosecutors said that they need to know the general criteria and that they have never seen any guidelines. Other prosecutors mentioned specifically that they would like to know the number of images needed, what specific acts are necessary, or what prior offender history is required, or that they believed interstate commerce or multijurisdiction cases should always be accepted. Clearly, the decision to refer these cases for federal prosecution is complex and needs more clarification.

Prosecuting Sexting Cases

Another issue prosecutors encounter is whether to prosecute sexting cases. Sexting refers to cases with sexual images produced by juveniles (with no adult involvement) and may include creating or distributing such images. Sexting often falls within states' legal definitions of child pornography: images depicting sexually explicit activity involving minors. Since the National Conference of State Legislatures began tracking sexting legislation in 2009, twenty states have enacted bills to address youth sexting.[54] Generally the legislation aims to educate young people about the risks of sexting, deter them from engaging in it, and impose appropriate penalties by protecting youths from harsh sentences under child pornography statutes, which were created to protect youths from sexual exploitation by adults.

A number of reviews have explored why many current laws are problematic and pose challenges for prosecutors.[55] Yet no studies have examined how these types of cases are resolved once they reach prosecutors' offices. The N-JOV3 study found that the majority of state prosecutors in the sample (62 percent) that had worked on technology-facilitated crimes against children had handled a sexting case involving juveniles, and 36 percent of prosecutors in the sample reported that they had, at least on one occasion, filed charges in these cases.[56] When prosecutors handled these cases, they presented minors with a wide range of alternatives to being charged: 59 percent of prosecutors in the sample had offered education classes or counseling, 42 percent had offered community service, 31 percent had offered loss of cell phone or computer, and 16 percent had offered the teen to write an essay or letter.

Of those prosecutors interviewed in the N-JOV3 study who had filed charges, 62 percent had charged at least one juvenile with a felony related to a sexting case. In the majority of those cases (84 percent), the prosecutors had charged the juvenile with a child pornography production felony. This charging sometimes occurred even in cases where images did not show sexually explicit conduct or exhibition of genitals, according to 17 percent of prosecutors who had filed charges. And 16 percent of prosecutors who had filed charges in these cases had, at least on one occasion, a sexting case that resulted in the defendant being sentenced to sex offender registration. It is important to keep in mind that this sample of prosecutors is a convenience sample and does not reflect national estimates about how often prosecutors handle these cases. The range of outcomes found in the N-JOV3 prosecutor study (alternatives to charging, not filing charges, charging with child pornography felony, requiring sex offender registration) mirrors the wide range of types of cases seen by law enforcement. Prosecutors are handling these types of cases, seeking alternatives in some cases, but also charging minors with felonies in other situations.

Conclusion

Although there is increasing sophistication in techniques used to identify and charge child pornography offenders, child pornography crimes pose unique investigative challenges for law enforcement and prosecutors. In many parts of the United States, law enforcement agencies and prosecutors have technological advantages in terms of identifying, arresting, and prosecuting these offenders. Clearly there is an expectation that these cases will facilitate identification of child victims and generate valuable evidence of sexual exploitation crimes against children. Additional assessment and research is needed to ascertain to what extent these child pornography possession offenders are also exploiting identified children offline.

The data from the three waves of the N-JOV study demonstrate that child pornography crimes are diverse and increasing, although it is not possible to say whether this reflects a growth in the population accessing child pornography or an increase in law enforcement mobilization around this issue. As technology continues to change, it is likely that child pornography crimes will continue to evolve and law enforcement investigators and prosecutors will need to continue to adapt. But the data also suggest a growing, more sophisticated, and informed law enforcement response to the problem. In 2009, proactive investigation of online child pornography trading generated more arrests than reports from the public. Law enforcement agencies were aggressively pursuing the online child pornography trade by proactively targeting offenders. Also, the number of law enforcement agencies trained to respond to technology-facilitated child sexual exploitation crimes has increased. About 45 percent of child pornography production arrests were made by Internet Crimes against Children Task Forces and affiliates, which receive specialized training in technology-facilitated crimes. Having adequate resources is clearly a critical tool in the response to child pornography crimes. Budget resources to hire experts and to access computer forensic specialists appear to matter when prosecuting child pornography.[57] One important policy question is how many resources to allocate to this type of crime and how much of a priority this type of crime should be for investigative agencies.

Although the vast majority of these crimes were prosecuted, with the federal government involved with the prosecution of about one-third of child pornography possession arrests, these cases often pose challenges for prosecutors, including practical challenges, lack of clarity of the role of federal prosecutors, and definitional challenges. The N-JOV3 study indicated that practical challenges include the lack of timeliness of the computer forensics exam, lack of equipment or training of officers, and issues with search warrants. This suggests the need for continual investments in laboratories, equipment, technicians, and training of police in child pornography investigation. Another challenge concerns the lack of clarity surrounding the role of federal prosecutors. Although many state prosecutors have referred cases to federal officials, many prosecutors nonetheless want guidelines about what cases will be accepted. Prosecutors are often not at all clear which cases federal prosecutors are willing to accept. To ensure that prosecutors are consistent when filing charges in these types of crimes, more attention is warranted on the distinction between charging locally or federally.

The largest definitional challenge is in sexting cases. Both law enforcement investigators and prosecutors reported handling sexting cases. In this sample of prosecutors that had worked on technology-facilitated crimes against children, one-third had filed charges in sexting cases. Given the diverse nature of sexting cases, it is likely beneficial to have a range of outcomes available to investigators. On the other hand, in order to ensure some consistency in investigations, it is likely beneficial to have specific statutes that clarify nuances and definitions. With the changing definitions and dynamics of child pornography, research needs to continue to help law enforcement investigators and prosecutors develop tools and strategies to most effectively handle the types of cases they encounter.

Law enforcement investigators and prosecutors are a crucial link in efforts to discourage the creation and dissemination of child pornography. As technology and criminal behavior changes, research needs to continue to help law enforcement investigators and prosecutors develop tools and strategies to deal with these complex crimes.

NOTES

1. A convenience sample is simply one in which the researcher uses any subjects that are available to participate in the research study. This type of sample does not truly represent a population and generalizations are limited.

2. JANIS WOLAK, KIMBERLY MITCHELL & DAVID FINKELHOR, METHODOLOGY REPORT: THIRD NATIONAL JUVENILE ONLINE VICTIMIZATION (NJOV3) ARREST STUDY 1 (Crimes Against Child. Res. Center 2011).

3. WENDY WALSH, JANIS WOLAK & DAVID FINKELHOR, METHODOLOGY REPORT—3RD NATIONAL JUVENILE ONLINE VICTIMIZATION STUDY (NJOV3): PROSECUTION STUDY 1 (Crimes Against Child. Res. Center 2012).

4. This chapter focuses on child pornography crimes involving the Internet. When child pornography statistics are described they refer to child pornography involving the Internet.

5. JANIS WOLAK, DAVID FINKELHOR, ET AL., TRENDS IN ARRESTS FOR CHILD PORNOGRAPHY POSSESSION: THE THIRD NATIONAL JUVENILE ONLINE VICTIMIZATION STUDY (NJOV-3) 1, 1 (Crimes Against Child. Res. Center 2012).

6. JANIS WOLAK, DAVID FINKELHOR, ET AL., TRENDS IN ARRESTS FOR CHILD PORNOGRAPHY PRODUCTION: THE THIRD NATIONAL JUVENILE ONLINE VICTIMIZATION STUDY (NJOV-3) 1, 1 (Crimes Against Child. Res. Center 2012).

7. Melissa Wells, David Finkelhor, Janis Wolak & Kimberly J. Mitchell, *Defining Child Pornography: Law Enforcement Dilemmas in Investigations of Internet Child Pornography Possession*, 8 POLICE PRAC. & RES. 273 (2007).

8. *Id.* at 270.

9. WOLAK, FINKELHOR, ET AL., *supra* note 5, at 2.

10. WOLAK, FINKELHOR, ET AL., *supra* note 5, at 3; Janis Wolak, David Finkelhor & Kimberly J. Mitchell, *Child Pornography Possessors: Trends in Offender and Case Characteristics*, 23 SEXUAL ABUSE: J. RES. & TREATMENT 22, 23–24 (2011).

11. Wells, Finkelhor, Wolak & Mitchell, *supra* note 7, at 276.

12. WOLAK, FINKELHOR, ET AL., *supra* note 5, at 2.

13. JANIS WOLAK, DAVID FINKELHOR & KIMBERLY MITCHELL, TRENDS IN ARRESTS FOR CHILD PORNOGRAPHY PRODUCTION: THE THIRD NATIONAL JUVENILE ONLINE VICTIMIZATION STUDY (NJOV-3) 1, 1 (Crimes Against Child. Res. Center 2012).

14. WOLAK, FINKELHOR, ET AL., *supra* note 5, at 2.

15. JANIS WOLAK & DAVID FINKELHOR, SEXTING: A TYPOLOGY, 3 (Crimes Against Child. Res. Center 2011).

16. WOLAK, FINKELHOR, ET AL., *supra* note 5, at 2.

17. Wells, Finkelhor, Wolak & Mitchell, *supra* note 7, at 276.

18. Melissa Wells, Law Enforcement Dilemmas in the Investigation of Internet Sex Crimes Against Minors 119 (2003) (unpublished dissertation for University of New Hampshire).

19. WOLAK, FINKELHOR, ET AL., *supra* note 6, at 3.

20. WOLAK, FINKELHOR, ET AL., *supra* note 6, at 4.

21. WOLAK, FINKELHOR, ET AL., *supra* note 6, at 3.

22. K. Babchishin, R.K. Hanson & C. Hermann, *The Characteristics of Online Sex Offenders: A Meta-Analysis*, 23 SEXUAL ABUSE: J. RES. & TREATMENT 105 (2011).

23. *Id.* at 105.

24. M.L. Long, L.A. Alison & M.A. McManus, *Child Pornography and Likelihood of Contact Abuse: A Comparison Between Contact Child Sexual Offenders and Noncontact Offenders*, 25 SEXUAL ABUSE: J. RES. & TREATMENT 388 (2012); J.A. McCarthy, *Internet Sexual Activity: A Comparison Between Contact and Non-Contact Child Pornography Offenders*, 16 J. SEXUAL AGGRESSION 191 (2010).

25. WOLAK, FINKELHOR, ET AL., *supra* note 5, at 4.

26. S.W. Cooper, *The Medical Analysis of Child Sexual Abuse Images*, 20 J. SEXUAL ABUSE 633, (2011); A.L. Rosenbloom, *Inaccuracy of Age Assessment from Images of Postpubescent Subjects in Cases of Alleged Child Pornography*. 127 INT'L J. LEGAL MED. 470 (2013).

27. Cooper, *supra* note 26, at 637.

28. *Id.*

29. Rosenbloom, *supra* note 26, at 470.

30. *Id.* at 469.

31. Wells, Finkelhor, Wolak & Mitchell, *supra* note 7, at 276.

32. WOLAK, FINKELHOR, ET AL., *supra* note 6, at 4.

33. M.A. Alderman & S.E. Ullman, *Creating a More Complete and Current Picture: Examining Police and Prosecutor Decision-Making When Processing Sexual Assault Cases*, 18 VIOLENCE AGAINST WOMEN 525, 541 (2012); T.P. Cross, W.A. Walsh, M. Simone & L.M. Jones, *Prosecution of Child Abuse: A Meta-Analysis of Rates of Criminal Justice Decisions*, 4 TRAUMA, VIOLENCE, & ABUSE 323, 334 (2003).

34. W. Walsh, L. Jones, T. Cross & T. Lippert, *Prosecuting Child Sexual Abuse: The Importance of Evidence Type*, 56 CRIME & DELINQUENCY 436, 444 (2010).

35. D. Bazelon, C. Yun Jung & J. Conaty, *Computer Crimes*, 43 AM. CRIM. L. REV. 259, 292 (2006); A. Carter & A. Perry, *Computer Crimes*, 41 AM. CRIM. L. REV. 313, 314 (2004).

36. K.V. LANNING, CHILD MOLESTERS: A BEHAVIORAL ANALYSIS FOR PROFESSIONALS INVESTIGATING THE SEXUAL EXPLOITATION OF CHILDREN 80 (Nat'l Center for Missing & Exploited Child. 2010).

37. T. Buzzell, *The Effects of Organizational and Community Context on Local Prosecution of Computer Child Pornography Cases*, 20 CRIM. JUST. STUD.: CRITICAL J. CRIME & L. & SOC'Y 391, 399, 402 (2007).

38. STEVEN W. PERRY, PROSECUTORS IN STATE COURTS, 2005. BUREAU OF JUSTICE STATISTICS BULLETIN 5 (U.S. Dept. Just., Bureau of Just. Stat. 2006).

39. Janis Wolak, David Finkelhor & Kimberly Mitchell, Third National Juvenile Online Victimization Study (2012) (unpublished raw data).

40. M. BRITZ, COMPUTER FORENSICS AND CYBER CRIME: AN INTRODUCTION (Pearson Prentice Hall 2004); R. CLIFFORD, CYBERCRIME: THE INVESTIGATION, PROSECUTION AND DEFENSE OF A COMPUTER-RELATED CRIME (Carolina Academic Press 2001); Jonathan Wolf, *War Games Meets the Internet: Chasing the 21st Century Cybercriminal with Old Laws and Little Money*, 28 AM. J. CRIM. L. 95, 101 (2001).

41. Katrien Jacobs, *Pornography in Small Places and Other Spaces*, 18 CULTURAL STUD. 67, 67 (2004).

42. T. Howard, *Don't Cache Out Your Case: Prosecuting Child Pornography Possession Laws Based on Images Located in Temporary Internet Files*, 19 BERKELEY TECH. L.J. 1227, 1239 (2004).

43. L. Myers, *Identifying the Required Knowledge Elements for the Effective Detection, Investigation, and Prosecution of High Technology Crime*, 14 CRIMINAL JUSTICE EDUCATION 245, 245 (2003).

44. WENDY WALSH, JANIS WOLAK & DAVID FINKELHOR, PROSECUTION DILEMMAS AND CHALLENGES FOR CHILD PORNOGRAPHY CRIMES: THE THIRD NATIONAL JUVENILE ONLINE VICTIMIZATION STUDY (NJOV-3) 2, 4 (Crimes Against Child. Res. Center 2013).

45. WOLAK, FINKELHOR, ET AL., *supra* note 6, at 1–4; Wolak, Finkelhor & Mitchell, *supra* note 39.

46. WALSH, WOLAK & FINKELHOR, *supra* note 44, at 2.

47. Damon A. King, *Methods of Proof: The 'Real Child' Issue in Child Pornography Cases*, Update 1 AM. PROSECUTORS RES. INST. 1, 1 (2004).

48. C. Cattaneo, S. Ritz-Timme, P. Gabriel, D. Gibeli, E. Guidici, P. Poppa, D. Nohrden, S. Assmann, R. Schmitt & M. Grandi, *The Difficult Issue of Age Assessment on Pedo-Pornographic Material* 183 FORENSIC SCI. INT'L 21, 22–23 (2009).

49. Buzzell, *supra* note 37, at 391.

50. Amir Efrati, *Making Punishments Fit the Most Offensive Crime*. WALL ST. J., Oct. 23, 2008, at 1, http://online.wsj.com/article/SB122471925786760689.html; Erika Goode, *Life Sentence for Possession of Child Pornography Spurs Debate Over Severity*. N.Y. TIMES, Nov. 4, 2011, at 1, http://www.nytimes.com/2011/11/05/us/life-sentence-for-possession-of-child-pornography-spurs-debate.html?_r=0.

51. I.N. Friedman & K.W. Supler, *Child Pornography Sentencing: The Road Here and the Road Ahead*, 21 FED. SENT'G REP 83, 84 (2008); T. Stabenow, *Deconstructing the Myth of Careful Study: A Primer on the Flawed Progression of the Child Pornography Guidelines*, (2009). http://www.lb9.uscourts.gov/webcites/11documents/Henderson_Deconstructing.pdf; *Citizen's Guide to U.S. Federal Law on Child Pornography*, U.S. DEP'T JUST. (Oct. 5, 2012), http://www.justice.gov/criminal/ceos/citizensguide/citizensguide_porn.html.

52. Buzzell, *supra* note 37, at 399.

53. WALSH, WOLAK & FINKELHOR, *supra* note 44, at 4.

54. *National 2012 Sexting Legislation*. NAT'L CENTER ST. CT. (Dec. 14, 2012), http://www.ncsl.org/issues-research/telecom/sexting-legislation-2012.aspx.

55. J. Bailey & M. Hanna, *The Gendered Dimensions of Sexting: Assessing the Applicability of Canada's Child Pornography Provision*, CAN. J. WOMEN & L. 405, 416 (2011); M. Levick & K. Moon, *Prosecuting Sexting as Child Pornography*, 44 VAL. U. L. REV. 1035, 1036 (2010); B. Ostrager, *SMS. OMG! LOL! TTYL: Translating the Law to Accommodate Today's Teens and the Evolution from Texting to Sexting*, 48 FAM. CT. REV. 712, 715 (2010).

56. Wendy Walsh, Janis Wolak & David Finkelhor, *Sexting: When Are State Prosecutors Deciding to Prosecute? The Third National Juvenile Online Victimization Study (NJOV-3)*, CRIMES AGAINST CHILDREN RESEARCH CENTER 1, 1 (2013).

57. Buzzell, *supra* note 37.

9 | A Critical Evaluation of the Federal Sentencing Guidelines for Child Pornography Offenses

Troy Stabenow

Federal law requires each judge to give careful consideration to something called the Federal Sentencing Guidelines. On the surface, these guidelines appear to sort child pornography offenders into clear categories based on the type of crime each committed and the various circumstances surrounding their crimes. In reality however, the guidelines result in dubious distinctions between similar offenders, resulting in enormously different sentences for defendants with comparable levels of culpability. The various circumstances the guidelines use to increase punishment apply to nearly all defendants, but even worse, they are largely unsupported by empirical study or common sense. This chapter will highlight the problems of a guideline sentencing by walking you through an imaginary, but typical case, as if you were the federal judge for that case.

The Facts of Mr. Smith's Case

Imagine you are a federal district court judge. Today you will sentence a young man caught with child pornography; we'll call that young man Mr. Smith. Like 97.1 percent of federal defendants nationwide,[1] Mr. Smith pled guilty without a trial. Like 82.5 percent of these defendants, Mr. Smith has no criminal history.[2] A federal magistrate judge handles your plea hearings, so this afternoon will be the first time you have ever laid eyes on Mr. Smith. Everything you know about this case will come from either the thin Presentence Investigation Report (PSIR), prepared for you by the probation officer, or from the arguments you will hear during today's hearing. As you sit down to lunch, you open the ten-to-fifteen-page report. You skim the procedural pages, and then, over the next twenty minutes, you read and reread several pages about Mr. Smith's life, the range of sentencing options available to you by statute, and a summary of the facts of the case.

According to the report:

> In November of last year, Mr. Smith decided to purchase a single, thirty-minute DVD entitled "12 Year Old Loves Showing Off" from two undercover postal investigators. The DVD's cover describes the movie as "a coming-of-age movie in which a blossoming young teen discovers her own sexuality." According to investigators, the DVD depicts thirty minutes of a young girl posing for the camera, stripping naked, and then masturbating.
>
> Mr. Smith sent a $20 certified check for the film to the sting postal address with a note requesting that the video ship in a plain envelope. A week later, one of the investigators, wearing a fake "Fed-Ex" outfit, delivered the package to Mr. Smith's door. Mr. Smith opened the door, commented, "I've been waiting for this," and signed for the package. He then closed the door. Two minutes later, agents knocked and immediately entered the house. As they entered, Mr. Smith was standing in his living room, about halfway between his 55″ television and the 13″ laptop computer he had sitting by his lazy-boy recliner. The investigators caught Mr. Smith just *after* he had opened the package, but just *before* he had started to watch the movie on either machine.

In indeterminate sentencing systems, such as those used in the United States military and in many (but not all) of our state courts, today's hearing might take a full day. Neither the prosecutor nor the defense attorney would know what sentence you are considering for Mr. Smith, so both sides would feverishly prepare a host of possible evidence and arguments to sway your judgment. With the full possibility that the accused could get twenty years in prison or no prison, the pressure would fall on both the prosecutor and the defense attorney to justify any sentencing recommendation with specific facts from the case. You would then decide an appropriate sentence based upon the evidence of the case.

As you might suspect, in indeterminate systems of that type, both sides closely evaluate the evidence to search for any possibly aggravating and mitigating facts. Does the accused have ten pictures of child pornography and one hundred thousand pictures of adult pornography, or vice versa? Are there any trends in the collection? For instance, did the defendant start with pictures of teens, then move on to picture of young children, and then progress to pictures exclusively of infants and child abduction? Or, conversely, does the collection appear random, where on any given day the defendant might have looked at any type of adult or child pornography by whim? In state or military courts, these facts matter; in federal court, facts like these are often undiscovered.

Because you are in federal court, you are part of a "semideterminate" system. Your system gives you some latitude in sentencing, but everyone at the hearing will tend to focus on a short checklist of approved sentencing factors. The facts you are supposed to consider relevant are listed for you in each case, and you are often discouraged from giving too much weight to other facts. Frequently, neither party will have looked at the forensic evidence any more than was necessary to "check off" the presence or absence of each established factor.

Although the statute may authorize you to impose a sentence of zero to twenty years, your actual sentence will tend to be "anchored" to whatever the United States sentencing guideline suggests as a "model" sentence for a generic case of this type. The United States Attorney's Office will almost always recommend a "guideline" sentence, and will tend to appeal any below-guideline sentence.[3] If you choose not to follow that recommended guideline, especially if you vary to any significant degree, you will have to explain yourself on the record. If the sentence you impose is considered too lenient by the prosecutor, or the reasons you give for the sentence are not standard factors, the government will likely appeal. Historically, circuit courts have more frequently overturned "lenient" sentences, and while above-guideline sentences tend to be overturned less often, within-guideline sentences are very rarely disturbed because they are presumptively reasonable.[4]

What then, is the single most significant sentencing factor for you to consider at today's hearing? What will likely drive Mr. Smith's sentence? What is the issue that the attorneys will devote the lion's share of their preparation and arguments to resolving? According to your probation officer, the most important disputed fact in this case is whether Mr. Smith intended to watch the movie on his 55″ television screen or on his 13″ laptop. You see, if Mr. Smith intended to use the TV, then the sentencing guidelines will recommend one sentence, but if Mr. Smith intended to watch the movie on his smaller, 13″ laptop screen, then the guidelines will probably suggest that you *add* two to three years to his prison term.

As you walk into the courtroom, you prepare to hear arguments about whether the defendant was actually closer to his TV or his laptop. You know that whichever way you decide, you will need to immediately explain to the defendant, his family, and the public why that fact should add or subtract several years to the amount of time Mr. Smith will serve in prison.

This is the type of dilemma federal judges face each time they impose a sentence for someone who possessed, received, or redistributed child pornography. Issues like these leave many judges feeling frustrated. While 85 percent of federal judges agree that the guideline system generally suggests an appropriate sentence for someone who *makes* child pornography, fewer than 30 percent have any faith that a guideline sentence is rational in the cases of possession or receipt (the lowest satisfaction rate of any guideline in the entire federal system).[5] But it isn't just the judges who are worried. The Sentencing Commission's Practice Group recently noted that "the marked propensity of our district judges to deliver sentences not within the guidelines . . . suggests that there's something wrong with the guideline, something seriously wrong."[6]

Even the Department of Justice has expressed these concerns, writing to the Sentencing Commission to explain:

> We think the report to Congress ought to recommend legislation that permits the Sentencing Commission to revise the sentencing guidelines for child pornography offenses . . . the changes in the use of technology and in the way these crimes are regularly carried out today suggest that the time is ripe for evaluating the current guidelines" and reforming the guidelines to "better calibrate the severity and culpability of defendant's criminal conduct.[7]

So why does everyone doubt the guideline range for these particular crimes? Why is it that while judges imposed a below-guideline sentence in just 1.9 percent of 2010 drug possession cases, they gave a below-guideline sentence in almost 60 percent of child pornography cases that same year?[8] As we shall see, there are compelling, logical reasons why this has become the least respected guideline in the entire federal system.

The Guideline in Theory

As a federal judge, your sentencing guidance comes from two sources, the first of which is a statute. 18 U.S.C. § 3553(a) instructs each judge to consider certain factors in every sentencing hearing. These factors include the nature and circumstances of the offense, the need for a sentence to reflect the seriousness of the offense, the need to protect the public from further crimes, the history and characteristics of the defendant, the need to promote respect for the law, and the need to avoid unwarranted sentencing disparities among defendants with similar records who commit similar crimes. As you can imagine, a judge may struggle to keep aware of how similar offenders are treated on the other side of the country. The sentencing guidelines represent the federal solution to this problem.

In principle, the sentencing guidelines serve as your second source of guidance by keeping you informed of developments around the country. As judges issue written judgments, the Sentencing Commission engages in an ongoing study of these decisions. The Commission should then adjust the applicable guidelines whenever research identifies a better method for evaluating the seriousness of a given case. In theory, any guideline endorsed by the Commission is based upon a review of thousands of pre-guidelines cases and correctly identifies the factors most judges find useful at sentencing for that type of offense. The presumption of an empirical basis to the guidelines may hold true for many offenses, but not for child pornography.

A guideline based on Commission research does not require a given sentence, but it should help you quickly identify the most important facts of the case. The guidelines should also suggest to you how much weight to give each aggravating or mitigating circumstance. Using the guidelines, a judge handling his or her first bank robbery case should theoretically tend to impose a sentence that is approximately consistent with what a more experienced judge in another state might impose. For example, all judges would start by determining that a bank robbery scores as an offense level 22 and that any injury to a teller or customer will add two to six levels based upon whether the injury was minor, serious, or life-threatening. Thus both new and experienced judges will be guided toward a similarly small range of sentencing options within the broad range of statutorily possible sentences.

The guidelines system works as follows: First, the manual establishes a "Base Offense Level" for different types of crimes. As the judge, you then add to that Base Offense Level based on various factors in the case (such as whether the defendant shot a teller during a bank robbery). You may also deduct based on recognized factors such as whether the accused pled guilty or was a minor player in the crime. You plot the final score on the "Y" axis of a sentencing chart. This is the Total Offense Level. Next, you rank the accused's prior criminal activity based on the nature and severity of the defendant's prior offenses. This produces the accused's Criminal History Category, which translates into a score of I-VI, which you plot on the "X" axis of the standard sentencing chart. Wherever the X and Y points intersect on the sentencing chart provides you with a recommended "guideline" sentence. So, assuming a first-time offender commits a bank robbery and shoots but luckily doesn't kill a teller, the Total Offense Level might be 25, the Criminal History Category would be I, and the corresponding Guideline range would be 57–51 months' incarceration.

The problem for child pornography cases is that the sentencing variables used to differentiate cases do not make sense and do not work. The Sentencing Commission had no significant body of historical cases to use as a baseline for determining important sentencing factors. As a result, the Commission had to invent sentencing levels without reference to a body of empirical data. The Commission was also not allowed to take the time to develop its own empirical approach that would meaningfully distinguish the severity of each case. Instead, Congress simply invented criteria and told the Commission to implement those ideas. Although these criteria are "objectively" measured and applied, they have proven largely useless when sorting and comparing relatively criminality. As things stand, the guideline criteria do not seem to correspond to the severity of the offense. Many of the criteria apply to the typical offender, and in such arbitrary ways that the worst offenders frequently score the same as, or even lower than, average defendants.

Guideline 2G2.2 in Practice

Mr. Smith's case demonstrates several (of the many) ways the guidelines' treatment of possession, receipt, and distribution of child pornography (Guideline § 2G2.2) actually obstructs a court's ability to fashion a rational sentence. As we shall see, the district where Mr. Smith lives, as well as minor differences in labeling the evidence in his case, will radically sway the sentence Mr. Smith faces for his misdeed.

1. Setting the Base Offense Level

First, you need to understand that you, the judge, do not control the Base Offense Level in Mr. Smith's case. Surprisingly, the Sentencing Commission does not exert much control on today's Base Offense Level either.

Instead, Congress granted the prosecutor the option to choose the Base Offense Level. The means by which the prosecutor exercises this discretion is to choose whether to charge Mr. Smith for the receipt of the DVD at his front door or for the possession of the DVD in his living room. The prosecutor's choice will then constrain your options at sentencing. This is the first flaw in the guidelines for child pornography cases. While 18 U.S.C. § 3553(a) directs you to impose a sentence that is "sufficient, but not greater than necessary," for the facts of this case, Guideline § 2G2.2 assumes that with identical facts, labeling a case as either receipt or possession necessarily changes what a "sufficient" sentence should be.

As you might guess, prosecutors can readily charge either possession or receipt in nearly every child pornography case. In 1996, the Sentencing Commission concluded an investigation of sex offenses with a report to Congress. As one of the recommendations, the Commission specifically requested permission to treat receipt and possession as equally serious offenses. The Commission explained that based upon a study of actual cases:

> There appears to be little difference in the offense seriousness between typical receipt cases and typical possession cases. Indeed, all the material that is possessed must at some point have been received (unless it was produced, in which case the defendant would be sentenced under the more severe production guideline).[9]

These findings came five years after the Commission first objected to a bill directing the Commission to treat receipt as a more serious offense than possession. At the time the rule was introduced in 1991, the Commission warned:

> Recognizing that receipt is the logical predicate to possession, the Commission concluded that the guideline sentence should not turn on the timing or nature of law enforcement intervention, but rather on the gravity of the underlying conduct. . . . Senate Amendment 780, unfortunately, would negate the Commission's carefully structured efforts to treat similar conduct similarly and to provide proportionality among different grades of seriousness of these offenses in a manner that will reintroduce the sentencing disparity among similar defendants and render the guideline susceptible to plea bargaining manipulation. . . . One primary reasons Congress created the Sentencing Commission was to devise guidelines that avoid

these unwarranted variances in sentencing for similar conduct. Amendment 780 will reintroduce the very problems the guidelines now prevent.[10]

If we recall that 18 U.S.C. § 3553(a) specifically directs federal judges to issue sentences limiting unwarranted sentencing disparities, then we can easily understand why the Commission argued to make receipt and possession equivalent under the guidelines. Nevertheless, to this day, Congress has forbidden the Sentencing Commission from adopting a more rational guidelines structure in which receipt and possession would yield similar sentences.

The 1991 prediction that this disparity would cause plea bargaining manipulation has proven prescient. While the guidelines were supposed to standardize punishments across the United States, what Guideline § 2G2.2 actually did was transfer arbitrariness into the hands of the prosecutor and into the background where it is difficult to observe or measure. Over the years, each district has adopted different charging practices, with some districts aggressively charging the more serious label of receipt, other districts using the threat of a receipt charge to force a defendant to waive certain sentencing arguments, and yet other districts opting to charge the lower offense unless the defendant proceeds to trial.

As a practical matter, the prosecutor's charging decision alters your sentencing options in two ways. First, the statutory range of punishment differs between the two charges. Both charges authorize a punishment of up to twenty years in prison. But while you can impose any punishment from zero to twenty years in a possession case, you *must* impose at least the mandatory minimum of five years for any conviction for the receipt of child pornography. As contrary as it sounds, if you know where a defendant got his or her child pornography from, then you must punish the recipient more harshly. On the other hand, if the defendant succeeds in hiding or shielding his or her source from law enforcement, that defendant may get a lower sentence. Not every case results from a sting like Mr. Smith's, so the result tends to be that defendants who confess and admit their source face a harsher mandatory minimum punishment (five years instead of none) than defendants who refused to talk.

Second, this bizarre system carries over to the guidelines' Base Offense Level as well. While the Base Offense Level for possession is 18, the Base Offense Level for receipt is 22. Although defendants who can prove they never intended to redistribute the images *may* get a two-level reduction (more on this later), at best they still face a Base Offense Level of 20. Again, defendants who hide their activities tend to receive an offense level two to four levels *lower* than those who confess and provide full disclosure.

Let us return then to the prediction about charge bargaining. As the Sentencing Commission warned in 1991, many prosecutors today use their arbitrary power to "charge bargain," or pressure defendant to plead guilty at the risk of facing much higher guidelines ranges. In fact, the Commission has discovered that although 97.5 percent of cases involved knowing receipt and/or redistribution, only 46.9 percent involved a conviction for receipt or distribution; 53.1 percent of cases were resolved as possession counts.[11] One judge described the behind-the-scenes dynamics of charge bargaining as it applied to a defendant named David Grober:

> This Court knows from its own experience about the problematic nature of charging discretion. . . . This year, the Court sentenced an offender under a plea agreement similar to the one offered to David Grober [which Grober did not accept]. . . . It is a chilling exercise to take an earlier defendant's plea deal and apply it to David Grober's case. His original indictment charged him with the same two offenses the government charged against an earlier defendant. . . . This court knows enough of the fact behind the earlier defendant's offense to be unpersuaded that there is an intellectually honest basis to distinguish what the earlier defendant did from what David Grober did.[12]

You might hope that the difference between possession and receipt could not prove that great and that behind-the-scenes posturing will not affect the sentence you will impose as a judge. But let us again consider Mr. Grober's case, where the court was fully aware of the facts in his particular case and where Mr. Grober refused to charge bargain his case and instead chose to go to trial (thereby losing an adjustment for pleading guilty and subjecting himself to the more seriously labeled charges). The court compared Mr. Grober's case to another similar case from the same time and noted, "What valid sentencing function transforms David Grober's conduct from warranting a sentencing range of 51 to 63 months to warranting a sentencing range of 292 to 365 months merely because he did not plead guilty?"[13]

In summary, the first step in this case is dictated for you; before you were even assigned this case the prosecutor chose how to set the Base Offense Level for Mr. Smith for reasons that you may never hear. At this point, you cannot appreciate the full effect of that charging decision until you calculate all of the enhancements, because the higher the initial offense level, the more a two- or four-level enhancement matters. For example, while a two-level enhancement onto a Base Offense Level of 18 might add six months to the prison sentence, the same two-level enhancement onto a Base Offense Level 32 might add thirty months. Whatever the Base Offense Level, though, it is a sure bet that number *will* rise rapidly as you begin to apply enhancements.

2. *Applying Enhancements*

Your next step is to consider each of the factors that § 2G2.2 claims will contextualize the offense and segregate run-of-the-mill offenders from those who are more dangerous or extreme. When applying the guidelines, your task as a judge is to do a simple, checklist-style review of the facts of the case. You answer yes or no as to whether each factor is present in this case and then score the case accordingly. In determining the guidelines enhancements, it does not matter whether the fact is only marginally present or is instead the defining fact in a case. For example, when determining if a sadistic or masochist conduct enhancement applies, a person who has one image of someone wearing a blindfold will score the same as someone who has a hundred thousand images of extreme bondage and torture of infants.

a. The "Use of a Computer" Enhancement

The first enhancement to consider is whether Mr. Smith used a computer. Guideline § 2G2.2 instructs you to increase the Total Offense Level by two levels if the defendant used a computer during the commission of the child pornography offense.[14] In effect, §2G2.2 directs you to treat the watching of a movie on a 55″ television as a much less serious crime than the watching of the same video on a 13″ laptop. Why?

In answering that question, you should keep in mind the friction between the desires of certain congressional leaders to look tough on crime and your need, as a judge, for some rational sentencing guidance. The "use of a computer" enhancement traces back to 1995, when Congress determined that mass producers and distributors of child pornography had created "lucrative businesses that reward people who would abuse children."[15] Congress directed the Commission to increase the punishments for those who use computers to mass-distribute child pornography and who use sophisticated computer technology to circumvent detection by postal investigators. These are both laudable goals. As it played out, however, by the time the bill became law Congress had decided to have the enhancement to apply to everyone, treating all computer use the same. The Commission warned the very next year:

> This adjustment does not distinguish between persons who email images to a single, voluntary recipient, and those who establish a BBS and distribute child pornography to large numbers of subscribers. . . . Not all computer use is equal, and sentencing policy should be sensitive to these differences in culpability so that punishments are tailored to fit the circumstances of each individual's case . . . the difference between print and computerized porn is not in the content of the images, but in the means of distribution. The seriousness of a crime involving computerized trafficking in child pornography depends in part on 1) The degree to which the computer use facilitates the widespread and instantaneous distribution of images, and 2) the degree to which it increases the likelihood that children will be exposed to the images. Different types of computer use have different effects on these two harms.[16]

Unfortunately, while the Commission warned that "what seems apparent is that a person's culpability depends on *how* they use a computer," Congress would not allow the Commission to change the application of the enhancement. Today, as in 1995, "the current statutory directive is aimed broadly at all persons who use a computer."[17]

Of course, the world has changed in many ways since 1995. Among the most profound changes is the fact that just about everything we do today involves a computer in some way. If two people exchange a picture of child pornography, they probably do so online. If not, they probably "met" or talked in a chat group using a computer, texted each other using a computerized cell phone, or checked the status of the package's projected delivery date using an online website. For that reason, 96.3 percent of offenders receive an enhancement for use of a computer.[18] Unfortunately, any of these activities result in the same "use of a computer" enhancement that would apply to a mass distributor who runs a commercial child pornography website.

While the number of people assessed this penalty has increased, evidence has emerged that use of a computer is not an aggravating factor in most cases.[19] Law enforcement agencies now find it much easier to discover child pornography online than in real life. Investigators can log on to public networks, spot a suspicious-sounding file, and use special software to examine the contents of the person's shared files without ever going into their home or seeking a search warrant. The online evidence is also easy to process, almost impossible to contest, and results in shorter investigations and faster pleas. There is even a growing body of evidence, recognized by the Department of Justice, linking access to offline, hard-copy child pornography with increased culpability and dangerousness.[20] The current thinking is that while people may "wander" into child pornography online, it takes far more forethought and planning to attempt to secure hard copies of child pornography, and such efforts are often designed to conceal the transactions from later investigation and scrutiny.

Suppose you knew this information as you prepared to sentence Mr. Smith. Knowing that the "use of a computer" enhancement is not just illogical as applied in *this* case, but that it applies to virtually all cases, and it tends to punish more harshly the least dangerous offenders, would you feel comfortable using this as a metric in your courtroom? No matter. Whatever your feelings, you must rule on the issue of whether Mr. Smith used a computer. If he was charged with possession and intended to use his 55″ TV, he will still face a Base Offense Level of 18. If he is charged with receipt and intended to use his 13″ laptop, you must start at an adjusted Offense Level of 24 (22 +2).

b. The "Number of Images" Enhancement

You must also apply an enhancement based upon how the DVD was formatted by the postal inspectors. Both the postal investigators and the Probation Office conducted a thorough investigation and determined that this single DVD is the only child pornography attributable to Mr. Smith. He has no history of child pornography offenses, so this sounds like an easy "collection" to evaluate. However, during the hearing, your probation officer approaches the bench and instructs you that she just recognized a tricky sentencing issue. Because of that sentencing issue, the guidelines sentence in this case will also hinge on your findings about how someone else formatted the DVD that Mr. Smith bought.

Under the current system, offenders receive an enhancement based upon the number of images they possessed, received, or redistributed. The enhancement ranges from a two-level to a five-level enhancement; the maximum enhancement applies if a defendant possessed more than six hundred images. The guidelines direct that each "video-clip, movie, or similar visual depiction shall be considered to have 75 images."[21] If the

DVD in this case consists of one thirty-minute-long movie file, then it counts as seventy-five images and gets a two-level enhancement. On the other hand, if the DVD consists of one "movie," subdivided into internal chapters that allow a user to select to watch portions of the movie, then each subchapter counts as seventy-five images. In other words, your finding on whether the DVD has been formatted with subchapters will determine whether the defendant receives only a two-level enhancement, or whether he will receive as much as a five-level enhancement.

You may ask why six hundred images warrants a five-level enhancement. The short answer is that there is no answer; literally no logical explanation or empirical evidence supports scoring offenses this way. The longer explanation is that it is difficult to articulate bright-line factors that will always make one child pornography case more serious than another. That is not to say that practitioners and judges cannot readily assess which cases are more serious. When faced with particular facts from particular cases, they can. The problem is that while it is easy to say what is particularly aggravating or mitigating about each case, it is much harder to write a bright-line rule that will apply in all cases. And without such a bright-line rule, it is difficult to declare that two cases, one in Oregon and one in Florida, are "the same."

During the 1980s and 1990s, the federal system tried to identify objective criteria for determining how significant a role a person played in a given criminal network, for any type of case. Quantity became the preferred method for comparing offenders in all criminal contexts. For example, a person who conspires to distribute one kilogram of marijuana is now treated as a low-level offender, while a person caught conspiring to distribute thirty thousand kilograms of marijuana is presumed to possess significant ties to major organized drug operations. Although this type of quantity calculus has come under repeated scrutiny, it quickly became a familiar component of federal sentencing.

In 2003, a young congressional aide decided that child pornographers needed to face more severe sentences. He wrote up a provision that would increase sentences based on the number of images, up to six hundred, that a defendant possessed. He conducted no research on whether that arbitrary number was tied to criminality or would usefully distinguish defendants. For all anyone knows, he chose the low number of six hundred with the specific intent that it would apply to most defendants.[22]

In short order, this aide convinced a first-term representative to attach the provision to a popular Amber Alert bill, and it became law. One problem was that neither the Sentencing Commission nor the courts nor the scientific community had any advance notice of the provision, and none had a chance to provide any input on the matter. No one studied the idea to determine whether the number of images really captures criminal culpability. Furthermore, there was no empirical basis for setting the tiered offense enhancements (+2 to +5) so that, for example, 149 images is considered significantly less serious than 151 images.

Another problem concerns the "market" for child pornography. Our gut tells us that there is a profound difference between someone who has ten images of child pornography and someone who has 150,000. As we consider other federal crimes, we might even think, isn't this similar to a drug defendant who is punished more for distributing 30,000 kilograms of marijuana than for one kilogram? The flaw in this logic is that such a comparison disregards an important feature of child pornography offenses—most defendants did not pay for the child pornography they possessed.

Defendants who acquire 30,000 kilograms of marijuana must utilize major drug networks, and they pump significant sums of money into the drug "market." We can presume that before they could buy drugs in that quantity, they had to build up relationships and earn the millions of dollars necessary to operate on such as a scale, presumably by first conducting smaller-level drug transactions. This type of logic fails utterly when applied to digital pictures and videos.

Today the Internet contains more free pornography, of all types, than a person could ever view in a lifetime. In addition, modern software makes such materials ever more readily available. Using a peer-to-peer program, a defendant can easily find and download hundreds, or even hundreds of thousands, of images in one thirty-minute session, at no cost. (Not coincidentally, the same method for finding and downloading files is used by law enforcement to discover and arrest many defendants).[23] Thus a defendant can acquire a large collection of images on his or her first day of activity, and the quantity of images collected often provides us no insight into his or her level of involvement, if any, in the child pornography community. At the very least, using six hundred images as a threshold for identifying "high-level" offenders is absurd.

Proof of this issue can be found in courtrooms around the United States. The untested and unverified enhancement for number of images now applies in 96.3 percent of cases.[24] As one judge who held hearings on the matter discovered when she questioned an experienced detective:

> Special Agent Chase recognized that that every one of her 180 investigations involved a possessor with 600 or more images. SA Chase

> testified that every one of the cases she had worked on '100 percent' – involved the use of a computer and of interactive computer service. Further, according to SA Chase, 'all' of the cases she has worked on involved images of prepubescent minors under age 12.[25]

The fundamental change in the nature of these crimes cannot be overstated. Thirty years ago, acquiring child pornography involved significant premeditation, planning, and expense. Child pornography was "difficult to find, . . . expensive to duplicate, and required a secure and private storage area."[26] In the 1970s, the size of a collection was a definite indicator of the scope of a defendant's involvement with other pornographers. Furthermore, because each image required both planning and payment, collectors tended to acquire images most representing their personal preferences.

Now it takes only marginally more time to download ten thousand images than it does to order a pizza, and the cost of acquiring ten or ten thousand images is likely the same: nothing. The nature of collecting has changed. As courts and research scientists have discovered, "because the internet is now the primary vehicle for delivering or consuming pornography (legal and illegal) and the number and type of images received is frequently accidental, it is thus a poor indicator of culpability. Most obviously this means of distribution facilitates the easy collection of a large number of images (triggering the enhancement for quantity)."[27] As a result of these dynamics, the size of a collection is now a poor indicator of criminality.

In my experience as a federal defender, the only defendants who don't receive the "number of image" enhancement today are the particularly savvy defendants. These defendants often use a variety of computer techniques to ensure that they minimize their digital "footprint," regularly clearing data off of their computers. They also use foreign servers and "cloud" data to obscure their connection to remotely accessible files. In other words, the defendants who do not receive enhancements are often the most capable defendants, who took the most time to plan their crimes in order to avoid detection. While these defendants may pose more of a threat to the community, these are the offenders least likely to face an enhancement for number of images.

At this point, we might remember that the smart "consumer" who hid his source and cleared his cache daily may now face only an adjusted Offense Level of 18, where the dumb consumer who talks to authorities and/or left a clear trail could now face an adjusted Offense Level of 29 (22 + 2 for the computer, + 5 for number of images). In our case, Mr. Smith may receive a two-level or the full five-level enhancement based upon possession of a single DVD. Again, the guideline system would instruct us that we have just used meaningful, objective criteria to distinguish the most serious offenders from the least serious offenders. Do you agree? Does Mr. Smith's case require a higher or lower sentence based upon how someone else formatted the DVD he never watched?

c. Enhancements for Sadistic or Masochistic Conduct and Depiction of a Prepubescent Child

While almost 97 percent of offenders receive enhanced sentences based on the number of images, so too do 96.3 percent of cases include at least one image of a prepubescent minor.[28] Again, this is due in large part to the changing nature of technology.

A study comparing child pornography offenders in 2000 to those in 2006 determined that the nature of acquiring pornography had changed by 2006. Over time, more and more users acquired child pornography using peer-to-peer (P2P) networks. Researchers discovered that with relatively little effort, P2P users acquired larger collections that also tended to "capture [violent or extreme] files even if offenders were not specifically looking for violent content" and despite "no evidence that P2P users were more deviant or criminal than other offenders" arrested for possession.[29] As one judge described the situation, using this new technology to free-download images results in situation in which "a defendant generally has very little control over the quantity of images he receives or the content of those images."[30]

It is entirely reasonable for citizens to worry most about defendants whose taste in child pornography involves particularly young children or children subjected to particularly cruel treatment. It therefore seems reasonable to add enhancements for any case that includes a file of sadistic or masochistic conduct or a file of a prepubescent child under the age of twelve. In practice, however, we must remember that § 2G2.2 is a simple checklist. Although a comparison of the focus and nature of a defendant's collection would tend to help you distinguish cases, that is not what you will do at this sentencing hearing. Instead, you will simply determine if any *one* image meets the criteria. In fact, the guidelines direct you to apply this enhancement "regardless of whether the defendant specifically intended to possess, access with the intent to view, receive, or distribute" these types of images. Thus, even if you find just one image, and even if you find *conclusive* proof that the defendant was completely unaware of the sadistic or prepubescent content, this is a strict liability provision you must apply to Mr. Smith.[31]

Suppose, then, that the DVD Mr. Smith ordered included an unexpected advertisement at the end of the movie. This thirty-second ad invites the viewer to buy a video called "Daddy Loves 11 Y.O. Daughter." In the advertisement clip, an adult man is seen rubbing his finger along the vagina of a smiling young girl who could indeed be eleven years old. If you find the existence of such an advertisement in the video, then you must apply a two-level enhancement based upon evidence that a file contained a depiction of a prepubescent minor or a minor under the age of twelve.

In addition, you must immediately consider applying an enhancement for sadism. The Sentencing Commission has never defined this term, but the appellate courts have consistently held that the enhancement applies whenever the creation of an image is likely to have caused physical or emotional pain.[32] As applied to a child under twelve, the courts have consistently determined that any sexual act involving an adult will necessarily cause emotional harm or distress to a young child, and thus the enhancement should apply.[33] Again, Application Note 2 of § 2G2.2 directs you to apply this enhancement regardless of whether Mr. Smith had any reason to know the advertisement was in the DVD he had yet to watch. Finally, if you are in the Ninth Circuit, you must also consider a two-level additional enhancement because the child was a "vulnerable victim." A single photo can trigger and require the application of three enhancements.[34]

d. Intermediate Tally

Now is a useful time for us to pause and compare the preliminary range of "guidelines" sentences resulting from the seemingly minor differences in the facts and our interpretations of the facts:

(i) If the prosecutor charged possession, Mr. Smith was standing closer to his television, and his one movie did not include an advertisement, then Mr. Smith's Base Offense Level is 18. One video file counts as seventy-five images, so he gets a two-level enhancement for having more than ten but fewer than one hundred images. We deduct three levels based on his plea, and the guideline range for a Total Offense Level 17, Criminal History Category I is 24 to 30 months in prison.

(ii) On the other hand, if the prosecutor charged receipt, you find Mr. Smith stood closer to his laptop, and the DVD was internally subdivided into four-minute "chapters" (that also contained an unseen ad), then Mr. Smith starts at a Base Offense Level 20, gets a two-level enhancement for use of a computer, a five-level enhancement for number of images, a two-level enhancement for a minor under twelve, and a four-level enhancement for sadistic conduct. He still gets three levels off for pleading guilty, but his Total Offense Level is 32 and his Guideline range is 121 to 151 months in prison.

Are you satisfied that the extra 97 to 121 months you would add due to these enhancements still expresses a sentence that is sufficient but not greater than necessary for the facts and circumstances of this case?

e. Enhancements for Intended Distribution

Although that is the end of Mr. Smith's case, the guideline checklist will score a typical defendant even higher than Mr. Smith. Remember that 97.4 percent of offenders use a computer and that in a great many cases, the way defendant used the computer was to download a picture off the Internet using some sort of filing sharing software such as Kazaa, Limewire, etc. These peer-to-peer (P2P) programs generally allow free and unrestricted access to search and download the content of other users. These programs also, as a default, set the computer to list and "share" any downloaded files with any other users looking for the same file. In internal testing, federal defender teams have found that even if a user turns off this function, the software still "shares" file that are in the process of downloading before putting the finished file into an "unshared" location on the computer.[35]

The guidelines mandate a distribution enhancement for "any act" that evinces intent to distribute, including "possession with the intent to distribute." Put another way, the distribution enhancement applies even if a defendant did not intend to distribute, so long as he possessed knowledge that by participating in a P2P file-sharing program whereby he could access other user's files, he was making his child pornography files accessible to others. Almost every federal court has concluded that the mere presence of file-sharing software on a computer automatically requires at least the two-level enhancement for possession with a willingness to allow redistribution of downloaded child pornography.[36] Unless the defendant can affirmatively prove he did not install the software or understand it was a file-sharing program, the courts will apply at least a two-level enhancement for unspecified distribution. Furthermore, every court will also consider applying the five-level enhancement for distribution "for the receipt, or expectation of receipt of a thing of value" if there was any evidence that the defendant used the file-sharing program and let his files be accessible to others specifically in order to gain access to more files or to faster connection speeds. Although "most offenders used open P2P file sharing programs that did not require the offenders to trade images in order to receive new images or videos from another,"[37] the five-level enhancement can still apply if there was any idea in the defendant's mind that leaving the default setting to "share" might result in easier access to other files. These enhancements do not require that any affirmative act of distribution occurred.

f. Final Tally

So, let us compare Mr. Smith with a typical offender:

(i) Mr. Smith talked to other child pornographers, sought secret sources of child pornography, arranged for a certified check, and then ordered child pornography from abroad (actually a fake, sting business). If he had been caught without us knowing his source, and if he had refused to talk to authorities, he would face a guideline sentence of 24 to 30 months. At worst, if law enforcement discovered his source and the prosecutor played "hardball," Mr. Smith could face a guideline sentence of 121 to 151 months in prison.

Meanwhile,

(ii) Mr. Jones, a typical offender, did not engage in any advanced planning, didn't know any child pornographers, and simply used a P2P program to download the exact same video as Mr. Smith from a shared folder he saw online. Mr. Jones was discovered by the authorities as the file downloaded to his computer. He confessed his wrongdoing. Mr. Jones automatically faces the same "use of computer," "number of images," "prepubescent," and "sadistic" enhancements as Mr. Smith. He should also expect to receive at least a two-level, if not a five-level, enhancement for distribution. If Mr. Jones is lucky, his guideline range will be as low as 151 to 188 months, but if the court concludes that he understood his computer might be sharing files, then his guideline range will be 210 to 262 months.[38] Mr. Jones is representative of the typical offender;[39] more than 65 percent of defendants receive a "distribution" enhancement.[40]

These child pornography guideline ranges are very long when compared to the average sentence for other sexual offenses. The average guideline sentence for fondling a child is 44 months, the average guideline for statutory rape is 32 months, the average guideline range for prostituting a child is 171 months, and the average guideline range for raping a child under twelve is 176 months.[41] In other words, according to the guidelines, Mr. Y deserves at least 34 months more in prison for swapping one video clip over the Internet than he would have deserved if he had targeted and actually raped a young child or if he had "pimped" his neighbor's child into prostitution.

You may now understand why judges complain that Guideline § 2G2.2 has failed its purpose.

g. Adding a Term of Supervised Release

In addition to a term of incarceration, you must also impose a period of supervised release. Supervised release is similar to probation or parole, but it follows after prison. It allows you and your probation officer to closely supervise and monitor all defendants after their release. If the defendant screws up, even if the problem is minor, you can send him to back to prison again and again until he stops causing problems. While the statute allows you to impose as little as five years or as much as a lifetime of supervised release,[42] the guidelines offer you no guidance when determining who needs more or less supervision. The guidelines recommend lifetime supervised release for all sex offenders "blindly and without careful consideration of the specific facts and circumstances of the case before it."[43] Does it make sense to supervise all offenders the same way?

Can Variances from the Guidelines Correct for Empirical Failures?

At this point, you may feel that Mr. Smith or Mr. Jones deserves to join the 62.2 percent of 2010 defendants[44] who received a below-guideline sentence. After all, you take very seriously the "parsimony" provision of 18 U.S.C. § 3553(a) requiring you to impose the lower of any two sentences that would both serve the statutory sentencing purposes. Unfortunately, the guidelines do not work the same way in each circuit.

If you are a sentencing judge that works in the Second or Third Circuits, you enjoy full authority to disagree with Guideline § 2G2.2 on policy grounds. For example, in the Second Circuit case of *United States v. Dorvee*, the appellate court agreed that § 2G2.2 was seriously flawed, noting that "the 2G2.2 sentencing enhancements cobbled together through this process routinely result in Guidelines projections near or exceeding the statutory maximum, even in run of the mill cases" and thus "an ordinary first-time offender is therefore likely to qualify for a sentence" approaching the statutory maximum sentence "based solely on sentencing enhancements that are all but inherent to the crime of conviction."[45] That the guideline enhancements routinely resulted in such high sentences for all offenders led the court to conclude that "2G2.2 eviscerates the fundamental statutory requirement in 3553(a) that district courts consider the 'nature and circumstances of the offense and the history and characteristics of the defendant' and violates the principle, reinforced in Gall, that court must guard against unwarranted similarities among sentences for defendants who have been found guilty of dissimilar conduct."[46] The court went on to state not only that sentencing courts may sentence outside the guideline range for child pornography defendants based on policy disagreements with the guidelines, but it also encouraged courts "to take seriously the broad discretion they possess in fashioning sentences . . . bearing in mind that they are dealing with an eccentric guideline of highly unusual provenance, which, unless carefully applied, can easily generate unreasonable results."[47]

On the other hand, if you work in the Fifth, Sixth, or Eleventh circuits, you may not sentence Mr. Smith or Mr. Jones below that guideline range simply because you disagree with the policies underlying the guideline. Those appellate courts have decided that it is irrelevant that the congressional directives to the Sentencing Commission to change § 2G2.2 were not supported by empirical data or seem illogical. The fact that the guidelines policies originated with Congress, according to these courts, means that you must give them special weight. As one of these courts explained, "it is normally considered a constitutional virtue, rather than a vice, that Congress exercises power directly."[48] The court went on to explain: "It is true that the Commission did not act in its usual institutional role with respect to the relevant amendments to 2G2.2. But that is because Congress was the relevant actor. . . . It is Congress' prerogative to dictate sentencing enhancement based on retributive judgment."[49] In other words, if you think that Mr. Smith and Mr. Jones should not serve more time in prison than child rapists, you will struggle to be able to alter their sentences unless you work in a certain circuit. Your location, as much as any particular fact, affects your ability to disagree on policy grounds with the problematic guidelines provisions we have identified during the hearing.

A Final Word on Failures in the System

If you as a judge are frustrated by the guidelines' approach, you may decide to conduct your own sentencing hearing and form your own judgment about the appropriate sentence in this case based the facts presented by both sides and based on arguments about the relevance and relative importance of those facts. This is the process that would occur in a state or military sentencing hearing. Unfortunately, there are a number of obstacles to holding such a hearing in the federal system, obstacles created by the obsession with guidelines checklists.

In particular, neither party will be able to provide you with the comprehensive facts you will need for such a hearing. While FBI agents often devote hundreds and even thousands of hours to evaluating evidence in a simple social security fraud case, the formula for investigating child pornography is to "checklist" the enhancement factors, then close the case. For that reason, few agents know much about the facts of their case. The evidence is also held at offsite locations, often far removed from the courthouse. In most districts, the defense must make an advance appointment to review any of the evidence. The defense attorney and his or her forensic computer specialist can only look at the evidence when government agents are present. These government agents watch every keystroke, so the government will immediately learn of any unfavorable discoveries made by the defense attorney. In this context, the defense is often unwilling to conduct a close review of the evidence for fear of the unknown or because they are unable to arrange access on a timely basis.

Two examples from this author's own experience highlight the scope of the problem: In the first case, the prosecution contacted defense counsel late on the Friday afternoon before a Monday morning sentencing. The prosecutor indicated she intended to introduce several images "sampled" from the defendant's collection. The computer lab was three hours away and was already closed for the weekend. When the sentencing hearing began that next Monday, the prosecution introduced four heinous images and one picture of a young child in her underwear. The FBI agent testified that the child in the final picture was the defendant's daughter. The implication was that the defendant was not merely a passive possessor but was in fact inclined to make child pornography of his daughter.

By stalling the hearing, counsel was barely able to get enough time for his in-house forensic analyst to go to the lab. The analyst conducted a forensic review while the sentencing hearing was in progress. The analyst then entered the courtroom. Counsel called him to the stand, not knowing what answer might emerge. The analyst then testified that the child's mother took the photo of the girl, *after* the defendant was arrested, and that the photo was from an entirely different location. It was one of a series of photos showing the child preparing for her first day at school. The sentencing judge scolded the government, and the defendant did not receive a sentence based on the misperception that he posed a risk to his own daughter. If defense counsel had not been fortunate enough to have a talented forensic analyst in house, however, counsel—and the judge—would never have discovered the truth.

In another case, local inspectors discovered a man who had sent a nude video of himself to a teenage girl. Investigators conducted a search of the man's home and reported the following evidence to the federal prosecutor and the probation officer:

> "Agents found hundreds of adult pornographic magazines, hundreds of sexually oriented advertisements for movies; and sex toys and aids, several of which advertised child oriented material such as Barely Legal . . . approximately 329 video tapes and DVDs containing thousands of pornographic movies, many depicting horror themes with violent sex, S&M, voyeurism, stalking, forced sex with prison/police themes, nearly all depicting females with shaved/partially shaved pubic hair, several depicting females portrayed as teens, dressed in school clothes, with braces or virgins."

It was only after counsel spent an entire day driving round-trip to a remote site in another state that everyone in the federal case learned that ALL of the "barely legal" materials were thumbnail-sized advertisements in the back of the defendant's subscriptions to the magazines "Juggs," "Playboy's Voluptuous Vixens," and "Hooters." Furthermore, all the "violent" sex scenes were fantasy movies involving vampires bought on Amazon.com, and all the females with shaved pubic areas and dressed in school clothes were clearly voluptuous, adult porn stars wearing "slutty" Halloween costumes such as a cheerleader outfits and pom-poms.

So long as many circuits continue to endorse the flawed policies imposed by Congress and contradicted by reality, and so long as the evidence is treated as so vile that it is not even worth examining in order to contextualize the offense conduct, your ability as a judge to get to the true facts of the case will remain in doubt. The current federal system discourages actual investigation and analysis.

A Way Forward

As the examples of Mr. Smith and Mr. Jones illustrate, there is much wrong with the federal law surrounding child pornography. The Sentencing Commission agrees that the statutory and guidelines sentencing scheme for child pornography "should be updated to better reflect the technological changes and new expert knowledge and also to account for current offenders' varying degrees of culpability."[50] With that starting point, this author hopes that Congress will eventually authorize some modifications to the system.

The first step in modifying the guidelines will be to build on scientific research about this subgroup of offenders. Until recently, studies of contact offenders—individuals who had physical contact with victims—were applied to this noncontact group. A growing body of evidence supports the proposition that people who possess and view child pornography are often quite different than contact offenders. They are also quite compliant under supervision. Studies also suggest that many, if not most, of these offenders would never "progress" to any "hands-on" offenses.[51]

At this point, it appears that the greatest predictor of danger to the community is not the size of viewed materials, or whether a person used P2P software, but is instead their past history of criminal behavior. For that reason, the Base Offense Level for these offenses might be better tied to past history than to whether a prosecutor arbitrarily charges "possession," "receipt," or "distribution."

Also, instead of applying dubious distribution enhancements to a majority of offenders, particular care should be given to those who directly encourage the creation of new images. The Department of Justice recognizes that "an offender who purchases child pornography from a commercial website . . . is not necessarily high-risk, and may even be an entry-level offender." These offenders often lack sophistication or ties to any pornography producers; they often buy images that are decades old.[52] Similarly, offenders using P2P technology signal a lesser risk than offenders who combine P2P file-sharing with the group activity with like-minded offenders. Enhancements could and should apply to offenders who participate in commercial or barter networks that directly target and solicit the creation of new "content."

Ultimately, our public deserves a sentencing system in which all misconduct is dealt with appropriately, one that makes sense. Rationale sentences, more than anything else, will promote respect for the law and tend to diminish unwarranted sentencing disparities.

NOTES

1. UNITED STATES SENTENCING COMMISSION, 2012 ANNUAL REPORT, chap. 5, p. 42, *available at* http://www.ussc.gov/Research_and_Statistics/Annual_Reports_and_Sourcebooks/2012/2012_Annual_Report_Chap5.pdf.
2. Melissa Hamilton, *Sentencing Adjudication: Lessons from Child Pornography Policy Nullification*, GA. ST. U. L. REV. (forthcoming) at 44 (citing unsourced U.S. Sentencing Commission statistics).
3. United States v. Biermann, 599 F. Supp. 2d 1087, 1101 (N.D. Iowa 2009) (noting that the U.S. Attorney's Office requested a guideline sentence in 1,524 of 1,526 cases).
4. United States v. Yirkovsky, 338 F.3d 936, 943 (8th Cir. 2003).
5. UNITED STATES SENTENCING COMMISSION, RESULTS OF SURVEY OF UNITED STATES DISTRICT JUDGES JANUARY 2010 THROUGH MARCH 2010 (2012), *available at* http://www.ussc.gov/research/research_projects/surveys/20100608_judges_survey.pdf.
6. U.S. SENTENCING COMMISSION, FEDERAL CHILD PORNOGRAPHY OFFENSES 12 (2012) [hereinafter U.S. SENTENCING COMMISSION, CHILD PORNOGRAPHY].
7. Letter from Jonathan Wroblewski (director, Office of Policy and Legislation) to Hon. William K. Sessions III, Chair, U.S. Sentencing Commission (June 28, 2010), at 5–6.
8. UNITED STATES SENTENCING COMMISSION, 2010 SOURCEBOOK OF FEDERAL SENTENCING STATISTICS, tbl. 28.
9. UNITED STATES SENTENCING COMMISSION, REPORT TO CONGRESS, SEX OFFENSES AGAINST CHILDREN 11 (1996).
10. 137 Cong. Rec. H6736-02.
11. U.S. SENTENCING COMMISSION, CHILD PORNOGRAPHY, *supra* note 6, at 166.
12. United States v. Grober, 595 F. Supp. 2d 382, 399 (D.N.J. 2008).
13. *Id.* at 400.
14. U.S.S.G. § 2G2.2(b)(6).
15. 141 Cong. Rec. H4122-01, 1995 WL 143978.
16. UNITED STATES SENTENCING COMMISSION, *supra* note 9, at 29.
17. *Id.*
18. U.S. SENTENCING COMMISSION, CHILD PORNOGRAPHY, *supra* note 6, at 209.

19. *See* Troy Stabenow, *A Method for Careful Study: A Proposal for Reforming the Child Pornography Guidelines*, 24 FED. SENT'G. REP. 108, 122 (2011).
20. *Id.*; U.S. SENTENCING COMMISSION, CHILD PORNOGRAPHY, *supra* note 6, at chap. 3 & 209.
21. § 2G2.2(b)(7) & Application Note 4(B).
22. *See* Troy Stabenow, *Deconstructing the Myth of Careful Study: A Primer on the Flawed Progression of the Child Pornography Guidelines,* January 1, 2009, at 19–21, available at http://www.fd.org/docs/Select-Topics---sentencing/child-porn-july-revision.pdf.
23. U.S. SENTENCING COMMISSION, CHILD PORNOGRAPHY, *supra* note 6, at 145.
24. *Id.* at 209.
25. *Grober*, 595 F. Supp. 2d at 397.
26. U.S. SENTENCING COMMISSION, CHILD PORNOGRAPHY, *supra* note 6, at 42.
27. United States v. Burns, 2009 WL 3617448, *7 (N.D. Ill. 2009).
28. U.S. SENTENCING COMMISSION, CHILD PORNOGRAPHY, *supra* note 6, at 209.
29. *See* Stabenow, *supra* note 19, at 120 (discussing Wolak, Finklehor, and Mitchell study).
30. *Burns*, 2009 WL 3617448 at *7.
31. U.S. SENTENCING COMMISSION, CHILD PORNOGRAPHY, *supra* note 6, at 35; U.S.S.G. § 2G2.2(b)(4).
32. Stabenow, *supra* note 19, at 126.
33. *Id.*
34. U.S. SENTENCING COMMISSION, CHILD PORNOGRAPHY, *supra* note 6, at 35.
35. For a detailed description of how P2P works in child pornography cases, *see* Chapter 3 of the Sentencing Commission's 2012 report on Child Pornography Offenses.
36. United States v. Conner, 2013 WL 1490109 (6th Cir. 2013); United States v. Durham, 618 F.3d 921 (8th Cir. 2010).
37. U.S. SENTENCING COMMISSION, CHILD PORNOGRAPHY, *supra* note 6, at 98.
38. The statutory maximum sentence will cap his sentence at 240 months.
39. U.S. SENTENCING COMMISSION, CHILD PORNOGRAPHY, *supra* note 6, at 148–52 & n.36.
40. *Id.* at 149.
41. *Id.* at 137.
42. 18 U.S.C. § 3583(k).
43. U.S.S.G. § 5D1.1(a)(1); United States v. Alvarado, 691 F.3d 592, 598 & n.2 (5th Cir. 2012) (citing United States v. Kuchler, 285 Fed. App'x 866, 870 n.2 (3rd Cir. 2008)).
44. Stabenow, *supra* note 19 at n.24.
45. United States v. Dorvee, 616 F.3d 174, 186 (2d Cir. 2010).
46. *Id.* at 187.
47. *Id.* at 188.
48. United States v. Bistline, 665 F.3d 758, 762 (6th Cir. 2013).
49. *Id.* at 763–64.
50. U.S. SENTENCING COMMISSION, CHILD PORNOGRAPHY, *supra* note 6, at 3.
51. Stabenow, *supra* note 19, at 117–21.
52. DEP'T OF JUSTICE, THE NATIONAL STRATEGY FOR CHILD EXPLOITATION, PREVENTION, AND INTERDICTION—A REPORT TO CONGRESS (Aug. 2010), *available at* http://www.justice.gov/psc/docs/natstrategyreport.pdf; Stabenow, *supra* note 19, at 116.

10 | Political and Empirical Controversies Threaten the Federal Child Pornography Guidelines

Melissa Hamilton

The moral panic over sexual predators targeting young children is often expressed in the punishment of child pornography offenders. The federal government's involvement began with its seminal statute criminalizing the commercial production of child pornography in the Protection of Children Against Sexual Exploitation Act of 1977.[1] Since then, Congress has continued to express concern that child pornography remains a national problem that harms children and society.[2] To that end, Congress has enacted numerous additional criminal statutes to cover nonproduction acts such as transportation, distribution, receipt, and possession of child pornography.[3] Leveraging its constitutional power to regulate interstate commerce, the federal criminal justice system has expanded its jurisdictional grasp over these crimes, which now are largely accomplished using online technologies and computer resources. The number of nonproduction child pornography offenders sentenced in the federal system has increased exponentially, from six dozen in the year 1992[4] to almost 1,800 in 2013.[5]

This book has outlined many areas in law and society in which crimes involving child pornography operate in special and usually contested manners. This observation remains true in sentencing, in which the punishment for child pornography represents perhaps the most controversial sentencing scheme in the federal criminal system today. The dispute has pitted several robust institutions against each other. Congress and the federal judiciary are vying for control over sentencing, and the agency created to foster mutual respect and uniform sentencing practices is struggling to maintain its authority. Congress created that agency, the United States Sentencing Commission (the "Commission"), almost thirty years ago. While Congress delegated significant policy authority to it and expected the agency to act as an independent expert body, Congress has since reminded everyone that the Commission is a subordinate operation.[6] The legislature and the judiciary have a different, though equally complex, relationship in which each operates as a check against the authority of the other, with neither obtaining primary authority in sentencing law. The question about whether sentences should be founded upon empirical study—meaning the result of skillfully calculating actual sentencing practices—is also eliciting debate in legal circles. This chapter explores these political and empirical controversies, points out differences in ideologies and legal conclusions that underlie them, and provides descriptive information about recent federal child pornography offending and resulting sentences. The overall inconsistency in sentencing across federal courts and, as will briefly be addressed, state sentencing schemes reflects differing definitional suppositions concerning the dangers child pornography viewers pose and the harms suffered by children and thus lead to differences in determining the appropriate proportionality of just punishments.

Federal Sentencing Basics

Three important governmental organizations are at odds over the power to manage sentencing practices in the federal criminal justice system. Congress, the United States Sentencing Commission, and the federal judiciary is each convinced of its own unique abilities to best judge culpability and to determine just punishments. As shall be addressed below, the debate is at a head with respect to nonproduction child pornography crimes.[7] To begin, though, a summary of the history of federal sentencing is necessary to set up the reasons for the recent controversy.

In the federal system, child pornography offenses have the potential to elicit long-term prison sentences. Transportation, distribution, and receipt offenses each trigger five-year mandatory minimum sentences and twenty-year maximums.[8] Possession of child pornography does not trigger a mandatory minimum but carries a maximum of ten years; if the material involves a prepubescent child or a minor under the age of twelve, the maximum increases to twenty years.[9] These sentences ratchet upward further if the defendant has a history of criminal sexual abuse. The selection of a particular federal defendant's sentence within those ranges is determined by a district judge subject to the constraints of statutory sentencing goals, the Commission's sentencing policies and guidelines, and constitutional law. All these provide standards that are designed to assist district judges in determining reasonable sentences to impose upon offenders.

The current federal sentencing system was established by legislation aptly named the Sentencing Reform Act of 1984, which overhauled what was an indeterminate system in which judges had great discretion to a more determinative system limiting such flexibility. This law created the United States Sentencing Commission, an agency to be staffed with professionals who would use their special expertise to craft uniform sentencing policies and guidelines. District court judges, essentially trial judges in the federal system,[10] would retain the authority to assign sentences in individual cases, but they were to be substantially influenced by guidelines issued by the Commission concerning the severity of the appropriate punishment for the relevant crime. To this end, the Commission crafted guidelines intended to encompass a reasonable sentencing range based on the idea that not all crimes are committed alike. For example, not all robberies are the same for the purpose of determining an appropriate punishment to match the level of the resulting harm and the offender's relative culpability. The goal was for the Commission to craft discrete sentencing ranges based on the offense committed, as modified by relevant facts or circumstances which the Commission determined either aggravated or mitigated culpability. These offense-related facts or circumstances are called specific offense characteristics ("SOCs"). Thus, under the guidelines the sentence calculation begins with a numeric base offense level for each type of crime (essentially a starting number), which represents the typical crime. Then points are added or subtracted for applicable SOCs, which increase or reduce the offense level based on facts related to the severity of the offense or the culpability of the offender. Basically, guidelines provide precise numerical methods for calculating final point totals, which are then matched against the defendant's criminal history score on a guideline table to determine the relevant sentencing range. Thus, the guidelines are expected to normalize sentencing practices by offering a regimented process to determine a recommended range of sentence. For example, the guidelines might indicate that a sentencing range of 100 to 125 months' imprisonment (approximately 8 to 10 years) was proper for a defendant who committed a certain type of robbery; it would arrive at that calculation by adjusting the base offense level for robbery using relevant SOCs, and then matching the final offense level with the defendant's criminal past on the guideline table.

Originally, Congress intended that the Commission's policies and guidelines would be presumptively binding on the courts. Yet the reform legislation itself contained two provisions that gave judges some flexibility. First, the law provided that federal judges retained some discretion to vary from a guidelines' recommended range for a fact or circumstance that had not already been considered by the Commission.[11] Second, the Commission's policies and guidelines would not embody the only criteria to be considered. Another statutory provision instructed that in determining a reasonable sentence, the sentencing judge must consider not only the guideline range, but also the nature and circumstances of the offense; the history and characteristics of the defendant; the need for the sentence imposed considering the seriousness of the offense, retribution, deterrence, and protecting the public; and the need to avoid unwarranted sentencing disparities among like offenders (collectively, "sentencing factors").[12] This flexibility notwithstanding, federal judges complied with guidelines' recommendations and abided by Commission policies a substantial majority of the time for nearly twenty years. Then, in 2005, the United States Supreme Court dealt the guidelines system a significant blow.[13]

In the landmark case of *United States v. Booker*, the United States Supreme Court rendered the guidelines advisory in nature, rather than presumptive, in order to remedy a constitutional issue with the mandatory nature of the federal guidelines structure.[14] Pursuant to *Booker*, a district judge now can now deviate from a guideline's recommended sentencing range if she determines that a different sentence is justified after consideration of the sentencing factors. The Supreme Court in the *Booker* decision clearly permitted a sentencing judge to vary for a reason related to the particular facts and circumstances in the individual case. A couple years thereafter, the Supreme Court went a step further when it approved the ability of a district judge to vary from a guideline's recommended range not due to any particular fact or circumstance relevant to the case at hand, but if the individual judge has a disagreement with a policy underlying that guideline.[15] For example, the Supreme Court allowed a sentencing judge in *Kimbrough v. United States* to categorically disagree with the guideline for crack cocaine trafficking, which was far more punitive than the guidelines for other drugs, including powder cocaine.

Together, *Booker* and *Kimbrough* might be construed to render the Commission itself, as well as its policies and guidelines, largely irrelevant. To the contrary, in a series of cases since then, the Supreme Court has reaffirmed that federal judges remain significantly circumscribed by the Commission's policies and guidelines, though the ability to vary for the reasons just mentioned survive.[16] Thus a district judge is still required in the first instance to correctly calculate the guidelines' range and also to consider Commission policies before considering whether to diverge from them after considering all of the sentencing factors.

As a result of *Booker* and *Kimbrough*, the compliance rate of issuing within-guideline sentences has continued to decrease in federal courts. The overall rate for within-range sentences fell from 72 percent to 51 percent from 2004 to 2013.[17] Notably, within-guideline sentences have decreased dramatically for child pornography offenses. The percentage of within-range sentences for child pornography offenses fell much farther, from 82 percent in 2004[18] to 31 percent in 2013.[19] The direction of variances for child pornography sentencing is decidedly in one direction: downward variances in issuing sentences (often, very far) lower than guidelines recommendations. The rate of below-guideline penalties in child pornography cases was 13 percent in 2004[20] and increased substantially to 68 percent in 2013.[21]

The current debate about child pornography sentencing has attracted widespread attention from various constituencies. In the last few decades Congress has regularly increased statutory maximum sentences and established higher mandatory minimums specifically for child pornography crimes.[22] Yet even with such numerical increases, Congress continues to be unsatisfied with the reduced sentences imposed by the judiciary in many cases. Thus, Congress has, on several occasions, statutorily required the Commission to make modifications specifically to the child pornography guideline. These have included mandates of specific offense level increases and changes to particular SOCs to enhance punishment.[23] Sentencing experts claim this is an unfortunate legislative intrusion into the operation of a purportedly independent agency and its expertise, an encroachment unique to child pornography crimes.[24]

The Commission itself is equally frustrated with the practices of courts and Congress in this regard. It has indicated its displeasure both with congressional edicts, which have changed the child pornography guideline, and with federal judges disregarding its mastery, which is exemplified by both the decreasing rate of within-guideline sentences and the criticism expressed in sentencing opinions. For their part, numerous federal judges regularly balk at the increasing length of sentences that the child pornography guideline has produced over the years; many now perceive this guideline as glaringly unhelpful in guiding the judge in determining a reasonable sentence.[25] To understand the judges' frustration, it is necessary to outline the common reasons among the judiciary and others for finding that the child pornography guideline's recommendations have become untenable.

Challenges to the Child Pornography Guideline

The controversies concerning the validity of the child pornography guideline converge upon several criticisms that are now oft repeated, at least by those who find fault. The discussion here will outline these common critiques, supplemented by certain numerical information derived from statistical analyses of the Commission data files for fiscal 2012 sentences.[26] First, the source of the child pornography guideline is at the heart of perhaps the most visible complaint. Judges who have varied downward often criticize the guideline as not resulting from the Commission's normal role as an independent agency conducting empirical study. Therefore, the argument continues, it cannot provide normative information about reasonable and consistent sentences.[27] Instead, the starting offense level and several of the SOCs were forced on the Commission by Congress.[28] Indeed, the Commission concisely describes this history in a comprehensive report on the evolution of the child pornography guideline:

> Congress has repeatedly expressed its will regarding appropriate penalties for child pornography offenders. Congress has specifically expressed an intent to raise penalties associated with certain child pornography offenses several times through directives to the Commission and statutory changes aimed at increasing the guideline penalties and reducing the incidence of downward departures for such offenses.[29]

Congress' penchant over the years to enact laws requiring fundamental changes to a specific offense guideline is virtually unprecedented. Its fixation on child pornography, a crime that has never made up more than 3 percent of the federal system's sentencing docket, is remarkable. Perhaps the allure of sex and violence involving the most protected segment of society—children—offers political advantage to support increasing sanctions for people perceived as child sex offenders. Even though such direct congressional influence over the guidelines is unusual, the fact that numerous judges eschew a guideline because of Congress' role in its development is not uncontroversial. That is because, as will be discussed further below, others believe that the ultimate authority over sentencing policy ought to be reserved to Congress, whose judgments should overrule any contrary views of the Commission or individual judges.

The second dispute concerns adjustments to the child pornography offense level. The current guidelines for child pornography offenses contain six categories of SOCs, which, if applied, can substantially increase the recommended length of imprisonment. Significantly, all the SOCs in this guideline are enhancements (rather than reductions). They include additional points for material involving prepubescent children or minors under age twelve; the use of a computer; sadistic or violent content; distribution activity; the number of images; and a history of prior sexual abuse. One of the most common complaints among critics is that several of the SOCs apply in virtually every case.[30] This is because most child pornography offenders use a computer to download and trade images, and the advancement of technology permits the collection of a large trove of material that likely will include very young children and violent content—even if the individual does not necessarily intend to collect those types of images. One problem with the high rate of applicability for multiple SOCs is that instead of acting as aggravating factors that isolate more heinous criminals, they merely represent the typical offender in contemporary times. Thus, the guideline fails to differentiate between more and less culpable offenders.[31]

The observation that some of the SOCs are almost universally applied is borne out by 2012 sentencing statistics.[32] At least 96 percent of defendants received points related to the enhancements for the material involving a minor, the use of a computer, and the number of images. Four out of five defendants received an enhancement for the sadistic or violent content of the images. Just over half of defendants were assigned a distribution-related enhancement. However, just one in ten received points for a pattern of activity of sexual abuse with children.

The problems associated with the SOCs exemplify the political and empirical focus of this chapter. Those SOCs that derive from Congress are not supported by any empirical study of actual sentencing practices. Further, as the Commission's report on the development of the child pornography guideline attests, even those SOCs not required directly by Congress are likewise not based upon any empirical analysis.[33] Instead, the Commission appears open to embracing SOCs that derive merely from various commentators' proposals. For example, the first two SOCs adopted in the child pornography guideline, involving material depicting a minor under twelve and distribution activity (which remain in existence today), evidently were made simply at the request of a Department of Justice representative. Another SOC change made shortly thereafter to trigger an enhancement for material involving a prepubescent minor came from a suggestion by a lawyer for an antipornography interest group, without debate or discussion.

Third, a related problem with many of the SOCs commonly invoked is that they act to ratchet up sentencing ranges significantly. This leads to recommendations for lengthy sentences, which many judges find to be unreasonably high. It has been observed that the resulting ranges tend toward statutory maximums, meaning that the guideline fails to adequately cover the full spectrum of potential minimum and maximum penalties, which again results in a failure to distinguish between various kinds of offending behavior.[34] Some say it seems illogical that Congress would provide a statutory range of five to twenty years for most child pornography offenses, yet the guideline routinely leans toward recommendations around the maximum.[35] Another method of articulating this criticism is that the child pornography guideline results in unwarranted similarity (i.e., extremely harsh penalties) for dissimilar cases and, as mentioned earlier, fails to adequately distinguish the worst (justifying twenty years) from the least culpable offenders (deserving five years).[36]

The final category of complaint is that, overall, the child pornography guideline tends to yield recommendations that are higher than other guidelines would provide for actual sexual molestation of children.[37] Judges adopting this view argue that it is senseless to punish offenses involving visual material more severely than actual contact crimes against children.[38] They also often believe that the child pornography guideline is disproportionate with guidelines' recommendations for other offenses. The guideline ranges tend to be longer for child pornography offenses than for such crimes as homicide, drug trafficking, and bank robbery.[39]

Individually and collectively, these criticisms have caused many federal judges to lose respect for this particular guideline, and the 2012 dataset analyses illustrate the problematic results. The 2012 sentencing data highlight the practice of varying from guideline recommendations, while also showing the result of disparities nationwide. Overall, 35 percent of child pornography sentences in 2012 were within guideline range. Almost two-thirds of child pornography sentences actually issued (approximately 62 percent) were below range. At the other extreme, slightly less than 3 percent were above range. While the sentencing guideline itself would seem to assure similar sentences across all types of offenders, *Booker* and *Kimbrough* have disrupted that result. Both decisions allow judges to reject the application of otherwise applicable SOCs and to vary from final ranges.

Several additional statistical measures highlight the result of variances. The mean prison sentence of for child pornography crimes in 2012 was ten years, which is not insignificantly lower than the mean guideline minimum sentence of over twelve years.[40] Yet there was great variation in individual sentences, ranging from a low of probation to a maximum of a life sentence. On the low end of this punishment spectrum, one-third of defendants in 2012 were sentenced to five years or less. Three percent received one year or less of prison time, with 2 percent receiving sentences of probation only. On the other end of the spectrum, 13 percent received sentences of at least twenty years. Separate regression analyses, not presented herein, also provide evidence of widespread disparities across the country even after controlling for relevant factors. Thus, perhaps because of the criticisms that the guideline improperly tends toward maximum penalties across the board, federal judges are using their newfound powers to achieve gradations in culpability and sentencing.

There are further statistics suggesting that many sentencing judges—but not all—find that the guideline produces punishments that are routinely too high. Even for the 35 percent of sentences in 2012 that complied with the guideline recommendation, most were oriented toward the lower end of the range. Of those sentences that were within range, 70 percent were exactly at the absolute guideline minimum sentence, while another 12 percent were within the lower half of the ranges. The combination of these statistical measures reveals two competing conclusions: First, there is a trend of deviating downward from this guideline. Second, there is also a lack of uniformity nationwide in complying with the guideline and, possibly, with the length of sentences actually issued.

Based usually on one or more of the foregoing complaints, judges often explain the basis of their downward variances as justified when considering all of the sentencing factors and the greater discretion afforded by the *Booker* ruling. The other common legal justification is that the child pornography guideline specifically deserves less deference and ought to be rejected as a matter of policy. This argument is tied to the *Kimbrough* decision referenced earlier. But whether *Kimbrough* legally permits such a policy rejection has resulted in inconsistent, indeed contradictory, conclusions by district judges across the country. Many, but certainly not all, judges find that the child pornography guideline is faulty and therefore unreliable. To make matters worse, the circuit courts of appeal are divided on the relevant legal issue, which partly explains the lack of uniformity in sentencing.

A Disputed Legal Question

Significant disparities in child pornography sentences may be related to an important legal disagreement among the federal courts that has emerged. The question is whether it is lawful for a district judge to vary from the guideline range based on a policy disagreement with the child pornography guideline. This legal question arose after the *Kimbrough* decision, in which the Supreme Court permitted a district judge to disregard the guideline for crack cocaine offenses because the judge disagreed with the principal policy on which that guideline was based. The sentencing judge in *Kimbrough* thought that the Commission's policy was unfounded because it was based not on any empirical study but on a highly questionable generic metric based on the weight of the drug. The Supreme Court's *Kimbrough* decision did not resolve two major issues that are now at the heart of the legal dispute in child pornography sentencing. One was whether a *Kimbrough*-type policy rejection is permissible for any other guideline that is not the product of the Commission's own policy conclusion. More specifically, the question is whether a court may reject a guideline policy when the disputed policy was mandated by Congress itself. The other issue is whether courts may reject only those guidelines that have not benefited from the Commission's empirical analysis. The reference to empirical analysis here refers to the expectation that the Commission would derive policies and guidelines only after undertaking statistical compilations of average sentencing practices across the country for the offense or SOC at issue. To be sure, the formative legislation did not compel the Commission to write guidelines that merely replicated past practices; the agency was also tasked with considering whether such sentences properly reflected the culpability and harm caused by the relevant offense. Still, many believe the Commission ought to at least study judges' decisions. To state this issue another way, the question is whether the ability to reject a guideline based on a categorical policy disagreement is limited to guidelines that do not reflect the Commission's study of normative experiences.

Legal rulings about the legal authority for a sentencing judge to reject the child pornography guideline for a policy-based reason have varied across the country.[41] Significantly, the federal courts of appeal have addressed this issue, resolving the question in three different ways. In one group, four circuits have explicitly denied lower courts the legal ability to reject the child pornography guideline for policy reasons.[42] These courts have offered several reasons for their denials. They tend to view Congress' involvement in the child pornography guideline as a reason to be respectful of the legislature's view that such crimes are serious and ought to be severely punished.[43] One appellate court clearly believes that the fact the child pornography guideline represents congressional will is a reason to consider *Kimbrough* as distinguishable and therefore inapplicable.[44] That court explained that it is not legally permissible to reject the child pornography guideline based on legislative influence because Congress maintains ultimate authority in setting sentencing policy.[45] For three circuit courts in this group, the argument that sentencing policies ought to be based on empirical studies is unpersuasive, with the appellate judges noting that determinations of reasonable sentences never necessitated a statistical analysis.[46] Another appellate court in this group concludes that the child pornography guideline cannot be rejected, but it offers a somewhat conflicting perspective, asserting this guideline actually *was* the subject of empirical support, though the court is unclear about the foundation for such assertion.[47]

On the other end of the spectrum is the group of appellate courts, also numbering four, that have explicitly condoned a policy-based rejection of the child pornography guideline.[48] One appellate circuit construes Congress' involvement in directly and indirectly amending the child pornography guideline as problematic because it undermines the Commission's normal empirical study, leading the court to conclude that this guideline lacks credibility in guiding reasonable sentencing practices. Indeed, this court refers to the child pornography guideline as "eccentric," of "highly unusual provenance, and "fundamentally different" than other guidelines.[49] Another circuit is in substantial agreement. It points out that when a guideline fails to represent the Commission's deliberative process and instead is substantively influenced by congressional directive, it deserves even less respect.[50]

The third group in the dispute on the legal authority to reject the child pornography guideline for policy reasons includes three circuits that have taken an equivocal stance.[51] These courts theoretically accept the ability of a district judge to reject a guideline for policy reasons but at the same time they have expressed serious reservations about the prospect of rejecting the child pornography guideline. These circuits appear unwilling to adopt a definitive stance on the institutional clash, though they seem inclined to defer to Congress and the Commission. For instance, one court in this group opines that arguments that the child pornography guideline recommends overly harsh sentences ought best to be addressed to the Commission or Congress, rather than the judiciary.[52] Another circuit has expressed discomfort with the notion of rejecting a guideline that represents Congress' clear policy choices.[53] The last circuit's position, while not precluding or condoning a policy rejection of the child pornography guideline, expresses a generic deferential stance to congressional choices on punishments, while also opining that legislative preferences need not be empirically based.[54]

Statistical analyses of the Commission's 2012 dataset indicate that this circuit split is correlated with the length of sentences being imposed. The mean sentence in the circuits supporting a policy rejection of the child pornography guideline was about eight years, while in the other circuits it was eleven years. These numbers suggest that the dispute over whether a court may reject the child pornography guideline is related to the lack of national uniformity. Widespread disparities have caused conflict among various institutions in the federal justice system.

Institutional Conflicts

To be clear, some of the conflicts discussed in this chapter are not necessarily limited to child pornography sentencing. There is an ongoing, broader discussion about which federal sentencing institutions may engage in policymaking and, more specifically, whether one of those institutions may trump the others if there is a conflict. Some believe that Congress, as the elected representative body of the people, naturally holds the overriding power.[55] Others prefer the Sentencing Commission, pointing to its institutional advantages for empirical analysis and professional judgment, though not necessarily eschewing congressional oversight.[56] If the guidelines are more akin to mere "sentencing suggestions," as some have suggested is the current state of affairs, then perhaps the Commission should be abolished.[57] Still other experts insist that sentences are most just when judges are able not only to consider the Commission's expertise, but also to gather relevant information and engage in individualized sentencing.[58]

Notwithstanding the larger debate over federal sentencing, child pornography sentencing presents its own singular tensions. Congress continues to press for increases in penalties for child pornography crimes, as well as for decreased judicial discretion. The federal judiciary pushes in the opposite direction by varying downward from guideline recommendations in a significant portion of cases. In a politically charged hearing on the state of federal sentencing after *Booker*, the then-chair of the House Judiciary Committee remarked that "[a] criminal committing a federal crime should receive similar punishment regardless of whether the crime was committed in Richmond, Virginia, or Richmond, California. And that's why I am deeply concerned about what's happening in federal sentencing."[59] He focused not just on regional differences in sentences generally, but on high disparity rates for particular crimes, singling out child pornography sentencing as having the most extreme downward variance rate among federal judges. The conflict has caught the attention of the media, with numerous newspapers, magazines, radio shows, and other news outlets reporting on it. For example, legal reporters have recognized that Congress has micromanaged sentencing policy to an exceptional degree with child pornography penalties.[60]

Other constituencies interested in the debate and in its resolution are obvious: prosecutors, victims, the defense bar, and defendants themselves, all with sometimes conflicting interests. The American Bar Association has called for an overhaul of the child pornography guideline, claiming that its sentences are too severe and disproportionate considering they yield sentences longer than drug trafficking, white-collar crime, and some offenses involving luring children into sexual acts.[61] At a recent congressional hearing, an American Bar Association representative further opined that federal judges and the Commission ought to have a more symbiotic relationship; if the judiciary is consistently varying from a guideline, that fact should be considered significant in convincing the Commission that changes are required.[62] The Department of Justice also seeks an overhaul of the relevant guidelines, believing them to be outmoded, though it is not necessarily supporting the downward variance rate or a reduction in sentence severity overall.[63]

For its part, the United States Sentencing Commission appears torn between the constituencies it was designed to serve.[64] On the one hand, the Commission seeks to provide relevant guidance to federal judges in crafting sentences and thereby fostering national uniformity. It clearly recognizes the high variance rate and is displeased with it. A comprehensive review of the validity of the child pornography guideline has been a listed priority of the Commission since 2009, and the agency in 2013 officially expressed its continuing investigation into possible changes. On the other hand, the Commission was created by Congress. Although Congress delegated significant authority to the Commission, the Commission recognizes that Congress retains ultimate authority over sentencing policies and guidelines.[65] In its recent lengthy report specifically addressing the child pornography guideline, the agency reminds Congress that one of the Commission's legal duties is to examine sentencing data and to make modifications in light of feedback from the judiciary, including from their sentencing decisions, which in the area of child pornography have been dominated by a high variance rate in recent years.[66] Because the Commission evidently believes that prior congressional action in this area constrains it from overhauling the child pornography guideline on its own, it politely asks Congress for official approval to do so. Curiously, the Commission seems to have taken a conciliatory position in this respect. Instead of providing specific recommendations regarding discrete offense levels and SOC point adjustments, it vaguely refers to potential changes. Further, instead of offering modifications that would not infringe upon prior congressional dictates, the report seems to invite legislative approval before any official action is taken. In sum, the situation seems at a standstill, with the agency awaiting some clear congressional response.

Unfortunately, the Commission's ambivalent position in its recent report means that a significant variance rate and sentencing disparities will continue in the meantime. Indeed, the Commission's stance may actually create further trouble. Jurists who find fault with the guideline may seize upon the Commission's suggestions and experiment in implementing them in actual cases, creating even greater discrepancies in sentences nationwide for similarly situated offenders. The fact that there is a circuit level conflict on a major legal issue only muddies the situation.

Overall, this chapter provides reasoning, empirical data, and legal arguments that substantiate wide disparities in sentencing for federal child pornography offenses. Clearly, the various sentencing institutions in the criminal justice system are divided in judgments on culpability, which will lead to continuing differences in opinion on sentencing policy between and within institutions. In addition to the political controversies and empirical questions discussed, two further perspectives may be useful in assessing the current conflict over federal sentencing of child pornography offenders: a comparative analysis of criminal sentencing from other American jurisdictions and competing ideological perspectives.

Comparative Perspectives

Comparing sentences across jurisdictions creates a fuller understanding of the various political and empirical positions of punishment in our federalist system. The U.S. Sentencing Commission is generous in making available much of its data for researchers to analyze, including the statistical analyses in this chapter. Other sentencing agencies are not as transparent, which unfortunately makes it difficult to conduct a comparative analysis of sentences across multiple American jurisdictions. But there are alternative, albeit weak, methods, to ferret out where the federal system stands in comparison to other jurisdictions. One potential comparator is within the federal government itself: the military. The military justice system operates substantially autonomously from the criminal system for civilians. For the limited purposes needed here, the most relevant distinction is that military sentencers are not bound by the Commission's policies and guidelines. Though there is no publicly available database of sentences in the armed forces, much anecdotal evidence suggests that sentences in the military for child pornography offenses deviate from the civilian regime. A review of available case law in the past few years indicates that sentences for child pornography crimes in the military system are relatively minimal—generally far less severe than in the civilian system. Across the case opinions, sentences of less than two years appear to be the most common (e.g., ninety days,[67] four months,[68] five months[69]). The case law review suggests that sentences greater than that rarely are present unless additional crimes were involved, such as actual child molestation.[70]

No database exists, either, that permits an easy comparison of actual sentences imposed for child pornography offending in the various states. Two reporters have investigated potential differences in their geographic areas. Comparing federal sentences with Pennsylvania state sentences for federal and state child pornography offenses, one reporter found that half of those sentenced in Pennsylvania state court for child pornography offenses in 2009 did not receive any sentence involving incarceration, while of those that did receive some prison term the longest sentence was approximately eight years. The reporter compared these results to the average seven-and-a-half-year sentence in federal courts during the same time period.[71] A journalist for a Louisville, Kentucky, paper compiled years of statistics to compare sentences for federal child pornography offenders adjudicated in the local federal district court, not with state child pornography defendants, but with child sexual molestation defendants sentenced by the local state court.[72] He concluded that the average sentence for child pornography offenders in the area's federal district (from 2006 to 2011) was almost four times as long as the sentence received by offenders in the local court for sexually assaulting children.

This author's own analysis of Texas data for the offenses of possession and promotion of child pornography offenses yielded an average sentence of almost ten years, though with a range of six months to life. Yet this statistic is not exactly comparable considering it was a dataset of all offenders incarcerated in Texas state prisons as of February 2013. It included prisoners who were sentenced from 1997 onward and did not include probation-only sentences or those no longer in prison, and the dataset thus may have overrepresented lengthy sentences. A better comparison may be the average sentence imposed: The fiscal 2012 federal average was ten years. The average sentence imposed in Texas for child pornography offenses from January 1, 2012, through February 5, 2013, was about seven years. Again, though, this figure does not include probation-only sentences or those who were already released or for some other reason not then incarcerated in Texas' prisons despite being sentenced during that time period.

In sum, these small-scale and simplistic comparisons yield different conclusions. Comparing federal and state child pornography offending sentences, the Texas experience appears to be closer to the federal one, while the Pennsylvania sentencing system appears to impose far more lenient sentences. The local Kentucky review showed that federal child pornography defendants received sentences on average about four times as long as state defendants did for contact molestation crimes, suggesting the federal system is much more punitive for noncontact child sexual exploitation offenses.

An alternative, though admittedly also somewhat lax, method for a comparative analysis is to consider statutory sentencing schemes across state systems. Recall that the penalties in the federal system generally range from probation to ten years for possession and five to twenty years for receipt, distribution, and transportation (not including increases for prior sexual offending). A review of the fifty states' sentencing schemes for nonproduction child pornography crimes shows that there are widespread inconsistencies—some to a dramatic degree—in potential punishments across the country for child pornography crimes.[73] The comparative analysis herein focuses on distribution-type offenses, though many states gradate sentences for possession offenses much lower.

Overall, minimums and maximums vary to large degrees. In many instances, the ranges of punishments between different states do not even overlap. Many states permit sentences for distribution of no term of incarceration, including, among others, Florida, Iowa, Maryland, Michigan, Oregon, Pennsylvania, and Rhode Island. Other states appear to require some period of incarceration. For example, Louisiana, Mississippi, and New Jersey have five-year minimum thresholds, while the minimum in Massachusetts is ten years. In contrast, the maximum statutory penalty for possession and distribution in California is only one year, two years in West Virginia, and three years in Kentucky. Notwithstanding, several states permit more extreme punishments. Montana law allows sentences up to one hundred years, Alaska up to ninety-nine years, and Wisconsin and Mississippi each sanction forty-year sentences.

The range of possible terms of incarceration in any state varies greatly as well. Montana and Alaska offer the widest sentencing schemes with ranges of zero to one hundred and zero to ninety-nine years, respectively. A few other states provide wide ranges of punishment as well. Idaho's permitted sentence ranges from zero to thirty years, Mississippi from five to forty years, Illinois from six to thirty years. To the contrary, a handful of states dictate very refined sentencing options, notably New Mexico with a fixed six-year sentence and, at even lower levels, North Carolina provides for twenty-to twenty-five months and Kansas dictates thirty-one to thirty-four months. In general, all of this evidence indicates substantial variations in statutory declarations of culpability for child pornography offenders, as well as significant variations in sentencing, across the country for similar offenses based on both geographical and jurisdictional criteria.

Still, there is some evidence that the discrepancies in a guidelines-based system with sentences actually imposed may be unique to the federal system, at least in the child pornography area. In a recent survey of a representative sample of prosecutors nationwide who pursued child pornography cases, almost 80 percent reported that in their experience judges abided by state sentencing guidelines for child pornography possessors almost all the time.[74]

The foregoing reflects tensions among officials in defining appropriate punishments for child pornography offenders. Discrepancies in legal opinions between and within federal institutions and in sentencing laws across jurisdictions highlight the troubling results that otherwise similarly situated defendants may face differing sentences depending on the jurisdiction, region, and judge involved. Perhaps ideological contrast may help explain them as well.

Ideological Perspectives

Notwithstanding the importance of legal and empirical debates in explaining variations, the disparities in sentencing for child pornography offenders appear also to be founded upon fundamental differences in sociopolitical perspectives. It appears that the diversity of opinions in sentencing, which inherently also imbeds various judgments of culpability, is regularly tied to whether one concentrates upon depictions of sexual abuse of young victims or, instead, on the defendants and their behaviors.[75] Those who reiterate that the images depict the horrific sexual exploitation of the very young likely favor more severe punishments to appropriately account for the tremendous suffering of the children. In this view, the consumption of the images operates to victimize the children over and over again. A lens focusing upon the minor victims seems often to embrace the market thesis, that consumption fuels a market for further production and the search for new bodies, necessarily leading to additional incidents of sexual abuse of children. Under this thesis, strong punishment is considered necessary to deter even the casual possessor. Moreover, the market thesis posits that the availability and consumption of material involving child victims creates a greater risk of harm to society in general by normalizing adult-child sexual relations or, even more broadly, normalizing a view of children as appropriate objects, perhaps also holders, of sexual desire. Thus, even outside the area of illegal pornographic materials, the proliferation of these images is thought to beget more sexual activity involving minors. Notably, in this society, the mere idea of children engaging in sex is culturally abhorred. A victim-oriented focus can more easily ignore the offenders themselves. Because their crimes are related to the sexual exploitation of the most protected members of our society, child pornography viewers are universally reviled and therefore undeserving of empathetic concern.

On the other hand, supporters of reduced punishment oftentimes orient more towards the offenders. For example, federal judges often describe individual defendants as good family men with decent jobs, positive community ties, and no prior offenses.[76] Again, statistical runs using the Commission's 2012 dataset supports the observation that federal child pornography offenders as a group are far different than other federal defendants on certain risk-relevant measures. The vast majority of them are white males, American citizens, highly educated, and with no criminal history. Even the demographic characteristic of age indicates a less risky group; the mean age of child pornography defendants is forty-one years, and over one-quarter were age fifty and above. An additional explanation given why these defendants fail to pose a substantial risk to children is that the conduct is not necessarily indicative of deviant sexual interest in children; other, less nefarious motivations are in play. These alternative motivations include an original interest in adult pornography that led to collecting child pornography, in part because of technological advances in modern times.[77] The Internet offers what has been called the "triple A engine"—anonymity, availability, and affordability—that has fueled addictive behaviors in online activity, including cybersex.[78] Ease of access and efficient downloading capabilities offered by new technologies mean that individuals online do not always control all the materials that are available to them or that become part of their digital collections. This perspective downplays the market thesis because the defendant's individual collection is seen as contributing little to the global market for child pornography materials. It also reflects a judgment that there are gradations of culpability among downloaders.[79] Evaluations about culpability variations essentially involve findings that possession is a lesser crime than distribution and that distribution is a more serious crime when it is done for profit than when no financial consideration is involved.[80]

Ideological divides occur, as well, in how to conceptualize the risks and the harms of child pornography. It is possible that proponents of harsh sentences are using child pornography consumption as a proxy to punish undetected child molestation. To the extent child pornography is plainly being used as a substitute, critics argue that child pornography crimes should not be embraced as a sort of inchoate crime, and that it is unjust to punish what a person has not done (here, child sexual assault) or may in some merely speculative sense do in the future.[81] It may also be that the distinction between child pornography and child sexual assault has been negated by the new conceptualization of a broader umbrella of "child sexual exploitation crimes" that consolidate contact crimes together with child pornography offenses in a single category. This umbrella widens the lens to defining all those who engage in child sexual exploitation crimes as directly responsible for the harms caused to child victims, whether or not the offenders had physical contact with them. Indeed, child pornographers may even be characterized as having greater culpability considering that their crimes likely involve not one but many victims.[82]

Conclusions

As long as the Commission and the guideline structure remain intact, perhaps the preferred philosophy is to value the advantages that can be obtained. The Commission's data analysis can still foster coherent standards reflecting national uniformity. At the same time, the decisions of individual judges can act as checks on Congress and the Commission, while, in turn, Congress' ability to enact mandatory minimums that are generally enforceable on all institutions constitutes a substantial check.[83] Indeed, experts worry there might be a causative link—that if district judges exercise their *Booker* discretion and/or *Kimbrough*-style policy rejection to vary in a high rate of cases, it may lead Congress to react by implementing mandatory minimum sentences[84] or even abolishing the Commission and/or the guidelines entirely.[85] Such fears reflect what has already happened in the area of child pornography sentences.[86] This struggle over power between the sentencing practices of judges and the potential for Congress' corresponding backlash, while theoretically applicable to the entirety of federal sentencing, is at its zenith with the child pornography guideline. The sheer magnitude of the downward variance rate, together with Congress' unique and repeated attempts to counteract judicial discretion, is most striking with this guideline today. This makes the child pornography guideline important for the various reasons discussed herein, but also means it is at the cutting edge of federal sentencing policy for the future. At its core, the debate is about defining just punishment for a crime in which legal and ideological opinions are in direct conflict.

NOTES

1. Pub. L. No. 95-225, 92 Stat. 7 § 2 (1978) (codified at 18 U.S.C. §§ 2251–2253).
2. Chapter 6, Audrey Rogers, *The Dignitary Harm of Child Pornography—From Producers to Possessors.*
3. U.S. SENT'G COMM'N, THE HISTORY OF THE CHILD PORNOGRAPHY GUIDELINE 7–9 (2009).
4. U.S. SENT'G COMM'N, FEDERAL CHILD PORNOGRAPHY OFFENSES 126 (2012).
5. U.S. SENT'G COMM'N, 2013 SOURCEBOOK tbl. 17 (2014). References to annual sentencing data utilize fiscal years (October 1–September 30).
6. *See generally Uncertain Justice: The Status of Federal Sentencing and the U.S. Sentencing Commission Six Years after* U.S. v. Booker: *Hearing Before the H. Comm. on the Judiciary*, 112th Cong. (2011) (statement of F. James Sensenbrenner, Chair).
7. The term child pornography in this chapter refers only to nonproduction offenses, such as transportation, distribution, receipt, and possession.
8. 18 U.S.C. §§ 2252, 2252A.
9. 18 U.S.C. §§ 2252, 2252A.
10. As relevant to this article, the federal judicial system contains three hierarchical levels of judges/courts. The district judge is essentially the trial (and sentencing) judge, the circuit judge is an appellate judge with the authority to review district court rulings upon appeal, and the highest level is the supreme court.
11. 18 U.S.C. § 3553(b).
12. 18 U.S.C. § 3553(a).
13. U.S. SENT'G COMM'N, REPORT ON THE CONTINUING IMPACT OF UNITED STATES V. BOOKER ON FEDERAL SENTENCING pt. A, at 3 (2012).
14. 543 U.S. 220, 245 (2005). The Supreme Court found that the federal sentencing system operated in an unconstitutional manner by permitting judges to find facts that increased the punishment beyond what was authorized by facts admitted in the defen-

dant's plea or found to be true by a jury. Bestowing advisory status was the Supreme Court's remedial fix for the constitutional violation that had the added benefit of allowing the federal guidelines system to survive.

15. Kimbrough v. United States, 552 U.S. 85, 111 (2007).

16. Peugh v. United States, 186 L. Ed. 2d 84, 95 (2013).

17. U.S. SENT'G COMM'N, 2013 SOURCEBOOK tbl. 27 (2014); U.S. SENT'G COMM'N, 2004 SOURCEBOOK tbl. 27 (2005).

18. U.S. SENT'G COMM'N, FEDERAL CHILD PORNOGRAPHY OFFENSES tbl. 6-5 (2012).

19. U.S. SENT'G COMM'N, 2013 SOURCEBOOK tbl. 28 (2014).

20. U.S. SENT'G COMM'N, FEDERAL CHILD PORNOGRAPHY OFFENSES tbl. 6-5 (2012).

21. U.S. SENT'G COMM'N, 2013 SOURCEBOOK tbl. 28 (2014).

22. U.S. SENT'G COMM'N, FEDERAL CHILD PORNOGRAPHY OFFENSES 25–29 (2012).

23. *See generally* U.S. SENT'G COMM'N, THE HISTORY OF THE CHILD PORNOGRAPHY GUIDELINE (2009).

24. *See generally* TROY STABENOW, DECONSTRUCTING THE MYTH OF CAREFUL STUDY: A PRIMER ON THE FLAWED PROGRESSION OF THE CHILD PORNOGRAPHY GUIDELINES (2009).

25. SpearIt, *Child Pornography Sentencing and Demographic Data: Reforming Through Research*, 24 FED. SENT'G REP. 102, 102 (2011).

26. The author ran statistical analyses using the Commission's fiscal 2012 data file using standard statistical software.

27. United States v. McElheney, 630 F. Supp. 2d 886, 890 (E.D. Tenn. 2009).

28. United States v. Kelly, 868 F. Supp. 2d 1202, 1204–05 (D. N.M. 2012).

29. U.S. SENT'G COMM'N, THE HISTORY OF THE CHILD PORNOGRAPHY GUIDELINE 6 (2009).

30. Troy Stabenow, *A Method for Careful Study: A Proposal for Reforming the Child Pornography Guidelines*, 24 FED. SENT'G REP. 108, 110 (2011).

31. United States v. Martin, 2012 U.S. App. LEXIS 3911, at *3 (9th Cir. Feb. 27, 2012).

32. U.S. SENT'G COMM'N, GUIDELINE APPLICATION FREQUENCIES FOR 2012, at 40–41 (2013).

33. *See generally* U.S. SENT'G COMM'N, THE HISTORY OF THE CHILD PORNOGRAPHY GUIDELINE (2009).

34. United States v. Hanson, 561 F. Supp. 2d 1004, 1011 (E.D. Wisc. 2008).

35. United States v. Riley, 655 F. Supp. 2d 1298, 1305 (S.D. Fla. 2009).

36. United States v. McElheney, 630 F. Supp. 2d 886, 890 (E.D. Tenn. 2009).

37. *See* chapter 5, Carissa Byrne Hessick, *Questioning the Modern Criminal Justice Focus on Child Pornography Possession*.

38. United States v. Cruikshank, 667 F. Supp. 2d 697, 702 (S.D. W.Va. 2009).

39. United States v. Hahn, 2011 U.S. Dist. LEXIS 577, at *39–49 (D. Neb. Jan. 3, 2011).

40. Any statistic herein concerning the average sentence or recommendations imposed a cap of 470 months as typically representative of a life sentence.

41. U.S. SENT'G COMM'N, FEDERAL CHILD PORNOGRAPHY OFFENSES 238–41 (2012).

42. This group comprises the Fourth Circuit (United States v. Vanderwerff, 459 Fed. App'x 254 (4th Cir. 2011)), Fifth Circuit (United States v. Miller, 665 F.3d 114 (5th Cir. 2011)), Sixth Circuit (United States v. Bistline, 665 F.3d 758 (6th Cir. 2012)), and Eleventh Circuit (United States v. Pugh, 515 F.3d 1179 (11th Cir. 2008)).

43. Carol S. Steiker, *Lessons from Two Failures: Sentencing for Cocaine and Child Pornography Under the Federal Sentencing Guidelines in the United States*, 29 LAW & CONTEMP. PROBS. 28, 41–43 (2013).

44. United States v. Bistline, 665 F.3d 758, 764 (6th Cir. 2012).

45. *Id.*

46. United States v. Miller, 665 F.3d 114, 121 (5th Cir. 2011).

47. United States v. Pugh, 515 F.3d 1179, 1201 n.15 (11th Cir. 2008).

48. The four circuits in this group include the First Circuit (United States v. Stone, 575 F.3d 83 (1st Cir. 2009)), Second Circuit (United States v. Dorvee, 616 F.3d 174 (2nd Cir. 2010)), Third Circuit (United States v. Grober, 624 F.3d 592 (3rd Cir. 2010)), and Ninth Circuit (United States v. Henderson, 649 F.3d 955 (9th Cir. 2011)).

49. United States v. Dorvee, 616 F.3d 174, 188 (2nd Cir. 2010).

50. United States v. Grober, 624 F.3d 592, 608 (3rd Cir. 2010).

51. The three circuits include the Seventh Circuit (United States v. Garthus, 2011 652 F.3d 715 (7th Cir. 2011)), Eighth Circuit (United States v. Hyer, 498 Fed. App'x 658 (8th Cir. 2013)), and Tenth Circuit (United States v. Herget, 2012 U.S. App. LEXIS 18443 (10th Cir. Aug. 29, 2012)).

52. United States v. Garthus, 652 F.3d 715, 721 (7th Cir. 2011).

53. United States v. Hyer, 498 Fed. App'x 658, 661 (8th Cir. 2013).

54. United States v. Nghiem, 432 Fed. App'x 753, 757 (10th Cir. 2011).

55. Stephanos Bibas et al., *Policing Politics at Sentencing*, 103 NW. L. REV. 1371, 1388 (2009); Benjamin J. Priester, *Apprendi Land Becomes Bizarro World*, 51 SANTA CLARA L. REV. 1, 70–72 (2011).

56. Rachel E. Barkow, *Sentencing Guidelines at the Crossroads of Politics and Expertise*, 160 U. PENN. L. REV. 1599, 1614 (2012).

57. William G. Otis, Prepared Testimony before the Subcomm. on Crime, Terrorism, and Homeland Security, Committee on the Judiciary, U.S. House, Oct. 12, 2011, at 7.

58. Amy Baron-Evans & Kate Stith, *Booker Rules*, 160 U. PA. L. REV. 1631, 1742 (2012).

59. *Uncertain Justice: The Status of Federal Sentencing and the U.S. Sentencing Commission Six Years after* U.S. v. Booker: *Hearing Before the H. Comm. on the Judiciary*, 112th Cong. 5 (2011) (statement of F. James Sensenbrenner, Chair).

60. Alan Vinegrad & Jason Levine, *Guidelines Gone Awry*, 246 N.Y.L.J. 3 (2011).

61. AM. BAR ASSOC., REPORT OF THE AMERICAN BAR ASSOCIATION IN SUPPORT OF THE NEED FOR REVIEW OF THE FEDERAL SENTENCING GUIDELINES FOR CHILD PORNOGRAPHY OFFENSES (2011).

62. *Uncertain Justice: The Status of Federal Sentencing and the U.S. Sentencing Commission Six Years After* U.S. v. Booker: *Hearing Before the H. Comm. on the Judiciary*, 112th Cong. 126 (2011) (statement of James E. Felman, Liaison to U.S. Sent'g Comm'n, American Bar Association).

63. U.S. Dep't of Just., Letter to the United States Sentencing Commission, March 5, 2013.

64. *See generally* U.S. SENT'G COMM'N, FEDERAL CHILD PORNOGRAPHY OFFENSES 126 (2012).

65. U.S. SENT'G COMM'N, THE HISTORY OF THE CHILD PORNOGRAPHY GUIDELINE 6 (2009).

66. U.S. SENT'G COMM'N, FEDERAL CHILD PORNOGRAPHY OFFENSES i–iii (2012).

67. United States v. McKinley, 2011 WL 2586748 (N.M. Ct. Crim. App. June 30, 2011).

68. United States v. Astacio-Pena, 2010 WL 2265592 (U.S.A.F. Ct. Crim. App. April 30, 2010).

69. United States v. Tessier, 2011 WL 2279613 (U.S. Army Ct. Crim. App. June 7, 2011).

70. *E.g.*, United States v. Mullins, 69 M.J. 113 (U.S. Ct. App. Armed Forces 2010).

71. Terri Morgan, *Feds, Pa. Differ on Kid Porn*, THE TIMES LEADER, Jan. 16, 2011.

72. Andrew Wolfson, *Are Child Porn Laws Unfair? Viewers' Sentences Can be Worse than Molesters'*, COURIER-JOURNAL (LOUISVILLE), March 25, 2012; *see also* Chapter 8, Wendy Walsh, Melissa Wells & Janis Wolak, *Challenges in Investigations and Prosecutions of Child Pornography Crimes* (providing information on differences in potential sentences at the state v. federal levels).

73. U.S. SENT'G COMM'N, FEDERAL CHILD PORNOGRAPHY OFFENSES app. F (2012).

74. WENDY WALSH, JANIS WOLAK, & DAVID FINKELHOR, PROSECUTION DILEMMAS AND CHALLENGES FOR CHILD PORNOGRAPHY CRIMES: THE THIRD NATIONAL ONLINE JUVENILE VICTIMIZATION STUDY 9 (2013).

75. Chapter 6, Audrey Rogers, *The Dignitary Harm of Child Pornography—From Producers to Possessors.*

76. United States v. Cruikshank, 667 F. Supp. 2d 697, 701 (S.D.W.Va. 2009).

77. United States v. Grober, 595 F. Supp. 2d 382, 403(D.N.J. 2008).

78. Al Cooper, *Sexuality and the Internet: Surfing into the New Millennium*, 1 CYBERPSYCHOLOGY & BEHAV. 187 (1998).

79. United States v. Beiermann, 599 F. Supp. 2d 1087, 1103 (N.D. Iowa 2009).

80. United States v. Kelly, 868 F. Supp. 2d 1202, 1206 (D.N.M. 2012).

81. United States v. Marshall, 2012 U.S. Dist. LEXIS 90487, at *4 (N.D. Ohio June 29, 2012).

82. United States v. Miller, 665 F.3d 114, 121 (5th Cir. 2011).

83. John Gabriel Woodlee, *Congressional Manipulation of the Sentencing Guideline for Child Pornography Possession: An Argument for or Against Deference*, 60 DUKE L.J. 1016, 1054–56 (2011).

84. Stephanos Bibas et al., *Policing Politics at Sentencing*, 103 NW. L. REV. 1371, 1372 (2009).

85. Thomas M. Hardiman & Richard L. Heppner Jr., *Policy Disagreements with the United States Sentencing Guidelines: A Welcome Expansion of Judicial Discretion or the Beginning of the End of the Sentencing Guidelines?*, 50 DUQ. L. REV. 5, 34 (2012).

86. United States v. Jager, 2011 U.S. Dist. LEXIS 21203, at *37–38 (D.N.M. Feb. 17, 2011).

Contributors

Amy M. Adler is the Emily Kempin Professor of Law at NYU School of Law. She is a specialist in the legal regulation of sexuality, art, and speech. Her scholarship focuses on the intersection of law and culture; her work draws on an array of fields, primarily from the arts and humanities, to explore legal questions. Professor Adler's recent articles have included analyses of nude dancing, obscenity, pornography, child pornography, "sexting," moral rights, and art. She teaches art law, First Amendment law, feminist jurisprudence, and gender jurisprudence. She is also on the faculty of the Visual Culture Department at NYU. Professor Adler has lectured to a wide variety of audiences, ranging from artists to psychoanalysts to the Federal Bureau of Investigation.

Prior to joining the faculty at NYU, Professor Adler was an attorney at Debevoise and Plimpton, and then a fellow at the Freedom Forum Media Studies Center at Columbia University. She graduated summa cum laude from Yale University, where she was elected to Phi Beta Kappa and where she received the Marshall Allison Prize for promise in the arts and letters. She also graduated from the Yale Law School, where she was a senior editor of the Yale Law Journal. She clerked for Judge John M. Walker Jr. of the United States Court of Appeals for the Second Circuit.

Paul G. Cassell is the Ronald N. Boyce Presidential Endowed Chair in Criminal Law at Utah University's S.J. Quinney College of Law. He teaches criminal procedure, crime victims' rights, criminal law, and related classes.

Professor Cassell received a BA and a JD from Stanford University, where he graduated Order of the Coif and was president of the *Stanford Law Review*. He clerked for then-Judge Antonin Scalia when Scalia was on the U.S. Court of Appeals for the D.C. Circuit (1984–85), and for the Chief Justice of the United States, Warren Burger (1985–86). Cassell then served as an Associate Deputy Attorney General with the U.S. Justice Department (1986–88) and as an Assistant U.S. Attorney for the Eastern District of Virginia (1988 to 1991). Cassell joined the law faculty at the University of Utah in 1992, where he taught full-time until he was sworn in as a U.S. District Court Judge for the District of Utah on July 2, 2002. In November 2007, he resigned his judgeship to return full-time to the University of Utah to teach, write, and litigate on issues relating to crime victims' rights and criminal justice reform.

Jeremy M. Christiansen is currently a law clerk to Justice Thomas R. Lee of the Utah Supreme Court. He graduated with Highest Honors from the University of Utah's S.J. Quinney College of Law in 2014, where he was a member of the Executive Board of the *Utah Law Review* and was elected Order of the Coif. During law school he worked extensively with Paul Cassell and James Marsh on child pornography restitution cases in the U.S. Courts of Appeals, ultimately culminating with *Paroline v. United States* in the United States Supreme Court. Following his clerkship in Utah he will clerk for Judge Jay S. Bybee of the U.S. Court of Appeals for the Ninth Circuit during the 2015–16 term. The views espoused in Mr. Christiansen's contribution to this book are his own and do not reflect the views of his current or future employers.

Melissa Hamilton received a JD and PhD in sociology from the University of Texas at Austin. She currently is a visiting criminal law scholar at the University of Houston Law Center. Dr. Hamilton has published in law reviews and social science journals on interdisciplinary perspectives on interpersonal violence. Her current research interests focus on issues of risk, mental disease, and culpability of child pornography defendants and contact sexual offenders. She has published a number of articles on child pornography law.

Dr. Hamilton served as a law clerk to Judge Sam Johnson of the U.S. Court of Appeals for the Fifth Circuit. Prior to attending law school, she worked as a police officer and corrections officer.

Carissa Byrne Hessick is Professor of Law at the University of North Carolina School of Law. She specializes in criminal law and criminal punishment. Her work on child pornography has been published by the *Washington University Law Review*, the *Indiana Law Journal*, and the *Federal Sentencing Reporter*. That work has been discussed in the *New York Times* and the *Boston Globe*, and it was quoted in the U.S. Sentencing Commission's 2012 report to Congress on child pornography crime.

Before joining the faculty at UNC, Professor Hessick taught as a Climenko Fellow at Harvard Law School and as a tenured professor of law at Arizona State University and the University of Utah. She served as a law clerk to Judge A. Raymond Randolph on the U.S. Court of Appeals for the D.C. Circuit and for Judge Barbara S. Jones on the U.S. District Court for the Southern District of New York. Professor Hessick also worked as a litigation associate at Wachtell, Lipton, Rosen & Katz. She is a graduate of Yale Law School and Columbia University.

Mary Graw Leary is a professor of law at the Catholic University of America. She is the former deputy director for the Office of Legal Counsel and policy consultant at the National Center for Missing and Exploited Children (NCMEC), and the former director of the National Center for the Prosecution of Child Abuse (NCPCA).

Before joining academia, Professor Leary worked primarily on issues addressing the exploitation of children and women, child pornography, child prostitution, computer-facilitated crimes against children, and the investigation and prosecution of family violence cases. As both a state and federal prosecutor, Professor Leary focused on family violence and sexual assault. She is a former Assistant U.S. Attorney and has served as deputy chief of the Domestic Violence Unit for the Middlesex County District Attorney's Office in Cambridge, Massachusetts. She also served as an assistant district attorney in the Family Violence and Sexual Assault Unit of the Philadelphia District Attorney's Office. Early in her career, Professor Leary clerked for the Hon. Sue L. Robinson in the U.S. District Court for the District of Delaware.

Professor Leary's scholarship focuses on the intersection of contemporary social problems, technology, criminal law, and criminal procedure. She focuses on areas of exploitation and abuse of women, children, and vulnerable peoples. Her work has been published in several journals including those at the University of Pennsylvania, University of Virginia, Duke University, and the American Criminal Law Review. A sought-after commentator, she has been quoted in numerous media outlets including National Public Radio, C-SPAN, the *Legal Times*, and the *New York Times*. She is a graduate of Georgetown University Law Center and Georgetown University.

James R. Marsh is currently a partner at Marsh Law Firm PLLC, where his practice focuses on representing victims of child pornography and child sex abuse in criminal restitution and civil cases in federal courts nationwide. He is also the founder, former executive director, and current cochair of the emeritus board of the Children's Law Center in Washington, D.C. He is an experienced trial attorney and frequent commentator and author on legal issues affecting children. Mr. Marsh is a graduate of the University of Michigan Law School.

Audrey Rogers is Professor of Law at Pace Law School. She teaches criminal law, family law, civil procedure, and computer crimes. She has written a number of articles on child pornography, which have been published in *Villanova Law Review*, the *Baylor Law Review*, and the *Pace Law Review*, among others.

Professor Rogers is actively involved in the legal and outside community, currently serving on the Merit Selection Panel of the United States District Court for the Southern District of New York, and the Board of Directors of the Graham School Foundation. Prior to joining the faculty at Pace, Professor Rogers was an associate at Siff, Newman, Rosen & Parker, P.C., where she specialized in appellate practice.

Troy Stabenow is an Assistant Federal Public Defender for the Western District of Missouri. In 2008, Mr. Stabenow authored an article on federal sentencing, "Deconstructing the Myth of Careful Study: A Primer on the Flawed Progression of the Child Pornography Guideline." The article received nationwide attention, generated published opinions in nearly every circuit, and contributed to a drastic change in the way courts sentence child pornography offenders. In 2012, Mr. Stabenow published a follow-up article analyzing the current science and offering proposals for reform. He is one of the nation's foremost experts in child pornography crimes.

As a military prosecutor in Germany during the 1990s and 2000s, he worked with the Bundeskriminalamt (the German equivalent of the FBI) on computer crimes. He also trained military investigators and prosecutors to better investigate and prosecute these offenses. In 2003, he returned to the United States, and began litigating and teaching from the defense perspective. In 2005, Mr. Stabenow transferred to the U.S. Army Reserves and joined the Office of the Federal Public Defender. Until he became a professor in 2011, Mr. Stabenow defended child pornography cases in federal court during the week, and then prosecuted them for the military on the weekends.

Mr. Stabenow is the author of the four-volume series "West Federal Forms for District Courts—Criminal." He serves as an adjunct professor at both the University of Missouri Law School and at the Army's JAG

School. He is a member of the Eighth Circuit's Criminal Law Jury Instruction subcommittee.

Wendy Walsh is Research Associate Professor of Sociology at the Crimes against Children Research Center at the University of New Hampshire. Her research focuses on evaluating child abuse prevention and intervention programs and examining the criminal justice response to child abuse. Her research areas include children's advocacy centers, Internet crimes against children, child pornography victims, statutory victimization, and unwanted sexual experiences during college. She is the author and coauthor of numerous articles about child victimization and service use, the impact of victimization, and criminal justice outcomes and disposition time. She has worked on numerous national child victimization projects, including the Multi-Site Evaluation of Children's Advocacy Centers, the National Juvenile Online Victimization Studies, and the National Survey of Child and Adolescent Well-Being. She also works with the Carsey Institute on studies exploring the child welfare response to child maltreatment.

Professor Walsh received her PhD in sociology and a master's degree in family studies from the University of New Hampshire. She received her BA from Bates College.

James Weinstein is the Amelia Lewis Professor of Constitutional Law at Arizona State University's Sandra Day O'Connor College of Law. Professor Weinstein's areas of academic interest are constitutional law, especially free speech, as well as jurisprudence and legal history. He is coeditor of *Extreme Speech and Democracy* (Oxford University Press, 2009); the author of *Hate Speech, Pornography and the Radical Attack on Free Speech Doctrine* (Westview Press, 1999); and has written numerous articles in law review symposia on a variety of free speech topics, including free speech theory, obscenity doctrine, institutional review boards, commercial speech, database protection, campaign finance reform, the relationship between free speech and constitutional rights, hate crimes, and campus speech codes. Professor Weinstein has litigated several significant free speech cases, primarily on behalf of Arizona Civil Liberties Union.

During law school, Professor Weinstein was a member of the *University of Pennsylvania Law Review* Board of Officers. After graduating, he served as a law clerk to James R. Browning, Chief Judge of the 9th U.S. Circuit Court of Appeals, and then practiced civil litigation in Los Angeles for several years before joining the Arizona State faculty in 1986.

Melissa Wells is Associate Professor in the Department of Social Work, College of Health and Human Services at the University of New Hampshire. Her research focuses on child maltreatment outcomes and other components of adolescent victimization within families, online victimization and harassment among high-risk groups of adolescents, and mental health challenges and use of social media among foster care alumni.

Professor Wells received her BA and PhD from the University of New Hampshire and her master' degrees in social work from the University of Minnesota Duluth.

Janis Wolak is a Senior Researcher at the Crimes against Children Research Center of the University of New Hampshire. She is the author and coauthor of numerous articles about child victimization, Internet-related sex crimes, and youth Internet use. She is a coprincipal investigator and director for the First and Second Youth Internet Safety Surveys (YISS-1 and YISS-2), the National Juvenile Online Victimization Studies (N-JOV1 and N-JOV2), and the National Juvenile Prostitution Study.

Professor Wolak received a BA in sociology from New College in Sarasota, Florida, a law degree from Southwestern University School of Law, and a MA in sociology from the University of New Hampshire.

Index